Men of Wealth

THE STORY OF
TWELVE SIGNIFICANT FORTUNES
FROM THE RENAISSANCE
TO THE PRESENT DAY
BY

John T. Flynn

19 41

Simon and Schuster, New York

MANUFACTURED IN THE UNITED STATES OF AMERICA
BY H. WOLFF, NEW YORK

Contents

Foreword

WHAT FOLLOWS IN this volume is obviously a series of biographical essays. They present the outlines of the lives of eleven men and one woman. They are offered as twelve significant fortunes since the Renaissance.

It would have been a simple matter to have made a somewhat different selection. I might have chosen one of the Medici or Sir Thomas Gresham or Jacques Coeur instead of Jacob Fugger in the dawn of the capitalist system. At a later period I might have written of the Brothers Pâris or Samuel Bernard rather than John Law. I might have chosen Ouvrard, the financier of the French Revolution and Napoleon, as well as the Rothschilds. What excuse, someone will ask, can there be for including Cornelius Vanderbilt and not John Jacob Astor, Mark Hanna and not Carnegie, Hetty Green but not Jay Cooke or Jay Gould? And what reason can there be for leaving out Henry Ford and Andrew Mellon and the du Ponts?

In the course of the book I hope to make plain to the reader my reason for these choices. After all, the cast of characters of this or any other work having the same end must be determined upon some central principle of selection. I might have selected merely the dozen largest fortunes, in which event I would have left out not only Mark Hanna and Robert Owen, but J. Pierpont Morgan and, indeed, almost all of the others save perhaps Rockefeller, Vanderbilt, and Hetty Green. In fact, upon this standard of choice, it may be that Rockefeller alone could have been included.

Generally, what I have had in mind was to write of those figures in the history of wealth whose fortunes were, upon the whole, fairly representative of the economic scenes in which they flourished and whose methods of accumulating wealth offered the fairest opportunities to describe those methods. I have also tried to place these money-makers in certain important eras, putting more emphasis upon the latest. Having chosen Mr. Rockefeller as obviously the most important from any point of view in the period between 1870 and 1911, it was not possible to include Andrew Carnegie or Philip Armour or any of the oil barons in this country or Europe, however great the temptation. Having decided upon Vanderbilt I could not, without duplication, have added Gould or Huntington or Hopkins or Harriman or a score of other railroad kings.

Having chosen my subject my aim has been to make, as clearly and vividly as possible within the limits of a single essay, a picture of the economic system of the time; the means by which wealth was produced and the devices by which large amounts of it were siphoned off into the strongbox of the man of wealth. I have made, in part at least, one or two departures from this standard of choice. Hetty Green was selected because I wished to include at least one miser's fortune and one woman's fortune and happily she combined both. As for the omissions, I have left out several men whose lives I was sorely tempted to examine. Among them there was at least one Oriental fortune. There were one or two immense land fortunes. I omitted them because, after all, I felt they belonged not so much to the times in which they appeared as to a departed or at least a vanishing system of economic life. In the case of Mr. Ford—and this will hold for several others—I did not include him in obedience to a rule I made before I began my studies: that I would deal with the fortune of no living person.

I have been guided not merely in my selections but in the method of treatment by my conceptions of the means by which wealth is created and the mechanisms by which it is drawn off into the hands of rich men.

Wealth is created by labor—but by directed labor. It is created by labor working with tools and reinforced and multiplied by many skills—skills of hand and mind. It is created by this labor working upon materials. Putting it all together, we may say that wealth is created by labor working with various skills, with tools, upon raw materials, and under direction. The completed product is the composite of the materials, the common labor, the skills, the tools, including the whole technological endowment of the race and the direction of organizers.

No man working with his own hands, upon materials of his own possession and creation, with tools of his own fabrication, can produce enough to make himself enormously wealthy. The problem of becoming rich consists in getting a fraction—large or small—of the produce created by the collaboration of many men using all these energies.

The whole history of wealth accumulation consists in tracing the devices by which one man or a small group of men can get possession of this fraction of the produce of many men. In the beginning, when there were no machines, no money, no intricate inventions of credit, no man could establish a right to a share of the products of other men save through a simple and bald assertion of ownership over the materials and the men. Landownership and human slavery were the first instruments of the acquisitive. And as no man could acquire dominion over enough land and enough men to become rich save by an assertion of divine political power, we find the first rich men were kings.

As society grew and developed, men became individually more productive, on the one hand, and, on the other, the invention of money and credit enabled private individuals to establish claims upon the labor of ever-larger groups of men. We may say that the whole history of the art of accumulating wealth is the story of the invention of machines and the invention of the instruments of credit. Indeed, the two forces that distinguish the older world and its appalling scarcities from the newer world and its growing abundance are technology and credit.

Scientists and scholars slowly added one scrap of knowledge

to another, one mechanical device to another, gradually wresting from the earth its undreamed-of resources and multiplying the productivity of men. At the same time businessmen were slowly discovering and perfecting the devices of credit. They began with the simple transaction of lending a quantity of grain out of one crop to be repaid out of the next. They invented money as a measure of value. They got around to making loans of money. Then they reduced the money-loan transaction to a written record and then to a written record that could be negotiated. The layman who takes modern business methods for granted scarcely dreams of the immense advances made with this dynamic energy of credit. At first, when one man loaned a hundred drachmas to another, the drachmas had to be in existence before they could be loaned. We have proceeded so far that now we have the modern miracle of the bank loan in which *money is actually created by the very act of lending it,* so that we have the phenomenon of a nation using for its money the debts of its people.

In the chapters that follow I have kept these facts in mind. And as these historic Moneybags move across our stage I hope we may be able to see men fingering these inventions of credit and exchange, then strengthening and refining them—money, credit, notes, interest, bills of exchange, discounts, banks of deposit, then banks of discount, property titles, mortgages, clearances, stocks and bonds, and finally all the innumerable gadgets of the modern corporate world.

My aim has been to present the histories of these men and their times as nearly as possible in terms of our own day. We are apt to think of the problems of our time, with its depressions, its armies of unemployed, its farmers crying for higher prices, its burdensome debts, its social devices for dealing with poverty, its programs and plans, as unique in history. We may suppose that the stratagems by which our bewildered leaders have sought to elude fate and social disaster are quite new and untried. But it is not possible to wander through the market places and bourses and forums and slums of old cities and, indeed, ancient ones, without being struck by the parallels between their crises and our own. We shall see depressions in Florence, and France struggling against debt in the days of Louis XV, poverty tormenting farmers and workers in the Middle Ages and their sovereigns and premiers conferring and programming vainly against forces they did not understand which were changing their societies. We shall see businessmen and public officials quarreling about monopoly and government control and taxes and public debt and workers' claims and government spending. We shall behold economic messiahs with their gospels of peace and plenty all through the eras of Fugger and Law and Rothschild down to our own day. Men have been muttering about the same social ailments, the same disturbances, the same indignities and irritations for untold centuries.

These parallels, of course, can be pushed too far. The temptation is great. And because this will be evident I am eager at the outset to make it clear that I have faithfully sought to use no material that I have not laboriously examined and for which there is not ample support in history.

One further point. In the course of these several histories of rich men, questions have arisen and points have come to my mind which, it seemed to me, ought to be noticed. And yet I could not quite see how this could be done without interrupting the narratives with discussion that would serve only to distract the reader. I have attempted to solve this problem by including between some of the chapters certain interchapters in which I have offered brief observations on such of these questions and points as have interested me. The reader will find them in the interlogues so arranged that if he is sufficiently interested he may peruse them, and if he is not he may skip them without losing any of the essential parts of the twelve histories that follow.

JOHN T. FLYNN

February, 1941
Bayside, L. I.

Illustrations

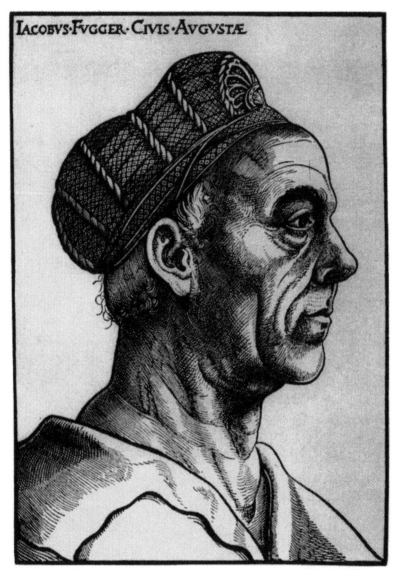

IACOBVS·FVGGER·CIVIS·AVGVSTÆ

Historical Pictures

JACOB FUGGER

CHAPTER I

Fugger the Rich

ORGANIZER OF CAPITALISM

— I —

JACOB FUGGER, surnamed the Rich, was the most important and imposing figure in the dawn of the capitalist era. Starting out to be a priest, he ended by becoming the greatest millionaire of the sixteenth century—greatest of merchant adventurers, first important industrialist-promoter of the modern world, banker to emperors and popes, whose countinghouses, warehouses, and factories spread to every city and port along all the trade routes of Europe.

Born three decades before Columbus discovered America, Fugger came into the world at a moment when men everywhere saw with dismay that their world was mortally sick. A monstrous internal growth was splitting the womb of feudalism. A new set of bones and muscles and nerves was drawing life from the disintegrating tissues of the old social system. Life and vigor were already in the blood of the infant ism that would take over the world for the next five centuries and that now, in its turn, seems gray and feeble and finds within its own womb struggling for birth a whole litter of new systems. Men were groping for new forms and patterns under which to live, and new instruments of organization suited to ordering these new ways. Profit, the modern merchant, and the middle class had come upon the scene to challenge the scholastic ethics and economics of Aquinas, the political theories of Albertus Magnus, the acquisitive techniques of the brigand nobles. And in the organization of the commercial instruments of this new era Fugger played a role not unlike that of Rockefeller and Morgan in giving direction and form to the new

3

corporate civilization which got under way in America in the early 'seventies.

Perhaps European society could have done nothing better for itself than feudalism in all the circumstances of the time. But essentially feudalism did not represent an effort at growth. It might be described as a vast shelter, a refugee haven into which the harried and starving and disordered masses of the first centuries following the destruction of the Roman Empire fled for safety. It was an escape from violence and want.

The terror of Europe in those early years was famine. Hallam records that in the seventy-three years in the reign of Hugh Capet and his two successors, forty-eight were years of famine and that from 1015 to 1020 the whole western world was almost destitute of bread—a frightful interregnum of barbarism when, as Hallam records, mothers ate their children and children their parents and human flesh was sold "with some pretense of concealment" in the market place. People sold themselves into slavery to escape hunger. In the presence of persistent hunger the outer crust of civilized morals crumbles and falls away, leaving only the unclothed savage man, pining for food. To him a precarious liberty seems a small price to pay for safety and meat.

Meantime, many of the stronger chieftains took to brigandage. Not yet emancipated from the ethical concepts of their northern paganism and the worship of gods who were little more than divine gangsters and celestial thugs, they broke upon the weak with that strange outpouring of cruelty that has marked man's journey from the beginning. The only refuge for the weaker peasant was to sell himself into the servitude of a stronger feudal baron.

In time, of course, this system became organized, strengthened, crystallized. And it was this system which was now dying. A new system that would symbolize not escape and flight but growth and development was to take its place.

The world of the Middle Ages was a rural world in which men lived in little clusters of 50 to 500 souls. The unit was the manor. It was a communal microcosm made up of a small number of families clustered around the castle of the lord. The castle, the cottage, the orchard, the fields, the pasture, the wood; these were the physical constituents of this tiny society. It was isolated from other societies. There might be a village but it was just a part of the estate. In a few places there might be a town.

The society within that little cosmos was, as to its domestic affairs, totalitarian. It was a collectivist society. It was a society in which the lord was the master and the state.

The manor produced the wealth that was created in the Middle Ages. It was a community organized for subsistence. And that is all it got—little more for a family than one gets on relief in depression-ridden America. The fields yielded grain, a few vegetables (carrots, cabbage, turnips, and, perhaps, some peas, beans, onions, celery, garlic, parsley). There was probably an apple and pear orchard and a vineyard. The flour was ground in the small estate-owned mill, the wine pressed in the estate-owned press. There were craftsmen who might be farmers also, and who exchanged their services for other services or for the products of others. Furniture was made, wool raised, carded, and woven, hides cured and formed into shoes and jerkins and belts upon the estate. But the produce of the estate was limited by the ability of the handicraftsmen to make things with very crude tools and out of limited raw materials. There are more *kinds* of things upon the shelves of a modern grocery than was to be found in the whole of Germany. All that vast multitude of commodities and merchandise which forms the necessities of the twentieth century was unknown. There were more different kinds of monkey wrenches made in predepression America than there were articles of merchandise in the feudal Holy Roman Empire. As someone has observed, more freight sweeps over a single railroad in a single night in one direction than poured through the Tirol passes in a year in the age of Frederick III. When the season's produce was available and all accounted for, the dwellers of the feudal commune had a modest subsistence while, by a variety of proscriptions and ordinances and dues and taxes, a certain amount of all that had been produced trickled into the bins and barns and cellars of the lord.

But since the lord commanded a fraction of the produce of only a small population of tenants, his whole share was not sufficient to make him rich. Only those lords who owned immense manors, comprising a town or two, or who owned a dozen or a score or a hundred manors, as some did, extracted enough from their tenants to amount to riches. The richest, of course, were those princes who possessed extensive domains and drew tribute from the tenants of hundreds of manors.

On the manor there was and could be nothing of this thing called abundance which the modern politician juggles before the hungering eyes of his constituents. Barring the visitation of famine or disease there was enough to eat, but little more. Life was inexpressibly dull. To the manor courtyard came at intervals the wandering acrobat and juggler and magician with their tricks; the pilgrim with his tales; the minstrel with his songs and sagas, and the peddler with his few exotic wares and spices and his gossip. But these were infrequent interludes in a world of dullness.

It was this world that was cracking up. And the force which was doing it was money, the merchant, and the town.

Imagine a little town—part of the estate of some flourishing lord. Within its walls is a jumble of rude dwellings, the homes and shops of craftsmen—weavers, glovers, armorers, smiths, perhaps glassmakers, or, mayhap, woodcarvers and other workers; the castle of the lord, with its retinue of workers, villeins, men at arms, and knights. Outside these walls, in some sheltered spot, is a cluster of merchants, with their carts and benches in the open air. As time wears on, these servile and declassed bargainers set up their dwellings, fix their headquarters there, and, after a while, form a small commercial community. Within are other thrifty craftsmen who assume the functions of merchants, handling their own and their neighbors' products with these outlanders and at the market places and fairs. In time these merchants, within and without the walls, find they have common interests, common wrongs to resist, common rights to support against the exactions of the lord. They organize. And thus the *bourgeoisie* is born—the *bourgeoisie* and the Chamber of Commerce which is to inherit the earth. This *bourgeoisie* clamors for a voice in affairs. It spreads and grows until it swallows the town. It organizes guilds. It sets up demands. It takes over from the lord the function of governing the towns either by free charter or by violent assumption of power. It regulates trade, prices, production, competition. Imposing guild houses rise in these new towns all over Europe. These merchants grow moderately wealthy. They build stouter houses behind more impregnable walls. By the middle of the fourteenth century they were already challenging the power of the feudal lords. Thus they not only laid the foundations of the modern city, set in motion the money economy, and launched the capitalist system, but they brought into being the first rudimentary techniques of representative government, though it was a long time before the constituency represented would be a popular one. Thus the modern town was born, and out of it came that ogre which ate up the philosophy, the ethics, the slavishness, the ways of life of the almost frozen medieval system.

And thus a new kind of rich man came into the world. The rich man of the feudal system was the hereditary lord who in an outlaw world swapped with the peasant and burgher protection and order for a share of their product. He took part of their product and part of their labor directly, in places taking as much as three days out of six. He demanded fines and dues and tribute, making almost every event in his own life and his vassals' births, marriages, and deaths the excuse for some new kind of levy.

But little by little gold and silver was flowing into this world of barter. By small degrees Europe found herself shifting to the money economy with consequences that her untutored social philosophers could not fathom or foresee. And as the towns spread out, the merchants began to accumulate money in exchange for a wholly different service from that performed by the feudal lord. After a few centuries they would take over the earth and set it spinning "down the ringing grooves of change" until one day a new force would arise to threaten the entrepreneur as he in his time challenged the lord.

————————————————— II —————————————————

It was about this time, in 1380, that a simple Swabian weaver named Hans Fugger left his small village of Graben to try his fortune in one of these growing towns—the free city of Augsburg. At the end of his life he was still a weaver, but he was more merchant than weaver, buying raw cotton for himself and his neighbors from Venice and selling his fustian and theirs to other cities.

When he died, he was succeeded by his two sons, Andreas and Jacob. They in time split off into separate enterprises and, indeed, separate dynasties. They became respectively the heads of the two Fugger houses—the Roe Fuggers and the Lily Fuggers. The Roe Fuggers, headed by Andreas, became prosperous first and disappeared quickly from the chronicles of the times. Jacob's descendants became the Lily Fuggers (so named because of their arms). He built a flourishing business, married the daughter of a Franz Basinger, a prosperous merchant and Master of the Mint, and set up in a handsome house in the chief street of Augsburg opposite the guild house of the weavers. When he died in 1469 he was ranked seventh among the wealthy men of the city.

Jacob Fugger II, his youngest son, was born March 6, 1459, in this imposing home. He had two older brothers, Ulrich and George, who were already employed in their father's counting room when he died. Ulrich at this time was 28, George 16. Jacob was but 10. But they were fortunate in the presence of an intelligent mother who was also a good businesswoman and who was able to direct her young sons wisely until they were able to take hold with a sure grasp. Jacob, however, was marked for holy orders. He proceeded as far as his first vows and was prebendary in Herrieden when his strong-minded mother decided he should forsake the sanctuary for the countinghouse. He left the cathedral in Franconia and went to serve his apprenticeship at Venice. In 1478, aged nineteen, he returned to Augsburg and took his place as a partner in the business which was then known as Ulrich Fugger and Brothers.

Thus Jacob did not start from scratch. It was into a very flourishing enterprise he stepped as a partner when he began his business career. His brother Ulrich, an able business administrator, had greatly enlarged the business and had actually made that connection with the House of Hapsburg which was later to prove of so much importance in the career of Jacob. He had already spread the firm's branches to a dozen European trading cities and had established it as a collector of papal revenues in Scandinavia. However, while Ulrich and George were businessmen of marked ability, Jacob's powers were of the highest order. And, despite his youth, he was not long in the firm before his influence began to assert itself. Before the fifteenth century had ended he had become the leader in the rapidly growing enterprise.

He was one of those men who not only possess great talents but exhibit them in their bearing and countenance. He had that kind of imperious manner and Jovian visage that marked the elder Morgan and made lesser money grabbers tremble in his presence. He possessed that inexhaustible vitality, that tranquil and unruffled temper, that immense talent for organization that characterize the greater industrial barons of our own day. In his lifetime he was assailed with varying degrees of fury as a monopolist, an enemy of German interests, a selfish and greedy hunter after profits, a foe to the established morals of the church and the state. Luther denounced him upon numerous occasions. And it was, indeed, Fugger's fate to find himself mixed up in that fatal adventure in papal finances that precipitated Luther's revolt. But through all this he preserved the perfect composure of the man who believes himself to be the special child and instrument of the deity. Just as a later-day industrial saint, John D. Rockefeller, said, "God gave me my money," the pious and acquisitive Fugger said: "Many in the world are hostile to me. They say I am rich. I am rich by God's grace without injury to any man."

Beginning as a theologian and then as a merchant, he became in turn a banker, a promoter, an industrialist, a commercial statesman. He was a dynast. But he had no ambition to found a family of noble and unproductive *rentiers*. He looked with unmixed satisfaction upon the function of the entrepreneur and the profit by which he lives. He put aside the suggestion of retirement into tranquillity and ease with the observation that he "wished to make a profit as long as he could." His ambition was to create a rich and powerful dynasty of bankers and industrialists. He consorted with princes, emperors, and popes, but he never fawned upon them. He could write to an emperor who owed him money—the most powerful potentate in Europe—to remind him that he owed his crown to Fugger's financial backing, that his majesty owed him money, and he begged that he would "order that the money which I have paid out, together with the interest upon it, shall be reckoned up and paid, without further delay." He lived amid magnificence, surrounded by priceless objects of art and the greatest library in Europe and with a collection of estates which he deemed becoming to a great prince of trade.

After his death the capital of the Fugger company, according to an inventory made in 1527, was 2,021,202 golden gulden. And twenty years later (1547) the firm, under the leadership of his nephew Anton, a man of ordinary abilities, had a capital of five million gulden.

III

The foundation of the Fugger fortune, of course, was merchandising. For a long time big merchants had been shouldering in among the swarms of peddlers who roved over Europe. The peddler's cart had left its wheel ruts along new roads, and these, with the remnants of the old Roman roads, became the nerve system of the Renaissance. Along these trade routes new cities rose and old ones took on new life. Transport companies were formed and navigation canals were opened. These peddlers were changing the face and stirring the heart and lungs of Europe. They made it possible for the beekeeper in some remote Thuringian manor to exchange his honey for a few ounces of pepper or cinnamon from the spice islands of Asia. Through their profit and coin-hunting expeditions it became possible for the fustian weaver of Augsburg to buy the product of the silversmith of Florence, the silks of Venice, the brocades of Lahore, and the perfumes of Alexandria. Two great streams began to flow around Europe: one a stream of goods made up of every sort of product of every clime; the other a stream of money coined in the little mints of hundreds of petty princes. These fustian makers and wool weavers and tool mongers began to have a wider market for their wares and they began to produce more. Men flocked to the towns. The capitalist system, with its money and its freedoms, was becoming the reigning ism, even though that word was unknown and the only isms men heard of were those which described the bloody and warring armies of religion.

Men like Fugger were coming to be a need. The smaller merchants, moving in an incessant stream over the growing network of European trade routes, had depended upon the customers they found at the manor gates, at the market places and the fairs. They were bringing to merchandising the utility of place. But a different sort of merchant was needed to confer upon it the utility of time and who would add the function of the wholesaler or jobber.

This called for a special kind of talent, the sort that in later years accounted for the huge fortunes of the early Astors, the English merchant adventurers, the Stewarts, the Wanamakers, the Selfridges and Strauses in this country and England. They had to have something more than mere instinct for bargaining. They had to have not only a capacity for organization and for accounting, but the spirit of adventure—unlike the modern merchant who reduces all to formulas called the science of merchandising and who thrusts the element of risk upon other shoulders. These large-scale entrepreneurs were putting on respectability. Already some English merchants like Sir William de la Pole and Sir Richard Whittington had attained to knighthood, and in Florence the Medici had achieved nobility and become the rulers of the city. The merchant, who had been hardly distinguished from the pirate and whose morality, says Nietzsche, was merely the refinement of piratical morality, now emerged like the traders of Tyre, "the crowning city, whose merchants are princes, whose traffickers are the honorable of the earth."

The Fugger firm handled a large number of commodities and products. Fustian, a sort of rugged cotton textile of which corduroy is one type, was in wide demand, and Augsburg was a great center of fustian manufacture. Fugger supplied the weavers with raw cotton that was picked up at Mediterranean ports, chiefly Venice, and brought by sumpter mule through the Tirol. In turn he bought their product and supplied it all over Europe. He was something more than merchant; he was also a manufacturer, of the contractor type, operating on the putting-out system, furnishing the wool and taking the cloth from some numerous hand looms—3500, some historians say.

He was a large importer of metals, spices, silks, brocades and damasks, velvets, herbs, medicines, works of art, rare and costly viands, fruits, and jewels. He purchased large diamonds, some costing as much as 10,000 to 20,000 golden gulden.

First among this merchandise was luxury goods. The princes, nobles, gentlemen, and the richer merchants were his customers. The lords and gentry and well-to-do townspeople were collecting their dues and fines and taxes in money, and there was a growing volume of silver and gold to spend. The lords had a constant flow of moneys which were for the most part dissipated. The income of Europe was beginning to pile up in the hands of the large merchants.

Inevitably these men were bankers—bankers to other merchants, to farmers, to weavers, and to governments large and small. When any government wanted money it customarily went to its rich merchants.

--- IV ---

In the infant capitalist world of the fourteenth century the closest approach to big-business technique was the spice trade. Spice played the role that copper was to play in the fifteenth century and oil in the twentieth. There was not much variety in the foods of the time and the means of preserving them were even less developed. The palate took refuge from the monotony of a limited diet in a jolt of pepper or some other spice. Spices came into widespread demand and merchant captains roved the seas looking for spice supplies with something of the adventurousness of the modern wildcatter hunting for petroleum.

For many years Venice was the center of the European spice trade. But Portugal, following her conquests in India, got control of a supply that transferred the world's spice capital from Venice to Lisbon and later to Antwerp. Here is the way this business operated. First of all, it was a royal monopoly. The Portuguese king, like most monarchs of the time—and since—continually needed funds. He would make a contract with a merchant to outfit a vessel at the merchant's own expense for an expedition to the spice regions of the East dominated by Portugal. The merchant loaned the king a sum of money proportioned to the amount of spice or pepper he hoped to bring back. When he returned with his hold loaded with pepper, cinnamon, and other spices the king paid off the loan with the cargo. These were called pepper contracts or spice treaties. Obviously they were highly speculative, since it was a long voyage, in primitive vessels, across seas menaced by storms and pirates. The empty-handed skipper, of course, lost his loan.

Fugger dealt in spices, but for most of his life he looked upon these spice adventures and their treaties a good deal as John D. Rockefeller looked upon the oil producers. Rockefeller preferred to buy their oil after they had fetched it out of the ground, and Fugger preferred to buy spices from the successful shippers after they had brought it safely back. A man had to buy pepper at a distant point, pay for it in advance in the form of a loan to the king, haul it at his own expense and risk, and take the chance in a fluctuating market that it would be worth what he paid for it.

This was not the sort of business Fugger relished. But the other merchants of Augsburg, chiefly the great Welser firm, were active in this. When the Portuguese conquered India, a consortium of Augsburg merchants led by the Welsers made a pepper treaty with the king to equip a fleet and made an immense profit. Fugger took only a small piece of this.

But in the end he succumbed, as the refiners succumbed to wildcatting for oil. Magellan, after a three-year trip around the world, returned, having made various conquests. He took possession of the Moluccas, the fabulous Spice Islands, for the crown of Spain. Jacob Fugger sought a spice contract with the Spanish king. With his fellow South German merchants, he equipped two voyages, one led by Sebastian Cabot and one by Garcia de Loaisa, to bring back pepper from the Moluccas. Both voyages were complete failures. But Fugger died before they got well under way and never lived to see the wisdom of his earlier restraint vindicated. He lost 4600 Spanish ducats on this venture.

—————————— V ——————————

These rising magnates were not without dishonor in their own times. They were economic revolutionists. They were as obviously at war with the established order as the inventors of the power loom at a later day or the makers of modern corporate finance capitalism in the last century or the protagonists of the planned capitalist society in our own day. An old dogma of economic ethics, hoary with age and heavy with the benediction of the church—the principle of the "just price"—was being hustled out of civilization.

Europe had been operating on the economic and social ethics of Saint John Chrysostom, remodeled and adapted to the times by Saint Thomas Aquinas, for centuries. There was a ban upon the unrestrained pursuit of wealth as something inherently evil. Profit and interest were the twin devils of the scholastics as they were of the atheist Marxians four centuries later. Chrysostom had said: "Whoever buys a thing in order to make a profit selling it, whole and unchanged, is the trader who is cast out of God's temple." "What else is trading," said Cassiodorus, a monkish jurisconsult and sort of ghost writer to Theodoric, "but buying cheap and wishing to sell dear at retail? . . . Such traders the Lord cast out of the Temple." This was fourth- and sixth-century Christianity. The great Angelic Doctor amended this to permit a profit—but at a "just price." "Trading in itself," he said, "is regarded as somewhat dishonorable, since it does not involve a logical or necessary end." "Gain," he argued in his *Summa The-ologica,* "which is the end of trading though it does not logically involve anything honorable or necessary, does not involve anything sinful or contrary to virtue; hence there is no reason why gain may not be directed to some necessary or honorable end; and so trading will be rendered lawful; as when a man uses *moderate* gains acquired in trade *for the support of his household or even to help the needy."* (Question LXXVII, Article IV.)

Out of this grew the doctrine of the just price which was supposed to inspire the trade of Europe until the eighteenth century. But as Saint Thomas himself had said, the "just price is not absolutely definite but depends rather upon a sort of estimate." Society therefore contrived a legal agency for ascertaining and proclaiming the just price. The merchant's guild became the arbiter. The trader and craftsman were supposed to be content with an income fitting their station in life. And in fixing the just price the guild was supposed to be guided by the interest of society and not the interest of the entrepreneur, which is one point of difference between the ancient guild and its modern editions—the twentieth-century trade association. Under the influence of this philosophy the guilds set up as code authorities in a medieval NRA and proceeded to subject medieval trade to the most extensive and exacting regulations. Everything was formalized. Trade itself was caught in hard and fast jurisdictional ruts. In Frankfort there were 191 crafts—eighteen in the iron industry alone. And as regulation begets regulation, the feudal town became enmeshed in a tangle of rules and formulas and ordinances and red tape that utterly constricted the economic system.

Everything had tended to become frozen. The merchants sought to hold the workmen to long hours, low wages, and protracted apprenticeships. There was a resistance to new men coming into the merchant's and master craftsman's ranks. High fees were imposed to keep the newcomers out. A tinker in Brussels was charged 300 florins for the privilege of starting up his own shop. The apprenticeship and journeyman stage was lengthened sometimes to twelve years.

Every form of progress had to fight against the established rulers of manor and town. Poverty was appalling. Workers lived in hovels. Abortive proletarian uprisings appeared all over Europe. Peasants rose without success in Saxony, Silesia, Brandenburg, Illyria, Transylvania. English laborers demanded to be paid in money. Journeymen guilds arose under cover of religious and technical-instruction associations—bootleg unions, like American speakeasies during the prohibition era disguised as dramatic and literary clubs.

For a century a quiet, unostentatious, cautious, and inarticulate resistance to these multiplying fetters was under way. New ways of life, new demands of trade, the changes made by the expanding money economy were forcing growing alterations in the general acceptance of these theological concepts of trade.

For one thing, in a growing money economy credit was necessary, even to the pope and the abbot who thundered against interest. Pope John XXIII died with his miter in hock to Giovanni de' Medici for 38,500 florins. When John died his successor demanded the miter back under pain of excommunication. Indeed, one monarch who possessed what was believed to be the crown of thorns that had pierced the brow of the crucified Christ pledged it to a Venetian banking house for a loan.

This need for credit expressed itself at first in a toleration of the Jews. The new monarchs assumed new powers without the financial means of supporting those powers. The religious orders, embarked upon grandiose programs of cathedral and monastery building, had to have money. Christians could not lend since the church forbade it. This offered an opening for the Jew, who was not bound by Christian ethics. And so, being excluded from other forms of trade, he became the moneylender of Europe. It is of more than passing interest that Aaron of Lincoln, one of the earliest known English Jewish moneylenders, had advanced funds to the St. Albans minister at Lincoln and at least nine other Cistercian abbeys. When he died the monasteries owed him $24,000, which the good King Henry II piously declared forfeited, at the same time confiscating Aaron's property and cash, which he used to wage war against Philip Augustus of France. Many such instances are recorded.

For this pretty situation Saint Thomas had provided a convenient ethical shelter. The great theologian held lending at interest to be a sin and an injustice to the borrower who was the victim of usury. "The usurer sins in doing an injustice to the one who borrows from him upon usury. But the borrower upon usury does not sin, since it is not a sin to be a victim." But, asked the theologian, does not the borrower induce the lender to commit a sin by offering him the occasion? "It is lawful," expounded the Angelic Doctor, "to use sin for a good end." He adds, with what might be called a naïve, almost holy sophistication, that "He who borrows money upon usury does not consent to the sin of the usurer, but uses it; nor does the taking of usury please him, but the loan, which is good."

And what end could be better than the building of a monastery or a cathedral or the support of a Christian monarch? As to the confiscation of the property of the usurer, is not the sinful man subject to punishment? It is not possible to excommunicate a Jew. But it is possible to deprive him of the means whereby he or his tribe commits a sin. To take his funds is like disarming a brigand.

As the new methods spread under the influence of the expanding money economy, the need for credit by businessmen and sovereigns grew to the point where funds more formidable than the Jew could supply were needed. Moreover the merchant class was accumulating money savings which they were eager to put out at interest, and so the Christian banker appeared upon the scene and the Christian ethic lost some of its plausibility. Society divided into two schools, those who stood by the old scholastics and those who took the fork in the road behind the leadership of the humanists. The old-timers roundly denounced Jacob Fugger and his colleagues in trade. They carried the war into the Diet and into politics. There were great cities whose security depended upon the power of the guilds, like Constance and Basle and Lübeck and all the Hanseatic towns. There were some others, like Augsburg, and the Flemish towns, and many in France, which were building their prosperity upon the independent capitalist.

The Hanseatic League, which comprised 150 cities at its height, forbade any man to buy grain before it was grown, cloth before it was woven, herring before it was caught. It regulated prices, submitted its members to the most minute regulations, arranged all to perpetuate the place and power of the "Little Man," backed its policies and rules with assemblies, tribunals, police, fleets of ships protected by a navy, flew its own flag, and maintained foreign branches where its branch managers and clerks lived in barracks under an iron discipline. Despite its power, such merchants were cruelly handicapped against the free, unfettered devices of the independent merchant. Hence they denounced the rising Fugger. At Constance the Ravensburg Company, until then the greatest trading corporation in Germany, demanded that no one should be permitted to have a capital exceeding 100,000 gulden, though its own was not less than 140,000. The Council of Nuremberg would restrict it to 25,000 gulden. In the German Diet it was said that the wealthy were reproached with "destroying all chances for work of the small trader on a moderate scale." In France a similar movement was afoot. Jacques Coeur, the erratic but powerful French millionaire, was indicted as one "who had impoverished a thousand worthy merchants to enrich one man." This sentence, in endless variations, was destined to go echoing through the succeeding centuries. In the American Congress, about the time John D. Rockefeller was born, a Mississippi representative would bewail "the death of so many small establishments which might separately and silently work their way into honorable existences" and "one great establishment rises on the ruins of all the surrounding ones."

Fugger soon concluded, as John D. Archbold and John D. Rockefeller did, that his philosophy needed an apologist. And he found the ideal one in Dr. Konrad Peutinger, the humanist, whose home was in Augsburg. Peutinger was a more formidable champion than Chancellor Day of Syracuse University or the flock of prosperous preachers who took Rockefeller's gold and used scripture to defend him. He was a sort of combination of Samuel C. T. Dodd, Rockefeller's verse-making and philosophising counsel and Elihu Root, who spread his own respectability thinly over the hated monopolists of his time.

He was a lawyer and, like most lawyers of that era, a theologian who had taken his place with that school which believed that the philosophy suited to a human society must seek its criteria and data in the affairs of men rather than in the abstract contemplation of the spirit. He was Fugger's chief adviser. He wrote: "Every merchant is free to sell as dear as he can and chooses. In so doing he does not sin against canonical law; neither is he guilty of antisocial conduct. For it happens often enough that merchants to their injury are forced to sell their wares cheaper than they bought them." He defended cartels and monopolies, profit and interest. He was indeed the first great philosophical

evangelist of the profit system. He drafted laws for the Emperor
Maximilian I in conformity with his beliefs and the interests of
his powerful client.

Thus always the reigning acquisitive group must have its philosopher. Rameses found his in the temple. Nicias had his Hiero.
The corporations of Rome had their Cicero. Saint Thomas turns
up providentially to build a fortress of philosophy around the
feudal lord whose regime depends upon the suppression of the
merchant. And Dr. Peutinger appears upon the scene to refute the
Angelic apologist when his ethics no longer fit the prevailing process
of wealth getting.

As a matter of fact, even the great Angelic Doctor himself had
left a large loophole for the collectors of interest. He held that
while a man could not receive interest, yet if he received a gift
"not asking it and not according to any tacit or explicit obligation,
but as a free gift, he does not sin; because even before he lends
the money he might lawfully receive a free gift, and he is not put
at a disadvantage by the act of lending." (*Summa Theologica,*
Lesson LXXVIII, Article II.)

Here is pretty thin skating upon the theological ice, and inevitably the ice cracked first by the use of the "gift," then by an
understanding, by means of the bonus, much as interest-rate laws
have been evaded in our own time, and finally by frankly throwing
overboard the whole Aquinian luggage. For when Fugger writes
to Charles V for payment of his *loan* he asks plainly that "the
money which I have paid out, together with *the interest upon it,
shall be reckoned up* and paid, without further delay." (Author's
italics.)

Certain it is that Fugger, the pious Christian merchant, stood
in need of an ethical basis for his enterprises, since he reveled in
profit and interest upon a most extravagant scale. His biographer,
Jacob Strieder, estimates—using Fugger's own figures—that in
1494 he and his two brothers invested a capital of 54,385 golden
gulden in their firm and that seventeen years later (1511) this
had grown to 269,091 golden gulden. Here was an increase in

capital of about 400 per cent, or 23.5 per cent a year. But this does not measure the profit, since it takes no account of the sums withdrawn during those seventeen years by all the partners.

However, in 1511 a new accounting is begun. Various sums were taken out of the business to pay off female heirs. The firm made a fresh start in 1511 with a capital of 196,791 golden gulden. After Jacob's death, the inventory made by his nephew Anton, which took nearly two years to complete, revealed a capital of 2,021,202 golden gulden. This represented a profit of 1,824,411 golden gulden, or over 900 per cent. Here was a profit over a period of sixteen years of well over 50 per cent a year. But again it is necessary to add a considerable percentage to this account for that part of the earnings withdrawn for the extensive expenditures necessary to support the Fuggers' magnificent way of life.

VI

The long struggle to break up the old feudal system and the primitive guild ethics of the towns and set in motion the capitalist society lengthened out into a series of steps. First there was the slow infiltration of money. Next came the shattering of public acceptance of the scholastic ethics. Then came the rise of free competition and the long retreat of the old guild trade monopolies. Next was the development of modern banking. Then came the rise of the large-scale industrial operator. It is because Fugger played a leading role in all these stages that he stands as the most important figure at the dawn of the capitalist era.

It is not easy to name the precise date when modern banking begins. It is simple to say that it begins when loans are made, not in cash, but in bank credit. Banks there had been in the earliest times. And indeed the famous Mercato Nuovo or the Vendi Tavolini in the Florence of the Medici did not greatly differ in appearance at least and in most functions from the bankers' locations on the street of Janus on the north side of the Roman Forum. In the latter the moneylenders occupied a large ill-lighted apartment and sat in rows on high stools with their coins spread out before them behind a bronze screen. In the Mercato Nuovo, which still stands, the bankers sat on lower stools behind their tables covered with green cloth, ordinary paper parchment for notations, scales, a bowl for silver coins, and with their gold in pouches at their belts.

The early Roman banker was primarily a moneychanger. A time came when he accepted deposits which he loaned out for his clients.

The Florentine banker was also a moneychanger. But he was far more a lender of money. He loaned primarily his own money. But he accepted funds from others which he used in his business and which use he paid for.

There is a hiatus—a long period in the early Middle Ages— when all traces of banks are lost. The moneylender—and chiefly the Jewish moneylender—alone is evident, a lone figure moving through an unfriendly world from fair to fair and town to town, a prey to knights and kings and brigands.

It is about this time, however, that banking again shows itself in the business world. It appeared among the Lombards at Asti, Chieri, and other towns, and later at Florence. These men did a sort of pawnbroker business like the Jews, taking valuables of various sorts as collateral.

We then find the larger merchant-adventurers drifting into the banking business. They were compelled to do a certain amount of moneylending in connection with their activities at fairs. The banker-merchant posted himself at the fair. Merchants went about buying and selling goods. Sometimes they operated by means of exchanges of goods, sometimes with coins—perhaps to the extent of 40 per cent. But there were merchants who had to have credit until they had disposed of their whole cargo. And so they took their vendors to the banker who either guaranteed payment or actually made payment to be repaid later. Out of this developed the practice of bills of exchange.

Always there were people or institutions or rulers who felt the need of a safe depositor for their moneys. The English king deposited his funds at times with the Knights Templars and so did other princes and lords. It was a logical survival of the ancient custom of keeping funds in the temples. In time the bankers became more than mere lenders of their own funds. They accepted the deposit of others' funds. These they were at liberty to lend out. Such deposits were treated as demand loans to the bankers. There were times, however, when the depositor came for some of his money only to find the banker did not have it available. Under these circumstances the banker would take his client to another banker with whom he had a deposit or enjoyed credit and thus honor the client's demand. After a while it became unnecessary for the banker to go in person to another banker to arrange this withdrawal. He would give his client a written order upon a neighboring banker for the funds he lacked. Thus checks came into use. And the next phase was for the client himself to give to another a written order upon his banker for funds. Thus the general use of checks came into vogue.

All the time, the banker served to accommodate the kings and the petty princes and lords who needed money. When the king required funds on loan he might get them from a single usurer at first. But later he would be aided by a consortium of merchants who would subscribe to the loan, usually under the leadership of one of large means and influence among their number. Such a one was Fugger. And thus, we see the rise of the international banker.

Cities, supported now by orderly taxation, would in need sell their revenues in advance to tax farmers who, not infrequently, raised the funds as the old Roman tax corporations did, by subscriptions among the well-to-do merchants. One finds running through all these early years ordinances and edicts and laws and regulations of cities and kings and public bodies and guilds covering the subject of checks and deposits and bills of exchange and negotiable certificates of deposit and bank examinations and balance sheets. Double-entry bookkeeping was perfected at Venice, where Fugger served his apprenticeship. The Italians, chiefly the Florentine bankers, were inventing names for various instruments

and transactions—*casa, banco, giornali, debitore, creditore*—which
were to become the daily countinghousehold words the world over.
Thus men were slowly forging the instruments, weapons, and the
jargon of the modern capitalist state that would become in time
the mold of society. These old bankers were leaving their names
upon the institutions and streets of the cities of Europe. In Florence you will still find in the street names, the memory of the
Bardi, Peruzzi, Albruzzi, Grecci, and others—bankers all.

The Fugger family had followed this evolution—first weavers,
then lenders of money around the fairs and market places, then
international bankers—the greatest of their time. Jacob Fugger's
firm had a web of branches and factories extending from Naples in
the south and the Spanish peninsula to Hungary and Poland in
the east and Scandinavia and England in the west.

───────────────────── VII ─────────────────────

No canvas designed to depict the dawn of capitalism would be
complete without a brief place for what was perhaps the first
authentic strictly capitalist depression in Europe, produced largely
by the operations of these new bankers. The episode is generally
known as the failure of the Bardi and Peruzzi banks in Florence
and it produced consequences not unlike those attending the failure of Jay Cooke in America or Baring in England or the Credit
Anstalt in Vienna in 1931.

Florence had carried far the organization of her producing
energies. Wool textiles was one of her important products. The
homes of the townspeople and the villagers were turned into sweat-
shops to which the merchants sent the raw wool to be processed in
the homes. While the Church and her doctors thundered against
interest and profit, the village priests read pastoral letters threatening the workers with a denial of the sacraments if they resisted
the exactions of the wealthy usurers of Florence who dominated
the system.

A continuous supply of raw wool on the one hand and wide

markets on the other became essential to the city's economic safety. This probably led the Florentine banker-traders to England, where the best wool was produced. Two of the greatest Florentine houses, the Bardi and the Peruzzi, began extensive operations in England in the latter part of the thirteenth and the beginning of the fourteenth century. They made large loans first to Henry III and later to Edward II and Edward III, but mainly to the latter. In return they got the privilege of trading in England, which was otherwise closed to foreign merchants, and the privilege of buying wool for the Florentine market.

It is these loans to Edward III which are called by historians the cause of the failures of the Bardi and Peruzzi. But this is a very considerable oversimplification. By 1337, when Edward III launched that bootless century of struggle known as the Hundred Years' War by invading France, he owed the Bardi 62,000 pounds and the Peruzzi 35,000 pounds. But he immediately made enormous additional loans to finance his ambitious design to seize the crown of France from Philip VI. By 1343, when the first phase of that quixotic adventure came to an end, he is said to have owed 900,000 pounds to the Bardi and 600,000 pounds to the Peruzzi. Sapori, a recent student of this historic episode, thinks the sums exaggerated and that they were nearer 500,000 and 400,000 pounds each.

Edward had promised to pay the principal and interest of these loans in coin, and his undertaking was guaranteed by the Archbishop of Canterbury and the Bishop of Lincoln. So eager was the rash Edward for these sums that, upon completing the arrangement, Edward gave to "the merchants of the Bardi society" 30,000 pounds sterling, to the "merchants of the Peruzzi society," 20,000 pounds sterling, and "in consideration of the great help given the king," 500 marks to a Peruzzi agent in England and, for the same reason, 500 marks to the wife of another agent and to the wife of a Bardi agent. Wives of two other agents got 200 pounds each. It sounds as if two great American banking houses managed an American loan to the government of Chile on a 20 per cent basis, while the partners in the two banking houses got a several-hundred-thousand-dollar bonus from the Chilean president, who also distributed the largess among the South American agents of the banking houses and their wives. Thus, commercial bribery had already made its way into the investment banking business.

But all this time Florence, rushing forward in the first incident of uncontrolled expansion of the capitalist era, was moving deeper and deeper into debt. Merchants were making profits and depositing them with the Bardi, the Peruzzi, the Mozzi, the Frescobaldi, the Scali, and also investing in various bond issues underwritten and managed by these houses, but chiefly by the Bardi and Peruzzi. Competition with their wool industry was growing from England and the Flemish weavers. But as they produced ever more they were ceaselessly seeking to expand their markets. Florence, an economic unit like modern England, imported raw materials and exported finished products. She enjoyed her expansion through the strategic activities of her rich bankers, who grew wealthy milking European monarchs and princes and at the same time using their loans as weapons to force Florentine products into those old custom-sealed European countries and cities.

One market, among others, was of great value to Florence—the city of Lucca. This city was a commercial battleground between the merchants of Florence and Pisa. And out of this situation it became the victim of an episode that depicts strikingly the inheritance of violence that deformed the early struggles of primitive capitalism. A band of German mercenaries seized Lucca and offered to sell it to the city of Pisa. Pisa agreed to pay 60,000 golden florins and made a down payment of 13,000 florins, which it was destined to lose when Florence armed to balk this sale of its valued market to its chief rival. Later certain Florentine merchants and bankers —including beyond doubt Bardi and Peruzzi—offered the German mercenaries 80,000 florins. They would thus control Lucca as a market for their products and own its customhouses and its tax revenues. It was as if a few leading merchants and manufacturers of Philadelphia were to propose to buy Pittsburgh from a mutinous regiment of the New York National Guard that had seized the latter city and was now peddling it around the East. But Florence, still ruled by the remnant of the old Guelph spirit, protested against this immoral purchase of a city's population like so many slaves. Finally the captors of Lucca knocked the city down to a Genoese merchant-adventurer named Gherardino Spinola for 30,000 florins. The outcome of this was war between Florence and Pisa.

The first effect of the war was a demand for war loans, which the banking houses were called upon to float. And this came at a time when Edward III was marching his armies around Flanders and making new appeals for larger advances from the Bardi and Peruzzi.

The competition of the English and Flemish wool weavers had been undermining the trade of Florence much as the competition of the Carolinas cut into the business of the New England textile industry and as the competition of the East cut into the textile industry of Manchester. Production in Florence fell off. The streets were filled with the unemployed. Merchants who had large deposits with the Bardi, the Peruzzi, the Frescobaldi, and others were calling for their funds. Some of the smaller bankers failed. Indignation against all the bankers was rising. Florence faced a crisis not unlike that which faced America in 1933 or Germany in 1932. Nothing could save the great bankers but a moratorium. Disturbing rumors floated in from Flanders, where Edward's generals were having but small success. In this crisis this old city, where the popular party had always been strong, with its active *popolo minuto,* which hated the Ghibellines not only because they represented the philosophy of the economic royalist, but of external interference and domination, submitted to the device of dictatorship. In 1342 that fantastic adventurer, Walter of Brienne, a Frenchman who styled himself the Duke of Athens, was made dictator through the machinations of the bankers. He proclaimed a moratorium on private debt for three years, which saved them.

But, having come into power, he plotted immediately for complete mastery. He suspended payment of the interest on the public debt and planned gradually to extinguish it by progressive repudiation, which promptly brought upon his head the wrath of the bankers. In 1343 the distress of the city was so great, the fortunes of the war so melancholy, the anger against the dictator so general that the people poured into the streets in an unrestrained uprising. They looted the palace of the Bardi, taking it is said, valuables to the amount of 30,000 florins. The dictator was compelled to resign and flee from the city. Certain Neapolitan bankers who had loans outstanding in Florence called them. The news came of Edward's reverses that brought the Hundred Years' War to its first pause in 1343, and Edward delivered the crowning blow by defaulting upon his loans. Immediately the Peruzzi bank failed. And within a year the great Bardi bank crashed. They carried with them most of the bankers of Florence. The disaster shook all Europe and produced in those cities where capitalist organization had proceeded to any length, such as Venice and Genoa, the most depressing consequences. Excessive debt, overexpanded industry, concentration of money and power and wealth, the extravagance of governments, the destructive power of war had made for Europe its first great capitalist depression in the modern era.

VIII

Like most of the great bankers from Jacques Coeur and William de la Pole in the dawn of capitalism to J. P. Morgan and the Mitsui in our own day, Fugger found it essential to his larger schemes to maintain an intimate association with the sovereign. And the sovereign, as Fugger mounted to power, was Maximilian I, who, like all the rulers of history, from Pericles and Caesar to Roosevelt and Churchill, found it essential to maintain an intimate association with the sources of credit. Fugger established a close relationship with the impecunious and unstable Maximilian, the "last knight of Europe." When the hard-pressed Hapsburg needed funds the faithful Fugger with his seemingly inexhaustible resources was at hand. But if Fugger was a never-failing well of cash to the Emperor, his majesty was a never-failing source of new privileges and monopolies and profits to Fugger. If Fugger had in his vaults what Maximilian required, Maximilian had in his rich realm priceless metal and other resources that were indispensable to the acquisitive Jacob.

Maximilian was Emperor of the Holy Roman Empire, that pale imperial shadow of power which was slowly vanishing out of Europe. But of far more importance to him was the struggle for mastery that was going on in Germany, as in every other country, between the king on one side and the numerous feudal lords on the other. As in the thinly concealed struggle which smolders today in America between the local governments and the Federal government over the rising supremacy of the latter, Germany was turning to strong central government to solve her little-understood problems. The spirit of revolt in religion, the expansion of knowledge, the awakening curiosity of the masses, dynastic and commercial and technological and political energies kept the population in a ferment, but, perhaps, in the center of all this, accentuating and stimulating all the other elements of unrest, were economic forces.

Probably more than anything else the prime moving spirit of turbulence, controversy, and change was money. For at least two hundred years the feudal world was disintegrating. Men knew things were wrong. They debated and argued and fought over the causes and the cures. They held conferences all over Germany to inquire what was amiss and how it was to be set right. But they never seemed to get around to the real cause or even to talk about it. The struggle resolved itself now into bitter religious controversies, now into wars between princelings and estates, now into political debates. What they saw was a political upheaval, the effort of the king to make himself master against the savage opposition of the lords. They took measures against this. But they took no measures against the one potent energy that entered the system like a malevolent germ—money. So that as you examine the long history of the decline of the Middle Ages you are struck by the fact that nothing contributed so much to destroying the existing order as the measures that were taken by the politicians of the day to save it.

For several hundred years money—coins—had been trickling into the hands of rulers and people. After the downfall of the Roman Empire, coins began to disappear. It is estimated that in the year A.D. 518 there were about $370,000,000 of gold and silver in Europe. By A.D. 806 this had dwindled to $160,000,000, or about half. Whether these metals were destroyed or merely hidden away or lost cannot be said. But after A.D. 800 the production—chiefly in the Holy Roman Empire—was more than sufficient to make good the yearly disappearance, and in the fourteenth and fifteenth century the production was notably increased. Doubtless, much of the hidden precious metals began to reappear. Estimates of the precise quantities in use must be taken with a good deal of caution. Certainly as men became sensible of the value of these metals in exchange the hunt for them was quickened. All through these years one reads of the adventures of the alchemists who were being grubstaked by various wealthy men and rulers in the hope that they might produce the gold so eagerly desired. Kings began to impose and enforce the most drastic measures to increase the supply of precious metals in their kingdoms. In England, for instance, every merchant was compelled to import a certain amount of coin or bullion in every ship, and export of the metal was prohibited.

For a while these metal coins were little more than glorified commodities—gold, silver, copper—confronting, as Marx puts it, all other commodities. But coins were not consumed as other commodities were and they acquired a velocity other commodities could not have. Workers wanted their wages in coins. Farmers preferred to exchange their produce for coins where possible. They preferred to pay their dues and services in money, even their rent. The lords preferred to have it so. The lord could now indulge in luxuries. People bought more and more from merchants who in turn grew wealthy. The banker became important as credit grew. No longer could men—merchants, bankers, townspeople—

tolerate the disorders that grew out of the petty wars and feuds and brigandage of the numerous lords and knights. They turned to the crown for order, stability, and protection against the feudal barons. The king—Maximilian—had no revenues from the kingdom save those from his own estate—the Tirol. Soldiers he could get from his vassal lords by levy under their feudal obligations when he wished to fight the heathen or a foreign foe. But for use against the lords themselves in the great struggle for mastery of Germany, the emperor had to have a mercenary army, and this required cash. He could get enough cash only by borrowing from the bankers, who in turn, through consortiums, could raise the moneys amongst the merchants.

Thus king and towns and merchants were drawn together by the inescapable necessities of this new money economy. This immense need for money for emperor, and pope too, for that matter, laid too great a strain upon the old scholastic ethics of Aquinas, for king and pope needed the rich man as the source of credit, and this, in turn, brought about a frank abandonment of the "just price" and the proscription against money wealth and interest. And thus the merchants and bankers waxed mighty, became the most powerful subjects, challenged the power of the lords, built castles of their own, acquired titles and estates, and became, in time, the lords of creation.

Maximilian was one of those frail vessels into which is poured the destinies of a people in a moment of crisis. He was young, well proportioned, ruddy and healthy, restless, ambitious, and not wholly devoid of ability. He lived simply, ate moderately, and avoided those copious draughts of Rhenish wine and beer that besotted the German nobility. The Tirolese peasants adored him because he was brave and adventurous as a hunter and a glamorous figure in the courtyard tilts. He enjoyed immense popularity with the younger nobles, was gracious and charming in his personal relationships, encouraged artists and scholars, and, in general, exhibited the qualities of urbanity, heartiness, ebullient good nature and courage that became one who was called the "last knight of Europe."

But he was unstable, flighty, always plotting for supreme power. He engaged in one calamitous war after another. He was forever fabricating new devices for getting more money. Even as an old man in 1518 he was talking of another crusade against the infidel. Declining toward the end of his reign into the most humiliating poverty, embittered by the embarrassments to which it exposed him, he left the Tirol, traveled down the Inn and the Danube, where, prostrated by a long illness, he died.

It was to this unstable, chimerical, and tolerant prince that Jacob Fugger attached himself as chief banker. And the heights to which the great Augsburg banker rose in the Hapsburg hierarchy will be seen in the part he took in naming the successor to Maximilian's throne.

Charles I, King of Spain, was a Hapsburg. He was the elder son of the Archduke Philip, Maximilian's only son. Philip had married the daughter of Ferdinand and Isabella of Spain and died before those monarchs. His son succeeded them on the throne of Spain as Charles I. Maximilian had decided to make his grandson, Charles, Holy Roman Emperor to succeed him.

But there was another candidate in the field, Francis I of France. The selection of the emperor was in the hands of the electors, a small group of dukes and archbishops. The Margrave of Brandenburg, the Count Palatine of the Rhine, and the electors of Mainz and of Trier were practical gentlemen and their votes could be had upon one condition only—Maximilian had to be able to offer a bigger price than Francis. The fight started at the Diet of Augsburg in 1518. Maximilian was growing old. His treasury was empty. And though he talked of his plans to launch another crusade he could not pay the tavern bills of his courtiers. Nevertheless, there, supported by the financial resources of Fugger, Maximilian was able to secure the promise of support for the Spanish king.

The negotiations, reduced to the grossest commercial terms, reached a point where the Margrave of Brandenburg had the deciding vote. Fugger undertook to purchase the noble miscreant. Francis had offered him a rich French wife with a large dowry. But Fugger countered with the granddaughter of Maximilian—the sister of Charles of Spain—and 300,000 Rhenish gulden. Fugger guaranteed to deliver 100,000 in coin as a down payment as soon as Charles was elected. Large sums had to be provided from various sources, including immense amounts to be collected in Spain to complete the purchase of the other electors. Maximilian had commissioned Fugger to carry out these arrangements.

But the aging Maximilian died shortly thereafter, and Charles I assumed the direction of his own campaign. Almost his first act was to displace Fugger. He turned over to the Welsers, Fugger's chief rival in Augsburg, the task of moving over 300,000 gulden collected in Spain to control the election.

Fugger was enraged at this. His whole position as the banker for the most powerful royal house in Europe, the Hapsburgs, was threatened. He lost no time acting. He let Charles know that he had but to throw his support to the French to blast the expectations of the refractory Spanish monarch. He got in touch with the electors. Soon Charles learned that an election consists not merely in making promises to those who have votes to sell but in convincing the purchased electors that the promises will be kept. When Charles' agents got down to brass tacks with the electors they made it plain that they wished Fugger to manage the financial arrangements by which they had to be bribed not to sell the crown of their country to a Frenchman. They insisted that they would be satisfied with nothing less than Fugger's guarantee of the payment of their respective shares.

Fugger was called back to the helm in triumph. In the discharge of this important commission, which resulted in the election of Charles of Spain as Holy Roman Emperor under the title of Charles V in 1519, Fugger extended credits of over half a million gulden in gold. His fame now reached its highest point. After this he remained the undisputed chief banker and financial adviser of the Emperor. Augsburgers said with pride that the name of Fugger was known throughout the world. He became almost a legendary figure. Luther related, with a touch of awe despite his hatred of Fugger's predatory class and his feud with Fugger himself, how the Bishop of Brixen, one of Peutinger's literary companions, had died in Rome, leaving a scarcely legible scrap of paper, and how Pope Julius sent it to Fugger's agent in Rome to be deciphered. The agent recognized it as evidence of a deposit of several hundred thousand gulden which the good Bishop had with the Fugger house. When the Pope asked how soon the money could be sent, Fugger's factor replied: "At any hour." The Pope turned to the French and English cardinals present and asked: "Could your kings also deliver three tons of gold in an hour?" When they said no, his Holiness replied: "But that is what a citizen of Augsburg can do."

The astute Augsburg banker made more than his interest and his "gifts" out of his sovereign. The function of banker—everready and loyal banker and financial adviser—opened for him the door to priceless privileges in Maximilian's ducal domain of the Tirol, rich in natural resources—that same Tirol with its mines which stimulated the patriotic yearning of the twentieth-century German statesmen for *Anschluss*. He obtained from the debt-ridden royal spendthrift those invaluable copper and silver monopolies that became the chief source of his great fortune.

It would be unfair to Fugger, however, to say that his loyalty to the Hapsburgs was the mere fruit of his predatory plans. He was banker, merchant, industrialist, Catholic and German. What were the percentages in which these ingredients fused in his imperious nature, it is not, of course, possible to say. He felt a strong tie to the Hapsburg house. His political philosophy, based upon his commercial interests, drew him inevitably to the monarch whose struggle against the principalities and estates advanced the cause of order and stability in a stronger central government, so essential to the rising merchant class. He gave to the Hapsburg drive for strong central government that kind of zealous support that the industrial magnate of Mark Hanna's day gave

to McKinley and Taft and that their successors today give with
equal vigor to the champions of local rule against the forces of
Federal power, because their changing interests now have shifted.
But he doubtless felt a strong personal attachment to Maximilian. Through all that bewildered sovereign's battles against
the old order, his frantic efforts to obtain military and financial
aid from the hostile lords, in Diet after Diet in which, as in Augsburg, the estates refused his appeal for arms and men or at Trier
when they refused his request for the common penny, Fugger
stood by his side and, in the last extremity, always opened his
brimming chests of gold.

He must have been touched as he beheld his own growing
wealth beside the ever-increasing poverty of his sovereign. At
the Congress of Vienna, where Fugger, surrounded by his rich
agents and the members of his family, magnificently attired, conferred upon favored nobles rich gifts of gold and pearls and
other precious stones, the impecunious Emperor strode about
resplendent in costly jewels that his rich banker had secretly
loaned him to enable him to play more splendidly the role of
monarch.

Fugger must indeed have been fully conscious that he occupied
a sovereign eminence in a province within the empire—the new
province, the great principality of money. For we find him addressing the Emperor Charles V in terms used then only by great
and powerful vassals who, under the formal language of allegiance, talked to kings with the assurance of equals.[1]

---

[1] Charles V was slow in repaying the large sums advanced by Fugger to accomplish Charles' election to the imperial throne. Fugger, his patience taxed by the
royal delinquent, wrote to the Emperor the following extraordinary letter:

His Most Serene, All-Powerful Roman Emperor, and most Gracious Lord!
    Your Royal Majesty is undoubtedly well aware of the extent to which I and
my nephews have always been inclined to serve the House of Austria, and in all
submissiveness to promote its welfare and its rise. For that reason, we co-operated
with the former Emperor Maximilian, Your Imperial Majesty's forefather, and,
in loyal subjection to His Majesty, to secure the Imperial Crown for Your Imperial
Majesty, pledged ourselves to several princes, who placed their confidence and
trust in me as perhaps in no one else. We also, when Your Imperial Majesty's

He began to play the magnifico. In 1511 he was made a count. But already he had begun to acquire great estates. Before 1511 he had acquired at least four splendid domains—two of them from the Emperor himself, all in Swabia, and one of them very near to Augsburg. He had also an estate or two in the Tirol and in Hungary, and his magnificent palace in Augsburg, filled with the paintings and sculptures of the best artists in Europe, was a treasure house of art. Chiefest of all, like that other magnifico of the last century, J. Pierpont Morgan, he was an inveterate collector of valuable and rare and beautiful manuscripts and books. His library at his death was already the finest in Germany and after his death, through additions of his family, became the most famous in Europe. Indeed the greater part of its treasures was brought together by Jacob Fugger's successors. It is worth recording here that 125 years after Jacob Fugger's death, this famous library was sold by Count Philip Edward Fugger to the emperor for 15,000 florins—about a fifth of the sum that had been offered for it in an earlier day, and when the imperial libra-

---

appointed delegates were treating for the completion of the above-mentioned undertaking, furnished a considerable sum of money which was secured, not from me and my nephews alone, but from some of my good friends at heavy cost, so that the excellent nobles achieved success to the great honor and well-being of Your Imperial Majesty.

It is also well known that Your Majesty without me might not have acquired the Imperial Crown, as I can attest with the written statement of all the delegates of Your Imperial Majesty. And in all this I have looked not to my own profit. For if I had withdrawn my support from the House of Austria and transferred it to France, I should have won large profit and much money, which were at that time offered to me. But what disadvantage would have risen thereby for the House of Austria, Your Imperial Majesty with your deep comprehension may well conceive.

Taking all this into consideration, my respectful request to Your Imperial Majesty is that you will graciously recognize my faithful, humble service, dedicated to the greater well-being of Your Imperial Majesty, and that you will order that the money which I have paid out, together with the interest upon it, shall be reckoned up and paid, without further delay. In order to deserve that from Your Imperial Majesty, I pledge myself to be faithful in all humility, and I hereby commend myself as faithful at all times to Your Imperial Majesty.

Your Imperial Majesty's most humble servant,

JACOB FUGGER

rian went to Augsburg to fetch the collection to Vienna the town councilors prevented him at the instance of the creditors of the Fugger family, whose wealth and power and glory had by this time departed.

Jacob, like many of the wealthy Christian men of wealth of his day, was a generous but never secret dispenser of philanthropy, giving to monasteries, churches, almshouses, and the poor. For one of these benevolences he is indeed famous. This was his erection of a model housing project—fifty cottages housing two families each, still known as The Fuggerei—in the suburbs of Augsburg to offer, at very low rents, decent homes to the underprivileged workers of the city. It is perhaps the first instance of a low-cost housing enterprise in Europe. And that the job was well done is attested by the fact that the houses remain in good condition and are still tenanted.

Always it was Fugger's wish to enlarge and embroider the visible evidences of his wealth and power, partly, perhaps, to gratify his vanity, partly to add to the prestige of the House of Fugger.

For always this great House of Fugger assumed an identity in his mind separate from that of its members, and the proud merchant studied ceaselessly to ensure its immortality and its magnificence.

The Fugger partnership contract was built around this dynastic dream. The three Fugger brothers were equal partners. Upon the death of any brother the remaining brothers were to act as directors and to select from among the male heirs one worthy to be trained to take his place as a director when needed. When all of the brothers were dead the two directors, thus named from among the heirs, would assume command and train a third for the succession.

Female heirs and those in orders were excluded from the business. All heirs were compelled to leave their inherited share in the business for three years, after which they could, if they wished, withdraw it only gradually. The great mining interests were seg-

regated from other enterprises, and only male heirs were permitted to inherit them. Various devices with penalties were
contrived in the business structure to ensure its permanence.

But Fugger, who knew so well how to manage the great craft
he captained, knew little enough of the perils of the seas it sailed.
Anton Fugger, a nephew, succeeded to the chief directorship on
Jacob's death. Before he died in 1560 the great Fugger house
was as deeply morassed in the financial adventures of the House
of Hapsburg as the Bardi and Peruzzi were in the finances of
Edward III. When Anton's son Marcus took over the reins, he
saw the Fugger riches slipping out of the company's hands. Most
of the wealth amassed by Jacob was dissipated in the lifetime of
his grand-nephew. A century later the only part of that wealth
that remained was what had been invested in lands.

------------------------------ IX ------------------------------

Greater than any emperor, richer in revenue than any temporal
monarch, was the pope of Rome. The papacy was then, as it is now,
a highly organized superstate with its branches in every village,
its parochial, provincial, and national officials, diplomats, armies,
secret agents. Its primary function was the salvation of souls,
but in the performance of that duty it had contrived an immense
machine. Its founder had administered his great enterprise with
literally no plant capacity beyond the open fields, the blue sky,
and the simple habiliments of a mendicant. But the modern
Church continued his ministry from the palaces of its wealthy
prelates and a vast physical structure that required an endless
flow of revenues into its treasury.

Inevitably the Church had developed an extensive system of
papal taxes originating in little contributions from every corner
of the world, flowing into larger pools in the numerous dioceses,
finally making their way to Rome.

For several centuries the pope had employed the services of
various bankers—chiefly Italians. But after 1502 Jacob Fugger

elbowed all other rivals aside as the foremost fiscal agent of Rome. He collected the papal revenues in Germany, Holland, Hungary, and the Scandinavian countries. He made advances to the pope, recouping his loans out of these collections. Similarly he transported papal moneys to diplomats, monarchs, generals, missions all over Europe.

His place in history in connection with this traffic, however, rests chiefly upon the part he played in the collection of indulgence money and the sums paid by wealthy candidates for Church benefices for their promotion. His role here was a sinister one. There seems little doubt that he artfully established himself as what in modern American parlance would be called the "contact man" with the Holy See in the distribution of Church honors and benefices in Germany. The ambitious cleric seeking the purple of the *monsignori* or the pallium of the archbishop as a rule had "to see Fugger." He was required to put up an immense sum with the Roman dataria, and Fugger was the gentleman who knew how to make the best terms for him, how to provide the money and the means of repaying it. Indeed, Fugger once boasted that he "had been concerned in the appointment of all the German bishops."

It was out of this traffic, denounced openly as simony by the Church, but practiced behind the scenes by its prelates from pontiff down, that Fugger got for himself a dubious immortality in that historic episode that precipitated Martin Luther's break with the Catholic Church.

In the fall of 1517, faithful Catholics gathered in the Catholic churches in the diocese of Mainz to hear a famous preacher portray for them the inspiring theme of a great mother basilica for Christendom—St. Peter's at Rome—which Pope Leo X planned to complete. What the preacher wanted was funds—money for the holy project. To those who would contribute, the Pontiff had offered a plenary indulgence. The faithful gave, at least for a while. But the success of the campaign for funds was interrupted by an exposé of the sinister facts behind it.

Young Albrecht, Margrave of Brandenburg, had an inordinate

ambition to collect archbishoprics for himself. Having achieved through the influence of his brother, the Elector of Brandenburg, the see of Brandenburg, he next succeeded in becoming archbishop of Magdeburg, in 1513, at the age of twenty-three. This was a hitherto unheard-of achievement. But he decided to seek also the archbishopric of Mainz when that post became open, in 1514, by the death of its incumbent. To command three dioceses was an exhibition of ecclesiastical greed which the avaricious Florentine party in power at Rome knew how to exploit. The dataria— the sacred bureau concerned with graces and benefices—informed the audacious Albrecht that the business could be arranged if he could raise 10,000 gulden in addition to the fifteen or twenty thousand which he would ordinarily have to pay for such a diocese. Albrecht's chance of raising so much money out of the overtaxed communicants of Mainz was slim, since that see had had two short-lived archbishops, each of whom had paid fourteen thousand ducats for his elevation. The diocese was bankrupt and hence would not yield further funds to the ordinary appeal. Some more effective squeeze was necessary.

The matter, apparently, was arranged in Rome by Johan Zinc, the Augsburg ecclesiastic who was in the pay of Fugger. Albrecht would borrow the 10,000 gulden needed from Fugger. Pope Leo would grant to him in Mainz and Brandenburg a plenary indulgence, ostensibly for the building of St. Peter's. In fact, however, the "gate" would be split fifty-fifty between the Pope and the Archbishop, like one of those American prize-fight benefits for the Milk Fund where the Milk Fund gets a modest percentage while the promoters and fighters get the rest, and all the ballyhoo is on the Milk Fund.

With this privilege granted to him, Albrecht was in a position to borrow the needed ten thousand from Fugger, while the banker, as security, took over the collection of the indulgence money. But it was important that there should be no mischance in selling the indulgences to the faithful. Therefore Albrecht and his banker-

managers did what an American Y.M.C.A. drive or Community
Chest campaign does. They employed a professional high-pressure
drive manager. There was at least one such person in Germany—
John Tetzel, the famous indulgence preacher, a sort of Billy
Sunday who had shown in other dioceses that he could bring the
pennies tinkling into the collection boxes. Tetzel made a specialty
of preaching indulgence drives.

With this organization—Tetzel managing the exhortation and
Fugger managing the money—Albrecht set out to gather in
Mainz and Brandenburg the ten thousand he had borrowed from
Fugger and the fifteen or twenty thousand he was to pay besides.
Tetzel went from town to town and from church to church. He
preached the gospel of the full remission of the temporal punishment due to sin for those who would contribute to build St. Peter's,
without disclosing the real object of the drive. The contributions
were put into sealed boxes, counted at Fugger's office in Augsburg
in the presence of representatives of Albrecht, and turned over to
the banker to be divided in accordance with the deal.

At this time Martin Luther was engaged in his rising controversy with the Church over this very question of indulgences.
The Albrecht-Fugger-Tetzel performances aroused his indignation, and he let fly at the whole incident in which an archbishop
"sent Fugger's cutpurses throughout the land" to collect money
under the guise of aiding a sacred cause to pay off a loan to the
Augsburg usurer. Luther denounced Fugger in the roundest
terms. He piled his scorn upon the banker's trade practices. While
Luther based his attack upon purely religious grounds, his ful-
minations found an answering echo in the minds of the practical
German burghers who saw in the whole indulgence and benefice
racket a scheme to gather up the all-too-meager supplies of German coin and drain it off under hypocritical pretenses to Italy.
The incident produced so violent an effect upon Luther's mind
that it precipitated his decision to bring the whole subject to an
issue, and, within two months of the commencement of the Tetzel

preaching campaign, the revolutionary monk nailed upon the gates of the town of Wittenberg his famous Ninety-five Theses.

— x —

If you will go back to the end of the fifteenth century to the ancient city of Neusohl, you will come upon something that strangely resembles in significance the Butte, Montana, of today or perhaps the oil regions of Pennsylvania in the 'seventies. As for the Augsburg of Fugger's time, it bore to the rising copper industry the same relation which Cleveland bore to the oil regions in Rockefeller's time. For there in Augsburg and in the copper country of the Tirol and of Hungary, Jacob Fugger was laying the foundations of the modern industrial system. There, the musty records of the era reveal, were the seeds of the coming industrial organization, its companies, its subsidiaries, its cartels, its patient and intriguing monopolists, its trust busters, its anti-monopoly drives with its prosecutions, investigations, and failures.

It would not do to assert that Fugger invented any of the devices that became the familiar tools of his monopolist successors, any more than it would be true to say that the Rockefellers, Morgans, Carnegies, and Harrimans invented the devices by which they built the corporate system of our day. But Fugger organized these devices, used them with audacity and skill. And through them he acquired most of the vast fortune that made him the richest man of his world. It was this role of industrial pioneer that gives him his chief claim upon history.

These activities were carried on in the copper and silver industries. The scene of these exploits was in the mining districts of Germany, in the Tirol, and in Hungary. From about the middle of the fifteenth century German merchants, chiefly from Augsburg, began to trade in the copper of the Tirol. The metal was produced by many small operators. The mines, of course, under the feudal system, were the property of the Duke, the owners holding them as feudal grants. The Duke, therefore, was entitled to a share of all the copper and silver taken out of them by the operators. Here was the foundation of the mineral and oil royalty that still persists.

The Augsburg merchants got into the business purely as traders, taking the product of the Tirolese operators. However, the Duke—Sigismund I—like all his contemporaries, constantly needed funds. He was an habitual borrower from merchants or a consortium of merchants in Augsburg, pledging his copper and silver royalties for the loans. Or, since he had the power to command the entire output of a mine, he might proclaim himself the only purchaser of the whole output at his own price and grant the handling of this to some merchant. These were called copper deals, silver deals, and so on.

Up to 1491 Hans Baumgartner, a rich Kufstein merchant, was the chief beneficiary of the Duke's copper deals. But in that year Fugger managed to shoulder Baumgartner out. From this point on Fugger felt the infection of that savage organism, the dream of the monopolist. And for the next thirty-two years he patiently schemed and bribed and intrigued to become copper king of the sixteenth century.

This, of course, he could not do unless he could control the resources of Hungary. But trade in Hungary was practically closed to the German merchant even if it were not too risky, for Matthias, the Hungarian king, was at war with the Holy Roman Empire. Maximilian, son of the Emperor, took the field against Matthias and defeated him after a bloody war, memorable for the fact that in it bombs were first used. Maximilian ended this struggle with a great victory, the death of Matthias, the elevation of Vladislav of Bohemia to the throne of Hungary, and the famous Peace of Pressburg. By this treaty Vladislav agreed that upon failure of male issue the crown of Saint Stephen should fall to the Hapsburgs.

With Hungary rendered safe for trade, Jacob Fugger made his entry. There an able engineer, Johann Thurzo, had risen to importance in the metals industry. He had perfected a method of rescuing flooded mines by means of a hydraulic pump and he had made great advances in the art of separating metals. What Thurzo needed was money. Fugger needed Thurzo's technical skill, and so they united to form the Fugger-Thurzo Company, much as John D. Rockefeller, the money man, united with Andrews, the practical oil refiner, to form the first unit of Standard Oil. And this company, backed by the political influence of Maximilian and the power of Vladislav, acquired a dominating position in Hungarian copper and silver production.

But Fugger never relaxed his intrigues to hold that position and to consolidate it. His strength lay in his relationship with the Hapsburg rulers and, of course, his own growing fortune. He wished to leave nothing to chance or to take the risk of any repudiation of the Pressburg convention. Accordingly, he schemed for years to unite the heirs of Maximilian with the daughters of Vladislav. And this he succeeded in doing at the Congress of Vienna in 1515, when the daughter of Vladislav, Anna, was betrothed to the grandson of Maximilian, Ferdinand. Fugger's biographer records that Fugger's expense account charged to the Fugger-Thurzo firm at this Congress was 10,000 gulden.

The Hungarian copper and silver trade was dominated by a subsidiary company, one half of which belonged to the Fugger Company and the other half to the Thurzo Company. It was known as the Fugger-Thurzo Company and it engaged entirely in the mining, smelting, and production of copper. Its entire product was sold to its constituent companies. The Fugger Company took half its product; the Thurzo Company took half. These two companies then sold their respective shares and pocketed the proceeds.

The Fugger-Thurzo Company operated mines, some of which they bought and some of which were leased. They handled the ores in their own smelting plants and treated the product in their own rolling and plate mills. They had three principal plants, at Neusohl, at Hochkirch, and at Fuggerau—an industrial town, forerunner of the modern Gary. The company employed several hundred workers in the mines and mills. This was probably the largest-scale business which had developed up to that time.

All through this period one perceives the continual efforts of Fugger to widen and cement his dominion over copper. Like the modern American trust barons whose first experiments in monopoly were made through trade agreements, Fugger's first efforts were made through cartels. As early as 1498 he made a cartel agreement with Herwart and Gossembrot of Augsburg and Hans Baumgartner of Kufstein. They pooled their supplies of Tirolese copper and sold them in Venice wholly through Fugger's factor, Hans Keller, thus eliminating competition and keeping the price and profits up.

In 1515 the Emperor Maximilian granted the entire copper product of Schwaz, richest mining district of the Tirol, to a consortium of Fugger and Hochstetter. Thus Fugger controlled the copper output of the Tirol through this consortium and of Hungary through the Fugger-Thurzo Company. It was agreed that Tirolese copper was to be sold only in upper Germany and Italy and the Hungarian output only in the Netherlands. These machinations became known, and Fugger found himself greeted by a howl of rage from the small businessmen of Germany. Frequent attacks were made upon him in the German Reichstag. Finally the imperial advocate or attorney general instituted proceedings against him for violating the antimonopoly laws of Germany. The great German merchant had to open the doors of his palace to the process server. The technique of subpoena dodging had not yet been perfected. About the same time, the town fathers of Augsburg rose against him and started proceedings to bring him to book.

In this crisis Fugger did what the American trust magnate has always done. He mobilized his lawyers and turned the heat of political influence upon the officials. He communicated with Emperor Charles V who was at Burgos. Charles wrote to the chief advocate directing him to end his prosecution. He wrote also to the Archduke Ferdinand to quash the court action. But this did not satisfy the insatiable Fugger. In May, 1525, the Emperor

Charles V issued a decree, prepared for him largely by Fugger's imperial lobbyists, declaring that hereafter ore contracts granting monopoly rights to merchants would not be considered monopolistic and that such merchants might sell their ores to one buyer, under monopolistic agreements, without violating the Reichstag decrees. Even this did not quiet the imperious Jacob. He did not rest until, five months later, the Emperor issued another decree declaring that his two copper contracts in 1515 and 1520 did not involve "criminal enhancement of prices."

But despite these strenuous stratagems to defend the structure of wealth he had reared, the clouds were gathering over the relentless monopolist. The flames of religious strife spread over distracted Germany from the torch of Luther. The Anabaptists were in eruption, the peasants rose, the castles and estates of nobles and men of wealth were destroyed. Fugger saw many ancient families forsaking the old Church for the standard of Luther, who lost no opportunity to denounce him and his "cutpurses." And as he sat in his splendid palace scheming to escape further damage and humiliations from the antimonopoly crusaders, the gravest news came from Hungary. That unhappy and backward country lay under the shadow of the Turk, for Sultan Suleiman had already captured one of the fortresses of Belgrade and merely awaited a favorable surcease from some of his other warlike enterprises to swoop down upon the land where Jacob had built his great industrial edifice.

But Hungary itself was in a state of political confusion while its people wallowed in the most degrading poverty. Vladislav, Fugger's royal friend, had died, leaving a boy of ten on the throne and a flock of courtiers and politicians struggling for control. A powerful nationalist movement sprang up. The half-starving peasants united with the small nobles to rise against the "foreign" capitalists who were exploiting their land and draining away its resources.

In the midst of these disorders Alexis Thurzo, who succeeded his father Johann as factor of the Fugger-Thurzo Company in Hungary, became treasurer of Hungary. The king was loaded with

debts partly growing out of the indemnities or "reparations" payments of the treaty of Pressburg and others of his own making, a
good deal of which was due to the Fugger firm. The country itself
groaned under a crushing debt. Thurzo brought about a devalua-
tion of the currency. It did not affect Fugger's credits since they
were payable in gold, but it did enhance in Hungary the value of
his copper holdings. In any case, a storm of indignation against
Fugger swept over Hungary which, added to the general hatred of
the foreign concessionary, brought the mobs swarming to the Ofen
and Neusohl plants of the company, which were sacked and looted
with immense losses. The young King Louis summoned Thurzo
and forced him to sign an agreement canceling the royal debts to
Fugger, renouncing all claims for damages to the Fugger-Thurzo
plants, and agreeing to furnish to the king 200,000 Rhenish golden
gulden.

When the news of these disasters reached Fugger at his desk in
Augsburg it filled him with wrath. He lost no time in the pursuit
of vengeance and restoration. He did precisely what the American
or British oil concessionary does in Mexico when the government
seizes an oil well. He appealed directly to the Emperor, Charles V,
who was then in Spain. The Emperor promptly notified the Hungarian king that he would support the claims of Fugger to the
uttermost. Menaced by the Turk on one frontier and the outraged
monopolist on the other, Louis yielded. But the masterful merchant
prince and banker was at the end of his labors. Worn out by all
his ceaseless adventures in pursuit of wealth upon so many fronts,
before the Hungarian business could be repaired, Jacob Fugger
lay dying in his Augsburg palace. The Archduke Ferdinand, who
represented the Emperor during his absence, proceeding to the
opening of the Diet at Augsburg with his train of courtiers and
guards, ordered the drums and trumpets silenced as the royal procession passed the house of the dying merchant.

Fugger breathed his last December 30, 1525. The next year
Suleiman with his Turks swept down upon Hungary, annihilated
its small army, devastated a fourth of the country, and departed,

carrying with him 107,000 captives. But in the one decisive battle where Louis' futile army was destroyed, the King himself was killed. The Hungarian monarch died without a son, and under the treaty of Pressburg, the crown of Saint Stephen fell into the lap of the Hapsburgs. In 1526 Archduke Ferdinand was elected King of Hungary. The Fugger dynasty, now ruled over by Anton Fugger, Jacob's nephew, came into complete possession of the Fugger-Thurzo interests and once again into complete domination of the Hungarian copper resources.

Fugger was buried in the beautiful chapel that, like a Pharaoh, he had begun to build fifteen years before. How differently these two men—Maximilian and Fugger, his banker and counselor—looked upon their deaths and monuments! Maximilian, feeling within him the signals of age and dissolution, had for four years carried around with him wherever he went a stout oaken coffin. Before his death at Innsbruck he left minute directions for his burial. He ordered that his hair be cut off, all his teeth extracted, pounded to powder, and publicly burned in the chapel of his palace. He ordered his corpse to be exposed to the people as a royal instance of mortality. He commanded that his body, put into a sack of lime swathed in silk, should be put into the oaken coffin and buried under the altar of his chapel so that the priest, daily saying his Mass, would humiliate the mortal remains by walking over the head and heart.

But the proud merchant of Augsburg provided for himself a magnificent mortuary chapel gleaming in marble and color and gold, decorated by artist and sculptor, and bearing the epitaph for which Fugger had provided both the text and the artist before his death, amazing in its brazen egoism:

TO GOD, ALL-POWERFUL AND GOOD! Jacob Fugger, of Augsburg, ornament to his class and to his country, Imperial Councilor under Maximilian I and Charles V, second to none in the acquisition of extraordinary wealth, in liberality, in purity of life, and in greatness of soul, as he was comparable to none in life, so after death is not to be numbered among the mortal.

JOHN LAW

CHAPTER II

John Law

MONEY MAGICIAN

———————————————— I ————————————————

JOHN LAW, the goldsmith's son, was born in Edinburgh, Scotland, in April, 1671. Having escaped from prison in London, where he was held after conviction of murder in his early twenties, he toured Europe, earning his living as a professional gambler, and then achieved the most amazing leap in history. He bounded in one immense flight from the gaming table to the highest office in France —a country of which he was not a citizen and from which, a few years before, he had been ejected by the minister of police because of his suspiciously consistent winnings. He had operated a gaming table in the house of a notorious actress and courtesan. And when he assumed the role of financial dictator of France he had the satisfaction of succeeding the very gentleman who as minister of police had invited him to clear out of Paris.

Law discovered and perfected the device that has played, perhaps, the most important role in the growth of what we now call finance capitalism. Here is what he discovered.

On the first day of January, 1939, the banks in America had on deposit, guaranteed by the government, the money of their depositors to the extent of fifty billion dollars. But the balance sheets of these banks showed only seventeen billion dollars in cash. A closer examination, however, reveals that not only was the fifty billions in deposits a myth, but the seventeen billions in cash was equally a fiction. There is not that much cash in America. The actual amount of cash—currency—in the banks was less than a billion dollars.

49

John Law did not invent the device that makes this miracle possible. But he discovered its uses and gave it to the world. Experimenting with it, he climbed one of the most dazzling peaks of material success, accumulated a vast fortune, engineered one of the dizziest adventures in the history of national finance, and ended by dying in poverty in Venice.

His father was a goldsmith. The goldsmith was the tadpole whence the modern banker sprang. He made a moderate fortune lending money at usurious rates. Thus the boy's first years were spent in the home of a moneylender and a Scot. He was educated with the greatest care with particular attention to mathematics. When he was twenty he left Edinburgh for London to taste the pleasures of the wicked capital of William and Mary.

He got access to the smartest circles. He was a young man of education and culture, handsome, quick-witted, a good athlete excelling at tennis, a graceful dancer, and a redoubtable talker. He spent his mornings in the city, where he got a reputation for skill in speculating in government paper. He passed his afternoons in the parks, his evenings at the opera or theater, and the later hours at the routs, balls, masquerades, and gaming houses. He played for high stakes and won large sums. He was a man with a system. Had he lived in our time he would have been in Wall Street with an infallible formula for beating the market.

The end of this was a duel which cut short his career in England. He got into a quarrel with an aging dandy known as Beau Wilson. Whatever the cause, which remains obscure, the two gentlemen met in Bloomsbury Square, April 9, 1694. It was not a noble performance. Apparently there was but a single pass when Mr. Law put his blade an inch or two into the breastbone of the ancient coxcomb, who died on the spot. Law was thrown into the Old Bailey, tried, convicted of murder, and sentenced to death. But presently he was let out somehow, until, on the demand of the victim's relatives, he was recommitted to jail. But very quickly he escaped from prison, was rowed down the Thames to a waiting vessel aboard which, as fate would have it, he made his way to

Amsterdam. A reward of fifty pounds was posted for his capture. But probably the headsman did not hanker too hungrily for his head, the law against dueling having been sufficiently vindicated by his conviction. This was in 1694.

In Amsterdam he established some sort of connection with the British resident there. And thus he found the opportunity to observe the working of the famous Bank of Amsterdam. Here the modern bank was being hatched. This historic institution was playing a decisive role in modeling the system of finance capitalism that attained its full flower in our time. Law liked money as an instrument of power. But he was deeply interested in it also as a social mechanism. He pondered its uses, its vagaries, and, above all, its limited quantities.

He was more than gambler. He was a fabricator of theories. By 1700—when he was twenty-nine—he was back in Scotland with a plan for rescuing her foundering economy. He printed a book— *Proposals and Reasons for Constituting a Council of Trade in Scotland.* He pressed it upon his countrymen, who rejected it. Whereupon he went back to the Continent, where for fourteen years he drifted around Europe amassing a fortune at roulette and cards and weaving his expanding financial theory for every public man whose ear he could reach. This theory was that the economic system of that day was being starved because of insufficient supplies of money. And, using the Bank of Amsterdam as a model, he had a scheme for producing all the money a nation needed. He was accompanied by his wife and his young son and daughter. Like that fabulous Don Louis, the Marqués de Vincitata, in *Anthony Adverse,* the restless gambler traveled about in an elaborate coach. For the greater part of fourteen years this unwearied coach rumbled all over the trade routes of Europe, from metropolis to metropolis, wherever people of wealth and fashion could be found in clusters seeking pleasure and profit at the gaming table. Everywhere he mingled with the most important and the noblest persons. He played with ministers of state, won their silver, and lectured them upon the virtues of his economic theories.

In 1705 he was back in Scotland with another book and another plan for saving his unwilling countrymen. But, despite the support of such powerful persons as the Duke of Argyle, they would have none of it. By 1708 he was in Paris. There he made a great stir. He had a large capital. Everywhere he won. He became a sort of legendary figure at all the fashionable salons—in the Rue Dauphine, at the Hôtel de Grève, in the Rue des Poulies. He set up a table for faro at the salon of Madame Duclos, variously described as famous comic actress and courtesan. The rich and noble gamesters of Louis XIV's Paris thronged to this salon. He struck up a friendship with the Duc d'Orléans. The Duke presented him to Desmarets, Minister of Finance, who listened with enchantment to Law's project for recasting the financial system of France. Desmarets took the scheme to Louix XIV who rejected it out of hand.[1]

Law made his appearance at the gambling salons in the evenings with two large bags of specie. He played for such high stakes that the existing coins became burdensome, so he had cast a large coin of his own mintage to facilitate the handling of the stakes. People marveled at his invariable luck. It was not luck, he said. He had a system. It was mathematics. Others whispered, as was inevitable, that it was something more than either luck or mathematics. The Chief of Police, M. d'Argenson, took notice of the audacious and dashing stranger. He told M. Law that he would do well to quit Paris. But it is only fair to say of him that he has the testimony of the perspicacious Duc de Saint-Simon, one of his critics, that he was not a trickster.

The coach again took up its ceaseless wanderings, to Germany, to Genoa, to Florence, to Venice, to Rome. At Genoa Law was again requested to move on. His fortune was growing. He was a millionaire. Stories clustered about his name throughout Europe. At Turin he was presented to Victor Amadeus, King of Sardinia. Law buzzed his system into the sovereign's ear. But the wily Italian

---

[1] Louis is said to have rejected the plan because Law was not a Catholic. This is hardly credible since Samuel Bernard, Louis' chief financial agent, was a Huguenot.

told him he should go to France. France had need of a financial miracle worker. Old Louis XIV was coming to the end of his reign. And Law was watching that port again. When Louis XIV died Law hurried to Paris and in an amazingly short time gained the confidence of the Regent, his acquaintance, the Duc d'Orléans, and set in motion, with the freest hand, all his theories which resulted in what Law and the French then called the System and what history has dubbed the Mississippi Bubble.

It did not last long, but in its course Law rose to the highest powers in France. Throughout, the roving gambler kept his head with singular poise and dignity, as one born to rule. He literally exercised all the powers of government. He was surrounded by flatterers. Expensive equipages jammed his roadway. His anteroom was filled with the rich and the noble begging for an audience. His son was admitted to dine with the young King Louis XV. His daughter gave a ball, and the most exalted nobles intrigued for a bid, some for her hand.

He was, of course, a Protestant, but in order to become Comptroller General of France, he embraced the Catholic religion. He was invariably courteous, affable, good-humored, profoundly convinced of his theories. And at one time, indeed, he saw about him in France such an upsurge of confidence, so many evidences of a rising boom, that he was justified in his illusion. Indeed one British nobleman told the French that Louis XIV had not been able to take away from France as much as Law could restore.

Law accumulated a vast fortune, but he invested it entirely in the securities of his companies and in a string of splendid estates in France.

His public career was brief. He opened his bank in 1716. He was driven from France amid the execrations of the people in 1720. He entered France worth 1,600,000 livres made chiefly at cards. He left it empty-handed after the crash of the greatest gamble in history—in which, as Voltaire said, a single unknown foreigner had gambled against a whole nation.

This was the man who reached a degree of power under Louis

XV which had not been held by any man since the days of Richelieu.

––––––––––––––––––––––––––––– II –––––––––––––––––––––––––––––

Law's famous Mississippi Bubble was something more than a mere get-rich-quick scheme. To understand it you must have a clear idea of the theory which lay at its base.

This theory consisted in two propositions. One was that the world had insufficient supplies of metal money to do business with. The other was that, by means of a bank of discount, a nation could create all the money it required, without depending on the inadequate metallic resources of the world. The bank Law had in mind was nothing more or less than the kind of banks we now do business with universally. But this was a unique proposal then.

Law did not invent this idea. He found the germs of it in a bank then in existence—the Bank of Amsterdam. This Law got the opportunity to observe when he was a fugitive from England.

The Bank of Amsterdam, established in 1609, was owned by the city. Amsterdam was the great port of the world. In its marts circulated the coins of innumerable states and cities. Every nation, many princes and lords, many trading cities minted their own coins. The merchant who sold a shipment of wool might get in payment a bag full of guilders, drachmas, gulden, marks, ducats, livres, pistoles, ducatoons, piscatoons, and a miscellany of coins he had never heard of. This is what made the business of the moneychanger so essential. Every moneychanger carried a manual kept up to date listing all these coins. The manual contained the names and valuations of 500 gold coins and 340 silver ones minted all over Europe.

No man could know the value of these coins, for they were being devalued continually by princes and clipped by merchants. To remedy this situation the Bank of Amsterdam was established.

Here is how it worked. A merchant could bring his money to the bank. The bank would weigh and assay all the coins and give him a credit on its books for the honest value in guilders. Thereafter that deposit remained steadfast in value. It was in fact a deposit. Checks were not in use. But it was treated as a loan by the bank with the coins as security. The bank loaned the merchant what it called bank credit. Thereafter if he wished to pay a bill he could transfer to his creditor a part of his bank credit. The creditor preferred this to money. He would rather have a payment in a medium the value of which was fixed and guaranteed than in a hatful of suspicious, fluctuating coins from a score of countries. So much was this true that a man who was willing to sell an article for a hundred guilders would take a hundred in bank credit but demand a hundred and five in cash.

One effect of this was that once coin or bullion went into this bank it tended to remain there. All merchants, even foreigners, kept their cash there. When one merchant paid another, the transaction was effected by transfer on the books of the bank and the metal remained in its vaults. Why should a merchant withdraw cash when the cash would buy for him only 95 per cent of what he could purchase with the bank credit? And so in time most of the metal of Europe tended to flow into this bank.

It was what Professor Irving Fisher now demands for America—a one hundred per cent bank. For every guilder of bank credit or deposits there was a guilder of metal money in the vaults. In 1672 when the armies of Louis XIV approached Amsterdam and the terrified merchants ran to the bank for their funds, the bank was able to honor every demand. This established its reputation upon a high plane. The bank was not supposed to make loans. It was supported by the fees it charged for receiving deposits, warehousing the cash, and making transfers.

There was in Amsterdam another corporation—the East India Company. A great trading corporation, it was considered of vital importance to the city's business. The city owned half its stock. The time came when the East India Company needed money to build ships. In the bank lay that great pool of cash. The trading company's managers itched to get hold of some of it. The mayor, who named the bank commissioners, put pressure on them to make loans to the company—loans without any deposit of money or bullion. It was done in absolute secrecy. It was against the law of the bank. But the bank was powerless to resist.

The bank and the company did this surreptitiously. They did not realize the nature of the powerful instrument they had forged. They did not realize they were laying the foundations of modern finance capitalism. It was Law who saw this. Law perceived with clarity that this bank, in its secret violation of its charter, had actually invented a method of creating money. He came to the conclusion that this was something which should be not merely legalized, but put into general use to cure the ills of Europe. He also saw clearly that this bank had brought into existence a great pool or reservoir of money and that he who controlled this supply could perform wonders. This was to be one of the most powerful weapons of the acquisitive man of the future—the collection of vast stores of other people's money into pools and the capture of control of those pools.

Here is what Law saw. It is an operation that takes place in our own banks daily. The First National Bank of Middletown has on deposit a million dollars. Mr. Smith walks into the bank and asks for a loan of $10,000. The bank makes the loan. But it does not give him ten thousand in cash. Instead the cashier writes in his deposit book a record of a deposit of $10,000. Mr. Smith has not deposited ten thousand. The bank has loaned him a deposit. The cashier also writes upon the bank's books the record of this deposit of Mr. Smith. When Mr. Smith walks out of the bank he has a deposit of ten thousand that he did not have when he entered. The bank has deposits of a million dollars when Mr. Smith enters. When he leaves it has deposits of a million and ten thousand dollars. Its deposits have been increased ten thousand dollars by the mere act of making a loan to Mr. Smith. Mr. Smith uses this deposit as money. It is bank money.

That is why we have today in the United States about a billion dollars in actual currency in the banks but fifty billion in deposits or bank money. This bank money has been created not by depositing cash but by loans by the bank to depositors. This is what the Bank of Amsterdam did by its secret loans to the East India Company, which it hoped would never be found out. This is what Law saw, but more important, he saw the social uses of it. It became the foundation of his System.

— III —

Law had in him that restless demon that drives those possessed to shape the world to their heart's desire. Gambler, lover of leisure and of easy money, he was yet a reformer. He looked upon a problem that has baffled men ever since the Middle Ages. When things go to pot the merchant finds he cannot sell his goods because there is not enough money in the hands of his customers. The remedy for this, he thinks, is more money. And how to produce more money has fascinated the minds of amateur economists for centuries as depression has followed depression. Always there comes forward a savior with a plan to produce more money purchasing power. It has never failed from Law to Major Douglas. They never fail to collect a vast train of loyal followers. Their remedy has always this supreme virtue: it is easy. It was Dr. Townsend's evil genius that prompted him to propose a scheme for raising all the old people to prosperity with pensions but planned to raise the pension money by the hard way of taxes.

Law made his first appearance as a reformer in Edinburgh in 1700. Scotland was in a severe depression. He came forward with an outright proposal for national planning. He urged a Council of Trade made up of three nobles, three barons, three commoners, three representatives of the Indian and African companies, and a neutral chairman—thirteen in all.

He then proposed a national fund for spending to be raised by taxes of about two and a half per cent on all manufactures, lands, rents, inheritances, and clerical benefices and ten per cent on all wheat and agricultural products. An additional million pounds might be borrowed in anticipation of these revenues.

Of this sum 400,000 pounds would be employed to promote the trade of the Indian and African companies and the balance would be used for various relief and recovery projects—public works, pegging farm and manufactured-goods prices, to lend and contribute to corporations and to fisheries, to encourage manufactures, and to make charitable payments to people in distress. There were to be import duties. Monopolies were to be regulated. There was to be free coinage of gold and silver at a fixed ratio and fixed standards of weight at His Majesty's mints.

This will have a familiar sound to those familiar with economic history and the devices of mercantilism and of Colbertism as well as to those who will see here the prototypes of the various alphabetical agencies of the New Deal. But as yet Law had not got around to producing the money by bank issues. Unlike the New Deal, he proposed paying the bills out of taxes.

This plan the Scottish government rejected. Law had put it into a book bearing one of those wordy eighteenth-century titles— *Proposals and Reasons for Constituting a Council of Trade in Scotland.* Such books published today bear such cryptic titles as *$2500 a Year for All, The Way Out, Every Man a King.*

The money theories are missing from this first plan for the rehabilitation of Scotland. It must have been after this that Law began to have a clear idea of the system he later sold to the Regent of France. Those theories he finally put into a book he published in Scotland in 1705, which is his principal contribution to the literature of economics. It was called *Money and Trade Considered, with a Proposal for Supplying the Nation with Money.*

After a brief examination of the nature of metallic money, Law in this volume lays down the proposition that the increase of money makes increase of trade and that an excess of exports over imports results in a large supply of money for production. As trade depends on money so the increase or decrease of a people depends on money.

Scotland has little trade because she has little money. This was good mercantilist doctrine.

There can be no doubt that the new capitalist money economy was greatly handicapped by a lack of sufficient supplies of money. There was no money but coins. We may see in this country how greatly handicapped our commercial activity would be if we had nothing above the metallic money which circulates. This is never above six billion, while our banks have fifty billion in deposits.

Law argued that all sorts of measures had been used to increase money but none had succeeded. Banks, he said, were the best instruments for accomplishing this. He then referred specifically to the Bank of Amsterdam and proposed that his bank do generally what the Bank of Amsterdam did only secretly for a single company—make loans in excess of its cash deposits. He proposed also that the bank should be permitted to issue notes in excess of its cash deposits. He noted that "some are against all banks where the money does not lie pledged equal to the credit." But he reminds the reader that "if 15,000 pounds is supposed to be the money in the bank and 75,000 pounds of notes are out, 60,000 pounds is added to the money of the nation, without interest."

Law was arguing in substance for the thing that is now common practice in our banking system and that, indeed, is one of the cornerstones of modern capitalism.

He then propounded his theory that the basis of paper money should be land rather than gold and silver. Silver was defective because the quantity is destined to increase. But land is of limited volume and is therefore destined to increase continuously in value; as a base for money it would ever become sounder.

Along with all this he revived his proposal for a commission for Scotland. Among other things this commission would have power to coin notes by lending on ordinary land values up to half or two thirds of the value of the land. Thus he would flood Scotland with new money. And for this system he obtained the support of the Duke of Argyle, the Marquess of Tweeddale, and other powerful noblemen and of a strong court party known as the Squadrone. But the Scottish parliament rejected it, saying in its resolution "that to establish any kind of paper credit, so as to oblige it to pass, was an improper expedient for the nation." Another reason given was that the plan might reduce all the estates in the kingdom to dependence on the government, which would become the universal creditor. But with this new edition of his plan of salvation for Scotland, Law had come around to be the New Dealer of his day.

With this brief outline of Law's theories we are now prepared to see how he sold them to France and, in a brief time, set France upon one of the most amazing financial adventures in history, gave to her the first great financial panic of the modern banking system, and, during the life of the episode, became almost the dictator of that country.

—————————————————— IV ——————————————————

Louis XIV set the stage for John Law. The unscrupulous and spendthrift monarch made way for the evangelist of easy abundance. It was necessary that France should be ruined before she would turn to so fantastic a redeemer. Louis XIV ruined her.

No man has been dealt with so generously by history as Louis XIV. He has been taken at his own estimate with small discount. He is recalled as Le Grand Monarque. In truth, he was the worst of kings. He used a power that had been put into his youthful hands, consecrated by the Church and sanctified by tradition, to ravage France. He was a shallow, egotistical, pretentious coxcomb. He achieved the effect of grandeur by means that are open to any adventurer with the power to squeeze taxes and loans out of a compliant people to be expended on projects and wars, displays, corrupt servants, and an army of shirt stuffers to produce the proper stage effects for what kings call their glory. The power he got was an inheritance from his forebears through the genius of two corrupt ecclesiastics—Richelieu and Mazarin. The money he got through ministers with a talent for inventing ever-new and subtle devices for taxing the impoverished people.

He squandered money with unrestrained abandon. On one palace alone—Versailles—he spent 116 million livres. His ministers, satellites, and the grafters who waxed rich through his bounties and incapacity imitated their betters. These vulgar displays were designed to exhibit the monarch and his satellites in the character of gods fit to rule the herd. Immense bounties were handed out to a swarm of poets and literati to exploit the grandeur and virtues of the King. When the King recovered from an illness the odes and apostrophes poured out in a flood from the horde of scribblers who ate from the King's bounty. Even the young Racine broke into thanksgiving verse.

The source of all wealth in France was the peasants upon their small farms and the artisans in the city. The machine had not yet come. Large-scale industry was still unheard of. There could be no pretense that the production of wealth at the hands of these humble toilers was stimulated and directed by the creative genius of inspired entrepreneurs. Hence there were few men of very large means who accumulated their wealth through owning and directing the processes of production. The wealth of the people, translated into money, flowed to the King through oppressive taxes. And most of the private fortunes were in the hands of men who knew how to tap this stream of public money on its way to the government. The nobles still held their hereditary lands and squeezed the last drop of tribute from their tenants. But the business fortunes were accumulated by men who drew them from the public revenues through contracts, monopolies, graft, gifts from the sovereign or from bankers who exploited the public treasury. They were strictly parasitic fortunes.

The peasants lived in mud houses with low roofs and no glass. A farmer got a pair of shoes for his wedding, and these had to last him a lifetime. But most of them went barefooted. They slept on straw, and boiled roots and ferns with a little barley and salt for food. Undernourished, they became prey to such diseases as typhoid and smallpox. Thousands swarmed toward the cities, and mendicancy and vagrancy became a scourge. Hospitals had to be closed for want of funds. Despite the fact that the people languished in hunger and rags, there was overproduction, the curse of the capitalist world. In places there was insufficient barley to feed the people, but no one could buy even the small supply. Peasants who had wine could not sell it to impecunious neighbors and could not ship it because they had no horses for transport.

Out of the meager substance of these wretched people the ministers of the Grand Monarch found the means to wring by taxes and loans nearly all the savings of the thrifty and a cruel fraction of the earnings of all. Slowly the money income of the nation was drawn in an ever-increasing stream toward the throne. But millions never reached it. Colbert found that out of 84 millions of taxes collected in one year only 32 millions reached the royal treasury. The rest found its way into the pockets of the farmers of the revenues. What reached the King in taxes and loans provided immense profits for war contractors and gifts for favorites. Indeed, even the virtuous Colbert died worth ten millions, all of which he said was derived from royal gifts and the legal prerequisites of his office.

There were extraordinary fortunes in the poverty-stricken France of that day. The treasurer of the imperial household was accused of appropriating to himself a tenth of the pay of the guard for years, and he had 1,600,000 livres invested abroad. Châtelain, a groom in a convent, took service with an army contractor, later set up for himself, had sixty mounted clerks scouring the country for grain for the army, and accumulated a fortune of over ten million livres. Crozat rose from a footman to be the greatest merchant in France, flourishing on government monopolies. Samuel Bernard, the great banker, had a fortune exceeding thirty million, made in the handling of government finances. Bouret, purveyor to the army, is supposed to have got together over 40 millions, while the more or less fabulous Brothers Pâris de Montmartel came to be worth, according to some estimates, as much as a hundred million. The Chamber of Justice found six thousand men who were by their own estimates worth well over a billion livres, a sum equal to about ten billion dollars in our time.

These parasites, with the gilded coxcomb at their head, had drained the nation. In the last fourteen years of Louis' reign he had spent two billion livres more than he had collected in taxes. By various devaluations and other devices this had been reduced to a debt of 711 million when he died. As his long reign neared its end and his prestige declined he felt something must be done to revive his glory. This wrong-headed poseur could improvise no better stratagem than to stage some dazzling fetes. Fetes cost money, however, and the treasury was empty. But Desmarets, the Comptroller, was ordered to find money. A twist of fate saved him. He discovered two of his servants inspecting his papers and communicating the details secretly to certain important stock jobbers. Desmarets planned an issue of thirty million livres. He put this paper in the hands of Samuel Bernard to sell. He purposely left upon his desk the secret outline of a royal lottery to pay the issue of securities. This was promptly communicated to the speculators. When Bernard offered his shares the jobbers bid up the price. When all had been disposed of and the lottery failed to materialize, the securities fell to a low level. Louis XIV's government was driven to this shabby and fraudulent fund-raising expedient to put on a great spectacle to exhibit to the desperate people of France the splendor of the aging and obscene sovereign.

He died on September 1, 1715, leaving the country he had raided in a state of appalling want and the treasury bankrupt. When the news of his death reached the roving Scottish gambler, he lost no time packing his family and his baggage into his much-traveled coach. He directed the postilion to head for Paris.

v

About the middle of September, 1715—about two weeks after Louis XIV died—the Duc d'Orléans, Regent of the child Louis

XV, sat with his newly formed cabinet. They were grave-faced and bewildered. A proposal had been made that the Regent should declare the nation bankrupt. France was indeed in ruins. The treasury was empty. The army was unpaid. The expenses of the government for the preceding year came to 148 million livres. The receipts were trivial. Besides, 740 million livres in obligations would fall due in the year. So high-minded and wise a man as the Duc de Saint-Simon had urged a proclamation of bankruptcy. Industry and trade had almost ceased to function. France had come to the end of a road, as America did in 1933, save that she was impoverished in substance as well as in the collapse of her economic mechanisms. But the Regent rejected the shame of a public confession of bankruptcy. Instead he sought to accomplish the same end by a less frank device.

Upon the death of Louis XIV all the directions of his will were rejected and Philippe, Duc d'Orléans, virtually took possession of the government as Regent of the boy king. This act completed the series of events that it was necessary for fate to weave for the appearance of Law. She had created for him a ruined nation. Now she marched upon the scene a ruler who would open the door for the promiser of good things.

Orléans was one of those nimble persons who liked the surface of ideas. He was a dabbler. He posed as a painter, an engraver, a musician, a mechanician. He composed an opera that was played before the King. He tinkered with chemistry. But he loved to play with ideas, was known to have an open mind—open at both ends— a dilettante's interest in the masses, and an unfailing talent for making bad choices of servants.

At such a moment, when the one obvious and desperate need of the government was money, John Law appeared like an angel from heaven. In a disordered world in which every statesman was at sea, he alone had a plan. And it was a plan which called, not for sacrifice or for painful surgery, but for a pleasant journey along the glory road to riches. As Law himself said, it was a perfect dispensation in which the king, instead of being an omnivorous taxer and an insatiable borrower of the people's substance, was to become the dispenser and lender of money. Here was to be a New Deal—the first New Deal of the capitalist order.

Moreover, Law had access to Orléans. The Regent had taken a fancy to him years before. Law's plan had become greatly expanded under the productive influence of innumerable conversations. He was a facile talker and a superb salesman. And he completely sold the Regent. His plan for a royal bank was submitted to the Council on October 24, only about seven weeks after Orléans assumed power. But a majority of the Council opposed it. He persisted. He declared that, if permitted, he would establish a private bank and finance it himself if he was authorized by a royal patent to establish it—the Banque Générale. And on May 2, 1716, the royal patent was granted and the Banque Générale was established privately and financed largely by Law himself.

It began on a small scale. But it was an entering wedge. It was such a bank as we now have on almost every corner of the business districts of small American towns. It was to receive deposits and discount bills and notes; it could make loans and issue its own notes. Law and his brother William set up the bank in Law's house. The company issued 1200 shares of 5000 livres each. The subscribers were to pay for the shares in four installments—one fourth in cash and three fourths in *billets d'état*. This was a master stroke. It invented a use for the *billets d'état*, or government securities, which were worth no more than twenty or thirty livres on the hundred. The amount of cash thus brought in was small, so that the bank was scarcely larger than the First National in any little American town. It did not seem formidable and this diminished opposition. It gave Law the chance to experiment with his idea. The Regent let it be known that he was its patron and that he would be gratified if merchants would open accounts with M. Law.

This institution had an almost instantaneous success. The value of a depository was great. The advantage of introducing certainty into the value of bank money, as in the Bank of Amsterdam, encouraged all merchants to bring their metal money there. It was not long before M. Law's bank money was quoted at a premium over cash. The bank discounted bills at six per cent instead of the extortionate rates, as high as thirty, which the usurers charged. Furthermore, the bank guaranteed always to deliver in exchange of its own credit or its notes the same amount of silver as was deposited. And in a country living continuously under the fear of inflation this was a great inducement. The deposits rose enormously. Law was able to reduce the interest rate to four per cent. His reputation rose. He was no longer looked upon as an adventurer. His influence with the Regent grew. His bank notes were circulating around France, the best money in the kingdom.

A year after the bank was founded (April 10, 1717) the Council of State ordered all agents of the royal revenues to receive the bank's notes in payment of all government dues and to cash at sight its notes to the extent of their available funds. Every government office became a sort of branch of the bank. The Parliament of Paris ordered the revocation of this decree, for Law had active enemies. But the Regent compelled the Parliament to annul its order. Law by this time had become the greatest figure at court.

While things went thus well for Law, they went badly for the government. When, after his accession to power, the Regent rejected the proposal for national bankruptcy, he employed an ancient stratagem to achieve the same result. He devalued the livre, coining 1,000,000,000 livres into 1,200,000,000. He called in the 682 million livres in *billets d'état* and issued in their place 250 million at reduced interest—four per cent. But this helped only a little. The government's paper was worth 20 per cent of par before this drastic operation and the new securities were still worth only 20 per cent.

The next move of the government was drastic in the extreme. The Duc de Noailles, Comptroller General, ordered every person who had made a profit out of state offices or contracts during the preceding twenty-seven years to make an exact accounting. A

Chamber of Justice was set up. Rewards were offered to informers. And for more than a year some 6000 persons—farmers of the revenues, high officers, government contractors—were dragged before the Chamber of Justice. These constituted the richest and most powerful men in the kingdom.

Wealth became a crime. People of wealth were in panic. They hid their money. They attempted to flee. They tried bribing judges —and some succeeded. But the spoliation of the rich and corrupt parasites who had robbed the state for a generation went forward ruthlessly. Burey de Vieux-Cours, president of the Grand Council, admitted possessing 3,600,000 livres. He was fined 3,200,000. All the rich bankers were heavily taxed—all save the Brothers Pâris de Montmartel, who actually were made inspectors of the visa. Of the six thousand persons examined, some 4110 were condemned. They confessed to having 713 millions and were fined 219 millions. Perhaps half the fines were collected. This ferocious invasion of the rich was carried on not by a revolutionary government of radicals but by the royal government of Louis XV.

But all this aided the staggering administration only slightly. In May, 1718, after two years of futile, even savage expedients, the livre was devalued again. This time it was cut 40 per cent, amid the opposition of parliaments and to the accompaniment of riot and bloodshed all over France. In the last sixteen years France had witnessed forty-two changes in the price of gold and silver and over 294 in the preceding four centuries. The silver in the livre had been cut from twelve ounces to less than half an ounce. The people of France, by successive devaluations, had been robbed by the government of over seventy times the amount of money in circulation in the country.

In the midst of the disasters, Law's reputation alone seemed to rise as his bank established its utility. And this, combined with the desperate state of French finances, brought on the moment for carrying into execution the grand scheme he had been meditating —the scheme which was destined to be known as the System.

―――――――――――――― VI ――――――――――――――

Here we enter, almost for the first time in history, the complicated labyrinth of modern finance. But it can be made quite simple and clear if we will discard the personal and historic incidents that clutter it up.

It will be remembered that Law had set up his bank with a subscription of six million livres—three fourths payable in *billets d'état* worth only about 20 or 30 livres in the hundred. The bank succeeded, the deposits grew, and Law paid dividends. Subscribers were delighted. Their all but worthless *billets d'état* were transmuted into profit-making shares.

His second venture was into trade. Crozat, a sort of eighteenth-century Cecil Rhodes, had enjoyed a monopoly of colonization and trade with Louisiana and Canada, France's possessions in North America. He had made a great fortune as a merchant and government contractor but did not do so well with the French East India Company, through which he operated his monopoly in the New World. Law, through the Regent's favor, took over this enterprise. He formed a new corporation—the Company of the West. He issued 200,000 shares at 500 livres each—100 million livres. But he used the scheme which had worked so well with the bank. He accepted payment for the shares in *billets d'état*. These *billets d'état* the Regent converted into government *rentes* at four per cent. The company was thus insured of an income of four million livres a year. This was in August, 1717.

Then in 1718 the company got the farm of the tobacco monopoly from Law's friend, the Regent, for which the Company of the West paid 2,020,000 livres. This was expected to produce a yearly profit of four million livres. This, with the four million in interest from the government, would mean an income for the company of eight million. But the company was also selling "lots"—for the Mississippi Company, as the Company of the West was called, was a great real-estate development scheme. Lots a league square

were offered at 30,000 livres, and some persons invested as high as
600,000 livres. This added to the income, though it went quite
slowly at first.

Then by the end of 1718 and the beginning of 1719, the company took over three similar companies—the Senegal Company,
the China Company, and the East India Company, with the same
kind of trading privileges as the Louisiana Company in different
parts of the world. Law then organized a new corporation—the
Compagnie des Indes (the India Company)—which took over all
of these adventures, including the Mississippi Company and the
tobacco monopoly. It became the master holding company. The
new company issued 50,000 new shares at 550 livres each, netting
27,500,000 livres. The original shares of the Company of the West
were called mothers. These were called daughters.

We must not make the common mistake, however, of supposing
that what was called the Mississippi Bubble of Mr. Law was just
a real-estate development. It was indeed the smallest part of the
whole episode. It was called the Mississippi Bubble because the
company that carried on all the enterprises was popularly known
as the Mississippi Company and those who bought its shares were
called Mississippians. It got its name from the great river which
ran through its principal domain, though the company was never
legally called the Mississippi Company. The real basis of the
mania of speculation that we are now to see lay in wholly different
fields. At this point John Law, the gambler of three years before,
had become the autocratic master of a vast domain extending from
Guinea to the Japanese Archipelago, Cape of Good Hope, East
Coast of Africa washed by the Red Sea, the islands of the Pacific,
Persia, the Mongol empire, Louisiana, and Canada. And he proceeded by all sorts of extravagant promotional and advertising
methods to push the sale of lands and the colonization of parts of
this empire.

About the same time—December 4, 1718—the Banque Générale
was transformed into the Royal Bank. That is, the state took it
over. The stockholders who had paid for their shares one fourth

in cash and three fourths in almost worthless *billets d'état* sold their shares to the government for cash and at par. Thus the man who bought a share for 5000 livres—1500 livres in cash and 3500 livres in *billets d'état* worth only 1000 livres—had actually paid no more than 2500 livres for his share. Now he got 5000 livres in silver for it, a profit of 100 per cent plus the dividend. But the bank was now a royal bank and Law was head of the royal bank and the man closest to the Regent. And what is more, the limitation in the original charter upon the issue of notes was no longer effective.

Then came the series of events that startled France. On July 25, 1719, the India Company took over the royal mint and got the privilege of coining money. This was estimated to be worth as much as ten million livres a year. It paid fifty million livres for the royal privilege and Law put out another 50,000 shares, this time at 1000 livres per share, to raise the money.

On August 25, the company took over the profitable privilege of collecting the indirect taxes. Law had enemies within the government. The most industrious was M. d'Argenson, the former police chief who had expelled him from France and was now Comptroller General. Inevitably Law's success would stimulate others to use the same method. D'Argenson conspired with the Brothers Pâris to organize a corporation to farm the taxes. The Brothers Pâris were the richest businessmen in France. Sons of a poor tavernkeeper of Dauphine, they started transporting provisions to the army of the Duc de Vendôme, rose rapidly, became purveyors to the army and so powerful and rich that even during the ruthless visa of the Duc de Noailles they remained untouched. And now they formed a corporation issuing 100,000 shares at 1000 livres each payable in annuity contracts.

This company bid 48,000,000 livres for the revenues, which it got through the influence of d'Argenson. This was called the Antisystem. They hoped to collect a vast sum in taxes—perhaps a hundred million, paying only 48 million to the king. Law had this contract annulled and new bids taken. He outbid the Brothers Pâris, paying 3,500,000 livres more than they, and got the contract for the revenues. D'Argenson resigned. The Brothers Pâris were now in complete disfavor and retired to one of their estates. A few days later Law got the contract for the direct taxes. By this time his position was amazing. He had complete possession of the vast colonial possessions of France, the monopoly of coining money, the collection of the revenues, the tobacco monopoly, the salt monopoly. He was, besides, complete master of the finances of France as head of the Royal Bank and he was the undisputed favorite of the Regent.

He now began to speak in imperious tones about his plans. He would rid the king of France of his debts—the debts that had ridden kings for a century. He would make the king independent of the parliaments, of the people, of everybody. Instead of making the king dependent on the taxpayers and the moneylenders he would make the king the giver of all funds and the universal creditor. Therefore he announced in September his greatest coup —the company would buy up the entire public debt of France. The king would have but a single creditor, the company, his obedient servant. The outstanding debt was 1,500,000,000 livres. Law therefore planned an issue of company stocks of 300,000 shares. These would be sold at 5000 livres, bringing in the required 1,500,000,000. Meantime the bank would advance the money. The bank had been printing bank notes and issuing them for various purposes. It had made loans on stock of the company, had invested in company stock, had made loans on other projects. Now it would issue enough notes to buy up the public debt. Meantime the India Company would issue shares and with the proceeds pay off the bank loans.

France's debt of a billion and a half livres, measured against her resources, was hardly less than America's debt of fifty billion dollars today. And Law's proposal to rid France of her debt by buying it through the Mississippi Company is comparable to the proposal of Mr. Roosevelt, in our own time, to extinguish the public debt of America by purchasing it through the Social Security Board.

In the meantime, by various devices, Law had manipulated the market price of company shares until people were offering 5000 a share for them. So he offered these shares at 5000 livres. But hardly had he done this when the shares advanced in price. They sold for 10,000. And they were gobbled up in short order. When this point was reached at the end of 1719, Law's company, in addition to all its other possessions and powers, was the sole creditor of the government.

This marked the peak of the great adventure. Here is how the capital of the India Company stood:

	NO. OF SHARES	NOMINAL PRICE	ACTUAL PRICE	AMOUNT PAID IN
1st issue	200,000	500	500	100,000,000
2nd issue	50,000	500	550	27,500,000
3rd issue	50,000	500	1000	50,000,000
4th issue	300,000	500	5000	1,500,000,000
Total	600,000			1,677,500,000

Law had been manipulating the stock prices until the shares were selling at 5000. After the rout of the Antisystem and the capture of the national revenues they went up to 10,000 livres. If a man had bought a share of the Company of the West at 500 livres in *billets d'état* or 150 livres in money, he would now at 10,000 livres have a profit of 660 per cent. Before the bubble burst shares went to 18,000 livres. This was the financial part of the famous System of Law in operation. Now let us see what happened to it.

VII

In the Paris of that day was a little street called the Rue Quincampoix. It was in fact a small alley, 150 feet long and very narrow. It ran at one end into the Rue des Ours; at the other into the Rue Aubrey-le-Boucher. Here the bankers had their houses, and men who had bills of exchange or *billets d'état* or other paper to buy or sell went from door to door seeking the best terms. This became the center of excitement when, during the visa of the Duc de Noailles, rich contractors rushed there to divest themselves of the evidences of their wealth. It was this little street that became the stage for the public scenes and manifestations of the Mississippi Bubble. It became the symbol of the speculation as Wall Street became the symbol of the orgies that flamed up in the 1920's.

The other scene of this extraordinary comedy drama was the Mazarin Palace. Law purchased this splendid edifice in the Rue Vivienne for the headquarters of the company and the bank when it was made into the Royal Bank. He added seven other houses adjoining. Here Law directed the moves on all the many fronts of his System.

This is what Law was doing.

First, he was managing a new type of inflation—pumping bank funds into the economic system, very much as Mr. Roosevelt is doing in America today and with very much the same instrumentalities.

Second, he was creating employment by numerous projects of public works, as Pericles did in Athens, as Roosevelt, Hitler, Mussolini, and Chamberlain did in 1939.

Third, he was attempting to stimulate the release and flow of hoarded savings back into business.

Fourth, he was attempting, by exploiting France's colonial empire, to make markets for her products.

Fifth, he was attempting to relieve the embarrassments of a debt-ridden government.

Sixth, he was making money for himself and his patrons.

He was engaged in trying to sell shares in the company that held France's colonial empire, and also trying to sell land there to investors and speculators. To do this he resorted to the most sensational methods of promotion. Indians were brought to France and paraded about. Departing emigrants were feted and paraded. Finding it difficult to get emigrants, young men were taken from the jails and girls from the streets and marched off garlanded to the strains of music as if they were honest citizens. Pamphlets, prospectuses, dodgers were circulated depicting the fabulous riches of the new lands. All this helped both shares and lots.

In the prosecution of the adventure we see many of the devices which serve the operators in the markets of today. Rumors were set afoot. It was whispered about that diamond mines had been found in Arkansas and gold and silver mines in Louisiana, rivaling the riches of New Spain and Peru. Stories of the fabulous sums being made by speculators and of the important persons who were buying shares "leaked" out.

The preferred list made its appearance. With each issue of shares persons of power and influence near to Law and the Regent were allowed to subscribe at the issuing price. Thus when the 300,000 share issue was offered, the Regent got 100,000 shares. He subscribed at 5000 livres. He could have sold within two months at 10,000 livres. It was by getting shares at the issuing price and selling later at the higher prices that many fortunes were made.

Moreover this served to limit the floating supply of shares in the Rue Quincampoix, since the subscribers held their shares off the market and thus the market prices were boosted.

The modern warrant or right came into use. Law himself paid 40,000 livres for the right to subscribe to a large number of shares at par six months later.

Street loans had their birth. The Royal Bank made loans on India Company shares at low rates of interest to stimulate speculation. When the bubble burst the bank had outstanding 450 million livres of loans on shares. The bank itself also invested in shares. In July, 1719, as Law was maturing the taking over of the national debt and the issuance of 300,000 shares, he announced that in 1720 the company would pay a 12 per cent dividend.

Ever since the issuance of the first shares of the Company of the West there had been much traffic in them in the Rue Quincampoix.

These little scraps of paper became the perfect instruments of gambling—gambling sanctified by the name of business and dressed up as investment. This was better than the counters on the tables of the Rue des Poulies or the Hôtel de Grève. As the new companies came along and the promotion assumed statelier forms, the activity in the street increased.

Almost unnoticed, the inflation that Law had been nourishing began to spark. By midsummer of 1719 about 400 million livres of bank notes had been issued. An air of enterprise appeared. People took confidence. Timid savings came out of hiding. The velocity of money increased. Law made extensive loans through his bank for enterprises of all sorts. Also he advanced sums for huge government projects.

Barracks were built for the first time to rid the people of the burden of housing the soldiers. A canal was built up the Seine, the Canal of Burgundy, the Bridge of Blois, new public buildings, new hospitals—there was to be a hospital at every six leagues—roads, the restoration of neglected farm lands, aids to businessmen in debt, and plans for free instruction at the University of Paris supported by part of the postal revenues, which brought the youth of Paris into the streets parading in gratitude to the great giver of all good things—M. Law. Various kinds of nuisance taxes were abolished, taxes burdening industry were mitigated or ended. Barriers to trade within the nation were struck down.

Here was a New Deal indeed—the old curse of harrying taxes gone, work for the artisans, succor for the farmers instead of levies, the spirit of enterprise reborn, the king himself emancipated from his creditors, the state become the foster father of all, the fountain of blessings rather than the aggrandizer of the people's substance, money flowing out mysteriously and flooding the market place. It is not to be wondered that for a few brief months Paris hailed the magician who had produced all these rabbits from his hat. Crowds followed his carriage. People struggled to get a glimpse of him. The nobles of France hung about his anteroom, begging a word from him.

By June or July, 1719, the crowd flooded into the Rue Quincampoix. Doctors, lawyers, businessmen, clergymen, coachmen,
scholars, and servants—people who had never seen it before—
came trooping in to buy a few shares and sell them on the rise.
The shares which had been 500 a little more than a year before
were now 5000 and in two months more they were 10,000.

As the crowds pressed into the street the demand for office space
became a problem. Small rooms rented for as high as 400 livres
a month. A house rented for 800 livres; one with thirty rooms
turned into offices fetched 9000 livres per month. Shopkeepers
rented space amid their barrels. Boxes were set up on a few roofs
and rented. The brokers worked in the street. The managers in
offices sent information to their agents in the street by means of
signals from the windows or by bells—as in the old Curb Market
in New York's Broad Street.

The noise of the spectacle spread through Europe. Speculators
flocked to Paris. In October the *Journal de Régence* reported at
least 25,000 had come from the leading commercial cities in a
month. Seats in the diligences to Paris were sold two months ahead,
and men began speculating in coach seats.

As Christmas, 1719, approached the excitement became almost
a public scandal. M. Law, a few days before the feast, was accepted
into the Catholic faith at the Church of the Recollets in Melun,
and on Christmas Day he and his children received communion
at St. Roch's, his parish church. He was made a warden to succeed
the Duc de Noailles. He made a princely gift of 500,000 livres to
complete the edifice and another of 500,000 to the English at
Saint-Germain-en-Laye. Then on January 5, M. d'Argenson, the
former police chief who had sent Law out of Paris in 1708, resigned as Comptroller General, and Law was named to that office,
equivalent to Prime Minister of France. At this moment his power
was almost supreme.

Immense fortunes were being made. Fantastic stories are recorded of the sudden flight to riches of barbers and coachmen.
How many are true it would be difficult to say. Madame de Chau-

mont, widow of a physician of Namur, made sixty million livres. Fargez, a private soldier, made twenty. The Duc de Bourbon made a vast fortune, much of which he reduced to cash, re-established his financially embarrassed house, acquired many new estates, set up a stable of 150 race horses, and continued as one of the richest men in France. Other noble persons—the Duc de Guiche, the Prince de Deux-Ponts, the Prince de Rohan accumulated immense sums. Count Joseph Gage made a fabulous winning and offered the King of Poland three million livres to abdicate in his favor. The Regent had a hundred thousand shares subscribed for at 5000 livres which he could have sold for ten thousand or more. He had a paper profit in January, 1720, of 500,000,000 livres. It is doubtful if he realized any of this.

But the last act in this tragedy-comedy began before the curtain had descended upon the triumphant scene in the preceding act. Well before Christmas, 1719—perhaps as early as late October— the little cracks and fissures in the hollow walls of the structure began to appear. Law perceived them. The base of his System was the accumulation of all the metal money in the hands of the System, the issuance and control of the paper currency, and the creation of additional funds by means of bank loans. Perhaps in October Law saw that, for the first time, gold and silver were leaving the Royal Bank. Therefore when he renounced his ancient faith at Christmas and became Comptroller General, it was not merely to crown his triumph with the trappings of high office, but to put into his hands the supreme power he required to begin the battle to save his System.

All the men who played this desperate game were not fools. A fairly rosy estimate of the probable income of the India Company was roughly 80 million livres. A more optimistic but unsound estimate looked for as much as 156 million. But 80 million would not come within many leagues of paying a five per cent dividend on 600,000 shares valued at 10,000 livres. Indeed 156 million profits speculators saw this quickly enough and began to unload. Groups would pay only a little more than half the dividend. Wise foreign of them formed to peg the market at higher prices than 10,000 livres while they quietly withdrew. Their example was soon followed by Frenchmen with the necessary wit. As they sold their shares they withdrew specie from the bank and transported it to other countries. Law saw this. By January the movement of money from the bank grew. The sellers were scornfully called realizers. They have appeared just before the last act of every boom from the golden age of Law to the New Era of Coolidge and the New Deal of Roosevelt. And with his elevation to the Comptroller Generalship Law began a losing battle to save the System.

Here was his problem: for a brief moment he seemed, as one commentator put it, to have solved the philosopher's dream of making men despise silver and gold. They preferred to louis d'or the paper promises of the three-year-old bank. Law's paper livres would buy five per cent more in a trade than the metal coin of Louis XIV. But now quite suddenly the wiser ones were recovering their taste for silver and gold. Law's problem was to check the flow of gold out of the country and into hoarding, to support the price of the shares, to save the value of his paper notes.

Through January the tide flowed heavily against him. The drain on metal became alarming. The inflation became more fevered. Prices of goods that were around 104 in 1718 and 120 before Christmas, 1719, went to 149 in January. Wages lagged far behind. The nongambling populace began to murmur. The Parliament of Paris became more hostile. Serious men like Saint-Simon, Marshal Villeroi, La Rochefoucald and Chancellor d'Aguesseau, who had held aloof from the gamble, now became more severely critical.

On February 22 the Royal Bank was suddenly turned back to the India Company. By this time over a billion in bank notes were outstanding. The issue had increased by 400 million since Christmas. Then on February 27 an edict was issued that no man would be allowed to have in his possession over 500 livres of specie —even goldsmiths and the clergy—and payments in specie could be made only in transactions of less than a hundred livres. This was difficult to enforce. But for the moment this did bring large amounts of specie back to the bank—perhaps as much as 300,000,000 livres.

Thus balked, the realizers now turned to real estate, furniture, plate, anything of solid value, as a refuge for their profits. One man bought up an entire edition of a dictionary. The inflation was in full flow in March. Prices were fixed but the attempt was futile. The hack coachman's fee was thirty sous, but he openly demanded sixty. Candles were fixed at eight sous, six derniers per pound, but sold at twenty. The general index rose to 166. On March 5, another debasement of the coin was ordered.

Law now sought to introduce a deliberate uncertainty into metal currency while stabilizing the price of paper by edict. On March 20, the shares were falling rapidly from a peak of 18,000 livres. An edict announced that shares would be stabilized at 9000 livres. At this price the bank would exchange shares for bank notes or bank notes for shares. Two bureaus were opened. The crowds swarmed to them with their shares. They demanded notes for their shares.

By this means the bank became the owner of an immense amount of its own shares, while the flood of paper notes was enormously augmented. It gave the inflation another boost and prices soared to 179. The Rue Quincampoix was in the wildest disorder. The frantic bargaining went on late into the night. The sober citizens of Paris muttered deeply against the scandal. Many robberies and acts of violence added to the apprehension and indignation. Then suddenly one of those irrelevant outrages intruded into the scene. Count Horn, a young Flemish nobleman, related distantly to the Duc d'Orléans and to several royal European houses, lured a speculator into a tavern at night, murdered him, and made off with his 150,000 livres. This crime shocked Paris. It gave Law an excuse to close the Rue Quincampoix and drive the gamblers away. Speculation was forbidden in the streets. The Count was arrested, convicted, and broken on the wheel in the Place de Grève. But the trading went on in side streets, alleys, hallways, and at night. Slowly it reappeared in the Place Vendôme. Then Law paid

1,400,000 livres for the Hôtel de Soissons and its spacious gardens and permitted stockjobbing in the numerous pavilions of the gardens, which were rented to stockbrokers at 500 livres per month.

By May the situation was desperate. The use of gold specie was forbidden beginning on May 1, and this was to apply to silver specie on August 1. The circulation had now soared to 2,696,000,000 livres. The general discontent was deepening. Prices had gone up, but wages had by no means kept pace with them. As June neared prices were at 190 but wages were only 125. Business was disrupted by the uncertainty of money values, the difficulty of getting coin, and the swiftly fading taste for paper. Political agitation was growing. The parliaments were becoming increasingly hostile. Law's enemies—d'Argenson and the powerful Abbé Dubois, corrupt and ambitious, scheming for power now—succeeded in weakening his prestige with the Regent. At this fatal moment they were able to force an edict that sounded the doom of the System.

The edict, issued on May 22, announced that the price of stock would be lowered to 8000 by July 1 and at the rate of 500 livres per month until December when it would be stabilized at 5000. Bank notes were also to be reduced in value from 10,000 to 8000 livres and at the same pace to 5000 by December 1. Thus the promise that the bank notes would remain stable was broken. The whole paper structure collapsed. Men ran wild-eyed to the bank to beg for specie. Soldiers blocked the way. Parliament demanded revocation of the edict. On May 28 this was done, but it was too late. The damage was done.

Law went to the palace and asked the Regent to relieve him of his post. His resignation was accepted. And the Regent directed two companies of Swiss guards to protect him from the fury of the crowds. His wife and children went to a near-by estate of the Duc de Bourbon for safety.

But that immense tangle of adventures without Law was a skull without a brain. He was recalled before May expired and named intendant and a member of the privy council. The disorders provoked by the suspension of specie payments at the bank were so great that an order was issued permitting the cashing of ten-livre notes and hundred-livre notes on alternate days, one to a person. They could be cashed only at the bank. Fifteen thousand people gathered at the Mazarin Gardens. Only a few note holders were admitted to the bank at a time. The crowd felt it was being played with. It broke through the gates. The soldiers fired, killing two or three men. This set off an explosion of wrath. The bodies were carried about to exhibit the cruelty of the "murderer" from England. In London brokers made bets that Law would be hanged by September. Law's carriage was torn to pieces.

After this the battle was hopeless. With the Regent Law tried to work out some sort of reorganization. A plan was formed to retire 600 million livres of the notes. New stock in the company and of the city of Paris was issued payable in notes. It was merely exchanging stock for money. The notes were destroyed in the presence of a committee of citizens.

Then another plan was attempted. It was proposed to issue annuities payable in notes. The bank was thus getting a long-term extension of its obligation to honor its notes. All notes above 100 livres in denomination could be used only to purchase these annuities. But nothing could save the System. By September prices of food and clothing were 270—they had been 120 the year before. Wages were only at 136. Actual wages—measured in purchasing power—had descended to 67. Thus the worker always is the sufferer by inflation. The demand for increased wages grew loud and angry. On October 10 an edict forbade the use of bank bills for currency. The stock of the India Company which had been worth 18,000 livres ten months earlier, was now sold for 2000 livres payable in bank notes worth only ten cents on the dollar. On November 1 the redemption of even small bank notes was suspended. All stockjobbing was forbidden on the eighth.

On December 10, worn out with sleepless struggles to save his System, the mob howling for his head, Law resigned. He retired to Guermande, one of his estates, six leagues from Paris. Sometime later two messengers arrived from the Duc de Bourbon bringing to him his unsolicited passports to leave the country. This was the royal invitation to begone. The Duke offered him financial assistance, but Law refused. He had just got 800 livres in gold from his box at the bank. This, he said, was sufficient. But he accepted the coach of Madame de Prie, the Duc de Bourbon's favorite. This nobleman, who had grown fabulously rich through Law's adventure, alone was willing to befriend him. He left France on December 21, accompanied by four equerries and six guards—his restless coach to take up again its wanderings. His wife joined him later, after remaining in Paris to put his household affairs in order and discharge the bills of tradesmen and servants.

The System itself, which had impoverished thousands and repeated the ruin of France, became a huge national bankruptcy. Duverney, an able but implacable enemy of Law, was charged with liquidating the disaster. The king, who was to be liberated from the curse of debt, was now more deeply in debt than before. When Law began his deliverance the national debt was 1,500,000,000 livres. Now it was, counting *rentes* and guaranteed stocks, over 3 billions. Instead of 48 million livres a year in *rentes,* the crippled government was saddled with 99 million. In January, fifteen boards were set up with 800 clerks to survey the ruin and demobilize it. Over 511,000 persons made claims amounting to 2,222,000,000 livres. They were reduced to 1,676,000,000. India shares were cut from 125,000—all that remained outstanding after being exchanged for annuities—to 55,000 shares bearing interest of 150 livres each instead of 360. The national debt was finally fixed at 199 million livres, and there was 336 million livres of specie in the bank against its multitude of claims. The trading business of the India Company was disentangled from the financial mess, the company was reorganized and continued to operate and in time even to flourish for many years in rivalry with the trading companies of England and the Dutch.

As for Law, the government confiscated all that he had left

behind in France, his numerous estates, art treasures, plate, his hundred-thousand-a-year annuity for which he had paid five million livres, his 4900 remaining shares in the India Company.

When he left France he went directly to Brussels. He was received with acclaim, entertained lavishly, appeared at the theater where a great throng greeted him. Then in a few days he set out upon his travels to Venice, to Bohemia, to Germany, to Denmark. He was sorely pressed for money. He, who the year before saw millions flowing through his hands, wrote the Countess of Suffolk, begging a loan of a thousand pounds. Later, at least one biographer reports, the Duc d'Orléans, the Regent, sent him yearly his old salary, which is variously reported as from ten to twenty thousand livres. But the Regent died in 1723 and this aid came to an end.

Before this, however—in 1722—Law went to London, invited thither apparently by the Prime Minister. He went aboard an English warship as the guest of its commander. In London his presence and entertainment provoked an outburst of criticism in Parliament against the Prime Minister, Walpole. But that statesman replied that Mr. Law was merely a British citizen who had come home to petition for His Majesty's pardon. Surely no fugitive from justice had ever returned quite this way before—an honored guest aboard His Majesty's vessel of war. It was indeed true, however, that his old sin—the killing of Beau Wilson—had dogged his footsteps. Apparently he had made earlier some composition with Wilson's relatives. He appeared now before the King's Bench attended by the Duke of Argyle and Lord Islay and others and was formally shriven of the old conviction.

He remained in England until 1725, from where he carried on a correspondence with the Duc de Bourbon, following the Regent's death, begging for the restoration of his fortune. Law never conceded that his System had failed. It had been ruined by enemies. He clung tenaciously to the hope, nay the expectation, that the Regent would summon him back to France. It is certain that gentleman always entertained a friendly feeling for his former minister. But the death of Orléans in 1723 ended these hopes. Law sank gradually in his pecuniary fortunes until toward the end he was not far removed from poverty. He died in Venice, March 21, 1729.

It is difficult to disentangle the fibers of Law the gambler and Law the reformer. His great reforms—his prodigious adventure in recasting the fortunes of a bankrupt empire—took much of its energy and substance from the gambler's art.

As a New Dealer he was not greatly different in one respect from the apostles of the mercantilist school—the Colberts, the Roosevelts, the Daladiers, the Hitlers and Mussolinis, and, indeed, the Pericles—who sought to create income and work by state-fostered public works and who labored to check the flow of gold away from their borders. He introduced something new, however, that the Hitlers, the Mussolinis, the Roosevelts, the Daladiers, and the Chamberlains have imitated—the creation of the funds for these purposes through the instrumentalities of the modern bank. Law is the precursor of the inflationist redeemers. Like all the inflationist salvations, his career was short. The others will not be long.

But he did develop a new technique of money getting. He did not invent, but he did perceive, the possibilities of two instrumentalities that have been at once the blessing and the curse of the modern world. The art of accumulating great wealth had consisted in sharing in a fraction of the labor product of a large number of people. The monarch had taken his by taxes; the politicians had taken theirs by intercepting the flow of taxes to and from the state; the slave owner had taken his by brute force; the landlord had taken his by owning the land that was the source of wealth drawn from it by many workers; the merchant had taken his by gathering into his hands the product of many small producers, finding a market, and taking a toll on each sale. The moneylender had got his portion because his loans enabled him to participate in the profits of many farmers, merchants, and producers. The wealth was drawn out of the *current income* of many people. But Law, by means of speculation in corporate securities, found the means of extracting from many men a part or all of their *savings*.

He exploited the eagerness of men to grow rich by making their profit, not in producing goods or creating utilities, but gambling on the changes in the price of investment certificates. He perceived also the uses of the bank as an instrument for creating an immense reservoir of savings funds as well as an instrument for actually manufacturing money—bank credit.

It would be a long time before the full possibilities of these weapons would be realized by the acquisitive man. Indeed it would not be until our own time that this would be done. But it has been done, and this civilization will not find its way to peace and grace until it learns how to get these implements out of the hands of the acquisitive enemies of society. Oddly, two hundred years after John Law, the gambler-philosopher, wrought upon society, one may see everywhere the good and the evil fruits of his brief adventure permeating our whole economic edifice. One may say of him as of Christopher Wren—if you would see his monument, look about you.

CHAPTER III

The Rothschilds

IMPERIALIST BANKERS

--------------------- I ---------------------

IN THE Rothschilds we come upon an elemental energy that can be described as nothing less than an organized appetite. The founders of this fortune were driven by nothing short of an acquisitive fury.

There were five brothers—Anselm, Solomon, Nathan, Carl, and James, in order of their ages—all devoted with a complete singleness of purpose to the hunt for money. One only possessed a mind of the first caliber—Nathan, to whose predatory imagination the house owned its dazzling rise. The House of Rothschild became in the Europe following the Napoleonic wars a five-headed octopus, an international banking house with headquarters in five countries—Nathan in London, James in Paris, Solomon in Vienna, Anselm in Frankfort, and Carl in Italy, listed in the order of their importance. The central office was in Frankfort and Anselm was the titular chief. But always Nathan was the real chief, and London during his life was the real capital of the Rothschild empire.

They were coarse, unlettered, graceless. Friedrich von Gentz, the hired shirt stuffer in chief, who sold his brilliant pen to gild their lowly origins, said privately that "they were vulgar and ignorant Jews" who pursued their craft "in accordance with the principles of naturalism, having no suspicion of a higher order of things."

There are such things as "vulgar, ignorant Jews," just as there are vulgar and ignorant Germans and Italians and Americans. The Rothschilds were coarse, illiterate, and brash.

86

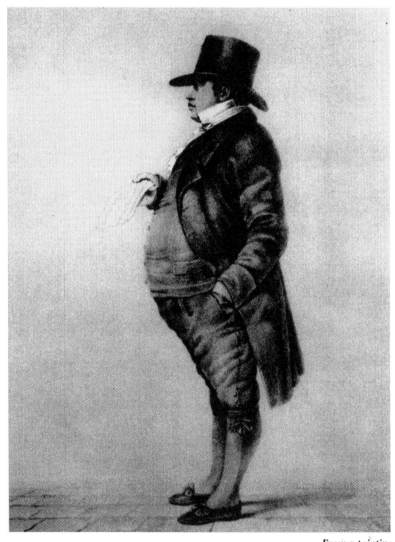

From a painting

NATHAN ROTHSCHILD

Nathan said of his children that he "wished them to give mind, soul, heart, and body to business." They were interested not in business but in money. They sought money not to enjoy power; but power in order to make money. Veblen's diagnosis of the acquisitive urge, as the craving to have what others have, to match the possessions of others, and to procure and exhibit the evidences of those possessions, did not apply to the Rothschilds any more than it applied to Hetty Green or Russell Sage. The rich James, escaping from the squalor of the Judengasse of Frankfort into the Paris of Napoleon, took quarters in a humble flat until he learned that he could do more business in the magnificent palace of Fouché. The time came when the brothers saw that palaces filled with works of art were better instruments of money getting. But they went in for magnificence to make more money and not for money to acquire magnificence.

They came upon the scene when a revolution greater than the French Revolution was changing the way of the world—the industrial revolution, out of which vast fortunes would be made. But it touched them not at all, as little, indeed, as the French Revolution touched an industrial genius like Robert Owen. They founded no industries, produced nothing, created nothing, invented nothing. The popular notion, fostered by some of their hired apologists, that they were the founders of the modern banking system, that they invented modern methods of foreign exchange, that they were the first international bankers, that they were the first to perfect the modern technique of distributing shares, and that they are entitled to the dubious glory of having first perfected the methods of security manipulation, is utterly without foundation.

There were international bankers two centuries before their time—the Fuggers, the Medici, the Frescobaldi, and the Bardi. There were great and powerful bankers in their own day against whom they were compelled to contend—the Barings in England and the brilliant Ouvrard, financier of Napoleon, in France; even in their own native Frankfort there were Gontard and Bethmann, ancestor of that von Bethmann-Hollweg who took the Germany of Kaiser Wilhelm into the First World War.

Their immense success was due to their immense preoccupation with the business of making money and to the acquisitive genius of one of their number. Certainly that success was almost fabulous. When the French mobs poured into the streets of Paris to destroy the Bastille and prepare Louis XVI for the headsman, the Rothschilds were isolated in the ghetto of Frankfort, matching in servility any of their neighbors in stepping from the sidewalk before the passing Christian Frankforter. When the Bourbon Louis XVIII returned to Paris after the Revolution and the Napoleonic eruption had run its course, he went to his throne with a million francs of expense money supplied by the Rothschild brothers. By that time they were the richest men in Europe.

II

Over the origins of the Rothschild fortunes some obscuring vapors hang—pestilential vapors partly, blown there by that archliar of history, the shirt stuffer.

How much falsehood history owes to the hired biographers and apologists of monarchs and statesmen and money kings! How the rich Maecenases in all ages, "patrons of art and letters," have been responsible for the mendacious chronicles of their time that have flowed around their feet from the pens of grateful poets, essayists, historians, and even philosophers!

As the Rothschilds grew in wealth and power, and statesmen and noblemen and even kings hungered for their pounds and gulden, they could never rid themselves of the dark veil of race and culture which hung between them and their noble clients. The rich banker Bethmann of Frankfort might treat familiarly with Solomon in his office or at the Boerse, but Bethmann's table was not open to him. The brothers might wear their ribbons and their titles and find themselves in the drawing rooms of impecunious finance ministers whose governments were in desperate need of funds, but there were still droves of snooty lords and ladies who drew away from the "upstart Jews" who still spoke with the crude accent of the Judengasse Yiddish, heavy on their consonants.

There was, therefore, one point on which they were most particular—the question of their origin. It was dogging their footsteps. In the salons of the great the brothers were unable to rid themselves of the odor of the old ghetto junkshop. They wished to have it settled, therefore, for all time that they were not upstarts, that they were as well born as some of those who lifted their nostrils at them; that they were the scions of a man of wealth, of high standing in the court circles of Hesse-Cassel, the financial adviser of a ruling house, bankers to whom the richest prince in Europe, when driven from his capital, had entrusted his whole fortune.

For this purpose they employed a gentleman, not unknown to fame, named Friedrich von Gentz. Gentz was the secretary of Metternich, Chancellor of Austria. He began life as a passionate supporter of the principles of the French Revolution; he ended as the aide of the most reactionary statesman in Europe. He was the author of many essays and several books, one of them a brilliant dissertation, *On the State of Europe Before and After the French Revolution,* which was translated into English at the time by John Charles Herries, Commissary General in the Liverpool cabinet, another intimate of the Rothschilds whom we shall meet anon.

Gentz was a man of scholarly attainments and charming manners who wrote excellent German prose. He made the perfect type of Tawney's predatory scholar, who aches for the sweetmeats of life and, not knowing how to make money himself, fastens himself upon some rich patron whose resources he can tap. Gentz was not at all discriminating in his patrons. He was a sort of literary street walker. He took money from everyone who had need of a sustaining paragraph or a scrap of influence at the foreign office. He was a thoroughly corrupt writer who jotted down in his diary with keen satisfaction the record of the bribes he received, the Rothschilds' name being among the most frequent.

Solomon Rothschild first met Gentz at Frankfort, preceding the Aix-la-Chapelle conference. The Rothschilds were seeking help in saving the Frankfort Jews from the cancellation of the privileges they had won under Napoleon's regime. When Metternich reached Frankfort, Gentz presented Solomon. Solomon handed him 800 ducats. For a number of years thereafter the Rothschild ducats flowed into Gentz' yawning pocket while the Gentz influence and tips flowed to the Rothschild banking house and the Gentz healing phrases flowed over the Rothschild fame.

In 1826 the Rothschilds paid Gentz a princely fee to plant in the popular Brockhaus *Conversational Encyclopedia* the story of the descent of the five brothers from the great banker of Frankfort. Solomon outlined what he wanted; Gentz wrote it in a pamphlet and contrived to have the pamphlet made the basis of the Brockhaus article. The article recounted the story of the flight of the wealthy Elector of Hesse before Bonaparte's advancing armies after having confided his whole vast fortune to Meyer Anselm Rothschild. So well did he manage the fortune in the Elector's absence that in its performance he sacrificed his own. When the Elector returned, old Meyer Anselm was able to restore the entire fortune intact with interest. And so grateful was the Elector that he insisted on Meyer retaining the use of the funds for several years more without interest.

This preposterous fiction has one prototype in modern burlesque humor—the story of the Jew who stood on Broadway throwing away five-dollar-bills while a Scotchman retrieved and returned them. For the Elector himself was the crustiest, most avaricious and suspicious gulden-squeezing old rascal in Europe. The whole tale is an invention fabricated by the Rothschilds—along with some other biographical fictions—to advertise the story that they were of excellent blood. There were many of excellent blood in the old Frankfort ghetto who bore their martyrdom with dignity and found surcease in the contemplation of the things of the spirit. But the Rothschild brothers were not of this number.

<hr>

III

<hr>

Meyer Anselm Rothschild, the father of these five dynamic sons, was born in the Frankfort ghetto in 1743. His father was a small tradesman who, perhaps, did a little moneychanging. The family, originally named Bauer, lived in a small, cramped ghetto dwelling that bore as its distinguishing mark a red shield. Thus they came by the name they later adopted.

Meyer was sent to a Talmudical college near Nuremberg to become a rabbi. But his father died when he was only twelve and he was forced to find work. He spent eight years in the bank of the Oppenheims in Hanover. His two brothers carried on the business in an even more crowded little shop that bore the sign of the saucepan. It sank to the level of a mere junkshop, dealing in the secondhand castoffs of the ghetto. Meyer returned from Hanover to join his brothers in trade. With the Oppenheims he had learned the business of coin collecting. He added this line to the secondhand trade. The brothers prospered after a fashion, the coin collecting forming but a small part of the business. The three made about two thousand gulden a year among them.

Meyer's coin collecting, however, brought him into touch with some of the noble families around Frankfort who could afford this hobby, among them the officials of the Landgrave of Hesse-Cassel. He sold rare coins to the Landgrave though he never met him. This added to the prestige of the small shop, however, particularly when the Landgrave conferred on him the title of Crown Agent. The title meant little, corresponding roughly to the English designation of a royal trader who may use the term "By Appointment to His Majesty."

He married the daughter of a prosperous tradesman—Guetele Schnapper, destined to be enveloped in a hazy glow of sentiment by

biographers of her famous sons. She bore him twelve children—
five of whom were those famous sons already named. In time one
of Meyer's brothers died and another drifted off for himself, leaving
Meyer in sole possession of the shop *zur Hinterpfan*. And there he
remained until 1785, when he was forty-three—a small tradesman,
dealing chiefly in tea, coffee, sugar, and spices, changing money
and expanding his coin-collecting business, getting along slowly.

In 1785 he moved to a new home which he bought. It was marked
by a green shield. Thus the family of the Red Shield found themselves living at the sign of the Green Shield. It is a narrow dwelling
—for it still stands—four stories high. The Rothschilds occupied
one half, a secondhand dealer the other. Meyer's shop was on the
first floor. The family lived in severely cramped quarters above.
And here in this small, crowded home in the Judengasse, with a
secondhand store for a neighbor, the elder Rothschild remained
until he died in 1812.

Meyer sought earnestly to get a little of the banking business of
the rich Landgrave of Hesse who had given him the empty title of
Crown Agent. He had struck up an acquaintance with Buderus,
the Landgrave's confidential financial agent. But even this failed
to bring him anything more than some coin sales.

It was not until 1795 that he began to make large profits. In
1790 his earnings, according to Berghoeffer, were from 2000 to
3000 gulden a year. By this time he had three sons in the business.
This was not a large annual profit to divide among four. But in
1795 the conquest of Holland by Napoleon had caused the collapse of the Amsterdam bourse and diverted much of that business
to Frankfort. A war trade had grown up as soon as conservative
Europe had launched her attack upon Napoleon in 1792. In 1795
Frankfort became the center of that trade. The three energetic and
aggressive sons—Anselm, Solomon, and Nathan, the last then
eighteen years old—were partners and had assumed the driving
control of the business.

Yet even then the business was a small one—trading in cloth,
sugar, tea, indigo, and textiles. It employed only the sons, two

daughters in the shop, and one daughter-in-law. Frankfort began to sparkle with the profits of the war boom. It was full of rich citizens—a few years later an estimate showed eight hundred citizens with unencumbered cash of more than 50,000 gulden each. But the Rothschilds still shared with the secondhand store the small building at the sign of the green shield. As late as 1810, with only two years to live, at the age of sixty-seven, after the sons had gone far in the amassing of war profits, Meyer reconstituted the partnership and in the articles put the firm's capital down as only 800,000 gulden. Two years later he died, still holding forth in his small shop, after several years of poor health. Whatever growth the business had after 1795 was due to the sons and not to Meyer Anselm himself.

— IV —

Before proceeding further we must pause to have a look at William, Landgrave—and later Elector—of Hesse-Cassel, with whose fortunes the first flights of the House of Rothschild were made. In a book of money-makers this curious old prince might well rate a chapter for himself.

Hesse-Cassel was a small principality in central Germany and just north of Hanau of which Frankfort was the principal city. The ruling house had worked up for itself one of the most impudent rackets for making money. For a hundred years the landgraves made a business of forming and drilling armies and hiring them out to other rulers for war work. The biggest haul made by these drovers of men was by the Landgrave Frederick II, who hired 22,000 Hessian troops to George III for £3,191,000. These were the celebrated Hessians who won such a dark immortality in our Revolutionary War. William IX was the son of this Frederick. He had a small subsidiary principality of his own before his father's death and, like a true scion of his father, he had his own small army which he too hired out to England, cleaning up a million or two for himself.

This William, however, had a special flair for finance and an acquisitive urge which amounted to a disease. He was a heavy investor all over Europe, particularly in England, a lender of money to tradesmen, financiers, and his fellow princes. So that in 1785 when his father died and he united his own fortune with the hereditary accumulations of his house he was, perhaps, the richest man in Europe.

As affairs on the Continent sank into the disorder which followed the French Revolution William kept a large part of his fortune in England. He invested heavily in consols, but he made numerous loans to statesmen, princes, bankers. The Prince of Wales borrowed £200,000 and the Duke of York and Clarence also owed him large sums. He made large advances to the Austrian emperor, the king of Prussia, and to most of the lesser potentates of the Holy Roman Empire. And if his brother rulers despised him for his traffic in his soldiers, he was none the less cultivated by them because they never knew when they would want access to the treasure box of this royal Shylock. But he did not overlook the small loan business. He spent his life haggling over notes and bills and interest rates, bargaining and scratching to squeeze the last drop of interest out of bankers and tradesmen and petty lords in his own domain.

He was a man of two passions. One was his gulden. The other was women. But apparently he was not a promiscuous roué. He adopted one mistress after another, but clove to her with a curious fidelity during her special chapter. He married Wilhelmina, daughter of Frederick V, King of Denmark. She brought him a dull soul and a frigid body. And so he turned for love to the wife of a master of his horse, whom, in turn, he turned adrift. Next he took up with the daughter of a commoner, by whom he had four children before his fidelity cooled and he tossed her back to her native purlieus. His next affair was with Rosa Wilhelmina Dorothea Ritter, educated, well born, assertive, who gave him eight children and forced him to give her an estate and a title— Frau von Lindenthal—before she incurred his displeasure by a flirtation with a subaltern. His next love was Juliane Albertine von Schlotheim, who added nine children to his collection of bastards. He induced the emperor to make her a countess and installed her in a palace. Thus he had twenty-four children, though less reliable historians endow the fecund old Turk with almost twice as many.

He provided for all these establishments. The support of so extensive a barnyard was a great burden, so the grasping prince who recruited an army and farmed out his soldiers like convicts shifted the burden of his bastard brood to the shoulders of his subjects by levying a special salt tax for their support. Some of his sons went into the military service of various kings. The most famous, or infamous, was that General Haynau—son of Frau von Lindenthal—who came to be known as the "Hyena of Brescia."

Into the treasury of this prince flowed a continuous stream of remittances from England, Austria, Prussia, and all the smaller states of Europe. They came in the form of bills of exchange. Meyer Anselm, for years, petitioned the Landgrave to grant him the privilege of cashing some of his bills of exchange. He did succeed in doing some of this business. But when Meyer sought to do a little of the Landgrave's banking business he was persistently excluded. As late as 1798, when Meyer was fifty-five, and William was making a loan of a million gulden to the Emperor of Austria, the Rothschilds could get no part of the transaction.

By 1800 the Rothschilds' fortune had grown. But it was the product not of Meyer but of his energetic and resourceful sons. They then began to do some profitable business with the Landgrave. They got from him a loan of 160,000 thalers in 1801 and of 200,000 in 1802. The next year they broke the ice in a state banking operation. They handled a loan from the Landgrave to the King of Denmark, his relative. William wished to remain anonymous because he had been showing a poor mouth to his family. Buderus arranged to have the transaction handled by the Rothschilds. After this the firm continued to render more and more services to the prince.

But this was accomplished by the simple expedient of taking Herr Carl Frederick Buderus, the Landgrave's confidential financial officer, into partnership. Put differently—the Rothschilds bought Buderus. This came to be the standard practice with the young men. They used money to buy what they wanted, including statesmen and their agents, as they were later to buy Gentz and as they bought sugar and indigo and other merchandise. Out of this corrupt arrangement Buderus became wealthy and died a millionaire.

They were now bankers and, to an increasing extent, thanks to Buderus' intercessions, bankers for a prince who, if not an important man, was at least a rich one who lent money instead of borrowing it. But they were far from being more than a third-rate house.

In 1806 Napoleon established the Confederation of the Rhine, adding Hesse-Cassel to the kingdom of Westphalia, which he gave to his brother Jerome. His armies under General Lagrange occupied William's capital and the terrified Landgrave, now raised to the dignity of Elector, fled for his life. He hid some 120 chests of papers and securities and valuables in his various castles and left his power of attorney with Buderus. He deposited with the Austrian ambassador for safekeeping several chests of live securities, bills of exchange, cash, and jewels.

This is the episode that Friedrich von Gentz made the basis of the yarn that the Elector had left his entire fortune in the keeping of the elder Rothschild. As a matter of fact, he left just two chests containing unimportant papers with the Rothschilds. The French immediately started a search for William's effects. They found the hidden chests in his castles. But Lagrange, the French commander, reported that the assets found were worth four million instead of sixteen million. He delivered the unreported assets into the hands of Buderus. For this he received a bribe of 1,060,000 francs. The Rothschild home was raided. But the Rothschilds had received a tip of the coming search from Dalberg, the head of the Confederation of the Rhine stationed in Frankfort and Napoleon's tool. The

Rothschilds had bought him too with a loan and kept him bought with a succession of loans. The search of the house revealed little and was terminated before it was finished by a bribe to Savagner, the French police chief, and a modest loan of 300 thalers to the officer in immediate direction of the search. The first thing the Rothschilds looked for on a minister or his agent was the price tag. They learned that their money could buy almost anything.

— V —

We are now to look at the larger ingots of the Rothschild fortune in the casting. Up to 1806 their riches were like a victory at chess —an accumulation of small advantages. These riches were now about to swell swiftly into an immense tumorous growth.

The Frankfort brothers were making their modest accumulations up to 1795 in small-scale moneylending, handling bills of exchange, but chiefly in trading, in textiles, coffee, tea, sugar, and, perhaps, indigo. England was the great market for these things. Save for textiles, they flowed in from her colonies. In textiles, the industrial revolution was well under way, and she had become the chief wool- and cotton-cloth weaver of the world. But with the rise of the war trade these Rothschild profits began to soar. Nathan, then twenty-two, was sent to Manchester as a sort of buyer of cloth. This was a stroke of fortune, for Nathan was the family genius, and England was to be the financial capital of the world.

The young, short, obese Frankforter, looking almost comical, speaking but little English heavily macerated by the strange Yiddish pronunciation of his ghetto German, was a blaze of business energy. He boasted that he quickly multiplied his £20,000 capital to £60,000—but he was a most mendacious witness when boasting of his prowess as a money-maker. However, he did prosper amazingly. In 1804 he went to London to extend his operations.

There had been a pause in the fighting in Europe after the Treaties of Lunéville in 1801 and Amiens in 1802. But in 1803 England resumed naval warfare on France and by 1806 the whole

Continent was aflame with the new assault upon Napoleon when Russia, Prussia, and Austria united in the attack. And once again, upon an even greater scale, the war profiteers proceeded to multiply their gains.

We now see Nathan leading his brothers in four swift episodes which were to land the five brothers among the richest houses in Europe. As late as 1810 they were unknown to official London as capitalists. In 1815 they were the bankers for the British government and the most powerful single unofficial force in Europe.

These four episodes were the smuggling trade against Napoleon's commercial blockade of England, the traffic in Wellington's bills and notes in the Peninsular war, the commission from the British government to convey funds to Wellington's army in Portugal and Spain, and, finally, the difficult job of transporting the British subsidies to her allies on the Continent.

--------------------- VI ---------------------

The first episode involved an adventure in large-scale smuggling. In 1806 Napoleon decided to crush England's commerce, to strike the despised shopkeeper whose flourishing trade nourished the armies of England. He declared his famous commercial blockade. England replied with an embargo and a blockade of all French ports. As the whole Continent needed British goods desperately, what had been a profitable war trade now became a more profitable smuggling industry. The Rothschilds had been making large profits in this war trade. They now, under Nathan's leadership, plunged into the smuggling adventure with all their resources.

Fortune favored them. With Nathan in England and the brothers on the Continent the firm was well equipped for the job. Moreover, Napoleon was soon to learn that the hand with which he sought to strangle England was also starving France; that the hated shopkeepers of perfidious Albion had upon their shelves merchandise that Frenchmen sorely needed. England too, which outwardly sealed the ports of France, found she needed markets in France and in Europe to create for her the credits essential to get funds to her allies. And so one necessity yielded to another. Napoleon, while publicly thundering destruction to the trade of England, managed to open a back door into France through which greatly needed supplies could be smuggled.

We had the spectacle of both governments winking at their decrees and smugglers actually squeezing past conniving officials the merchandise France wanted. Indeed, by a decree in the summer of 1810, the Emperor actually legalized and regulated the outlaw commerce. The bootleg captains clandestinely sneaked their contraband into France at Gravelines under the eyes and protection and patrol of the police at a port officially set aside for the traffic. The Rothschilds made the most of this.

But Nathan needed more capital. He saw with dismay the great profits others were making. His mind turned to the Elector of Hesse, an exile in Prussia. His brother Anselm was getting closer all the time to the Elector's good graces—thanks to Buderus. The Rothschild house in Frankfort was handling more of the Elector's loans and collections. And Nathan in London was managing the transmission of the interest on some £640,000 of the Elector's investments in consols. Continental business and investments were subject to grave perils. Why should not the Elector invest the immense sums in interest and in principal that were flowing to him in English consols—and do it through Nathan? Nathan pressed Buderus to aid with his influence. But for some reason the Elector seems to have been suspicious of Nathan. However, after much pressure, Buderus convinced the Elector to follow Nathan's advice. Thereafter an immense sum was put into Nathan's hands for investment in English consols.

How much he got is not precisely clear. Rothschild boasted that it was £600,000. It was probably something less, about £550,000. But it was not all sent in one remittance. It was delivered to Nathan over a period of several years—in three installments. This was authorized in February, 1809. But Nathan did not buy consols with it. Instead he used it for his own purposes—appropriated it to his own uses, feeling sure, of course, that he could restore it when pressed. Here we have the banker-agent of the avaricious Elector using for his own purposes the funds entrusted to him by his principal, on the advice of that principal's confidential financial official who was himself in the pay of the banker. And in the very month this was done Buderus' partnership in the Rothschild firm was reduced to writing.

As Rothschild purchased no consols it was impossible for him to forward the Elector receipts for their deposit in the Bank of England. William became uneasy. He demanded the receipts. He prodded Buderus. For over two years Buderus quieted his fears with one explanation or another. But in the end he lost patience and confidence. He demanded the instant delivery of the evidence that his funds had been used as directed and he gave orders that no further sums should be remitted to Nathan.

This was an audacious enterprise. That Nathan persisted for nearly three years in the face of the Elector's continuous demands is an evidence of his own daring calculations. The embargo furnished him a sort of excuse for his delays. And as consols were dropping in price he knew he could at any moment buy all that was needed to satisfy his noble patron. But the possession of these large funds was of the first importance to him in the enormously profitable smuggling and bill traffic during the period of the embargo. The profits of this were probably the chief source of the fortune the Rothschilds were rearing.

VII

The next episode has to do with the Rothschilds and the difficulties of the Duke of Wellington on the Peninsula. And this historians have managed to envelope in no end of fog. One minimizes it. Another accepts Nathan's own version that it was undertaken as a patriotic adventure to aid Lord Wellington in Portugal and Spain. Another describes it as the daring enterprise of a freebooter banker from which he made numberless millions and thus laid the groundwork of his whole fortune. And none clears up the procedure by which the enterprise was carried on. The facts as far as they may be unraveled follow.

In 1808 Napoleon forced his brother upon the throne of Spain. Madrid revolted and improvised a large army. England saw an opportunity in this to drive the usurper out of the Peninsula, and sent an army to Portugal. Wellington was one of its generals, but in 1809 became commander in chief.

The great problem was to get supplies to Wellington. Oporto and Lisbon were 600 and 800 miles from the nearest English port, and the sea was infested with enemy ships and privateers. Metal was too scarce to permit so much risk in its shipment, and Wellington needed money to pay his troops and purchase certain local supplies.

There grew up much the same bitter controversy about this as there had been between Lloyd George and the apologists of General Kitchener in the First World War over the inadequacy of supplies and funds. Wellington felt himself trapped. In desperation he began to purchase supplies from Portuguese merchants and to pay them with bills on the English Treasury. These bills were not much good in the hands of Portuguese and Spanish merchants until they were exchanged for gold or silver. Hence a trade sprang up in the notes, carried on by Sicilian, Italian, and Maltese bankers known as the "Cab," with headquarters at Malta. They bought the notes from the local merchants at small prices and relayed them through a series of hands and discounts until they reached London.

This made everything Wellington bought cost several hundred per cent more than even the high war prices in vogue. The Treasury protested. Wellington hurled back criticisms at the Treasury and the Commissary General. He said bitterly that the government cared nothing about his armies. His men, he wrote, remained unpaid for two months and had to sell their shoes and clothing for food and medicines. He intimated that England should abandon the whole expedition. "A starving army is worse than none," he complained. "We want everything and get nothing." He protested against the red tape and inefficiency of the Commissary which "must trace a biscuit from London to the man's mouth at the frontier." He went so far as to threaten to embark his army out of Portugal, leaving England exposed to the peril of an invasion, when her king would then learn something of the horrors of war.

Being in the smuggling trade Nathan of course knew all about this. This traffic in notes was too enticing to be resisted. And he went into it. How deeply he actually went in and how he managed it are by no means clear. One account has it that he summoned his brothers, Carl and Solomon, and later James; that Carl traveled to the Spanish border and bought up the notes with gold, then returned, meeting his brother Solomon halfway, exchanging his bills for a fresh supply of coin brought by Solomon, who then made his way to the French coast where he met Nathan, with whom he again exchanged notes for gold, Nathan taking the Wellington bills to London and exchanging them for guineas.

Another account is that Nathan had merely cashed some of the bills from the Cab and later planned to enter the trade—without actually doing so—in order to help Wellington.

What is doubtless nearer to the truth is that the Rothschilds did deal extensively in the Wellington notes and, probably, would have dealt far more extensively if another incident had not intervened. How much Wellington issued in bills seems not to have been fixed by fiscal historians. It would be a very surprising fact if the whole amount exceeded a million pounds. It is also certain that he did this not as a regular thing but only when pressed by necessity. It is also known that a number of bankers shared this trade among them, that it was in progress for some time before the Rothschilds entered it. It is therefore altogether probable that they got merely a share of this traffic. Indeed, the English Commissary Herries himself, who was closest to the whole business, said that the Cab had for a time managed to establish a monopoly of the trade. We may therefore conclude that the Rothschilds got a good deal less than half of this trade.

It is also difficult to believe that so much gold could be transported by a single traveler. A hundred pounds of gold would be a very onerous burden to a man traveling through hostile country, swarming with spies, under difficulties of transportation hardly conceivable today. The number of trips that must have been made to transport as much as a million pounds, or half that much, would be quite beyond the physical resources of the brothers.

While the profit was great, a number of persons had to share in the discount and many hands had to be greased. So that we may safely assume that whatever profit the Rothschilds made out of this has been grossly exaggerated. But they did make a profit and a large one and they were, undoubtedly, preparing to make a greater one by a more intelligent means of transmission of gold to Wellington when circumstances shaped themselves, almost with the appearance of destiny, to put these five young men upon the express highway to fortune.

VIII

This new turn of affairs arose out of the following facts. Rothschild's difficulty in the Wellington note traffic was gold. The guinea, said Herries, was an article of luxury. Every quarter of the globe was ransacked for specie. The Rothschilds, with their expanding trade areas, were doubtless able to gather a great deal. But there was a limit. In London a ship of the East India Company brought in a cargo of gold. According to custom, it was offered at public auction. Nathan Rothschild bought this for £800,000, using all the cash and credit he had, plus the funds of the Elector in his charge. In later years he said he planned to send this to Wellington. Some historians have accepted this version. But the notion that this predatory man entertained any such fantastic stratagem attended with so much risk is as preposterous as the yarn about his father sacrificing his whole fortune for the Elector and the Elector insisting on lending the Rothschilds all his cash without interest. He was merely planning to extend his traffic in the Wellington scrip and other war trade.

Rothschild was surprised to find himself summoned a day or two after this purchase to the office of John Charles Herries, Commissary General. The Commissary must have been no less surprised at the squat, blunt, Frankforter, looking and talking like a Jewish comedian taken from a London music-hall stage. Herries says that at this time Rothschild was wholly unknown in London official circles as a capitalist. Nathan was asked why he had bought the gold. What did he propose to do with it? It was the hour of fate for the Rothschilds. He might have lied—a course he would have pursued with as sweet a conscience as when he bought Buderus and other public officials. But he caught here a glance of the long turnpike of time. He told Herries why he had bought the gold—to buy Wellington's bills. Herries said the government wanted the gold and Rothschild promptly sold it to him at a large profit.

But how was the Commissary General going to transmit it to Wellington? Rothschild said afterward the government didn't know. Why not use the House of Rothschild to transport it? It had the resources. It had branches in England and on the Continent. It had agents in France and Spain. It had successfully transported gold overland to the traders who had taken Wellington's bills. It could do the same thing for the government in a way the government could not do for itself. The House of Rothschild was an ally, deeply devoted to the interests of the Elector of Hesse and to the Austrian Emperor, and Nathan himself was a citizen of Britain.

Rothschild outlined to Herries how he would proceed. Herries reported it to the Prime Minister and the Finance Minister, who approved the plan heartily. And, in a trice, Nathan Rothschild, the unknown smuggler-banker, was established in the headquarters of the ministry, supervising the delicate operation of sending money to the irascible and clamorous Wellington.

Just how Rothschild did this remains in some doubt. Count Corti, his most reliable biographer, meticulous in his citation of authorities, says, in this instance without giving adequate authority, that the English gold was transported across the Channel to France; that there the Rothschilds exchanged it for bills upon

certain bankers and thus, through a series of operations, got the
bills into the hands of Wellington who could exchange them for
specie with the bankers. The defects in this plan are too obvious
to discuss.

But Mr. Herries says that the Rothschilds took English bills of
exchange to Holland where they supervised the business of exchanging them for French coins. These coins were then sent by an
English warship from the port of Hellevoetsluis in Holland to
Lisbon. It would be bold indeed to say that Herries did not know
how it was done, since the whole business was managed from his
office. And if it is true it gives the lie to the whole romantic story
of the perilous journeys of the venturesome brothers over moun-
tainous country infested by brigands and armed enemy forces. We
find Herries writing to the Prime Minister telling him of the
"skillfulness and zeal" with which Nathan handled the transaction and how he had "already disbursed £700,000 in bills in
Holland and Frankfort without the slightest effect upon the exchange market."

But some gold was shipped across the Channel. Letters of James
to Nathan intercepted by the French police revealed that some
£120,000 had been sent to James at Paris. What is entirely probable is that the bulk of this business was done with bills but that
some gold, perhaps a considerable amount, was shipped also. What
the whole operation amounted to is also left to surmise. But we
know from another source that in the year 1813 the whole amount
of specie sent to Wellington by the British government amounted
to £1,723,936 and 339,432 Spanish dollars. Probably the bulk of
this was managed by Rothschild. And he doubtless was well paid
by the British government. His pay must have been a commission
and did not include the large profits in discounts. It was doubtless
a generous profit, but it could not account for the immense wealth
with which the Rothschilds appeared in Europe two years later.

But it did account for the most important advance they had
ever made. For they were now soundly entrenched with the British
government.

One incident of this operation, however, has not been sufficiently emphasized. It was one of those master strokes which exhibits these men as capable of strategic daring of the highest order. In the course of these transactions, either before or after the deal with Herries, James, the youngest brother, was sent to Paris. Solomon and Carl had been working more or less out of that center. But doubtless Solomon was needed at Frankfort. And it seems probable that Nathan saw the value of establishing a branch in Paris.

The brothers took advantage of the fact that Dalberg, primate of the Rhine Confederation at Frankfort, to whom they had made many advances for his personal account, was going to Paris upon the occasion of the birth of Napoleon's son. Anselm loaned the venal Dalberg 80,000 gulden for the trip and got from him a passport for James and a letter of introduction to no less a person than Mollien, the Finance Minister of Napoleon. James went to Paris and called on Mollien. He informed him that his brother Nathan in London, as the representative of their house, was doing a large business in English-Continental trade and that he was shipping gold to France through Gravelines. This information intrigued the French minister, for there was nothing France desired more than British gold. He encouraged the young Frankforter to continue this trade and expressed the hope that his story was true.

There could have been but one reason for this step. The Rothschilds were shipping into France gold that was going to Wellington. If discovered by the police they would have to make an explanation. Here was an explanation. What is more, it was an explanation made in advance of discovery—and made directly to the Finance Minister himself. It was a dangerous expedient. James was putting himself in the hands of the French. He was trifling with a resolute and ruthless enemy. A false step here might have brought him to the block swiftly enough. It was foresight supplemented by action of a very audacious kind. But it was more. It was also a plan to get a footing in France. After all, Frankfort was in the hands of Napoleon. The Confederation of the Rhine was his satrapy. The brothers were already operating in both camps, with

Nathan in England and the headquarters in Frankfort. Nathan was on terms of intimacy in the service of England; but Anselm was on terms of equal intimacy with Dalberg, Napoleon's ruler of Frankfort, while at the same time maintaining confidential relations with the dispossessed Elector of Hesse and seeking further relationships with Austria. The brothers had their feet in all camps and were prepared to capitalize upon any result the war produced. Beyond doubt these moves proceeded from the fertile imagination of Nathan, who was now the recognized leader of the house.

IX

The fourth episode revolved around the last mighty effort of England and her wobbly Continental allies to drive Napoleon out of France. The vast disaster of Russia had undermined the Emperor's strength and reputation. It was a terrible economic blow to France. England rallied the allies to another great exertion of their united resources. In January, 1813, England agreed to send to Prussia and Russia large grants of money. Prussia was to get £666,666; Russia over a million. Each was to put new large levies of men into the field. Later in the year Austria, under Metternich's leadership, abandoned Napoleon and threw in her lot with the allies. England promised Metternich a million pounds. Later this was more than doubled.

Herries, the English Commissary, was now charged with the difficult task of getting these sums to Prussia, Austria, and Russia. It was a delicate job. England could not send that much gold to the Continent out of her already depleted resources. But if she sent bills to her allies the effect would be disastrous on international exchange, particularly British exchange.

The reader would do well to understand this. If a man in England wishes to send a hundred pounds to a man in Berlin, he can send gold. But if he does not wish to send gold he may hunt around for some man in England who has a hundred pounds due him from a man in Berlin. This first Englishman may buy from the second his hundred-pound claim against the man in Berlin. He may then send that claim to the man in Berlin to whom he owes his hundred pounds. That Berliner may then collect the hundred pounds from the Berliner who owed the bill in England.

Thus in a city like Vienna there are always a number of merchants who have bills due to them by men in London. Bankers buy up or discount these claims against London merchants and sell them to other Viennese who want to pay bills in London. Thus there is always a demand in Vienna for bills due by men in England. And here is where the trouble begins. If the demand for the bills is small and the supply great, the price of these bills will drop. A man in Vienna who has a bill of a hundred pounds due to him from a Londoner may have to sell it for only ninety pounds because the supply of London bills is very great.

Now if England were to send to a city like Vienna £168,000 in bills, added to all the other bills in Vienna due by Londoners, the price of these London bills would fall disastrously. That, indeed, is precisely what happened. The Austrian finance minister complained that he had to sell a thousand-pound bill for six hundred pounds. Thus, while England sent a bill for a thousand, the Austrian government got only six hundred. The remaining four hundred was absorbed by the bill brokers and bankers.

As England had to send over many millions to Russia, Prussia, and Austria, she was anxious to find a way of doing this without depressing the price of British paper, so that her allies would receive a thousand pounds for every thousand-pound bill sent. To do this delicate job Herries again called in Nathan Rothschild. The banker was commissioned, first, to manipulate the foreign-bill market so that exchange would not be against England—that is, that English bills and pounds would not decline in price; and, second, that the money would be transmitted to her allies without loss and without upsetting the foreign-exchange market.

And this job Nathan, with the aid of his brothers, did with great skill in the face of many difficulties. He did this partly by "going around" the bill market and partly by manipulating it.

At this time a large trade was flowing between England and the Continent. Continental powers were buying more from England than they were selling. Therefore, the price of English bills on trade alone would have been favorable. But when to the bills due by England on commercial transactions were added the millions due by her on the subsidies she promised, the natural drift of the market was against English bills.

It was the bills for the subsidies which caused the trouble. But all these, so far as Prussia and Russia were concerned, were delivered to Rothschild. Thus, he had in his hands the surplus of English bills. Now if he could get in his hands also a large supply of the Continental bills, it would be possible for him to feed either English or Continental bills into the market as might be necessary to keep prices balanced. To put into his hands still further control of the exchange, he bought bills through his brothers and his agents directly from merchants in the leading European ports before these bills got into the regular bill market.

In this way, controlling enough of the two streams of bills—bills against England and bills against Continental countries—he was able to protect the English pound sterling from declining. Of course, he had to use a large amount of his own large resources on the Continent to purchase Continental bills and to hold them. And always, of course, there would be balances in gold to be settled by England. But these balances never got into the channels of trade. They did not have to leave England always. For the Rothschilds could receive the gold in their English house, retaining it there, and paying it out from their Frankfort or Paris houses. The whole transaction was complicated. But it was one which, as Herries said, kept Rothschild "in his [Herries'] rooms constantly." The value of these services was all the more apparent by contrast with the difficulties encountered by Austria, which persisted until the war was over, in negotiating these subsidy transfers through her own Viennese bankers, to her great loss.

But the Rothschilds besieged the Austrian government for the privilege of servicing the transmission of the English subsidies.

What they had done for the English government was quite unknown, the Wellington service remaining a profound secret, according to Herries, for twenty years. It was probably difficult for the Austrian officials to believe that these uncouth Jewish traders with their bad grammar, their harsh Yiddish, and their unlettered appeals could be such extraordinary financial wizards. Only one small transaction did they get from Austria—handling half of a remittance of only 9 million francs from Belgium. The Austrian finance minister explained that the whole amount was too large a sum for second-rate bankers to manage.

A mere incident was to turn the scales in their favor. Their rising wealth had stimulated the jealousy of both Christian and Jewish rivals in Frankfort. When Napoleon returned from Elba, every effort was made by Austria to draft the needed men for the troops. At Frankfort an effort was made to force two of the Rothschild brothers into the army. They appealed to Nathan. Nathan appealed to Herries. Herries wrote the Austrian ambassador at Frankfort. He outlined the immense importance of the work they were doing for Great Britain, the great sums involved, the delicacy of the operations, and "the English government is most anxious that this firm should not be annoyed in any way." This note was sent to the foreign minister. It opened his eyes. It revealed that if he did not know who Rothschild was, it was his loss. It broke the ice at the Austrian finance offices, and thereafter the Rothschilds began to handle the Austrian business, too.

Their resources had become enormous. After Napoleon's banishment Prussia was desperate for funds. Solomon Rothschild took £200,000 to the finance ministry himself from the British government. But the government said this was inadequate. On his own responsibility, out of the Rothschild funds, and without waiting for formal approval from England, Solomon handed over to the Austrian treasury another £150,000. Herries, of course, confirmed this. But this bold act and the display of large resources completely won the Prussian treasury. Solomon was made Commercial Adviser of the government.

Then came Napoleon's defeat and the entry of the allies into Paris. The Count of Provence, soon to be crowned Louis XVIII of France, was living in Buckinghamshire. He was broke and applied to the English government for funds to assure his march to the throne in the style becoming a king. Nathan accepted the English government's draft for five million francs in England, and when Louis arrived in France, James handed him the money. While all else had been done by Nathan in the darkest secrecy, this act he wished to be known. What more natural? The scion of a score of monarchs and a thousand years went to his throne with the francs of the poor and crusty bill merchant of Frankfort's Jew street jingling in his pockets.

With this event the Rothschilds could boast that they were bankers in the service of England, France, Germany, Austria, to say nothing of Russia and the smaller states. The great, gleaming, golden road was opened before them.

———————————— x ————————————

In the midst of all this Meyer Anselm, the father, had died in Frankfort. Long before his death the business had been literally swept out of his hands by his energetic sons. He had been ill for several years. He had drifted more and more to the comforts of his Talmud. He was a quiet man, amiable, wholly lacking in that fierce energy which drove his sons. He was stricken in the temple and three days later—September 19, 1812—died at the house of the green shield in the Judengasse, where he had lived over his small shop for so many years.

Two hoary fictions cling about that bedside. One is that his five sons, with their daughters and mother, gathered about while the dying man delivered to the boys the moral testament by which they lived and which is epitomized in their coat of arms—*Concordia, Integritas, Industria*. The other is that there he bequeathed to them, like an expiring emperor, the five great financial provinces of Europe which they ruled so long afterward—Germany, Austria, England, France, and Italy.

When the old man lay dying, Nathan was in England, while Solomon, Carl, and James were either in Paris or the country contiguous to it, carrying on their trade in the Wellington bills. Anselm alone could have been there and he doubtless was.

As for the bequest of Europe's five provinces, Carl did not go to do business in Italy until many years later, neither Solomon nor Anselm had done any business for Germany or Austria, James was a mere youth acting as Nathan's subaltern in Paris in connection with the English business. Nathan had built up a flourishing business in London, but of no great importance yet.

When the old man was stricken on September 16 he hurriedly made his will. He wished to keep the business in the hands of the sons who had created it. And when he died and the will was opened, it turned out, as in the case of John D. Rockefeller and many other American millionaires, that he no longer owned any part of the firm.

In 1810 he had reorganized it. He had made it into a partnership with fifty shares. He was allotted twenty-four, Solomon and Anselm twelve each; Carl and James one each. Nathan was left out— doubtless the shares of the old Meyer included Nathan's twelve.

But now in his will he declared that he had sold his interest to his five sons for 190,000 gulden—about $76,000—and that this constituted his whole estate. He left 70,000 gulden to his wife and the balance to his daughters. But he made it plain that after his death the sons were to be equal owners. He provided that the daughters should have no interest in the business or any right to see the books. He created, as Fugger did, a continuing dynasty or partnership, limited to those male heirs who took an active part in the business. And he enjoined upon all his children "unity, love, friendship." After his death the headquarters of the house remained in Frankfort. Anselm, the eldest, became the titular head of the firm.

XI

When Napoleon was definitively liquidated at Waterloo and Europe settled down to peace, every country was in a state of economic disorganization. Every country was loaded with debt. Every country was more or less dislocated by the changes that the industrial revolution was making in its economic structure. Every country was desperately in need of money.

At this moment the prestige of the Rothschilds, and particularly of Nathan in London, reached the highest point. No longer were they to be mere suitors for financial jobs from finance ministers. These lordly gentlemen were now to court the Rothschilds.

It is by no means clear precisely what was the chief source of their vast wealth. They had rendered invaluable service to the allies in transmitting large sums of money from one to the other. But they had not acted as lending bankers, though they did make occasional advances in the prosecution of the transmissal services. They were well rewarded, but it is difficult to believe that the reward was more than a commission and, though generous, could not account for the immense accumulations they turned up with when Napoleon went to St. Helena. They made large profits on the Wellington business, but that too could not have been the source of as large a fortune as they possessed. It is difficult to account for their wealth unless we conclude that the bulk of it was amassed in profits on war trade and the financing of war-trade profiteers and in speculation.

What they were worth is difficult to say. No accurate estimate exists. But all their biographers, most of whom are none too reliable, are agreed that they were, when the war ended in 1815, among the richest, if not the richest, men in Europe.

The brothers now wanted recognition. They had money; they needed prestige. They wanted ennoblement. And they proceeded to ask for their reward. They sought it from Austria, the last of the powers to recognize them. But just as the Rothschilds had groveled before these princely customers, now the ministers of Francis talked among themselves how they might hold the support of the powerful bankers. They were not left in doubt. The Rothschilds hinted that they wanted to be barons. It was embarrassing. What title could be given to these rich fellows: imperial and royal counselor? No, that was for eminence of another sort. Then let them have the prefix *von* before their name. But a privy counselor subjected this proposal to a devastating analysis. Why? he asked. What had these men done to command such distinction? They had performed the tasks entrusted to them well, but they had been in the employ of England and England had paid them well, doubtless, rewarding them with money, which is what they worked for. They had performed the service for which they were employed and had been compensated for it. What more should a businessman ask? All the talk about their punctual, reliable, honest, and efficient dealings—well, these are virtues expected of any banker. The argument that Austria should keep these men satisfied and friendly seemed to the privy counselor the silliest of claims. These men were businessmen. They had been begging Austria to give them its business. That is what they lived by. When Austria had profitable business, they would, like all bankers, jump at the opportunity for profits. When the business was not profitable, they would not touch it. They operated for profit. They would serve as long as that was available. But if it was deemed desirable for political reasons to reward these brothers —why, then, give each one a gold snuffbox bearing the emperor's initials in diamonds.

The privy counselor was right. In 1822 Austria needed money badly. She asked the Rothschilds for a loan of 30 million gulden. The Rothschilds said—yes, they would lend the money, but would have to have the bonds at 70 per cent with interest payable in advance. The finance minister analyzed their offer. It meant the government would have to issue 42,875,000 gulden in bonds to get 26,796,875 in money. The interest would amount to 7½ per cent. The bankers would make 3,215,625 gulden. The government discovered that Herr Solomon *von* Rothschild was preparing to rook the royal treasury. It made inquiries elsewhere and discovered that bankers who had not been honored, who owed nothing to the imperial throne, foreign bankers, indeed, and for nothing more than a mere profit, were willing to do better than the *von* Rothschilds. The von Rothschilds did not get the business.

But it was some years later that this proof came. In 1816 the privy counselor was not listened to. The emperor raised Anselm and Solomon to the dignity of being von Rothschilds and a week later conferred the same honor upon Carl and James. Nathan, being an English subject, was left out. But six years later—in 1822—after the Rothschild house had risen to undisputed eminence as the first banking house of Europe, all of the brothers were made barons, including Nathan. But Nathan, to his dying day, never used the title.

———————————— XII ————————————

It was at this point—when the war ended—that the Rothschilds moved into the upper altitudes of international banking in its most important sense, the issuance of government securities.

They had been bankers. They did a large bill-brokerage business. They speculated in bills. They made loans to all sorts of people. They handled a few small public loans for Denmark and some cities. They handled the funds of the Elector of Hesse-Cassel. They made great sums transmitting money for the great powers. But they had been rigidly excluded from the upper altitudes of banking, where the aristocrats of money reigned—the flotation of loans for governments. Their great wealth had been made in smuggling, in war trade, in financing war trade of merchants, in war bills, and in speculation in government securities.

Highly colored journalistic accounts of Nathan standing at his favorite pillar of the London Exchange, potbellied, somber, taciturn, inscrutable, sending the market up and down with his smiles and his frowns have been greatly overdramatized. The London Exchange was a market place for securities, but chiefly for government securities. Only a few corporate stocks were listed—those of the large trading companies. Government paper fluctuated violently at times during those troubled years and it was in this that speculation took place. Nathan carried on extensive operations on the floor in government paper and it is not at all improbable that the greater part of his fortune was made this way up to 1814. The art of manipulation had already been developed. The subtler and more delicate nuances of fraud for which exchanges are noted were well understood. These were not born with Daniel Drew and Jim Keane. Abraham Goldschmidt, "King of the Stock Exchange," could plant a false scrap of news, let out a flock of fake rumors and tips, jiggle an issue as neatly as the gentlemen who sent Radio and American Can and Case Corporation bounding up and down in 1929.

Nathan Rothschild came to be known as one of the most daring and successful speculators of his time. With his brothers on the Continent and his agents everywhere he was able to collect inside information and to transmit it swiftly, as Jacob Fugger had done three hundred years before. There is a legend that exalts and debases Nathan Rothschild; one that admirers who love proficiency in slickness have loved to repeat but which, fortunately for his fame, is not true. It is the story of how he stood on one hill in Belgium while Napoleon stood on another, the Emperor directing the Battle of Waterloo, the banker watching the tide of fortune, and how, when Napoleon's defeat was imminent, Rothschild fled from his high perch, made for the coast with relays of swift horses, set out in a chartered boat at night, and reached the Exchange next morning in time for the opening and before news of Wellington's victory was known. There the brokers saw him by his familiar pillar, simulating dejection, selling consols. Knowing his facilities for inside news, his action precipitated a panic and a wave of selling, while through his agents he gathered in all the government paper that was offered, making a fresh fortune.

The story, of course, is not true. A mere glance at the dates and time and distances involved reveals that the feat was physically impossible. The Exchange had the news when it opened for business. Nathan did indeed get the news of the victory an hour before the government and he had the satisfaction of sending to the ministry the first word of the great event. That is all.

After the war, the history of the firm became the story of a large and ever-growing international banking house with branches in five countries, richer, more powerful than others, but following the pattern of banking as it had been developing for three hundred years.

Anselm, the oldest brother, remained in Frankfort. A fine banking house there was the firm's headquarters. He himself managed the business of the firm with Prussia and Germany. But Frankfort became an unpleasant haunt for the Rothschilds for a while. The hot breath of hatred was on the poor Jewish family that had risen to such wealth. Napoleon brought to Frankfort at least one thing—legal equality for the Jews. This they bought from Dalberg, Napoleon's venal ruler in the city. The old Jew street remained, but those only lived there who wished to. The elder Meyer remained until his death. Guetele, his widow, continued there until her death many years later. The sons had made their homes and their business headquarters outside that old prison street. But now Dalberg was gone. The Germans were again in possession. They refused to ratify the liberal dispensations of Napoleon. The Senate actually considered measures to force all Jews back into the ghetto. This would include the Rothschilds with all their millions and power.

At this point Anselm and his brother Solomon considered emigration. They would go elsewhere. This was a serious matter for Frankfort. Anselm spent 150,000 gulden a year upon his home. He dispensed 20,000 gulden in charities to all sorts of people. A procession of rich and eminent persons filed daily into

Frankfort, seeking favors at the hands of the great banker, and
spent money in the city. It would not do to lose so profitable a
citizen. Accordingly, the family put pressure upon Metternich to
force the Frankfort Senate to remove the Jewish disabilities. And
in 1819 this was done, after a fashion. The ghetto was abolished
but the Jew could own but a single piece of property. The race
was limited to fifteen marriages a year. They were classified as
citizens but as "Israelitish citizens"—a special subclass of citizen
less favored than other Frankforters. But it was a great gain,
even though in a very small area—Frankfort—and the Rothschilds were responsible for it. They used their power at court and
their money. They kept the palm of Friedrich von Gentz, the
commercialized publicist-secretary of Metternich, well greased;
they loaned Metternich himself 900,000 gulden.

Solomon Rothschild found it necessary, because of the growing
business with the Austrian court, to establish a house in Vienna.
But Vienna was not free to the Jew. He therefore took quarters
in the Empire Hotel. When the freedom of the city was given him
in due course he took over the whole hotel and the adjoining
building as the Rothschild home and banking house. After Aix-
la-Chapelle in 1818 he became the chief banker of the Austrian
government. Metternich wrote of him as "my friend Rothschild."
Metternich, the archangel of legitimacy, and Solomon Rothschild,
the embodiment of upstartery, became fast allies for legitimacy,
and wherever the great Austrian champion of absolutism went
with his documents and his troops, the indispensable gulden of
Solomon Rothschild flowed along to nourish the project. Somehow
it got about that the fortunes of Austria and of the House of
Rothschild were inextricably intertwined. Bethmann, his great
rival banker, now completely overshadowed, said in 1822 that the
continued prosperity of the Rothschilds was necessary to Austria.

James Rothschild, the youngest brother, who had gone to Paris
when the affair of the Wellington bills was being managed, remained there, flourishing, after the best Rothschild manner. After
the Bourbons returned to power he forged rapidly forward to

become one of the first bankers of France. He moved from his modest flat and took over the palace of Fouché, Napoleon's chief of police. He filled it with treasures of art, costly furnishings, and plate, and became a sort of patron of men of letters. He entertained lavishly and made loans with great discretion to many leaders and statesmen. He established the closest relations with Louis XVIII and Charles X, his successor. But when Polignac staged his ill-fated *coup d'état* for Charles and Parisians rushed to their beloved barricades to drive Charles from his throne and put Louis Philippe there in his stead, James Rothschild could look with satisfaction upon a new king whose investments he managed, to whom he loaned money, and with whom he had dealt on terms of the greatest intimacy. Thus James in Paris could fall upon his feet with the alleged liberal revolution of Louis Philippe while Solomon in Vienna held the pursestrings of the most implacable foe of liberalism. And though France had her great bankers—Laffitte and Casimir Périer, Delessert, Mallet, Hottinguer, and Ouvrard—the House of Rothschild rose above them all.

The state to which these men had arrived may be sensed from the following account of James by the poet Heine. "I like best to visit him at his office in the bank, where, as a philosopher, I can observe how people—not only God's people but all others—bow and scrape before him. It is a contortion of the spine which the finest acrobat would find it difficult to imitate. I saw men double as if they had touched a Voltaic battery when they approached him. Many are overcome with awe at the door of his office as Moses once was on Mount Horeb when he discovered he was on holy ground."

This was the man who as a boy was taught in Frankfort that he must step off the sidewalk and bow when a Christian approached.

A revolt in Naples was the occasion of the establishment of the last of the Rothschild houses. The people of Naples and Sicily revolted against Ferdinand I, the King who had been restored to his throne when Napoleon's Murat had been driven away. They wanted a constitution. Ferdinand, under pressure, yielded. But Metternich promptly summoned a congress of monarchs at Leibach and got for Austria a commission to deal with Naples. Metternich sent an army of 40,000 men. But an army costs money, and Solomon Rothschild was asked to supply it. He did—first sixteen million and then much more. And Carl Rothschild was sent to Naples to act as financial adviser of the Neapolitan king. For four years Metternich's soldiers remained quartered on the people of Naples, at their expense. Carl paid the bills, taking the bonds of the Neapolitan state. And there in Naples he remained, setting up the fifth of the Rothschild financial colonies. Thus this extraordinary family, in a space of a score of years, rose from the estate of a small firm of bill brokers and traders to be the most powerful financial institution in the world, with England, France, Germany, Austria, and Italy as its provinces.

--- XIII ---

The first phase of this adventure in money getting had been, as we have said, like the progress of the chess player, an accumulation of small advantages. The next was a sudden flight upward to great wealth by processes and methods that were not quite open to those lordly bankers who had accumulated constricting dignities along with their money. The third phase was the emergence into the realm of public-security banking, where the profits were magnificent. The final phase was dynastic.

There is no point in recounting all the national loans in which the Rothschilds figured as Europe, which had borrowed herself into disaster by war, now tried to borrow herself out. It was a paradise for the bankers, and the Rothschilds found themselves handling the largest loans either singly or with others for England, France, Austria, Prussia, Russia, Italy, and the smaller states. And here they were able to sink their arms into those rich pools of invisible profits which are the source of most vast fortunes.

The banker got a commission for floating a loan. But this made but a part and frequently a small part of his rewards. He underwrote a state bond issue, taking over at 60 bonds with a face value of 100. Having taken the issue and handed the money to the state, he then proceeded to boost the price on the bourse by the well-known methods of manipulation which the stockbroker and banker of today still insist are essential to his trade. It was not possible for him to hang on to the whole issue, but he usually kept as large a block for himself as his resources and expectations justified.

The Rothschilds were in some cases able to drive issues up to par before they unloaded their own holdings. The modern American and English banker does the same with corporate shares. In the financial world the banker, the broker, the institution organized to perform some function gets paid, as a rule, some modest and justifiable compensation for that service; but behind the scenes and out of sight there are that collection of slanted, semidark, questionable devices for making huge profits, which give to finance too often the character and ethics, if not the external appearance, of the racket. Out of all these things the firm of Rothschild was now prospering amazingly. Bethmann, the Frankfort banker, said that he had it on reliable authority that the five brothers were making six million gulden a year. In another decade they were far outstripping that.

One secret of their enormous power in their several national dependencies was that, unlike the modern American banker at least, their clients were governments rather than corporations— kings and emperors rather than board chairmen. The governments of Europe had gone in on a large scale for borrowing. This was not new. It was merely that war had become more expensive. And thus the governments of Europe fell into the hands of the bankers as the railroads and utilities of America have done in our time. The bankers cultivated ministers, bribed them and their agents, baldly as they did Gentz, more subtly by loans as they did Metternich. They entertained them, showered gifts upon their

wives, as the Bardi and Peruzzi did three hundred years before.
Also they found it necessary to penetrate government departments,
as they did when they took Buderus into partnership, and as one
of our great American banking houses has done for decades, with
its members, its lawyers, its employees holding positions of importance and trust in the state and finance departments of the
government, while recruiting its partners from men of power and
influence in the administration of all parties. The ethics of the
city party gangs, perfumed and rigged out in a frock coat and
sprayed with the odors of sanctity, have characterized the public
morals of investment bankers the world over.

But the Rothschilds beyond all question had that kind of intui-
tive feeling for money, for risks, for the chances that rise out of
the elusive and generally unpredictable behavior of men that
amounts to genius. At least one of them had it and the others
were men of large talents in this one area of human activity.
The record of their performances attests this. In the very difficult years preceding the panic of 1825—1823 to 1825—the Baring
house made two loans, both of which defaulted. The Goldschmidts
made three and the Ricardos one, all of which defaulted, while
the Rothschilds made eight large international loans, all of which
stood up. Out of twenty-six flotations by leading English bankers
in those years, only ten escaped default, and eight of these were
made by the Rothschild house.

But the Rothschilds until late in their careers apparently took
little or no part in the creation of wealth in any country in which
they operated. In those years from 1790 to 1825, the most amazing
change in the processes of producing goods was taking place—
that industrial revolution which set the modern world off upon
the machine age and changed its manners, its habits, its tastes,
its governments. The revolution in the methods of producing textiles, wools, the introduction of steam, of railroads, of steam
shipping, and a host of other technological developments came
about rapidly. But the Rothschilds, so far as the records reveal,
took no interest or part in this until all the spadework had been

done. They did not finance industry. Indeed, few of the bankers did. And, above all, they stood aloof from corporate finance, which seemed to belong to a level below their lordly attention. Indeed Baring in the House of Commons denounced the growing flood of corporate stocks that was flooding the market, though it was quite small. In fact twenty years later, in the early 'forties, out of £1,118,000,000 of securities listed on the London Exchange, £894,000,000 were government issues and £46,800,000 were bank issues.

In later years, however, they did turn to industrial and commercial ventures, particularly as their vast resources increased and, as the result of industrial development, great opportunities appeared, involving less risk than in the earlier years of the new era—and when they saw the value of doing with corporate stocks what they had done with bonds, underwrite them, boost the price on the exchange, and unload at large invisible profits. Also they were drawn into certain large-scale private and semiprivate enterprises by reason of their close alliance with their respective governments. In England, Nathan's son Lionel, after Nathan's death, financed the purchase of the Suez Canal for England and backed the adventures in empire building of Cecil Rhodes. The French house came to the rescue of the Czar several times, on one occasion getting from him the important Baku oil concession that put the Rothschilds into competition with John D. Rockefeller until they sold out to Dutch Shell.

In France, James financed and built the Chemin du Nord, became its president, and it has remained in the family among its important possessions to this day. Later, in 1870, James' son Alphonse financed the transfer of the huge 5,000,000-franc indemnity of France to Germany.

In Austria Solomon did some not-too-successful railroad financing. He organized the Credit Anstalt, Austria's greatest bank until its disastrous collapse in 1931, and continued as the chief Austrian banker until his death.

Nathan died in 1836, leaving his son Lionel in command.

James lived until 1868. Solomon died in 1826; Carl and Anselm in 1855. James' son Alphonse assumed the leadership of the powerful French house. Anselm left no sons, and the house, managed by two nephews for a few years, gradually passed out of existence. Carl, in Naples, left his son Albert in control. But Naples was too troublous a spot. Italy was too much in ferment for successful banking under a banker who had little or no interest in his business. And so the Neapolitan house was closed. Gradually the Austrian branch sank into a place of unimportance. The French house became a mere investment trust for the extensive invested wealth of the family. The old banking house of Nathan in St. Swithin's Lane remained, active and influential, but far from first among London bankers. Today, Rothschilds do not control any of London's five big banks—the Midland, Barclay's, Lloyds, National Provincial, or Westminster. No Rothschild is on the directorate of the Bank of England, but Nathan's old enemy Baring is there.

Fortune magazine said a few years ago that there were then living thirty-seven persons of the Rothschild name. They are strangely different from those tough-fibered old gulden chasers of the Frankfort ghetto. A hundred years of wealth have softened some, mellowed some, vivified some. But the original energy is gone. The energy of those able three brothers, Nathan, James, and Solomon, has been succeeded now by the energy of mere money. There is no money-making energy like money itself. That vast bolus of wealth which two generations piled up is now endowed, through sheer investment, with more money-making power than the famed brothers possessed. The family is richer now than it was under them, but it is far from being as powerful. The Rothschild family is now just a bankroll.

It is difficult to leave these men without, like a symphonist, strumming for a few bars on one of the minor motifs of this piece. It has to do with the hardihood of the legends that have clustered about the Rothschild name. Nowhere is this better illustrated than in a single paragraph that appeared in one of our leading magazines several years ago. It represents in a nutshell the batch of fairy tales that three generations have had repeated to them over and over about the Rothschilds:

It was their guess about Napoleon that set them on their unique pedestal. The five brothers were clever enough to realize that for all his genius, for all his victories, Napoleon could not last. On that intuition they staked every penny. Nathan's fabled advance news of the Battle of Waterloo gave the Rothschilds an opportunity to buy depressed securities in London. Even without that coup the day after Waterloo was to find all the established governments of Europe deeply in their debt. . . . They, especially Solomon Rothschild, guessed right about railroads, became the railroad builders of Europe. While Calvinist clergymen thundered against the steam engine and country squires complained that the filthy little teakettles on wheels were ruining the countryside, the Rothschilds and their sons were pouring out gold to lay tracks.

It would be difficult to find anywhere in history so many insupportable statements packed into so few sentences. Literally every statement is wrong. Yet the writer can hardly be censured since he was repeating what is to be found in innumerable biographies, histories, and essays, having their origin at least in part in the industry of inspired writers beginning with Gentz.

The Rothschilds did not realize that Napoleon could not last and did not stake their all on this conviction. On the contrary, they took excellent care to protect themselves against any eventuality. Nathan in England worked with the English ministry, but Anselm and Solomon in Frankfort worked on equally friendly terms with Napoleon's rulers in Germany. They loaned nothing to the English government. They did make loans to Dalberg, head of Napoleon's Confederation of the Rhine, both personally and to his state. James went to Paris where, while operating in collusion with Nathan, he maintained the friendliest relations with Count Mollien, Napoleon's finance minister, and established an excellent reputation as a banker. Nathan, in London, observed the greatest caution in keeping under cover so that his activities would not injure his brothers on the Continent. They played the game safe and were in a position to capitalize on victory for either side. It was not until after the disaster at Leipzig and when Napoleon's star was definitely setting and all Europe was betting against him that the Rothschilds became openly opposed.

Of course the story of Nathan's Waterloo coup is pure fiction. And equally fictitious is the statement that the day after Waterloo found all the governments of Europe deeply in debt to the Rothschilds. No government owed them anything, unless perhaps the small government of Denmark, which is doubtful. Up to the defeat of Napoleon they played no part in the flotation of loans by European states. Had Napoleon routed Wellington at Waterloo, the Rothschilds would have lost nothing, save some good clients. Then follows the statement that they became the railroad builders of Europe. They built a single railroad—the Chemin du Nord in France. And this they built not when country squires were complaining that the filthy little teakettles ruined the countryside, but after most European railroads had been built and developed (there were at least seventy-five roads in England alone) by other men and the little teakettle locomotives had disappeared. There is a curious consistency in naming Solomon "especially" as the railroad builder. This fable is hoary with age. He built no road. He did finance in part a single road in Austria which had so unhappy a history that he quickly got out of it. James was the only one who built a railroad.

Interlogue One

COSIMO DE' MEDICI

THE TEMPTATION to include in this volume whole chapters about three men was not easy to resist. They were Cosimo de' Medici, Sir Thomas Gresham, and Jacques Coeur. The essentials in the stories of these men were quite the same. They were the chief pioneers in organizing the forms of the new capitalist system in Italy, England, and France, respectively. They seemed, however, interesting and romantic in their personal histories, but less significant than Jacob Fugger, and it was not possible to include more than one.

When we speak of the Medici we may choose one of three— Giovanni di Bicci, surnamed the Friend of the People, or Cosimo, his son, called Pater Patriae, or Cosimo's grandson Lorenzo, known as the Magnificent. Giovanni laid the foundation of the fortune. Cosimo, however, ablest of the three, accumulated that vast wealth that gave the Medici their power in Florence. Lorenzo advertised, paraded, luxuriated in that fortune and laid the foundation for its ruin. All of them were merchants, moneylenders, bankers, manufacturers. Cosimo, however, added to the techniques of these professions the role of politician and the devices of homicide. One does not use these brutal terms about such splendid persons. Yet if truth is to be served we must describe Cosimo and Lorenzo as bankers, merchants, manufacturers, statesmen, and murderers.

Giovanni actually established a large business with branches all over Italy, in the Levant, Constantinople, and other cities. He opposed the Albizzi, rulers of Florence, and was hailed by the people as their leader. The Medici remained continuously heads of what is called a republic for four generations—from 1434 to 1494—sixty years in which the republic ripened into a thorough tyranny.

Cosimo, shrewd, iron-willed, looking the esthete, gracious but cruel, refused office and ruled Florence as the invisible power functioning behind some nominated tool, as Dick Croker or Charlie Murphy did, save that they ruled a vast city and he a small one of 70,000 souls. He dressed in simple robes, sometimes like a poor guildsman, shrank from notice like Rockefeller, whom he resembled in some respects, whereas his grandson Lorenzo resembled J. Pierpont Morgan. He mingled the virtues of the chalice and the dagger. The problems of competition that have continued to torture industrial barons, he met with the singularly effective application of the knife. Persons of power who were in his way in the state or the market place were driven out of Florence; the less fortunate were murdered. An important source of his business growth was the finances of the popes. The Medici became papal bankers. The possession of these large funds served him as the possession of the funds of the emperor served the Mitsuis in Japan.

A devout Christian, Cosimo fraternized with the Franciscans whom he presented with a monastery, providing it with a cell to which he himself retired at intervals for meditation and prayer. When he was seventy-five he went to his last rest with the perfect tranquillity of the righteous man, not at all ruffled by the memory of his climb to wealth and power. His son Piero, surnamed the Gouty, succeeded him, and died after a futile career of five years. Into his shoes stepped Lorenzo, who proceeded to lavish upon Florence the wealth his grandfather had amassed.

Lorenzo made money, of course, for he possessed a great fortune, a great money-making machine, and enormous prestige. From Pope Paul II he got a monopoly of the alum recently discovered in the hills around Volterra, his Holiness justly protecting the monopoly by proclaiming excommunication against anyone who

competed by importing alum from the Turks. Thus excommunication was added to assassination as a defense against competition.
Lorenzo was a good Catholic, but a better moneylender. He loaned
Pope Innocent VIII 100,000 ducats for a year, taking as surety
two tenths of the stipends of all newly appointed priests, and
possession of the Città di Castello until paid. The Pope made
Lorenzo's fourteen-year-old son a cardinal and gave to Lorenzo's
daughter his own illegitimate son in marriage.

An attempt upon Lorenzo's life was made by two priests during
Mass, instigated by Pope Sixtus IV and the Pazzi, bankers.
Lorenzo's vengeance was swift. Certain of the Pazzi were hanged,
others butchered in the streets, some cast into the Arno. He became
an unrestrained tyrant, filled Florence with spies, was himself
excommunicated by the Pope. He showered gold and favors upon
painters, sculptors, poets, philosophers, enriched Florence with
their works, bought rare manuscripts, books, antiquities, covered
himself with the praise-giving of these subsidized flatterers, and,
dying, left his city upon the brink of ruin. His son Pietro ruled
disastrously for two years and was driven out of Florence to make
way for the theocratic Fascism of the monkish enemy of bankers,
national and international, Savonarola.

---------------------------- II ----------------------------

SIR THOMAS GRESHAM

The great businessman of England in the dawn of capitalism was
Sir Thomas Gresham, financial adviser to three Tudor monarchs
—Edward VI, Mary, and Elizabeth—founder of the Royal Exchange and reputed discoverer of Gresham's Law, known to every
crossroads store controversialist on money.

Son of a baronet who was a friend of Wolsey, born in 1519,
when Fugger was at the peak of his career, merchant-adventurer
by inheritance, studied at Cambridge—Thomas Gresham was the

prototype of the modern Peel-Hanna-Chamberlain-Mellon school of merchant-banker-statesman. Starting with an education amid members of the mercers' guild, who had but little, he spent twenty years as merchant and king's factor in Antwerp, money metropolis of Europe, where he learned more about money, credit, exchange, and speculation than any of his English contemporaries.

He went to Antwerp as king's agent in 1551 when Edward VI's ministers were looking ruefully down that bottomless hole known as the national debt. It was an external debt—more kings have fallen by it than by guns. English kings borrowed from Flemish, German, and Italian bankers. More money flowed out in usurious interest than flowed in in loans. Edward VI had to find 40,000 pounds a year for interest to foreign bankers. "How can the king be rid of his debt?" asked the ministers. Gresham's answer was an amazing one. "By paying them and incurring no new ones." Seemingly it had occurred to no one. It was the hard way. Politicians have a preference for the easy way—the primrose path down which they lead people to the ever-lasting bonfire. Gresham persuaded the ministers of Edward, Mary, and Elizabeth to try the hard way. It led to riches for England.

By skillful manipulation on the Antwerp bourse he got control of pound exchange over a considerable period, making it favorable to London. He induced the government to economize and to remit to him weekly sums for extinguishing the debt.

He had observed in Antwerp and Amsterdam that the worn and inferior coins drove out the good ones. England's slipshod coinage resulted in the continuous flight of the sound ones and of the precious metals. Gresham supposed he discovered this law. As late as 1857 H. D. Macleod, economist, supposed so, too. He gave it the name of Gresham's Law. It is probably the best known of economic principles. But actually Gresham did not discover it. It had been observed by others before him—Copernicus for one. To Elizabeth he said: "And it please your majestie to restore this your realm into such estate as heretofore it hat bene, your highness hath none other ways, butt, when time and opportunyty serveth, to bringe your base money into fine, of xi ounces fine. And so gowlde." This was done.

He perceived that foreign interest payments drained away England's metal money. Why not borrow from Englishmen at home? There was the canon law against it. But off in Augsburg Jacob Fugger and his personal philosopher Peutinger had already argued the ecclesiastical and secular validity out of that old Aquinian fetish. And so Gresham got Elizabeth to end the ban on interest in England. She fixed the legal rate at ten per cent.

Buying abroad and selling too little also took away England's precious metals. Gresham contrived to shift the base of England's trade from Antwerp to the free port of Hamburg. From thence he built a large trade into Germany. The Hanseatic merchants had had almost a monopoly of that. Gresham took away their hold upon England's export trade to Germany. Thus he weakened the Hanse merchants and drove the Steelyard out of London. Almost as important, he taught England a lesson. Wars are made, not merely with arms, but with economic weapons. But he did not neglect the value of weapons. In his role of adviser he taught Queen Bess that a navy was a thing of great value to England and proceeded to supply her with one in his role of merchant.

Lastly, Sir Thomas Gresham—knighted for his services—built out of his own funds the Royal Exchange to provide London merchants with a bourse such as he had seen in Antwerp. In 1571 the fine building was formally dedicated by the Queen, after dinner at Gresham's home.

Serious, severe, sober in his dress, he lived well, but not ostentatiously as did Fugger and the Medici. He had a home in Bishopgate Street and several in the country. He endowed a college—Gresham College—an almshouse in Broadstreet, and distributed alms to five prisons and four hospitals each quarter. He attained to no such wealth as Fugger or Medici. Moreover, he came on the scene after them and when the devices of the new flowering capitalist and mercantilist world had been much advanced. But he must rank as one of the great commercial figures of that era.

III

JACQUES COEUR

The great business leader has been called in order **Magnate**, **King, Baron, and now Tycoon.** The first title of adulation conferred upon him was prince. Hence Jacques Coeur was called the Merchant Prince of the Middle Ages. He was *in* but not *of* the Middle Ages. The smell of money was in the air in France. Men who had the feel of livres as some men have the feel of cards or dice were fingering livres and breeding them. They were not operating in accordance with the dying techniques of the Middle Ages but rather of the emerging capitalist world. Jacques Coeur was doing this in France, as Fugger was in Germany, Gresham in England, and the Medici in Italy. And, though there were no schools of business or professors of banking institutes, these gentlemen did very well. Most of them—Coeur, Fugger, Law, Rothschild, Rockefeller, Morgan—were already rich before the average young business-college graduate has emerged with his M.A.

Coeur was pre-eminently a trader—a merchant-adventurer. He flourished upon the swiftly growing intercourse between nations, the wider variety of products upon the market, and the means of gratifying the taste for them by means of money.

He was born in Bourges about 1400, the son of a prosperous small merchant, got some education—enough to get the tonsure of the clerk when he was past twenty—married the daughter of the Provost of Bourges, and turns up in the money-coining business about the time the Maid of Orléans was winning her battles for Charles VII.

Coining money was the king's prerogative in France, but he let it out upon a partnership basis to various *argentiers* in different sections. Ravent Ladenois had it for Bourges and a brace of cities.

And Ladenois found for himself a partner in each such town to operate the mint. Young Jacques Coeur was Ladenois' partner in Bourges. Ladenois and Coeur were arrested and thrown into jail on the charge of cheapening the king's money—that is, short-weighting the coins, pocketing the difference as profit. Unhappy M. Ladenois whimpered that so great had been the exactions of the king out of the business that this was quite necessary for him to make a profit. Young Master Coeur said he did as he was told. Both were convicted, fined 1000 livres each, the plea of necessity weighing heavily with the judges.

Coeur became a merchant. He turned up next as a merchant-adventurer. Shipwrecked in his vessel on a trip to the Orient, captured by pirates, he escaped, drove forward in business, became rich, and finally landed on both feet in the very palace of the king as Lord Steward of the household. He continued to expand his business and, we are told, spread his agents to all the important ports of the world. He had three hundred factors, his business in Bourges housed in thirty buildings, with several business buildings in towns like Tours, Marseilles, Lyons. He built a famous palace— Jacques Coeur House—in Bourges, surpassing any royal home in France. It still stands, a castle in splendor and beauty worthy of a twentieth-century economic grandee, filled with tapestries, paintings, gold and silver plate, and other works of art.

He received a patent of ennoblement from Charles VII, lived at court the equal of the greatest, had his son made archbishop of Bourges, and built his estates all over France. He went to Rome, one of the leaders of a great embassy, carted thither in eleven of his own ships, commanded by himself, pausing at Finale to deliver arms to the French and then going in to the Vatican to open the eyes of the Romans to the splendor of the ambassadors and their entourage, cantering in rich costumes to the court of Pope Nicholas V. When the king renewed the Hundred Years' War, Jacques Coeur advanced him 2,500,000 francs in metal money, though he had to borrow some of it.

Then, as ever, the love of the king for Jacques cooled. Almost out of a clear sky he was arrested in July 31, 1451, thrown into a dungeon of the palace, and charged with the poisoning of Agnes Sorel, the king's mistress, and some ten other crimes. Chief of them was that he had "sent coats of arms to the Saracen by means of which the Sultan had gained a victory over the Christian armies."

There was the odor of conspiracy in all this—charges coined to ruin Coeur. After all, there was a vast estate which was subject to confiscation by the crown. And there was probably some serious rift between Coeur and the king because of the quarrel between Charles and his exiled son, who would become Louis XI. And Coeur was suspected of being friendly to the Dauphin. The charge of poisoning was dropped. But Coeur was convicted on four of the remaining ten counts, including the arming of the Turks, despite his claim that he had a license from the Pope to ship the arms. Coeur sold the arms to the Sultan in order to get permission from him to bring out of Alexandria a large cargo of pepper.

His life was spared but his property was confiscated and sold at auction, the administration of the estate constituting probably the biggest receivership in the history of France to that time. Coeur ultimately escaped, went to Rome where he was received with honors by Nicholas V, who officially proclaimed his innocence. In 1456 he went with an expedition against the Mohammedans, was taken ill, died on the island of Chios, and was buried with honor in the chapel of the Cordelliers in 1464.

IV

THE ART AND INDUSTRY OF MAKE-UP

I

It is interesting to note, that in the very dawn of civilization, in ancient Egypt, when men were just beginning to learn the difficult business of living together, the art of make-up was much in use by the monarch and the ruling groups that surrounded him.

It is also worth noting that this, the oldest of the luxury industries, is the one that has persisted and grown so extensively that in
our age it becomes at once a prop of our economic life and the chief
weapon of our ruling figures for continuing their dominion over the
minds of men.

The world is now and has always been ruled by men of wealth,
and the most important instruments in the stratagems by which this
is achieved are the rouge pot, the haberdasher, the builders and dec-
orators, the dramatist and the showman, and, as we shall presently
see, that oldest of functionaries—the shirt stuffer.

Plato's sovereignty of the philosopher will never come until the
philosopher puts aside the humility of the scholar and assumes the
air of the conqueror, arranges the necessary pageantry, hires publicity men, and proceeds to sell himself to his fellows, in which very
moment he will cease to be a philosopher.

This is the trick the ruler and the rich man knew when we discover the first traces of him in the ancient monuments and which,
doubtless, he brought with him out of the jungle.

-------------------------------- 2 --------------------------------

We are all bank notes, observes Thomas Carlyle, representing
gold. But alas! he laments, many of us are forgeries. On this point,
however, he consoles himself with the thought that, after all, men,
in all times, especially in earnest times, have a talent for detecting
quacks and, indeed, for detesting quacks.

The sour old Scotch philosopher, who believed in the authenticity
of heroes and the necessity for them, had a theory to which this
reliance on man's perception in detecting quacks was essential.
Woe to the times, he said, which, calling loudly for its great man,
finds him not there.

Carlyle overstates the disaster. The times, in all ages, have had
a way of inventing their great men. The machinery and means of
producing men and women to our taste—and great ones, too—have
always been ready to hand. We have always been equipped to make

beautiful women, to hold back the wrinkles of age, to banish the silver threads from among the gold, to simulate youth and loveliness. But also we have been able to simulate intelligence and power, to make great scientists out of little pill mixers, to transmogrify bewildered little businessmen into great captains, and to inflate to the proportions of statesmen the meanest little spirits in our towns.

Somehow the hero worship that flourished in the ancient world still persists, despite education and newspapers and books. We have had a gargantuan spree of debunking, of stripping the wrappings and labels from our spurious miracle men, our pyramid builders, our treasure hunters and statesmen. We have seen a good many of the bank notes go to protest and—to mix the metaphor—to jail. But the equipment for turning out fresh forgeries seems to be inexhaustible.

These deceptions are achieved through that same more or less harmless theatricality by which men and women mitigate the errors of nature. No doubt originally devised to add to grace and charm, it has been cultivated extensively to give to cheapness and fraud the aspect of quality and authority and even greatness.

————————— 3 —————————

Civilization, as it moves slowly away from primitive barbarism, seeks to dress itself up for the part it would like to play.

This art of make-up probably was cultivated by remote tribes fifteen to twenty thousand years before it appeared on the banks of the Nile. And as it was one of the most important industries in the wealthiest of early nations—Egypt—so it continues to flourish as one of the most important of the great industries in the wealthiest of modern nations. It is doubtful if any single industry can match it in the number of persons employed and the sums expended in the vast business of dressing and beautifying the American man and woman.

Along the Nile and the Red Sea and across the Arabian Desert boats and camels transported the materials for ministering to Egyptian vanity, and this constituted the bulk of that country's trade. Today in America it is said the American woman's cosmetic bill is two billions a year. This is in addition to what she spends on clothes, furs, millinery, and jewelry. A thoughtful gentleman of my acquaintance who loves to toy with novel ideas has advanced the not wholly fantastic proposal that this nation, groping about frantically but futilely for a new industry to pull itself out of its depression, might accomplish this by merely extending the area of the oldest industry and inducing men to go in for beauty as women have done.

Oddly enough, man has never felt sure of himself in the nude. This in itself has made an end of the struggling cult of nudism. Men and women will never trust themselves to the opinions of their fellows, based on their unadorned bodies. People do not dress for modesty. Modesty, like many other excuses in our moral codes, serves a better reason.

Human beings wear clothes to shield their nakedness, to keep them warm, and to adorn themselves. But a woman can hide her nakedness in fifty cents' worth of cotton cloth. She can keep herself warm in six dollars' worth of wool. Nevertheless she spends fifty dollars for her coat and five thousand if she can afford it. This will serve as a measure of the relative importance of these three influences in feminine attire. People dress to conceal the defects of the body, to neutralize the onset of age, to hide the effects of gluttony and sloth.

The sums expended every year upon the mitigation of female defects and deformities is so great that were the sex as a whole to agree to suspend their make-up for a single year they would utterly wreck the economic machine of the world. Some wag with a flare for statistics has estimated that her ladyship dabs on her face 4000 tons of powder, 52,000 tons of cleansing cream, 7500 tons of nourishing cream, 25,000 tons of skin lotion, and 24,000 tons of rouge, all of which must be produced by workers, processed by factories, sold and dispensed and applied at beauty counters and salons, in-

volving the expenditure of billions in production and distribution
costs. Which leads to the observation that while vanity is vanity it
is also big business and indispensable to the continued functioning
of our economic world.

A German artist of the last generation made a devastating series
of drawings representing groups of important people in their most
admired and favored surroundings, posturing in their salons, strutting in their ballrooms, posing in all their pretension and hauteur,
looking wise and profound, staring through lorgnettes, loaded with
jewelry—but minus their clothes. The spectacle of withered old
men and women, with hanging paunches and drooping breasts,
wrinkled, flatulent, stooped, made an impression that would wring
from the most irascible hater of mockery and deception in dress a
cry for a return to those tons of creams and lotions and rouge and
layers of lace and fur and silk and wool. Let us expose their sins, let
us have at them with ink and jest and invective, but for God's sake,
let us not undress them!

---------------- 4 ----------------

Carlyle, in the opening chapter of his *French Revolution,* refers
to Louis XV being pictured to the French as leading his victorious
armies, winning battles, planning new campaigns and victories, and
charging the enemy when in fact he was a gouty, scrofulous cripple
being carted around with the army like so much baggage.

It is the way of the world with so many of its leaders. They are
invented; fictitious beings created for us out of the masculine imagination of the shirt stuffer operating upon the pliant feminine
imagination of the masses. It is one of the least pretty of our social
mechanisms.

Go about Italy, and wherever there is a plaza to hold it you will
see, mounted on a monstrous charger, a colossal warrior in bronze
or marble, with uplifted sword and a countenance of majesty and
power—the figure of Umberto Primo or Vittorio Emmanuele Sec-
ondo, thus advertising to the Italian mass mind the great leader-

ship of these two mighty sovereigns who were, in fact, just two little fellows whose capacities could have been duplicated among the lesser bureau chiefs of any town in Italy.

But kings must be great men. They must be wise, courageous, full of nobility and power. As they seldom have these qualities in larger measure than is to be found in the members of the local chamber of commerce, the political promoter has collaborated with the military promoter for centuries to invest these small fellows with the missing royal attributes. They have drawn upon the age-old arts of pageantry, costume, feathers, flags, and music. The populace, prepared by the proper prologue, sees a bewildered and sometimes blundering fool encrusted in gold and other metals, crowned with a towering shako, upon a richly caparisoned horse capering between lines of saluting privates, and attended by the brass of the band and the cheers of the people—it sees not the little man at all but the fictitious figure who does not exist. Of course, a philosopher, a statesman, and a priest may be counted on to write learnedly that all this is essential to the stability of the society, as the king, after all, is merely a symbol, a spiritual nucleus essential to the well-being of the multitude of moronic protons who revolve around him.

The church knows this. The great cardinal, heavy with crimson robes and flowing trains, mitered in gold, surrounded by surplus *monsignori* against a background of marble and brass, stained-glass windows, and the dim glow of candlelight and incense, and with the incidental emotional tremors of the organ—the cardinal thus made up can pretend with success to powers no one would credit if he lived in a cottage or dressed in a smock of cheap wool.

And, of course, presidents, politicians, businessmen with products to sell, bankers with securities to distribute understand this principle. All of the stratagems of make-up, of shirt stuffing, are employed to fill the imagination of the people with fictitious images of the men who must be sold to the public. Selling merchandise often depends first upon selling to the buyers the man who produces it. The priceless ingredient, proclaims one advertiser, is the reputation of the maker for integrity. Therefore, it is important to erect the manufacturer of things—drugs, foods, stocks, and ideas—into a being of purity and intelligence. Half the job of selling a bottle of ineffectual jalap for rheumatism is done if the great Mr. Bunkus, its maker, miracle man of the drug world, jalap king, great philanthropist, eloquent speaker at commercial banquets, doctor of law and of humane letters at Yale and Harvard, is behind the product. It is easy to sell the voters a bill of goods embracing the "abolition of poverty" or "the abundant life" if some "great" engineer or the great radio crooner is behind these respective emulsions. Throughout history we shall see that the great rulers, dictators, oil kings, steel kings, and money kings have employed the techniques of shirt stuffing to build themselves up to the proportions of heroes of one sort or another in the common mind. Once a man has made a million dollars, it is promptly assumed that because he knew how to make a million he knows also how to run a college, a church, a government. Presence on the board of the college, the vestry, or the cabinet of the government gave to the businessman a character that aided him in getting what he called "consumer acceptance" for his products. It has been easy to convince people affected with an abiding appetite for wealth that the man who has succeeded in accumulating it is capable of ruling them. Hence the rich man has tended to move into all the places of power—to dominate our education, to mold our theology, to form our culture, to modify our social thinking.

A definite technique has been perfected for creating any kind of character out of almost any man with enough money to hire the professional help. His name and picture are repeated over and over in the press until he becomes a member of our performing celebrities, his benefactions artfully and opportunely contrived and announced, with pictures, encomiums, editorials heralding his public spirit. Articles about him appear in the success magazines. Men are hired to write speeches for him to deliver at conventions, banquets, public gatherings, at colleges, and over the radio. He issues statements upon all sorts of subjects, has opinions about everything, all worked up and happily phrased for him by his hired shirt stuffers. It is an old stratagem. We have already seen Dr. Peutinger acting as apologist for Jacob Fugger. We shall see how other men of wealth have utilized the resources of religion, the press, the platform to build up their reputations for wisdom and patriotism as a prelude to exercising a dominating influence over the public mind. It is quite possible that the free society has no greater enemy than the shirt stuffer and that men will never be wholly free, in that higher and finer sense to which they aspire, until their minds shall be emancipated from the power of the rich to possess and control the instrumentalities by which opinion is made.

V

WRITERS AS MONEY-MAKERS

It would be an interesting speculation how far the history of the world has been obscured, twisted, and falsified as a result of the fact that writers, historians, poets, and even philosophers have depended upon the bounty of the rich and powerful. The very first writers, in order to eat, had to please the king or some powerful patron. Apparently the very earliest writings among the Egyptians, the Chaldeans, the Phoenicians were upon clay tablets by public officials to be read by the king, the priests, the court. The authors of the Pharaohs' day were attached to the temple. The first Chinese writers depended upon official appointments for their livelihood.

The audience of all ancient writers and even of modern ones up to a few hundred years ago was limited, since few had the art of reading. Even the circulation of the old Greek works was small and would have been impossible without the favor of certain rich men. Some philosophers in ancient Athens were paid incredible sums as teachers, some of them—Protagoras, Gorgias, Zeno—getting as much as 10,000 drachmas to educate a student. But these gentlemen were Sophists who taught the sons of wealthy Athenians how to get along, how to use their faculties to the end of success. There were no such rewards for the realistic searcher after truth. The Greek playwrights, however, had an audience and hence, in the free society of Athens, could command comparatively substantial sums for their work, while they enjoyed a corresponding freedom, discussed public affairs, discoursed on public and private morals, and did not hesitate to lampoon the head of the state himself. This was not altogether true in Rome when the state began to provide the populace with plays. Terence and Plautus could get for their plays sums which were not available to the poets and commentators, but they were paid public money by the aediles who were charged with providing dramatic productions for the people.

Men like Horace and Virgil got little or no money rewards from their works. Both depended upon the bounty of Maecenas. And Maecenas took up the role of the magnificent patron of letters as a means of fortifying the regime of Augustus. Horace speaks of his publisher, Socii, but laments that while the publisher made profit from his poems, Horace made nothing. But it is highly improbable that any publisher made very much in a world where books had to be written by hand and few of the people could read. Martial, the epigrammist, said that the sale of his poems brought him nothing. But he cultivated the friendship of the Emperor Domitian and became tribune. Quintilian, the rhetorician, had an income for a while of 100,000 sesterces from the Emperor. And, of course, in that ruthless dictatorship, there was no more place for the independent thinker or artist than there is in the tyrannies of Mussolini and Hitler. Before the empire dissolved all independent literary production had come to an end. And after that, the church succeeded to the role of literary dictator.

In the modern world the same thing held true for many centuries. It was perhaps worse than in certain periods of the ancient world, for there were times and places where even the wealthy and powerful could not read, when this faculty was limited to a handful of people. It is a singular fact that the authors of such universally famed productions as the *Edda*, the *Cid*, the *Nibelungenlied*, and the legends of King Arthur remain unknown, while various monarchs have come down to us as writers. Charlemagne is a case in point—a Frankish German of no education, who probably could neither read nor write, yet who is supposed to have composed a German grammar, poems, and even a work in medieval Latin on the worship of images. He did gather scholars around him and encouraged literature. But it is probable that his own compositions were the work of some of those shrinking persons with a passion for anonymity so dear to the hearts of rulers.

As writers appeared on the scene they might well be represented as grasping their pen in one hand and the king's bounty in the other. In France, Colomby, original academician, drew 15,600 francs as the king's orator and Jean Louis de Balzac 10,000 francs as the king's general eulogist. In Italy Petrarch counted his patrons among several of the ruling houses of Italy and was an especial ward of the Colonna family. Boccaccio, who learned something of his art from Petrarch, learned from him also how to cultivate the good will of the prince. He enjoyed the special favor of King Robert of Naples, and the *Decameron* was written for the King's family, as the *Heptameron* was written for the delectation of Francis I, possibly by his sister Margaret, but more likely by some anonymous spinner of yarns about the castle.

The dependence of the writer upon the political treasury and the favor of the lord or merchant continued to a late day. And some of them did quite as well for themselves as Horace and Virgil did in Rome. Jean Chapelain, author of a dreary and forgotten poem called *La Pucille*, died at the age of seventy-nine, leaving a fortune of 1,450,000 francs, which he got in gifts from Richelieu, Mazarin, and Louis XIV; and Boileau, famous satirical poet, who died in 1711, left an estate of $236,000 which he owed to the munificence of the crown.

In time, profits from publishing did make their appearance, but they were meager. The writer still had to look for his security to reliance on the government or a patron. Milton received but sixty-three pounds for *Paradise Lost*, but he got a thousand pounds from

Parliament for a political treatise. Gay, the author of *The Beggar's Opera,* James Thomson, Scottish poet, author of *The Seasons* and *The Castle of Indolence,* and Edward Young, author of *Night Thoughts,* like the more important Addison, Steele, and Swift, were the recipients of royal and noble favor. Gay got a job as secretary to the Duchess of Monmouth, tried his hand at the South Sea speculations, lost what he had, and became a dependent of the Duke and Duchess of Queensbury. Thomson, a very poor youth, began his career as the beneficiary of a noble Maecenas, got a sinecure at 300 pounds a year from the Lord Chancellor, and, when the Chancellor died, got another from the Prince of Wales at 100 pounds. Young, who started a school of graveyard verse, began life with a poem of disgusting flattery of George Granville upon his elevation to the peerage, and followed this with several others dedicated to one wealthy patron after another until he knocked off one to Walpole, celebrating his investiture with the Order of the Garter, and was rewarded with 200 pounds a year. He finally attained the heaven of army officers, ministers, and professors by marrying the daughter of an earl.

Addison, before he was thirty, got a pension of 300 pounds a year, and when the government wished to exploit the popular value of the victory at Blenheim, Addison obliged with his poem, *The Campaign,* which pleased his patrons so much that he got an appointment as Commissioner of Appeals. He held various offices and sinecures and, like Young, annexed as a wife a dowager countess. Thackeray said of this trio—Addison, Steele, and Swift—that "the profession had made Addison a minister, Steele a commissioner of stamps, and Swift almost a bishop." The sharp-tongued Swift felt that his services with his pen had merited something better than an Irish deanery.

But it was precisely when these men were drawing their sustenance from their political and social sponsors that another writer was demonstrating that England had come upon an audience which was willing to pay for what it read and that a man might earn a living as an author without putting on any man's collar. This was

Alexander Pope. He had some small means of his own, but he made a decent living throughout his life from his own labors. Samuel Johnson says he received 5320 pounds for the translation of the *Iliad*, from which he bought and enlarged the country estate at Twickenham where he lived until his death. After this period writers became more and more dependent upon the public that bought their books rather than the noblemen, businessmen, and statesmen who hired their pens and bought their souls. Even poor Bobby Burns could get between five and six hundred pounds for an edition of his works.

For some reason the playwright in France and England seems to have been as much at the mercy of the rich sponsor as the writer of poems and essays. Molière made money out of the stage, but he was playwright, actor, and producer. Shakespeare, too, made enough to leave a decent competency to his family at his death, but it was apparently as playwright, actor, and manager that he, like Molière, made his money. He did not seem interested at all in his plays as subjects for publication. He probably could have made little out of them.

But Ben Jonson, who was a mere writer for the stage, declared he had never made more than 200 pounds out of all his plays. In France both Corneille and Racine sought and got benefits from various patrons. Racine tried to make his plays pay. He met with a resistance that reveals a curious ethical attitude toward this whole subject at the time. He had got 40 francs a night from the theater for the use of his plays. But plays seldom went through many nights of performances. He demanded a thousand francs. Instantly there was a bitter protest from the stage. Madame Beaupré, an actress, complained that whereas with the smaller payment the theater could make money for all, now with Racine's extortionate demand it could not. The whole town echoed her resentment. Racine, it murmured, was attempting to trade on his poetic talents. How the poet could live they apparently did not consider. Nor did they suppose that he had but two choices, either to trade upon his talents with the audiences or with the politicians and the nobility. What did they suppose he was merchandising and to whom and for what when he got 140,000 francs for following the king during the royal military campaigns, or when he got 14,000 francs as royal historiographer or when he was granted a pension of 6900 francs by Richelieu? What was Corneille trading upon when he dedicated *Cinna* to the unscrupulous financier Montrauon?

Yet this curious moral notion persisted. It can be explained upon no other ground than that the emoluments of the writer were meager, that by abandoning them in favor of the sweeter viands of the patron the author was losing nothing, and that the ethical pretension that his gifts must not be prostituted by the outright sale of his product supplied him with a convenient defensive rationalization of his pension.

Even Voltaire, whose earnings might well have been large, and who was rich, did not acquire his riches from his works. He gave away the rights of his plays. He presented some of his works to his publishers, asking merely some author's copies beautifully bound. He presented his secretary with 12,000 francs, the proceeds of an edition of his works. His wealth he got through business adventures not unlike those carried on by our own Hetty Green. He loaned money to princes and to cities and bought national bonds. He speculated in lotteries, in grain, in foreign securities. He invested in contracts for army supplies, and is reputed to have had at one time an income of 350,000 francs a year.

It was Jean Jacques Rousseau who in France did what Alexander Pope had done in England. He disdained the generous offers of the wealthy. Instead he drove the best bargains he could for his works. Like many another author since, he wrote much inferior but popular material in order to obtain the means of devoting time to his more serious work. He got $2300 for the libretto of an opera which he turned out in a few weeks, which was something more than he got for *Émile* upon which he expended twenty years of thought and writing.

From this time forward the art of reading came into the possession of an ever-increasing number of people. And, with the new guarantees of freedom or at least the widening tolerances, the writer was able to find a larger market for his wares—a market that could afford to pay for them. The time came when all sorts of writers, emancipated from the clutch of the rich patron, could earn a good living, while some of them became as rich as some of the former Maecenases. Walter Scott got $20,000 for *The Lady of the Lake,* and Lord Byron collected $13,000 for three cantos of *Childe Harold.* From his novels Scott earned a princely income of around $75,000 a year. Victor Hugo was paid 40,000 francs ($8000) for each of ten volumes of *Les Misérables.* Disraeli got $60,000 each for *Endymion* and *Lothair,* and George Eliot got $40,000 for *Middlemarch.* Alphonse Daudet collected $200,000 for a single novel, *Sappho.* And Charles Dickens was perhaps the largest earner of all.

The great sums collected by successful novelists and playwrights in our own day are too well known to be repeated here. If they earn these sums it is because almost universal literacy, rapidly spreading secondary and higher education, and an ever-increasing population furnish them with an enormous market, while their ability to collect their incomes from the whole public rather than a handful of powerful patrons is the guarantee of the highest form of freedom of expression.

CHAPTER IV

Robert Owen

THE REFORMER

———————————————— I ————————————————

THE LONG annals of money getting have produced but one Robert Owen. If you can imagine one of the largest employers in America —Mr. Henry Ford, for instance—becoming the leader of the labor movement, or Mr. Tom Girdler taking the field for factory reform, or Mr. Owen D. Young going up and down the land clamoring for a recovery scheme not unlike Mr. Upton Sinclair's EPIC plan; if you will conceive of a manufacturer, whose schooling got no farther than the three R's, becoming the most advanced educational reformer of his time, using the kindergarten before Pestalozzi or Froebel, antedating Marx in socialism and all the Victorian reformers in welfare work, you will have some idea of the sort of man Robert Owen was in the dawn of the industrial revolution. It was in amassing a fortune as a manufacturer that Owen saw the evils of the factory system flourish, saw challenging human problems flowing out of the same machines that poured out wealth for him and set him off upon his extraordinary career of unselfish evangelism for the creation of a better world.

There have been many men of wealth who have looked with questioning upon their possessions. Andrew Carnegie, as a young man, was deeply disturbed to find he had made fifty thousand dollars in a year and he wrote in a moment of pious possession that he would never permit himself to make more than this. It was a vow as useless as if Casanova had sworn himself to celibacy. Some have soothed themselves amid their treasures by giving after they were done with getting. But Owen, even as a young man, declared

ROBERT OWEN

war upon the system by which he was growing rich and, in the end, consumed his fortune in that struggle. He organized the first model factory system. He forced the passage of the first Factory Act. He built the first infant school. He pioneered in universal education. He built a utopian community in the New World. And he never ceased his pressure upon the public mind of England. When he was eighty-seven he wrote his autobiography. When he was eighty-eight he was still calling meetings and conferences. He was one of those rare souls who had caught a vision of the future and who kept his eyes all his life upon the far-off hills. Though it was a modest one, no fortune in history has had so profound an effect upon the course of human events.

II

Owen was born at Newtown, in Montgomeryshire on the Welsh border, on May 14, 1771, the son of the village saddler and iron-monger. He was born into an England that was overwhelmingly agricultural but alive with a score of professional and amateur mechanics and inventors who were tinkering with all sorts of clumsy little machines that would revolutionize the world and its way of life.

He had a business career that satisfied all the specifications of a Samuel Smiles success story. He got no more education than a bright boy under ten could get from a gentleman who apparently knew but little more than his scholars, and who was named Mr. Thickness—a name hardly surpassed by the schoolmaster of Dickens' Coketown, Mr. Choakumchild.

At nine he was assisting the schoolmaster.

At ten he set out, like Dick Whittington, for London, to seek his fortune, with but forty shillings in his pocket.

In a few months he was apprenticed to a Mr. McGuffog, a draper in Lincolnshire, an excellent and honest merchant who proved a sound exemplar. He attended the Presbyterian Church with Mr. McGuffog and the Church of England with Mrs. McGuffog, generating such a supply of tolerant piety that he was called "the little parson," but also acquiring a healthy skepticism of the creeds preached by the rival ministers.

At thirteen he was a clerk with Palmer and Flint, a drapery house on London Bridge, working from eight in the morning to midnight and often later. Palmer and Flint were pioneers in their way. They ran an eighteenth-century cash-and-carry store, with fixed prices and moderate markups.

At sixteen young Owen transferred his activities to a wholesale draper in Manchester. This was 1787. From across the Channel came the rumblings of the French Revolution that would stir England and particularly her young thinkers and writers like Southey and Wordsworth. But young Owen would remain untouched by this storm. He was far more interested in another revolution that was now in full swing—the industrial revolution. And Manchester was the scene of some of its most notable victories. In this feverish hive, filled with its new breed of self-made men, its boosters and Babbitts, the young neophyte of business was far more interested in getting along and ahead than in making over the world by such violent means as were being used by the Paris mob. In this year, at eighteen, Owen went into business for himself.

With a hundred pounds borrowed from a brother in London, he formed a partnership with a practical mechanic to manufacture spinning machinery. It ended quickly, Owen taking some of the machines they had made and starting by himself as a spinner. He prospered and was soon making six pounds a week profit. At twenty he answered an advertisement of a Mr. Drinkwater who owned a mill and wanted a new manager. Owen demanded £300 a year and got it. Thus at twenty this budding success-story hero found himself the manager of a plant with 500 hands and a contract for £400 the second year, £500 the third, and a fourth interest after that.

Two years later Drinkwater was negotiating to combine his interests with Samuel Oldknow, a rising cotton lord, and Owen was shouldered out of the promise of a partnership. He quickly formed another partnership with a new concern backed by two substantial

Manchester cotton firms. This was the Chorlton Twist Company. Owen found himself building a large mill in the Manchester suburbs that he later operated as managing partner. His duties forced him to travel about, and in these commercial wanderings he met at Glasgow a lady named Anne Caroline Dale. Her father was a banker and manufacturer who had built several cotton mills in Scotland. One he had put up at New Lanark in partnership with Richard Arkwright, famous for having introduced certain important spinning inventions. But Dale and Arkwright had parted company and Dale was looking for a buyer for the New Lanark mills. Owen, with his partners of the Chorlton Twist Company, bought the property for $300,000, payable $15,000 a year. And for good measure Owen married Dale's daughter. After a brief time he moved to New Lanark where he assumed the complete management of this, one of the largest cotton spinning enterprises in Scotland. This was in 1800. And here he was to round out his fortune, make large profits for his partners, and make the name of New Lanark famous throughout Europe and in industrial history.

But Owen's social experiments at New Lanark landed him in trouble with his partners. Before he got through he had three sets of them. All feared their investments were being imperiled by reform. The first set rebelled when Owen proposed to use company funds to build a school for the children. Owen dug up a fresh set of partners and bought out the original ones, paying them $420,000 for a plant that had cost them $300,000 and on which they had made five per cent a year and an additional $180,000 in profits.

The next set became alarmed when Owen's educational ideas clashed with their solid British orthodoxy. Also they saw an opportunity to grab a flourishing enterprise at a bargain price. They dissolved the partnership and demanded a public sale, circulated stories of the mills' difficulties, and insisted they were not worth forty thousand pounds. But at the auction they bid up to $570,000, whereupon Owen topped them with another $500 and got New Lanark. His third brace of partners comprised some wealthy businessmen with reform ideas, including Jeremy Bentham, the famous utilitarian philosopher, and the well-known Quaker, William Allen.

Then for another twelve years, Owen, with a freer hand, developed this industry until it was certainly the most famous, if not the greatest, in England. In the end—in 1825—his last batch of partners drew away from him, some seeing in his schools "a manufactory of infidels." His management of New Lanark ceased in 1825. He withdrew his interest altogether in 1828.

Owen became a very rich man. But no satisfactory estimate of his fortune has been found. It was, however, a modest fortune and is important, indeed epochal, not for its size but for the fruits it produced in Owen's mind, the things it enabled him to do to the very processes by which he got rich, the influence it enabled him to exercise upon the new industrial system in the very years of its birth. He spent it as freely as he made it, and after 1828 he ceased to make any more. It was finally exhausted in his numerous crusades, until at last he was wholly without funds and lived upon a modest allowance of £360 a year from his sons, who managed to disguise it as the fruits of some old investments.

III

The significance of Owen lies in the fact that he began his career as the industrial revolution appeared in Europe. England was fascinated by her new gadgets. They gave birth to the modern factory. The nation was preoccupied with driving the new machines, multiplying its wealth, perfecting the wealth-making organization and devices. Owen saw that these machines were doing something to the soul of England. He became preoccupied with that phenomenon.

The factory was a new economic weapon of profound importance. It enabled the acquisitive man to do something hitherto but little understood—to share in the fruits of the labor of many persons in the field of production. Hitherto this was possible only in agriculture, in merchandising, in finance. But the industrial producer had until now remained a more or less solitary worker.

The Cotton Lord was enabled to do in the field of industrial production what the Land Lord was able to do in the field of commodity production.

The factory was not wholly new. Cephalus employed a hundred and fifty men in his shield factory in Athens. There is a story of John Winchecombe—Jack of Newbury—in Henry VII's day, the "most considerable wit of fancy or fiction England ever beheld" who kept a hundred looms in his house, each managed by a man and a boy. But these were merely central shops. They were very uncommon and were of little economic importance.

Before this time the method of making cotton cloth was quite primitive. The raw cotton was picked and teased to remove the seeds. Then the fibers were combed out by hand. The next step was to twist these fibers into a thread by means of the old-fashioned spinning wheel that had been brought to England from India in the thirteenth century. The threads were then put upon a loom worked entirely by hand. And all this was done in the home of the weaver. The women and children did the seeding, combing, and spinning. The men managed the loom. The family was an organized industrial producing unit. The town merchant supplied the raw cotton and frequently the patterns for the cloth and bought the finished cloth from the weaver. This was indeed the pattern of all production. And under this old handcraft system it was difficult for anyone to share in the product of the producer.

But a series of inventions began to make its appearance in the eighteenth century. Kay invented the flying shuttle in 1738. Instead of throwing the shuttle by hand between the warp threads, the shuttle was now shot in each direction by a spring released by pulling a cord. Thus one man could do the work of two. In 1765 Hargreaves invented the spinning jenny, called after his wife, whose wheel gave him the idea. It enabled a person turning one wheel to spin eight spools at once. And before long this was eighty. Then came the inventions of Arkwright and Crompton, improving the spinning jenny, and later still the application first of water power and then of steam to the operation of spinning machinery and looms. Eli Whitney eliminated household seeding with his cotton gin and Dr. Edward Cartwright completed the process with his invention of the power loom.

The home was no place for these cumbersome machines. It was immediately obvious that the way to use them with the greatest profit was in clusters under a single roof. They made the factory inevitable.

It was into this rapidly developing industry that was producing its Manchesters and Birminghams and Glasgows that Owen stepped, with no education in economics or the social sciences. But he began to see very quickly that the factory was making deep marks upon the human beings it was using as well as upon those it displaced.

Manufacture of cotton was no longer spread out over many places. It became concentrated in lumps and clusters—in cities. And it grew around cities that had access to water power. It made production swifter and cheaper, so that England began to supply the world with cotton thread and cloth. It shaped the destiny of England, whose Cotton Lords clamored for more *laissez faire,* more freedom at home while they fought also for wider markets abroad, markets that England proceeded to acquire by capture and to subject to the most rigid control—an inconsistency extinguished by the wondrous solvent of patriotism.

This manufacture of cotton summoned to the surface very quickly a new breed of gentlemen who knew how to organize and manage and promote and get hold of capital. It augmented heavily the number of rich enterprisers. It reinforced the great middle class. It set up a new equestrian order in Britain. It made a powerful group of Cotton Lords—and later Iron Lords and Railway Lords and other categories of industrial nobles—who challenged the supremacy of the Land Lords. It unloosed a mania for money getting since it supplied a new and potent weapon. The predatory soul spun calculating dreams of wealth such as lit the flames of cupidity in Leonardo da Vinci's soul when he invented, of all things, a needle-making machine. "Early tomorrow," he writes, "I shall make the leather belt and proceed to trial. . . . One hundred times in each hour 400 needles will be finished, making 40,000 in an hour and 480,000 in 12 hours. Suppose we say 4,000 which at five elidi per thousand gives 20,000 solidi; 1000 lira per working day, and if one works 20 days in the month, 60,000 ducats the year." [1]

Owen saw all this with dismay and commented on "the love of luxury which had induced its possessors to sacrifice the best feelings of human nature in their accumulation."

On one hand this industry caused larger streams of money income to flow through the land, producing greater prosperity in good times and deeper distress in hard times. The capitalist found endless avenues for pouring his profits into new investment as fast as he made them. The worker was paid in money wages, and monthly there flowed out into the streams of business numerous rivulets of money purchasing power, so that England found herself wallowing in a new kind of prosperity.

In a generation England had undergone a profound change. In 1775 she was an agricultural country. By the census of 1811 the agricultural population was but a quarter of the whole. The cotton mill had done this.

And what had this done to the workers? They had been congregated into unwholesome clusters, into hot, ill-ventilated mills, where they worked long hours at low wages. They dwelt in foul houses. The mills devoured all the hands they could lay hold of—men, women, children. Money wages rose, but there was more need of them since the worker now produced nothing for himself.

Behold the dreary lot of the factory worker! At five in the morning the clanging of the factory bell drew the long streams of unrested slaves through the dark streets to their brick prisons. At seven there was a half-hour for breakfast—tea or coffee, a little bread, perhaps some oatmeal porridge; a scant mess with the tea bad and the infusion weak. A half-hour at noon for dinner—boiled potatoes in one dish, with melted lard for the poorer workers,

---

[1] *Technics and Civilization,* by Lewis Mumford, 1934.

butter for the better paid; for the most favored a few pieces of fat
bacon over the mess. For the factory worker the roast beef of old
England was just a phrase in a song. At seven or eight or nine in
the evening the streets were darkened again with the drudges trudg-
ing home to tea or maybe a glass of grog. The streets were narrow,
dirty, without drainage or scavengers. The houses were poor,
usually one room to a family. The slum at its worst had arrived.

Early in the factory era the parish board took to farming out
the pauper children. They were called pauper apprentices. These
wretched children, toiling for twelve, fourteen, even sixteen hours a
day, were far worse off than slaves. One observer said the children
"lived the life of the machine while working and at other times that
of a beast." Imagine, if you can, the lot of the child of ten who
went to work at five in the morning, with only a stop for breakfast
and dinner, and quit his machine at seven or later at night, and
getting for this brutal grind two shillings, twopence a week.

The discipline was rigid. There were rules and fines for every
infraction of them, ranging from one to six shillings; there were
fines for leaving an oil can out of place, fines for being found dirty
or being found washing, fines for leaving a window open or for
spinning with the gaslight on too long in the morning. The Cotton
Lord, who bent over his hymnal on the Sabbath and gave three-
times-three for the glories of *laissez faire,* bound his workers in a
harness of iron discipline beside which Owen found the life of the
American slave one of freedom and ease. The employer, indeed,
had now found something better than the slave. The slave must be
bought with a capital outlay and supported in all times. The factory
worker involved no initial investment so far as his body was concerned and could be laid off when times were hard.

IV

At twenty-nine years of age Owen assumed the direction and
part ownership of one of the largest of these modern juggernauts.
New Lanark was about thirty miles south of Glasgow on the Falls

of the Clyde which furnished its power. It consisted of four huge main buildings of graystone quarried near by, each seven stories high and surrounded by smaller workhouses. The buildings, set in a lovely circle of hills, were themselves gaunt, grim fortresses after the model of the large mills of that day.

Between 1800 and 2000 persons dwelt in the village and an additional five hundred pauper apprentices were housed in a separate building. Owen has described this population when he assumed control: "a collection of the most ignorant and destitute from all parts of Scotland, possessing the moral characteristics of poverty and ignorance . . . much addicted to theft, drunkenness and falsehood." The housing was bad—one family to a room and no sanitary arrangements—and the streets were narrow and filled with filth. The people hated the mills. There were no public houses, the former owner Dale being a rigid prohibitionist, but there were bootleg joints. Many different churches, each with a different creed, led to no end of hostility between the communicants.

Owen's first services arose out of the reactions of a generous and just spirit to these bad conditions. Yet bad as it was, New Lanark was one of the better mills, and Owen had seen much of the industry in which he had now been engaged for eleven years. He had not yet formed that social and economic philosophy that later brought him into collision with all the respectable elements in Britain. Generally speaking, he began with the assumption that these men and women and children had rights that employers were cruelly ignoring, and he made up his mind to respect those rights in his own mill. And this led him to that philosophy which characterized the welfare movement of the next hundred years: the spirit of *noblesse oblige;* the principle that the rich ought to be good to the poor.

In pursuance of this, Owen introduced a series of reforms into New Lanark which made it the first model factory.

At the outset he put an end to the employment of the pauper apprentices. He took in no more and let out those who were there as fast as their indentures expired. He employed no children under ten. He limited hours for all to ten and a half—though he believed they should be less, even eight, he was never able to cut them below ten and a half. He ended the fines and introduced an honor system. He greatly improved the houses and doubled the accommodations per family. He supplied playgrounds. He built two school buildings and gave the children the advantages of the best free education then found in England before they went to the mills, and thereafter provided evening instruction. He arranged for lectures, meetings, dances for the adults and threw open to the people for recreation the woods which the company owned. He provided for medical attendance, established a sick club, a savings bank, and summer courses of study in the open air for all. He made available meeting-houses where men of any denomination might speak, ensuring complete religious freedom in New Lanark. And this made a very dark item in the bill of particulars against him when his battles began.

No one in our day will see anything subversive in all this. Indeed even the more conservative employer provides more than this now. Yet it was the introduction of these reforms over a series of years that brought Owen into conflict with his partners, even those later ones who had joined him because of sympathy with his humanitarian objectives. But no one could question the fruits which appeared at New Lanark. The early, sullen hostility of the people had been broken down, a process that was completed when, in 1806, America put an embargo on raw cotton shipments to England. Owen and his partners decided it was best, rather than pay extortionate prices for speculative cotton, to shut down the mills. But for four months he continued to pay the employees their full wages.

Over 25,000 persons, educators, social workers, manufacturers, parliamentary and county and town committees signed the register book at New Lanark as visitors to inspect these reforms. Owen himself said in 1812 that this same population was "conspicuously honest, industrious, sober and orderly and an idle individual, one in liquor or a thief is scarcely to be seen from the beginning to the end of the year." And above all—miracle of miracles—the company that sponsored all this was singularly prosperous and those who owned it grew rich from it.

V

Owen, disturbed by the evidences of inhumanity, cruelty, greed, injustice all about him, was nevertheless not so naïve as to suppose that the ignorant and debased proletarians of his day were capable of forming the better world he began to see beyond the far-off hills. He believed that the world had to be made a better place for men to live in dignity. But he was equally convinced that men had to be made better to participate in the treasures of such a world.

Apparently Owen started out with nothing more than a conviction that all children, as a matter of human justice, should have an opportunity to have an education. But he soon went beyond this and imported into his theory the proposition that this education should be of a very special kind; that, while training the mind for the benefit of the individual, the character should be formed upon a model designed to enable the individual to live in an enlightened society. The formation of character became the cardinal principle. And that, Owen believed, must take the direction of developing the social virtues—the human sympathies, an understanding of the rights of others, a hatred of the antisocial virtues of greed, acquisitiveness, dishonesty, private and public. Owen had long before abandoned any faith in any existing religion. But he held as a utilitarian principle that a cultivated modern society of free men cannot be operated successfully without a highly developed and universally accepted code of social ethics. And what is more, he believed this could be accomplished. His own statement of his educational principle ran as follows:

A man's character is a product of the circumstances in which he is born, lives and works. Evil conditions breed evil men; good conditions develop good men. Today man is surrounded by conditions which breed selfishness, ignorance, vice, hypocrisy, hatred, war. If a new world is to be born the first thing that must be done is to spread the truth concerning the foundation of character, namely that man's character is made *for* him and not *by* him.

It was to lay the groundwork for this dream of a world of socially educated men and women that he established in 1816 at New Lanark his Institution for the Formation of Character.

---------------------------------- VI ----------------------------------

The time came when Owen determined to compel his fellow manufacturers to clean house. They cheered heartily his plans to reduce the duties on raw cotton, but they turned a deaf ear to his proposals for humanitarian reform in their plants. Then he decided that the state should compel them to be good. He therefore prepared his famous Factory Act, mild enough as we inspect it now but epochal in that it marked the beginning of the long struggle for justice to workers that is not yet wholly won.

Owen's act applied to cotton, wool, flax, and silk mills. It limited hours to ten and a half a day, prohibited employment of children under ten, fixed the working hours of children as sometime between five A. M. and seven P. M., provided for medical attendance in cases of contagious diseases, compelled a half-hour daily instruction period for children in a suitable place, and gave to justices of the peace the right of entry and inspection.

The introduction of this bill into Parliament was the signal for calling into action that intransigent reactionary energy known as the manufacturers' association. Manufacturers, like other men, are far from monsters and have their share of good and bad citizens. But the manufacturers' association is one of those ingenious inventions that enables the members to preserve their individual decencies while entrusting the promotion of their baser social elements to another. It was then, as it has generally been, the spirit of aggressive selfishness with its hired philosophers and economists and statisticians and publicity men. It proceeded to fight Owen's moderate proposals as it has since fought almost every step in civilized industry, even when its individual members were advancing; as it has since fought compensation insurance, child-labor laws, humane restrictions of female employment conditions, collective bargaining, wage and hour standards.

Owen, with his son, toured the mill towns and villages and painted for Parliament a dark picture of their indecencies—children working fifteen hours a day and more, some of them infants as young as four; foremen carrying leather thongs to get out of the young by flogging the compliance they extorted from their elders by means of fines; a fifth of the children in shoe factories crippled or otherwise injured by diseases and other abuses.

But the manufacturers' association was not idle. It investigated Owen and New Lanark. When he charged them with flogging little children, they replied with the impressive revelation that he permitted dissenting ministers in New Lanark meetinghouses. When he pleaded for a measure of Christian compassion for the poor and downtrodden, they countered with the charge that he was a heretic. They investigated not his business practices but his religious tolerance. They paid the expenses of a minister from New Lanark who testified that he had heard his wife quote what she had heard Owen say in a public speech. As the manufacturers' association today replies to all charges with the cry of "Communist," their predecessors in Owen's day cried "infidel." But they could not say he would ruin their industry, for, with far more exacting standards in his own mill and against an unrestrained competition, he had made notable profits for himself and his colleagues.

In a noble passage Owen depicted the narrow vision of the men who fought him:

I am well aware, my lord, of the claims which these propositions will at first call forth from the blind avarice of commerce; for commerce, my lord, trains her children to see only the immediate or apparent interest; their ideas are too contracted to carry them beyond the passing week, month or year at the utmost. They have been taught, my lord, to consider it the essence of wisdom to expend millions of capital and years of extraordinary scientific application as well as to sacrifice the health and morals of the great mass of the subjects of a mighty empire that they may uselessly improve the manufacture and increase the demand for pins, needles and threads; that they may have the singular satisfaction, after immense care, labor and anxiety on their own parts to destroy the real wealth and strength of their own country by gradually undermining the morals and physical vigor of its inhabitants for the sole purpose of relieving other nations of their share of this enviable process of pin, needle and thread making.

This from one of England's foremost thread makers.

Owen put his finger on one of the most amazing stupidities of the industrialists—their failure to see that their workers were also consumers and that while England carried on the mightiest efforts to win markets abroad, she excluded her own workers from the market place for the goods she produced, by giving them low wages and long hours. In our own time it dawned upon our own manufacturers, with the force of a discovery, that men buy nothing while they are at work; that much of their spendings occur in their hours of leisure, and that men with pauper wages who are fatigued beyond endurance by long hours can purchase nothing. Yet in the very struggle over the first Factory Act, a hundred and twenty-four years ago, this enlightened manufacturer warned his colleagues that "no evil ought to be more dreaded by a master manufacturer than low wages and long hours. . . . These [their employees] are in consequence of their numbers the greatest consumers. . . . The real prosperity of any nation at all times may be accurately ascertained by the amount of wages or the extent of comforts which the productive classes can obtain in return for their work." It has taken a hundred and twenty-four years to make employers see that, and, even yet, only imperfectly.

It would be unfair to say there were no manufacturers who sympathized with Owen. One, Sir Robert Peel the elder, greatest of the cotton lords, was a member of Parliament. He was entrusted with the handling of the bill. But he held conference after conference with his fellow mill men; he yielded on point after point. In the end—in 1819—the bill was passed, but frightfully diluted.

It was limited to cotton mills, the hours of work were raised to twelve, the age for children was reduced from ten to nine, no inspection was provided. Owen denounced this compromise and washed his hands of the bill. But it was a beginning and he alone was responsible for what was to be the first step in a long and fruitful struggle for the welfare of the masses.

VII

In June, 1815, the allied armies of Europe crushed Napoleon at Waterloo. But something else came to an end—the war boom in England. England fought Napoleon the way we fought the Kaiser, not only with men, but with guns, munitions, ships, and money loaned to her allies and spent for the most part in England. Birmingham and Manchester and London had boomed like Pittsburgh and Bridgeport and New York. Fortunes were made. But the war was the customer. When the war ended the customer vanished. The boom folded up in 1815 as it did in 1919. Warehouses and shelves were filled with unsalable goods. Mills closed down, or cut their wages and workers. Many were already idle because of the displacement of the hand spinners and the revived Enclosure Acts that drove farmers from their acres. Now the cotton and wool and flax mills poured their thousands into the ranks of the unemployed. The war had made the farmers rich—wool and wheat prices soared. Now they demanded that the government keep these prices up. A law was passed excluding foreign grain unless home-grown grain should rise above eight shillings per quarter.

Discontent flamed up menacingly. Poverty became a scourge. Crimes multiplied. By the middle of 1816 the situation was serious. Then the obvious step was taken. A conference was called—as was done by Mr. Hoover in 1929—of the lords of the realm, the Land Lords and the Cotton Lords. The radicals had a plan—parliamentary reform, ballots for people who cried for bread. The Land Lords had a plan—to raise a fund for charitable distributions. Mr. Owen was asked for his views. He gave them, but they were based upon certain fundamental maladies and disarrangements in the economic system. They were listened to with attention. But the conference ended by naming a committee to raise a fund and to enquire further. The Duke of Kent—Queen Victoria's father— was the chairman. Owen was made a member. He was asked to prepare a plan. He did. And when he presented his plan at a meeting of the committee presided over by the Archbishop of Canterbury it is not difficult to believe that that gentleman and certain others arched their noble and sacerdotal eyebrows. This plan marked the beginning of Owen's slide into the realm of utopian socialism, and he was proposing it to men who worshiped not a Trinity, but a quadripartite god—The Father, the Son, the Holy Ghost, and Property.

Here was his plan. Society had found a means of producing goods beyond the "revenues" of the people to buy. This disparity between goods produced and available purchasing power seemed to him the hub of the problem. Having more capacity to produce than to buy, manufacturers deemed it necessary to reduce capacity. Capacity consisted of men and machines. But the machines were cheaper than the men, so the men were let out. But the men let out were also consumers. The machines were not. Thus the ability of society to consume was once again diminished more than its capacity to produce.

The men let out became a charge upon the taxpayers, which still further added to the burden of the manufacturer.

Owen then offered a scheme. It will sound strangely familiar to American readers who recall Mr. Upton Sinclair's EPIC plan that inflamed the imaginations of some Californians and the terrors of others in 1934 to such an extent that Mr. Sinclair was almost elected governor.

Owen proposed first that the poor and unemployed be taken at a stroke off the backs of the taxpayers. This proved as enticing in Britain as it did in California, for the employer, having perched on the backs of the workers, now found that a large number of them in turn had climbed on his back. Owen proposed that the unemployed should be literally lifted out of the normal economic system and placed in a separate one. They would be settled in villages of co-operation. The village would produce what it needed for its subsistence. The villagers would be producers and consumers. Thus what the unemployed produced would not augment the supply of goods offered in the commercial markets. But by producing what they needed they would also supply themselves with purchasing power that would not be taken out of the pockets of the taxpayers. Many such villages would be established and financed by the government or by counties or cities or private organizations. The villages would exchange goods with each other.

A village would cost from sixty to ninety-six thousand pounds to organize. The homes would be erected at the center of the village —large apartments of modern construction. Thus, the people would live in communal dwellings; the meals would be prepared in a common kitchen; there would be playgrounds, schools, and the rest. And the fields would lie all around this communal garden center. The subscribers would lose nothing as the villages would be able to pay five per cent interest on the investment, though how they could do this without sending their goods into the general market was not disclosed. The Archbishop's committee quickly dropped this rather hot potato by referring it to a parliamentary committee. There it did not even get a hearing. Whereupon Owen took his plan to the country. And in the subsequent agitation he broke completely with the highly respected persons who had hitherto given their moral support to his humanitarian adventures.

———————————————— VIII ————————————————

Almost without knowing it, Owen was slowly drifting out of the troubled ocean of benevolent capitalism into a new sea, unknown, uncharted, little understood.

Owen was not an economist, but a social philosopher. He was a schematic philosopher whose reflections drove him to make blue-prints for the world of tomorrow. He was a utopian who set out to build his own Land of Nowhere.

His ideas were not, of course, wholly new. The dream of the City of Light and Justice was an old one with which men had played since Plato. Saint Augustine had described his own theocratic community—the City of God. Thomas More, recently canonized by that church which is today the stoutest defender of property, attacked the institution of private property, envisaged a planned society on the agricultural model in which the needs of the people would be the basis for calculating the volume of production, with a six-hour day and the exchange of goods between town and coun-try without a money medium. This was More's Utopia, discovered by his fictitious Portuguese scholar and sailor, Raphael Hythloday. He described a democratic government, widespread education, and that democratic ideal of the latter-day utilitarians—the greatest good of the greatest number.

After this came a whole string of explorers of the Land of No-where and founders of dream cities—Bacon with his Atlantis and his Solomon's House, forerunner of the House of Magic where scientists would invent a perfect world; Andreas' Christianopolis, peopled by artisans steeped in the higher learning, desiring peace and renouncing riches; and Campanella's City of the Sun, with a government of the elite, without riches or poverty and a commu-nistic dictatorship.

Behind all these visions, however, lay specific ideas—the effort to produce democratic equality, to create abundance, to redeem all men from ignorance, to secure peace. It was the ancient dream of ending war, poverty, vice, ignorance. And Owen, like many of the others, saw ignorance at the bottom of it all.

Before Owen, reformers of various types were playing with the idea of the labor theory of value—Babeuf, Étienne Cabet, and, above all, Saint-Simon and Ricardo. Others toyed with the concept of public ownership of industry, the principle that each should contribute to society according to his capacity and each should be rewarded according to his needs, as Le Blanc put it, or according to his services, as Saint-Simon put it. These ideas and a dozen others—Thomas Paine's inheritance tax, Thomas Spence's land tax (forerunners of the single tax), Prudhon's assault on property, Godwin's utilitarianism—filled the air, animated discussions, gave birth to movements.

It is a little difficult to determine just how Owen got hold of his various ideas. He had been an omnivorous reader in his youth, but had passed his mature years as a man of action in business and social reform. He had met, however, many of the eminent social thinkers of the time. Bentham was one of his partners. Ricardo was deeply interested in his plan. He knew William God-win and was undoubtedly greatly influenced by him. He may have got hold of the labor theory of value from Ricardo or he may have evolved it himself. It is entirely probable that he came himself upon the important truth about the grand flaw in the economic system. In a memorial presented to the conference of powers at Aix-la-Chapelle he said:

The grand question now to be solved is, not how a sufficiency of wealth can be produced, but how the excess of riches, which may be most easily created, may be generally distributed throughout society advantageously for all and without prematurely disturbing the existing institutions and arrangements in any country.

That question is still baffling the statesmen who are trying to find the magic formula for distributing all that we can produce within the framework of the capitalist economy. No one else at that time saw this so clearly or expressed it so decisively as the grand problem of the age.

Owen still believed it might be worked out *without prematurely disturbing the existing institutions.* The very use of the word "prematurely" indicates his suspicion that eventually the "existing arrangements" would be disturbed. He hated revolution. He hated violence. He hoped that gradually, by means of education and by slowly insinuating his villages of co-operation into the existing society, they would expand, increase, and finally supplant the society. Owen himself said he owed his plan for these villages to a John Billars who recommended them in 1696 and whose pamphlet *Proposals for Raising a College of Industry of All Useful Trades and Husbandry* Owen reprinted.

Owen appealed to public opinion to adopt his plan. And as he crusaded for it he began to make it plain that he regarded this plan not merely as a palliative to meet the emergency of the depression, but as a wholesome pattern for the organization of society upon a new collective model. Owen was becoming the first great socialist leader of England—a utopian socialist, it is true, but nevertheless a socialist expounding what came to be the standard socialist diagnosis of the capitalist system.

He wrote articles for the newspapers, outlining his plan, and bought thirty thousand copies of the papers a day, which he sent under the frank of an M.P. to the ministers, the members of Parliament, magistrates, and religious leaders in every city. He spent twenty thousand dollars for this alone. He printed pamphlets by the thousands and carried on an extensive propaganda by every known means. His plan was opposed by the Radicals—advocates of parliamentary reform. They called his villages "parallelograms of paupers." He was opposed by the Malthusians. Apparently he grew indignant at the opposition of the clergy. And so in a historic meeting he denounced the "gross errors that have combined with the fundamental notions of all religions." He said that by the aid of these errors man had been made "a weak, an imbecile animal; a furious bigot and fanatic; or a miserable hypocrite." "I am not of your religion," he told them, "nor of any religion yet taught in this world." Thereafter he lost the sympathy of a few high ecclesiastics like the Archbishop of Canterbury who had given him their support. It was possible then to demolish any proposal of Owen by calling him an "atheist."

But events were playing into his hands. The depression following the war continued to deepen. The unemployed thousands, the dispossessed farmers and farm hands, the underpaid and enslaved mill workers grew wrathful. The poor-relief system was breaking

down under the strain. Indeed, the whole subject of relief was just
such a nightmare as it was in America in 1932, or, indeed, as it is
today. England's poor laws had been fashioned in the dark times
of Henry VIII and Elizabeth; hence workhouses, the free materials
to be processed by the poor, the overseers of the poor, and finally
that most monstrous of all poor laws, the farming out of pauper
apprentices. This remained the backbone of the English system
until 1834. There was one more demoralizing addition—the allowance system, introduced in 1782, under which paupers were farmed
out, their wages collected by the county authorities and augmented
by a public subsidy. This demoralized the worker and made a
paradise for the employer who wanted workers for pauper wages.
England was spending ten million pounds on poor relief in 1783.
In 1818 she was spending thirty-nine million.

Workers sought to combine, but the laws still forbade it. The
wretched victims of relief and unemployment began to riot here
and there. There were outbreaks among the midland miners. Mills
were set on fire. The Ludites, named after Ned Ludite, a village
idiot who to be avenged on his tormentors broke some machinery,
began demolishing mill machines. The ministry was frightened.
It remembered the terrible anger of the Paris mobs. It held fast
to its confidence in the iron hand. Rioters were disbursed by hus-
sars. The jails were filled. The habeas corpus act was suspended.
Meetings were forbidden. The circulation of pamphlets was ruthlessly crushed. All the sacred guarantes of the Magna Charta
were put under foot. Then came Peterloo. Some eighty thousand
unemployed assembled on the field of St. Peter outside Manchester.
It was an orderly meeting. The bands played *God Save the King*.
But the authorities were terrified. And when an orator attempted
to address the crowd, the soldiers were ordered to charge. Eleven
were killed, four hundred wounded—some women and children.
A thrill of horror swept over the country, horror in the breasts of
the lords of land and cotton, leading to more suppressions; horror
in the breasts of the poor at the death of their comrades.

In these desperate circumstances many responsible people in

England, not knowing where the cure for all this disorder lay, were driven to consider with tolerance the plan of Robert Owen, who was so eternally positive about its value. Another meeting was called about it, another committee named, headed by the Duke of Kent. And this committee actually recommended that a trial be made with one village. It recommended that a fund of five hundred thousand dollars be raised. Owen himself promptly subscribed fifty thousand. But no other considerable amount was forthcoming. The bright vision faded. And Owen turned his eyes to the New World.

IX

In 1826 on the banks of the Wabash River in Indiana, Owen established a village of co-operation on the model that he had been urging in England. New Harmony was already a co-operative community established by a group of German settlers. It was not, of course, formed upon the lines of Owen's plan. And it was for sale. He purchased it for $182,000, brought his four sons to Indiana, and set about bringing to reality in the New World, away from the commercial crystallizations of the old one, his city of the sun. It lasted about two years under his direction and ended in failure. It was in the New World, to be sure, but the settlers attracted to it were quite as deeply saturated with the social habits and thinking of the Old World as the countrymen they had left behind. Owen rightly attributed the failure to the fact that the men of his day— like the men of our own—were unprepared by education and environment to live in such a community. He lost forty thousand pounds on the adventure and returned to England, no whit discouraged and with undiminished faith in the ultimate emergence of the new moral world of his dreams.

X

But there was another cauldron in the United States when Owen was steaming up New Harmony—a pot out of which a very different brew was coming. This was Lowell, Massachusetts. Indeed, New Lanark in Scotland and Lowell in America must be looked upon as the generating plants of the forces that would grow and envelop our society and clash, as they do now, in a death struggle.

Lowell was forging the weapons that the acquisitive man of the next hundred years would use to work his wonders. New Lanark was forging the moral weapons that reformers and crusaders would use to fight those who were armed with the predatory munition of Lowell.

On February 2, 1822, a group of New England gentlemen organized the Merrimack Manufacturing Company. Francis Cabot Lowell was a graduate of Harvard. Kirk Boott had been a student there until he enlisted to fight in the Peninsular campaign with Wellington. Nathan Appleton was a graduate of Dartmouth. Their colleagues, Paul Moody, Patrick Tracy Jackson, Thomas N. Clark, and Warren Dutton were practical men.

They selected a site for the building of a planned industrial town. That town was called Lowell. They built a power-loom mill that stands and is operated to this day. They chose the site because of its nearness to the Pawtucket Canal. The Canal belonged to a corporation that was owned by five hundred stockholders scattered all over New England. The Merrimack Company wanted the water power of the canal. So it sent Mr. Thomas N. Clark around New England to buy up the shares secretly. The company wanted machinery, and therefore arranged to get the processes and patents of the Boston Manufacturing Company in Waltham. The two companies made an arrangement "to equalize the interest of all stockholders in both companies by mutual transfers of stock" which was their way of saying the companies were merged by mutual exchange of shares. Indeed, here was the first corporate merger—the Merrimack Company, the Pawtucket Canal Company, and the Boston Manufacturing Company—a device that promoters would use to blow billions in bubbles during the next few generations.

The Canal and Merrimack Falls developed more power than the

Merrimack Company needed. Also the company had more land than its mills and houses could occupy. Therefore, it formed a subsidiary—the Locks and Canals Company—with $600,000 capital and with Major George W. Whistler, U. S. army, and father of James Abbot McNeill Whistler, as chief engineer. To this company was transferred the operation of the water power and the construction and operation of a plant to build textile machinery. Thus the Merrimack Company became a holding company, owning all the stock of the Canal and Locks Company.

Here now was an integrated vertical enterprise which, for the first time, spun the yarn and also wove the cloth; it built its own machinery; it operated its own power canal, and it would, through the Canal Company, take a contract to build a textile plant, stock it with machinery, supply the site, and furnish the power to anyone who wished to embark in the same business.

It found the need for capital always urgent. It was, therefore, interested in an insurance company in Boston and in a bank, perhaps several, upon which it could draw for funds. In its numerous corporations, which grew in number, for it soon began to have an interest in other mills, it used the device of interlocking directorates. And it had begun to experiment with schemes for holding corporation meetings at times and in places that made it difficult for stockholders to attend.

It built company houses; sent a large bus around the countryside recruiting girls from the farms; built hundreds of boardinghouses managed by widows, where the girls lived. Naturally the little birds soon whispered in Boston tales of the goings-on of men and women in Lowell. A committee of ministers investigated the town and reported that the criticisms were unfounded, for here, happily, where a pious management worked the men and girls for eleven to thirteen hours, the creatures, in God's own good providence, were too fatigued at night for the sins of the flesh. It was a heavenly dispensation. The pious gentlemen had made the discovery that the fatigue that God-fearing manufacturers generated in their workers was the greatest enemy of the devil.

In fairness to these gentlemen, it ought to be said that Appleton, and perhaps Boott, had met Owen, and that in their hard, New England way, they set up certain welfare controls. But they were conceived not so much in the spirit of humane consideration for their employees as for the purpose of maintaining order and efficiency. And order meant religion. Hence they established a church—St. Anne's, which stands to this day. And later they built a Catholic church to bring the unruly Irish immigrants under some sort of discipline. They prohibited liquor in the boardinghouses and also "light and frivolous conversation." They started a library and meeting places for discussions and later established *The Lowell Offering*, perhaps the first corporation house organ, edited by the girls. Some trace of Owen's influence may have lingered here, for John Greenleaf Whittier sang of its "acres of girlhood," "flowers gathered from a hundred hillsides," "fair, unveiled nuns of industry," and a local chronicler spoke of them as "troops of liveried angels," which was probably laying it on thick for the benefit of pious Unitarian Boston.

But the chief significance of Lowell was that it forged the weapons of the acquisitive promoter and monopolist while New Lanark developed the weapons of the social reformer.

It is probably a fair estimate of the period to say that these two groups, added to those who had gone before—the Fuggers and Laws and a score of others—stocked the arsenals of the later rivals who would contend for the mastery of the world. The men of wealth now had the institution of property, the invention of money, the invention of credit, and, more important, the invention of bank credit, the corporation, the holding company, the subsidiary, the manipulation of corporations, speculation in corporate securities, the production of reservoirs of savings and the control of them, of bank and insurance and corporate funds—all this was ready to hand, this and the creation of the factory, of machinery, and of the techniques of management. With this the way was open for great numbers of ruthless and unscrupulous men to amass great fortunes.

At the same time, while philosophers and economists were fabricating the theory of individualism that created the perfect climate for their operations, another group, of which Owen was the great precursor and evangelist, was formulating the ideals and principles of social control in various forms, including collectivism, the theories underlying the claims of the workers, and finally the organizations through which the workers would challenge their masters and over many long and bloody decades wring from them one surrender after another. In that struggle, too, Owen was to take a pioneering part.

-------------------------------- XI --------------------------------

The labor-union movement got its first important impetus in England in 1824, just about the time Owen departed for America. It would not be true to say Owen had any part in this. He had shown no interest in unionism or in militant organizations of workers to exert pressure in collective bargaining against employers. He was not against this, but his interest was in a more fundamental rearrangement of society. He conceived of a system in which all the producing persons, from managers down, would be united in a common organization. But the plight of the workers admitted of no such delay as would be involved in realizing this dream. Workers were forbidden to combine. The Combination Acts dated from the sixteenth century. They were strengthened at intervals. The latest Act, made in 1800, forbade workmen to unite to force an increase in wages or reduction in hours or for other purposes, including pressure on another workman not to work. This law was rigidly enforced, and in the distress following the war jail sentences were invoked. Union to better the workers' lot was called "sedition." But in 1824, under the leadership of Francis Place, the Combination Acts were repealed and labor unions became legal.

The unions promptly united with the Radicals for parliamentary reform. Owenites had little interest in parliamentary reform. They were wrong in supposing that this was a futile step, since redress of the workers' grievances required first that they have political power. But they were right in realizing that mere parliamentary reform would not of itself bring an economic cure, as the workers discovered quickly enough. And this led the unions in the years between 1824 and 1829 to seek some more specific and effective remedy. They wanted some direct action. And the only proposals in sight were those of Owen—the principles of co-operation. Hence in those years there sprang up an ever-widening movement for co-operation on the Owen model. But pending this, co-operative societies were organized to unite the producing and purchasing power of the workers for their common benefit.

England was filled with Owenite leaders. Societies of all sorts, as well as the unions, journals, lectures, bombarded the British ear with the new cult of Owenism. And when Owen returned from New Harmony he was literally pushed into the leadership of this movement. It is an odd phenomenon in Owen's career that he thus became the head and front of a movement for co-operative buying and selling groups, in which he had little faith, and for militant trade unionism, in which he had perhaps less. It can be explained, in a man of Owen's uncompromising intellectual integrity, only on the theory that by thus going along with the workers he would ultimately lead them to the realization of his own dreams. And indeed the workers themselves were almost completely infected with this dream as an ultimate goal.

There is no point here in tracing the development of the trade union, co-operative societies, and co-operative-village movements thus all intertwined. It is a long story. But what is interesting and important here is Owen's attempt to establish labor exchanges upon a very radical model. The National Equitable Labour Exchange was launched in London in 1832. It was a plan for creating a co-operative market with the workers as producers and buyers. Members could bring their products to the exchange; they could also buy those products.

Most important was the means of payment. Owen had adopted the labor theory of value. He now conceived of labor as the standard of value. "The average physical power of men," he argued, "has been calculated; and as it forms the essence of all wealth, its value in every article of produce may also be ascertained and its exchangeable value with all other values fixed accordingly."

He therefore established a labor "standard" of value. He arrived at the estimate that sixpence was the average money value of an hour of labor. The value of any article was established thus: cost of materials plus cost of labor arrived at by multiplying hours by standard wage for that work plus one pence in the shilling for the cost of handling. The total was divided by six—sixpence being the average cost of labor per hour. This gave the amount of "labor time" incorporated in the article. For whatever this was worth, here was the germ of that doctrine of Marx that the use value in every article is the amount of socially necessary labor it contains or the social labor time requisite for its production. Here was an attempt by Owen to find a measure for that "jelly" of labor which is the essential value component of every article which Marx proposed.

Owen waxed enthusiastic as the unions grew in number and activity and he hailed the coming of the great era of co-operation. It took all sorts of forms, from efforts to establish villages to the creation of the great Builders' Guild which became a co-operative construction organization owned by the workers, who also hired the managers.

But all these great experiments failed. Owen's objective, of course, was to use trade unionism as an instrument of socialism. He himself came to see that it didn't work. He continued for many years with his community building and preaching the gospel of the New Moral World. He edited journals, wrote books, prepared and delivered lectures, petitioned Parliament, in support of his philosophies on remaking the world by education and sound moral ideas. He spent every dollar he had on these adventures in recreation. By the time he was seventy-three years old all his fortune was gone. For the rest of his life his sons, who had settled in America, paid him an annual income of about $1800 a year, based upon a fictitious debt of $36,000 that, through a carefully arranged but imaginary debt, they were supposed to owe him. This was done to spare his pride. Thus supported he went on preaching his doctrines in London, in Paris, in America to the end. When he was eighty-seven he was carried by four officers to the platform at a meeting in Liverpool to which he had traveled in great pain to proclaim once more his doctrines. When he arrived home he sank into unconsciousness. He recovered for a brief spell and died November 17, 1858.

CHAPTER V

Cornelius Vanderbilt

THE RAIL KING

--------------------------- I ---------------------------

A SMALL CATBOAT scudding the waters of the bay from Stapleton to Battery Pier; at the tiller a big hulk of a youth, large-faced, broad-chested, blue-eyed, bursting with health and blood and self-assurance. This is the sixteen-year-old ferryman of Staten Island —Cornelius Vanderbilt—who has just plunged into business for himself.

Down from a line of Dutch farmers who settled in Staten Island in 1650, this young Corneel has been working with his father, ferrying passengers and freight in a small boat since he was ten. That huge engine of muscle and gristle and nerves and blood in this lump of a Dutch boy has come from this loutish and thriftless father. But the motive power in the engine, the energy, the drive, the arrogance, the egotism and self-assurance have come from Phoebe Hand, his English-descended mother, who looked with a tolerant pride upon this self-willed and truculent son. As for him, perhaps the only person he ever really cared a tinker's damn about was this resolute woman who was his mother. Illiterate, boisterous, quarrelsome, cocksure, selfish, he was the perfect candidate for a marshal's baton in the age of brigandage that was about to open in American business.

He was born May 27, 1794, while Washington was still President. School irked him. At ten he began to help his father, for whose financial adolescence he soon developed a lusty scorn. At sixteen he borrowed a hundred dollars from the elder Cornelius and bought his own small boat.

178

CORNELIUS VANDERBILT

What happened there in the bay is the story of what happened in every town in America. A group of men driving buggies or stages or boats; one of them with an eye on the future buying the hack of another and presently owning three or five and then a livery stable or a general store; then, little by little, as the village grows into a town, getting a finger in every pie—in the bank, the creamery, the streetcar line, the gas company, ending as the town mogul and despot.

Thus it was with this sixteen-year-old boy, who would buy another boat and another. And presently the boats would be no longer small piraguas but schooners plying the Sound—blunt-bowed Dutch boats going up the Hudson to Albany.

In 1813 he married Sophia Johnson, daughter of his father's sister—a strange, unhappy alliance, touched with tragedy that flowed directly out of the ruthless, imperious nature of that loveless husband. He was not the man to tie his heartstrings around anyone or anything—wife, children, or country. When he tired of this woman he put her in a lunatic asylum. As for his country, he lived to be eighty-two and in all that time he voted but twice. His religion was a simple creed of his own forging in which the deity was Cornelius Vanderbilt.

In 1817, at the age of twenty-three, he had amassed a tiny fortune of nine thousand dollars and three good schooners. At the end of that year he decided to sell the boats and make a new start.

---------------------------------- II ----------------------------------

In the early months of 1818 a small steamboat—the *Mouse of the Mountain*—was putting in regularly at Battery Pier. Her skipper was Captain Cornelius Vanderbilt. He had gone up in the world—and down. Now he commanded a steamboat instead of a mere sailing vessel. But it was another man's, not his own. He was getting a thousand dollars a year salary instead of the three or four thousand he had made as his own master. But the important point to young Captain Vanderbilt was that now he was moving under steam power.

Robert Fulton had sailed his *Clermont* up the Hudson in 1807. Vanderbilt had watched with contempt the steamboats that plied the river. A man without vision, a know-it-all, he knew with the certainty of ignorance that steam would never supplant sails. But by 1817, facts—existing facts as distinguished from dream stuff and visions—were under his very nose. If he could not dream he could act. So he abandoned canvas for the steamboiler, even though it was impossible for an independent to go into the steamboat business—impossible because Fulton and Livingston had a monopoly of it.

Robert Fulton and Robert Livingston owned Fulton's steamboat invention. They were not content with this, however. Livingston was Chancellor of New York State and a political power. He had got from the legislature a monopoly for the firm for the operation of steam vessels in the waters of New York State.

Aaron Ogden was Governor of New Jersey. He got the franchise from the monopoly to operate steamboats between New York and Philadelphia, including New Jersey ports.

Thomas Gibbons, of Elizabethtown, operated several small steamers between New Brunswick and a point connecting with Ogden's line. The monopoly declared that because Gibbons fed Ogden's line, he must pay royalties to the monopoly, even though he operated wholly within New Jersey. Gibbons refused. Instead he launched with one of his vessels a line between New Brunswick and Battery Pier, New York City. Thus he challenged directly the monopoly. Ogden, backed by the monopoly, went to court and sought an injunction against Gibbons. The eminent Chancellor Kent granted it. It was this Gibbons boat—the *Mouse of the Mountain*—that young Cornelius Vanderbilt was commanding in 1817.

Vanderbilt had decided to go in for steam navigation. But it is characteristic of monopoly that newcomers cannot enter the trade it rules. And though newcomers are essential to the capitalist economy, its defenders for decade after decade have made it more and more difficult for newcomers to arrive, until in this year of grace in which I write it is all but impossible.

Vanderbilt had to look for a job with someone who had a boat. He picked Gibbons. He swapped the role of proprietor for that of employee in order to learn about steam. Thus he found himself jammed in the very center of the first great monopoly battle in America—and against monopoly. Vanderbilt, of all men, born monopolist! He was the very man for Gibbons. He had a reputation on the water front as its boldest, most warlike and formidable battler. He united the untamed truculence of the ruffian with those more terrifying qualities—an eye that blazed with resoluteness and wrath, a Jovian countenance, and a huge, loose-jointed body and ready fists. He was the sort of man who might have stood on the quarter-deck of a pirate ship and quelled a mutinous crew with his commanding anger. He had whipped every blackguard on the river front. He loved a fight. Gibbons was in a fight. Vanderbilt needed an education in steam navigation. And the deck of the *Mouse of the Mountain* was the school for him. But it must have irked the man who called his first schooner the *Dread* to be commanding a vessel called the *Mouse*. Vanderbilt induced Gibbons to rehabilitate the slattern craft and rechristen her the *Bellona*.

Vanderbilt's reputation as a manager rose rapidly. The conditions in which he operated the *Bellona* were difficult. The captain and his craft were pursued by process servers and sheriffs for months, while the litigation lasted. But he managed to evade them, keeping the *Bellona* in service despite the Chancellor's injunction. Meantime Gibbons had taken his case to the Supreme Court of the United States. And there he won it. The case of Gibbons vs. Ogden is one of the great landmarks of constitutional history. Chief Justice Marshall held that the United States government alone had the right to regulate traffic in the navigable waters of the nation. If, said Marshall, the Federal government did not have the power to regulate so essential a function then the Constitution would become "a magnificent structure, indeed, but wholly unfit for use."

The way thus cleared, Vanderbilt, year after year, extended Gibbons' line. He added boat after boat. If he did not have vision for perceiving the shape of things to come, he displayed magnificent talents as a manager of things as they were. He was now manager of the Union Line, as Gibbons' enterprise was called. He had an office at 457 Washington Street. And there, in an atmosphere of violence and blue profanity that made even the sailors wince, he roared orders at his employees and abuse at his rivals. He revealed here that quality which marked the brigand money getters of his day, an utter incapacity to envisage any reason against doing what he wanted to do. If men objected he brushed them aside. If they fought back he knocked them down. If laws intervened, why, they were damn-fool laws and not fit to be noticed. If officials blocked the way, why, buy them. If judges issued decrees, why, see that the decrees were on his side. Those who disagreed with him were blockheads. Those who resisted him were—why, Goddamn them! —they were hypocrites and blackguards and public enemies. This was the code with which he operated to expand the nine thousand dollars he had amassed as a ferryman to a hundred million before he died.

When Vanderbilt took his job with Gibbons he moved his family to New Brunswick. There his wife took over an old inn, renamed it Bellona Hall, and ran a tourists' tavern. Like himself she was illiterate; unlike him she was without ambition. She was an efficient drudge whose objective did not extend beyond making a go of Bellona Hall. But that she did. She scrimped and saved and slaved and bore to her husband with amazing regularity a flock of children until there were twelve. Vanderbilt saw little of them, thought less of them, indeed scarcely knew them. His home was on the bounding waves and in the little office in Washington Street where he too slaved sleeplessly. He looked upon his wife and her brats as hopelessly inferior to the expanding and altogether admirable figure into which he saw himself growing.

The Union Line was making $40,000 a year for Gibbons. Vanderbilt was not the man to go on making $40,000 a year for another man when he could do it for himself. The nine-thousand-dollar capital had by 1829, what with his earnings and those of Bellona Hall, swelled to thirty thousand. In that year Vanderbilt—thirty-five years old—went to Gibbons and, to that gentleman's horror, informed him he was quitting. He shut up Bellona Hall amid his wife's tears, moved his family to a small tenement in Stone Street in Manhattan, and once again went into business for himself.

III

Vanderbilt bought such boats as he could. He got some from Gibbons. He plunged into his enterprise with all his boundless vitality. He succeeded from the first. He succeeded because he was a manager of the highest ability. He grew rich fast. In the first five years he made thirty thousand dollars a year. The sixth year he made sixty thousand. He never made so little again. He built up a network of steamboat lines that covered all the ports of Long Island Sound and New York Harbor and extended to Bridgeport, Newport, New Haven, Providence, and Boston. Before he ended this episode of steamboating he owned a hundred vessels and was worth millions.

He was a ruthless competitor. He had two principal weapons—superior service and rate cutting. He drove weak competitors from the water. He threw his strength with abandon against the strongest.

He put a boat on the Hudson River. And here he first met that sinister man who was to be his foe in every business he attempted. You have to go to the pages of a novelist like Dickens for such a character as Daniel Drew. He was a compound of coarseness, illiteracy, vulgarity, meanness, dishonesty, and hypocrisy. He had risen through the levels of canvasman, animal trainer, clown in a circus, drover, keeper of the Bull's Head Tavern on the Boston Post Road and Twenty-sixth Street, to steamboating, speculating, banking, and railroading, battling Vanderbilt on every stage of this long ascent. He looked upon cards, the bottle, the theater, and dancing as things of the devil. But lying, duplicity, thievery, and greed were the passions of his life. Somewhere in the dark corners of his soul he worshiped some strange version of the Christian God, but there was no form of perfidy to which this vulgar old Goth could not descend with a pious ejaculation upon his tobacco-stained lips.

Vanderbilt started a rate war on the Hudson with Drew and drove him from the river. He tackled a much more formidable combination—the Hudson River Association—backed by the power of the Van Buren machine and led by Dean Richmond, with whom also he was to cross swords upon other battlefields. He could not drive them from the river. But with a rate war he could inflict heavy losses on them. They offered him terms, and for a consideration he agreed to quit the Hudson River route.

Soon Daniel Drew was back on the Hudson with a sensational vessel, the *Isaac Newton,* first of the great floating palaces, 300 feet long and with berths for 500. Vanderbilt promptly returned with an even more luxurious boat, the *Cornelius Vanderbilt.* "Live-oak" George Law, another lifelong antagonist of Vanderbilt, entered the lists with the *Oregon.* Which was the faster—the *Oregon* or the *Cornelius Vanderbilt?* That was a river bet until Captain Vanderbilt and "Liveoak" George agreed to fight it out. They ran a race as famous then as the great race between the *Robert E. Lee* and the *Natchez* years later. And Law's *Oregon* beat the *Cornelius Vanderbilt,* to the great disgust of the Captain. These two men were to meet many times again in more deadly struggles.

------------------------------ IV ------------------------------

During these years Cornelius Vanderbilt had been expanding personally. By 1849 he was forty-five years old. Yet he had scarcely begun his career. He had moved his family, of course, from the Stone Street tenement to a larger house on Madison

Avenue and then to a still more commodious one at 173 Broadway
and then, at the insistence of his wife, to a stately home and farm
on Staten Island. And by 1845 he built a splendid residence, at
No. 10 Washington Square, in keeping with his stature in the
community.

He had been promoted. It was a time when many a commanding
figure was found in Broadway. Men made up for their parts, with
their whiskers and frock coats, their cloaks and high hats. But
there was no more commanding figure there than this frock-coated,
high-hatted, side-whiskered Jove, tall, erect, alive, past forty but
moving with the stride of a younger man. It was ridiculous to go
on calling this imperious person merely Cap'n. So men began to
call him Commodore—and Commodore he remained. Time had
softened very little the bucolic curves of his accent or the illiterate
forms of his grammar. He was not a man to look himself over for
defects. He remained to the end a thoroughly ignorant man—
ignorant of everything save his business.

During these years there were terrible divisions in his family
which would have destroyed a more sensitive man, save that they
could not have happened to a sensitive man. He cared little or
nothing for his children. One of them had to be committed to an
insane asylum. His son William H. married, but was forced to
retire to a New Dorp farm to regain his health. Nothing could have
seemed to the virile Commodore surer evidence of weakness in a
man's character than a loss of health, and so he looked with contempt upon this febrile son.

Most serious was the dark gulf that widened between himself
and his wife. He was a heartless man. She was a weak woman.
She wept and seemed forever dissatisfied. Her health broke down.
She declined into fits of melancholy, due partly, beyond doubt, to
her physical infirmities but also in part to certain escapades of the
full-blooded Commodore that preyed on her mind. She whimpered
against moving back to Manhattan to the stately home being built
on Washington Square. They quarreled. The quarrels split the
family. And in the end Vanderbilt said she must be crazy. To sus-

pect it was to conclude it, and, against the protests of her daughters, he put her into a Flushing insane asylum. Members of his
own family charged that he did it to make way for some other
woman. It is a dark chapter in his life. It opens a crack in his shell
through which we may have a peep at the ruthless soul within.
The unfortunate woman remained in the asylum for two years,
after which, under pressure of his family, he permitted her to come
home. This was in 1847. Two years later he made up his mind
that he was done with steamboats. He turned his mind to other
fields.

V

In 1849 gold was discovered in California. Thousands flocked
to the coast. They went by covered wagon, and by clipper ships
around the Horn. Vanderbilt's old Hudson River foe, "Liveoak"
George Law, along with Albert G. Sloo, Marshall O. Roberts, and
others, organized the United States Mail, while Harris and others
formed the Pacific Mail Steamship Company. The first was called
the Sloo Line; the second the Harris Line. The Sloo ran from
New York to what is now Colón. Its passengers were sent across
the Isthmus of Panama, where the Harris Line took them to San
Francisco. The trip cost $600 first class and $125 in the steerage.
It was expensive but it was the quickest and most comfortable
route to the Land of Gold. The ships received juicy mail subsidies
and the companies were getting rich. Vanderbilt decided to enter
this trade. He planned to send passengers to Nicaragua by steamship instead of to Panama, across Nicaragua by canal, and then
by ship to San Francisco. It would be shorter and he knew he could
manage ships better than Sloo and Law. He went to England to
get financial aid and met with refusal. But he was not daunted.
He established the ship line from New York to Nicaragua and from
Nicaragua to Panama. He sent his passengers across the narrow
isthmus by steamboat on the San Juan River into Lake Nicaragua
to Virgin Bay. Then they went over the twelve miles to San Juan

del Sur, on the Pacific, by stage. He operated eight ocean-going ships in the Atlantic and Pacific and ran twenty-five handsome blue and white coaches over the isthmus connection. He could beat the Harris and Sloo lines by two days. And, in spite of their subsidies, he could carry passengers for $300 instead of $600 and make money. Steerage passage he cut from $125 to $35. He took two thousand passengers a month to California from New York and New Orleans, transported much of the gold, and made a million dollars a year. By 1853 he boasted to a friend that he was worth eleven million dollars.

This line to California he called the Accessory Transit Company. He sold stock in it, keeping merely enough to control it, less than a majority. In 1853, when all was running well, he went to Europe on an extended vacation with his family. He confided the operation of the Transit Company to the banking firm of Garrison, Morgan, Rolston, and Fretz. While he was away Morgan and Garrison quietly bought up enough stock to get control. When the old buccaneer returned he found that he had been boarded and scuttled. In a towering rage he wrote Morgan and Garrison a letter that is a model for brevity and meaning:

GENTLEMEN: You have undertaken to cheat me. I will not sue you because the law takes too long. I will ruin you. Sincerely yours.

He did not ruin them. But he did go quietly about buying up enough stock to regain control of the line. Then he threw them out.

He was to find the road to quick millions strewn with enemies. Hardly had he settled with Morgan and Garrison when he was confronted with a revolution in Nicaragua. A dashing young American filibuster, William Walker, overthrew the government and seized and revoked the Transit Company's charter. Such a crisis called forth Vanderbilt's natural ability as a general. He stopped all his vessels en route to Nicaragua and thus cut William Walker off from communication with America, whence he was getting men and supplies. Walker got himself elected President. Instantly the neighboring Central American "republics" were outraged. Vanderbilt armed and financed Costa Rica, Honduras, Guatemala. They poured hostile troops into Walker's new empire. He organized a filibuster under two notorious adventurers. He received aid from Buchanan. He drove Walker into a corner until he surrendered to a United States gunboat.

He got his Transit Company back. But by this time he was ready to quit Central America for other fields that looked greener and less troublesome.

His natural sense of justice based on its relation to the interests of Commodore Vanderbilt had been profoundly disturbed by the immense subsidies Harris and Sloo and Law were getting from the government—$900,000 a year since 1848. He thirsted for that money and had a vision of the means to get most of it. Having slashed the rates on his rivals, he had devoured most of their profits. He went to them and proposed that he would withdraw— but they must make it worth his while. He had done the same thing before to Dean Richmond when he fought the Hudson River Association. He forced Harris and Sloo to buy his boats at a good price and to pay him $40,000 a month as long as he kept out of that trade. A little later, by a threat to return, he compelled them to raise the price to $56,000 a month—$672,000 a year. He got all his investment back and drew $672,000 a year, most of the subsidy, without lifting a finger. He drained most of the subsidy away from Law and his colleagues and let them do all the work and supply all of the capital.

Then he built two magnificent vessels—the *Vanderbilt* and the *Ariel*—and entered the Atlantic trade, running his ships to Southampton, Bremen, and Havre in competition with E. K. Collins. He has been accused of being in a conspiracy with Collins to extort subsidies from the government. But there is no proof of this. He found there was no profit in this business. With all his capacity as a manager and his willingness to work men for the lowest wages, he discovered he could not compete with the Cunard Line which paid still lower wages and enjoyed large subsidies from the British government. And so the old Commodore, a multimillionaire, second in wealth only to John Jacob Astor, sixty-six years of age, bade good-by to the sea, but not to retire. He sold his ships to Allen and Garrison for $3,000,000—all but the *North Star*. And that calls for a word.

———————————— VI ————————————

In 1854 Vanderbilt built a magnificent vessel that he named the *North Star*. Whether this was primarily an ocean liner or a private yacht is not quite clear. It was certainly fitted out at first as a private yacht. But it was a ship of 2500 tons and almost as large as the largest transatlantic liners then in service.

In the early summer of 1854 Vanderbilt astonished New York by putting the elegantly appointed *North Star* into service as a private yacht. Into this Ark de luxe the skipper loaded his wife and his twelve children, a famous captain, and a fashionable chaplain. The chaplain wrote a book about this pretentious expedition, called *The Cruise of the Steam Yacht* North Star: *A Narrative of the Excursion of Mr. Vanderbilt's Party to England, Russia, Denmark, France, Spain, Italy, Malta, Madeira, etc., by the Rev. John Overton Coules, D.D.* The old Commodore literally knocked London's eye out. He was feted by the Lord Mayor. He and his wife rode around St. Petersburg in the Czar's carriage.

This was the vessel he reserved when he sold all his others to Allen and Garrison. It happened in 1859. The next year the South seceded and Vanderbilt, in a gust of patriotism, offered the *North Star* to the government. He intended it as a *loan*. The government went him one better and accepted the *gift*. Hell and damnation! Gift! He had made no gift. But this painful error put him in an embarrassing position and so he had to absorb the loss with the best face possible. But the mistake was to stand him in good stead later. When a country goes to war or is ravaged by a plague, there are always men whose first question is: what can I make out of this? The whole prewar era was one of vulgar dishonesty. It was not surprising, therefore, that men who had materials to sell or who understood the delicate mechanism of speculation should have sunk their hooks deeply into the public treasury while the rest of the country fought and suffered. It is a dark and sordid story. Vanderbilt managed to get himself smeared with some of this scandal.

The government planned in great secrecy an expedition to New Orleans under General Banks. It needed vessels to transport horses and men. Secretary Stanton asked Vanderbilt to look after the purchase of the needed vessels. Later an ugly scandal broke out about these purchases, which led to a Congressional investigation and an acrimonious debate in the Senate. The main charges were fully substantiated. Men who had vessels to sell were compelled to pay from five to ten per cent commission to Vanderbilt's agent, T. J. Southard. Old, outmoded, and even rotting ships were unloaded on the government at extortionate prices. Vessels utterly unfit for ocean service were rented at rates shockingly in excess of prices paid for the same boats in similar expeditions.

A resolution censuring Vanderbilt, his agent T. J. Southard, and Commodore Van Brunt of the navy was introduced in the Senate. The question was—did Vanderbilt know that Southard was taking this money? Was he personally aware of the nature of the vessels purchased?

It is fair to say, notwithstanding some of the bitter excoriations of Vanderbilt, that no evidence was produced to prove that he knew that Southard was grafting, although the latter's guilt was established—he even offered to return the money. What Vanderbilt was guilty of, however, beyond doubt, was shameful negligence and incompetence. He did approve the buying of boats at prices which he knew better than anyone else were indefensible. He most certainly bought and hired craft without reasonable inspection. His excuse was that they were adequately insured, to which Senator Tombs of Georgia replied that surely insurance could not cover the lives of the men committed to some of these rotten hulls. He did know that Southard had bought for the government some of his own boats at even higher prices than those paid for any others.

The whole transaction smelled of fraud. And had Vanderbilt been a man with a finer sense of public service it could not possibly have happened.

His name was expunged from the censuring resolution and it has been charged that he used political influence to effect this. But certainly that left-handed "gift" of the $800,000 *North Star* went a long way to save him from the branding iron of the Senate.

------------------------- VII -------------------------

When Vanderbilt sold his ships it was not to retire. He abandoned the sea for railroads. He was no pioneer. He was in no sense a man of vision. Other men dreamed. He went into action after their dreams had materialized. When he operated his schooners, he sneered at the steamboats that Fulton and Livingston and other men of vision were running. When he adopted steam he laughed with scorn at the little iron horses that puffed along the Hudson. He went into the Isthmian-California traffic after Sloo and Law and others had shown the way and the profits. In 1860 railroads were no longer experiments. He had no time for experiments. But he could see that they were potential money-makers and that the men who were running them were doing a bad job of operation.

One fable linked with the Vanderbilt saga is that he took a great number of little jerkwater roads and forged them into the great New York Central trunk line. The legend is overwrought. By 1860 the New York Central was an integrated line running from Albany to Buffalo. The work of consolidation had been nearly completed. Originally the traveler from Albany bound for Buffalo had to start on the Albany & Schenectady to Schenectady. There he changed to another road—the Schenectady & Utica—for Utica. At Utica he boarded another road for Syracuse. At Syracuse he scampered out again for another stretch on another road to Auburn. There he boarded the Auburn & Rochester for the latter city. And then, with a sigh of relief, he got a ticket on the Rochester, Lockport & Niagara Falls for Buffalo. In 1852 all these small roads, plus some more enjoying unused franchises, were consolidated into a single line called the New York Central. Then the management boasted that a man—after a sleepless night from Albany to Utica—might eat his breakfast in Utica, dine in Rochester, and sup with a friend on the shores of Lake Erie. As for the beginning of it all, the man who dreamed the dream was an aristocratic old gentleman named George W. Featherstonhaugh, who made the start with the first road from Albany to Schenectady when Vanderbilt was haw-hawing at the stupid fellows who thought they could make those dern things work. Most of the consolidating occurred when he decided to transfer his talents to steam.

He began, however, not with the Central but with two roads running out of New York to Albany—the New York & Harlem, and the New York & Hudson River. First he bought a controlling interest in the Harlem road. Its downtown terminus was at Tyron Square back of City Hall. Its cars were hauled by horses to Twenty-sixth Street where the locomotive was hooked on. Then it proceeded to Chatham where it connected with the Boston & Albany for the capital city. Like most early roads, it was mismanaged. In twenty-nine years it had averaged less than half of one per cent a year profit. Its road and equipment were badly run down. Vanderbilt bought control at nine dollars a share.

The Commodore's next step was to get for the Harlem road from the Common Council a perpetual franchise to extend its right of way down to the Battery. Out of this incident grew an unlovely comedy of duplicity, treachery, and fraud scarcely duplicated in our turgid business history.

While Vanderbilt sought his franchise from the Council, George Law—he of the Hudson River Line and the Panama episode—sought a similar one from the legislature. Vanderbilt bribed the corrupt Council known as the Forty Thieves. Law bribed the equally corrupt legislature's dominating group known as the Black Horse Cavalry. Vanderbilt got his franchise, Law got his, but Tweed's governor vetoed it at Vanderbilt's urging, doubtless implemented by cash. The stock of the Harlem shot up in price.

But Daniel Drew, who is entitled to a high place in American business' Hall of Infamy, entered into a conspiracy with the Council. Drew showed them how they could make a lot of money by betraying the old Commodore whose cash they had taken to give him the franchise. The members were equal to any infamy. The *North American Review* about this time described this august body as being made up of "pickpockets, prize fighters, immigrant-runners, pimps and the lowest of liquor dealers" to the "absolute exclusion of honest men." Under Drew's leadership they formed a pool to sell the Harlem stock short. That is, as the stock rose in price they would sell—stock they didn't have, of course—for future delivery. Then if the courts held the franchise to be unlawful, which was more than probable, the stock would promptly go down in value. If the courts did not hold it illegal the Council could revoke the franchise they had voted to Vanderbilt for bribe money. When the shares sank in price, Drew could buy cheaply all the shares he needed to make delivery to those who had bought at high prices.

The stock went to 100. Drew sold heavily as planned. But somehow the stock did not sink in price. Drew continued to sell in order to hammer the price down. But instead the price went up—to 120, to 150, to 170. Here is what happened. Vanderbilt got word of this conspiracy. Therefore, as fast as Drew sold Vanderbilt bought. It was, indeed, Vanderbilt who was buying all the stock Drew was selling. Presently Vanderbilt owned practically all of the 110,000 shares of the Harlem and the thousands of fictitious shares Drew had sold. Then he called upon Drew to make delivery of those shares. This meant Drew had to go out in the market and buy. But there was none for sale. Vanderbilt had it all. Drew had to buy from Vanderbilt. He went to his old enemy and begged for mercy. Vanderbilt turned the screw and compelled him to buy thousands of shares at $179. It cost Drew and his aldermen colleagues a million dollars in losses. It was nearly enough to make up for what Vanderbilt had paid for his control of the road. But he had lost the franchise.

Next he bought control of the New York & Hudson River, the river route to Albany and much the better line. Then he asked the legislature to authorize the consolidation of the Harlem and Hudson River roads. The Black Horse Cavalry had to be bought again. Here again the legislative leaders attempted to carry off a short-selling coup like that tried by Drew and the Council. They planned to defeat the act at the last minute and cover as the Hudson price sank down. But once again Vanderbilt duplicated his offensive against Drew. He found himself in possession of 27,000 shares more than existed. He compelled the legislative gamblers to settle at $285 a share and boasted with glee that he "had busted the whole legislature." He got his act, merged the two roads, and then turned to getting the New York Central.

In the Harlem and Hudson operation he did not so much join two roads as he did put one of them out of business. He began to build up the Hudson River route, double-tracking it, erecting new stations, and providing new equipment including the new sleeping cars. Everywhere the effects of new and capable management were visible.

Getting the Central was not easy. It was in the hands of tough-fibered men, with plenty of money—John Jacob Astor, John Stewart, and others, led by Dean Richmond, who had fought Vanderbilt with the Hudson River Association when Vanderbilt made him pay him to quit the Hudson for a while. Moreover, the Central had been shamefully overcapitalized. Its various component roads had cost $11,000,000 to build. But the capitalization was raised to $23,000,000 and at the consolidation to $35,000,000—sixty per cent water.

But Vanderbilt was a general of formidable talents in such a fight. He had driven old Drew from the field in a swift tactical maneuver and repeated it later against the corrupt leaders of the legislature, with that kind of swift decision with which he countered Walker's filibuster seizure of the Transit Company in Nicaragua and that sort of shrewd strategy with which he managed to make the Sloo and Harris lines fork over to him most of their rich subsidies from the government.

The Central had one weakness. It could get its passengers from Buffalo to Albany, but had no means of sending them to New York save over the Hudson River road in the winter and by the Hudson River steamers in the warm months. Vanderbilt had begun to buy stock in the Central, but when he found he could not get control he took swift and sudden advantage of this weakness. When the fall months ended and ice filled the river, the Central ordered the shift of its New York passengers and freight to the Hudson River line. But when the passengers got out of the Central trains, there were no Hudson River trains to receive them. Vanderbilt had ordered that the Hudson trains should not only not cross the river to meet the Central but should stop a mile away from their usual station. The Central passengers had to troop in the snow to their New York connection. The freight had to be hauled by drays, adding immensely to the cost.

The Central managers denounced him. The public joined the protest. The legislature ordered an investigation. It summoned Vanderbilt and asked him why he had failed to send his trains across the river. He bowled them over by producing a state law prohibiting his company from sending trains across the river. That settled that. But why had he stopped his trains a mile away on his own side of the river? He didn't know. He didn't give the order. "I was home," he said blandly. "I was playing a rubber of whist. And ye know, gentlemen, I never allow anything to interfere with me when I'm playing cards. Ye got to keep your attention fixed on the game."

Backed by the law, he held his ground. It was a costly strike against the Central. And in 1857 the stockholders compelled Richmond, Astor, and Stewart to surrender. They called Vanderbilt in and made him President. He began extensive improvements on this road too, and in two years asked the legislature to permit the joining of the Hudson River and the Central. This was his only merger

of roads in that continuous trunk line that he called the New York
Central & Hudson River road. He increased the stock from
$44,000,000 to $86,000,000. Each holder of a $100 share got a share
in the new company for $180. The eighty dollars was pure water.
As for Vanderbilt himself, he got for himself and his services six
million dollars in cash and $20,000,000 in shares, in addition to the
water he got on his own shares. Thus he embarked upon that
vicious and socially disastrous practice that was to be the curse of
American business to this day, of inflating the capitalization of
railroads, utilities, and corporate enterprises of all sorts.

VIII

There is a curious notion that enjoys much popular support in
this country. It might be called the brigand theory of progress. A
certain kind of lusty scoundrel, audacious, adventurous, taking
bold chances, not putting too nice a point upon questions of right
and wrong when it is a question of getting things done, is supposed
to be essential to business progress.

Such men do wicked things by the code of the casuist. They
engage in enterprises that involve fractures of many command-
ments. They enforce losses upon smaller men. They are cruel. We
need not condone all this. But we are told that we must recognize
that these are blemishes among many greater qualities. Indeed,
these very vices are but the by-products of the exuberant energy
which is essential to pushing forward great projects. They are
driven by a passion for doing things. And in a world of timid souls
and doubters, of human obstacles of every sort, of stupid laws and
venal officials and selfish interests balking progress, men of tough
fiber are needed to cut through all the physical and human fortresses that block them. Some people suffer, some lose as a result
of their methods, but out of their efforts emerge great works and
great institutions.

This precious gem of social philosophy is worth assaying. But
at least this we may observe: at the period of which we are writing

there appeared as fine a collection of rascals materializing railroads and other works through the processes of the brigand theory of progress as ever were to be found on the Spanish Main itself. Whether or not they were driven by a passion for getting things done, certainly they were driven by a consuming passion for getting other people's money. Whether the passion for achieving great works was stronger than the appetite for money, we may judge from the manner in which Commodore Vanderbilt ditched his Panama project in favor of a scheme under which he could wring $56,000 a month out of his opponents without all the trouble of operating a project.

Jay Cooke, banker, planned to build the Northern Pacific with money furnished by bond buyers while he and his colleagues took the stock and the ownership and control without putting up any cash (or only a trifling sum) and then got the government to give them an empire in land grants—44 million acres. Cooke ruined himself and his investors, plunged the nation into a panic, and doubtless delayed the building of the road for years. Then another group reorganized it, took 49 million shares of stock for themselves for which they paid nothing. In later years, when the road needed $11,000,000 in additional capital, another great banking firm supplied it from its clients and in return loaded the company with $58,000,000 in securities.

The Union Pacific was marked by a similar trail of failures, delays, corruption, and theft, including the infamous Crédit Mobilier, which bribed members of Congress and its Speaker, governors, editors, judges, and a candidate for the presidency. To build a railroad? No, to build the crooked capital structure by which they could exploit it. They made a contract between themselves and the roads to do the construction work and put in the way of the great project that most terrible of obstacles—prohibitive costs due to their own extortionate charges.

That other precious quartet of railroad titans—Charles Crocker, Collis P. Huntington, Leland Stanford, and Mark Hopkins—who built the Central Pacific, issued to themselves $33,000,000 in bonds and $49,000,000 in stocks in return for practically no investment and as representatives of the roalroad made a contract with themselves as builders to construct the road and charged the company three times the $27,000,000 it cost to build.

The proceedings of Messrs. Vanderbilt, Drew, Law, and others in the Harlem and Hudson River franchise and corners offer an excellent instance of the skulduggery to which these gentlemen resorted, not to build railroads, but to grab roads already built. The railroads, like the utilities, are a gift to us from countless devoted scientists who created the instrumentalities that make up a railroad, and of countless industrious operating engineers who dreamed them, built them, and later managed them all for very meager rewards, while the work of driving forward railroad development was actually hampered by the scoundrels who used the financial necessities of the roads to exploit them, rob their stockholders and bondholders, debauch their communities, and, in the end, ruin the roads themselves.

Indeed this whole matter of brigandage is a bit elusive. It is not always easy to know where the outlaw ends and the baron begins. One cannot detect with accuracy the moral boundaries that divide the pirate from the privateer and both from the racketeer and the promoter.

There is the outlaw—the man on the horse or sailing under the Jolly Roger, who defies society, denies its laws, and makes war on it—like Captain Kidd.

There is the racketeer who remains in society, scoffs at its laws, but assumes control of some of its operations and functions—like Al Capone.

There is the financial promoter who uses neither horse nor galleon, who does not defy laws but rather shapes them to his ends, does not make war upon society but corrupts its officials, adopts and exploits its machinery—like Jay Gould.

But all have the same objective—plunder. And all exist, where they do exist, because of a tolerance of them that persists as a strange anachronism in civilized society. It must not be forgotten that Henry Morgan was knighted not before he went astray as the most ruthless buccaneer of his time, but after. In a life of crime under the license of a privateer he assaulted and sacked one island after another, ending with his savage attack on Panama, where he burned the castle and the town and marched away with 175 mules and cattle loaded with treasure worth over a million and a half and 600 prisoners who were held for ransom. He defrauded his men and returned to England where he was knighted and appointed governor of Jamaica by Charles II.

We have conferred doctorates, positions of honor, built monuments, named streets and institutions after some of our own freebooters who were scarcely better than Sir Henry Morgan. I can explain it upon no other theory than that we are as yet but very imperfectly civilized. Our people as a whole have only a very rudimentary perception of the more subtle social virtues. They can understand and applaud only a few very rudimentary human virtues. They understand strength, courage, loyalty, generosity. Therefore, they can admire the political district leader who will fight at the drop of a hat, who always overcomes his enemies, who distributes largess to the poor and sticks to his friends. That he may rob the city, betray his official trust, accept bribes from the predatory enemies of the poor, mismanage and bankrupt the community is of no importance since these performances involve the exercise of social virtues and vices that they perceive but dimly.

How thin this line between the freebooter and the magnate may be, one may see in the following account of one of the most amazing episodes in American business history.

———————————— IX ————————————

The Erie Railroad runs from New York to Buffalo and on to Chicago. It competed in 1866—and still does—with Vanderbilt's New York Central. The poor old Erie had a long history of corruption and mismanagement. One group of directors after another had looted it. The road was organized in 1832 with a capital of $4,000,000. The state of New York put up $3,000,000; private investors the other million. The state got bonds; the private investors got stock. The state never received a penny of interest or principal on its bonds, and after ten years these were canceled. Another issue of $3,000,000 in bonds and $3,000,000 in stock was put out, and the Erie began another decade of mismanagement. By 1857 it was again in the hospital. At this point Daniel Drew, then a banker and broker in Wall Street, entered the picture. He loaned the road $3,480,000. It couldn't meet the loan so Drew took it over. For eight years thereafter it almost ceased to be a railroad and became a mere tool in the Wall Street kit of Drew, who ran its stock up and down at will and made millions out of gullible speculators.

Vanderbilt saw the possibilities of the Erie. Moreover, it competed with the Central. He determined to add it to his possessions. He began buying shares secretly. He accumulated 20,000. This was not enough. But John S. Eldridge of Boston controlled a large block of stock. A Boston group that he represented wanted to bring about a consolidation of the Erie with their Boston, Hartford & Erie. Vanderbilt induced Eldridge to unite with him, pool their shares, and seize control of the road. Eldridge agreed but exacted as a condition that old Daniel Drew should be ousted.

At the stockholders' meeting Vanderbilt's directorate was elected. Drew was left out, but two new men, Jay Gould and James Fisk, Jr., were named. Eldridge did not know it that day but he discovered very quickly that Vanderbilt had double-crossed him. The old Commodore, then seventy-two years old, made one of the most astonishing blunders of his long career. When Drew learned that Vanderbilt had the votes to win he went to Vanderbilt's Washington Square home. He was in tears. He begged Vanderbilt not to throw him out. He suggested that he be taken in as an ally with his large stockholdings and that the two men work together. No one knew Drew better than Vanderbilt. He knew him to be a scoundrel. Drew had tried to ruin him in the Harlem corner. He knew that Drew was merely a plunderer of every property and partner he dealt with. Why the Commodore listened to this oily old rascal pleading with tears in the name of their old "friendship" it is impossible to conjecture.

But he did yield. And he paid dearly for his folly. It was agreed that Drew would not be elected to the board. But as soon as the board took office, a dummy elected for the purpose was to resign and Drew was to be named in his place and made treasurer. Worse than this, Vanderbilt agreed to name two associates of Drew, two of the most unconscionable rogues ever thrown up by American business, which has been peculiarly fruitful of them. This was that incompatible and ill-assorted pair, Jay Gould and James Fisk, Jr. Never had two more unscrupulous rascals a sponsor worthier of their talents than Gould and Fisk found in Drew.

After a brief career in Pennsylvania where he operated a tannery and wrote a history of Delaware County, Gould appeared in New York with a patent rattrap he had invented. He gravitated to Wall Street where for the rest of his life his inventive genius was applied to bear, bull, and lamb traps from which he made uncounted millions. He was a small, frail, dark-bearded but pastyfaced man; sickly, gloomy, coldly cruel. Before he ended his career he had gathered under his power a web of railroads, steamships, the Western Union, the New York *World*, the New York elevated roads, comparable to that complicated and diverse empire that the Van Sweringen brothers assembled later.

Jim Fisk was the son of a Vermont peddler and in his early life traveled the Connecticut Valley in wagons brilliantly painted like circus carts, selling cloth, silks, tin, and baubles. Like Drew, he had enjoyed a brief career in a small animal circus. He got his start selling blankets to the army during the war at extortionate prices. He fell in with Drew for whom he negotiated the sale of his Stonington steamboats. The hard, dry, sanctimonious Drew was attracted by the gaudy, extravagantly dressed dandy, glittering with rings and other jewelry, his blond hair and mus-

tache elaborately pomaded and dressed. Drew aided him to set
up in Wall Street as a broker, where he met Jay Gould. What
was the attraction between Gould and Fisk it is impossible to
say, save that each supplied the qualities for adventure that the
other lacked. Gould was a man of powerful intellectual equipment, simple in his tastes, meticulous in his personal morals,
scornful of the world and those in it with whom he dealt, resourceful and merciless. Fisk was noisy, ostentatious, vulgar in his tastes
and morals, audacious, with the mental equipment of a New
England horse trader, but an able field general in a stock operation.

Gould and Fisk had a special object in establishing connections with the Erie road. In 1866 they bought a small road—the
Bradford & Pittsburgh Railroad. They paid $250,000 for it and
promptly issued $2,000,000 in bonds. They wanted to lease this
line to the Erie, forcing that already distressed corporation to
assume the new bonds. They did sell the road to the Erie and
received for the $250,000 investment $2,000,000 of Erie bonds
convertible into stock.

As soon as these three freebooters—Drew, Gould, and Fisk—
found themselves inside the Erie compound, with Drew as treasurer and the three of them on the executive committee, with Drew
representing Vanderbilt's interests, they proceeded to rob Vanderbilt. What they did to this wise, suspicious, and formidable old
warrior is a classic in duplicity and helps us form some idea of
what can be and is done to the less knowing and helpless investor.

First they undermined the Commodore with their fellow directors. They intimated that the objectives of the Commodore were
completely selfish, a disclosure that must have come as a great
shock to that choice collection of selfless souls. Vanderbilt was
tagged as an exploiter who wanted a monopoly of transportation.
He would make the Erie play second fiddle to the Central.
Hitherto it had been a mere jimmy in the tool bag of a safecracker.
Having gained the confidence of the new directors, Drew, Gould,
and Fisk induced that body of shocked altruists to issue ten million
dollars in bonds. These were almost all turned over to the three

saviors of the Erie in payment of various spurious claims. The Commodore, hearing of this, realized that they were bent on treason. He uttered a roar of wrath and hurried his lawyers off to Judge Barnard for an order commanding the looters to quit issuing bonds.

Meantime Vanderbilt redoubled his efforts to buy Erie stock to ensure control. His brokers bought right and left. But the supply seemed inexhaustible. In fact, it was—at least as long as the printing press of Gould, Fisk, and Drew kept running. For the ten million in bonds they had grabbed were convertible; that is, they could be turned into stocks on demand. The Unholy Three had their printer turn these bonds into stocks. And they dumped 50,000 shares on the market to be followed quickly by another 50,000. It was these Vanderbilt was buying, the millions he was paying flowing into the pockets of the conspirators. And Jim Fisk said with glee: "We'll give the old hog all he can hold if this printing press holds out."

When this perfidy dawned upon Vanderbilt he fell into a Jovian rage. Once again he rushed to his judge and got an order for the arrest of the villains for contempt. The judge who issued these orders must not pass unnoticed. He fitted into the comedy of the times as Harlequin in the pantomime. He was the Honorable George C. Barnard, a kind of human blackjack in the arsenal of Boss Tweed. Yale, maker-of-men, gave him to the world. He went to California and became a stool pigeon in a gambling joint. Later he was a blackface comedian. He returned to New York, where Tweed made him a magistrate and then a Superior Court judge in his kennel of justice. Tall, handsome, eccentric, boisterous, dressed in the loud and extravagant livery of a side-show barker, he sat on his judicial throne, whittling little strips of wood that his clerk kept piled on the desk for his amusement, spewing a stream of foul-mouthed impudence and abuse upon attorneys and litigants alike. Vanderbilt had bought him as he would an expensive horse. It was this gentleman who now ordered the arrest of Drew, Gould, and Fisk.

Getting wind of this, the three marauders hurriedly packed the records, account books, securities, and cash of the Erie Railroad, amounting to six million dollars, and like the hard-pressed ministers of a Balkan government fled in hacks for the border—for the Hudson River ferry and across to Jersey City, out of the jurisdiction of Judge Barnard.

They now enacted one of the most fantastic burlesques in the whole history of American business. They took over the Taylor Hotel. They made it into a fortress. They recruited a small army of thugs and armed them with rifles and small cannon, to repel what they believed was a threatened invasion of Jersey by the roaring and blaspheming Commodore. They called their citadel Fort Taylor. Fisk, as colorful a rogue as ever sailed the Spanish Main, assembled a fleet of vessels which he armed and of which he assumed personal command to check the invader before he reached the shore. Thus, the pirates with their army and navy awaited the assault of Vanderbilt. The whole town was aroused. The militia was mobilized to deal with the expected crisis.

But Vanderbilt had no intention of using force. The marauders were actually in a desperate plight and he knew it. At this point the command fell from the hands of the frightened Drew. Gould took it over. With $500,000 in cash he slipped quietly into Albany, where the legislature was in session. Somehow he got the ear of Tweed who up to this point was the ally of Vanderbilt. Gould gave Tweed $180,000 of Erie stock. He distributed large sums of cash among the members of the Black Horse Cavalry. A bill was introduced in the legislature to legalize the ten-million-dollar stock and bond issue. Barnard called it a bill to validate counterfeit money. Vanderbilt fought them with money and threats. Albany assumed the appearance of prosperity. The smell of money was in the air. All legislative business was suspended while the lawmakers gathered in groups and discussed the current quotations on votes. Rates fluctuated between two and three thousand dollars. The courts were drawn in. Gould and Fisk got a counterinjunction from Judge Cardoza. Thus, two Tweed justices—Cardoza and

Barnard—squared off in a duel of injunctions. Vanderbilt lost at Albany. The law legalizing the security issue was passed.

But Barnard still threatened the fugitives with jail for contempt if they appeared in his jurisdiction. And so, despite their victory, Gould and Fisk and Drew dared not enter New York. Vanderbilt, outwitted and beaten, had this advantage—his enemies were refugees from the haunts that were essential to their lives and plans.

Vanderbilt knew that Drew dreaded jail. He got word over to Jersey that Drew's time to talk business had come. Drew took the hint. He slipped one Sunday morning over to Vanderbilt's Washington Square home. Vanderbilt let him know that he would not relent until the hundred thousand shares he had bought were taken off his hands at what he had paid for them. Drew was willing to settle and proposed another meeting. Some days later he slipped again across the river to the home of Vanderbilt's lawyer, Judge Pierrepont. While he and Vanderbilt were in conference Gould and Fisk walked in. They had had old Daniel Drew shadowed and they followed to surprise him. There, with all the combatants present, Vanderbilt laid down his terms.

He did not get all he asked. But, all things considered, he did very well at the hands of these cutthroats. They agreed to take back 50,000 shares at 55, paying $2,500,000 in cash and $1,250,000 in securities. They agreed to pay a million dollars for the right to redeem the other 50,000 shares at 70 within six months. Thus, Vanderbilt recovered $4,750,000. He insisted this left him with a loss of $2,000,000.

But Gould and Fisk were not done with him. They began to beat the price of Erie stock down with heavy short selling. When it reached 35 they bought back in sufficient quantity to get control of the road while making another killing. And they found Vanderbilt glad to sell his remaining 50,000 shares at 40 instead of 70. They returned to New York, bringing with them the Erie headquarters, which they established in an elaborate white marble building at Eighth Avenue and Twenty-third Street. It contained a theater, which the incredible Fisk operated, finding thus an instrument for his exhibitionism and a recruiting station for his harem.

Vanderbilt had wanted control of the Erie. He wanted a monopoly of transportation in the territory served by the Erie and the Central. He got that control through his purchase of the shares the criminal trio had fed to him in the stock market. But having got it, he changed his mind. At the moment he was probably more interested in ruining his enemies. By forcing them to pay him $4,750,000 and leaving them with the rotting hulk of the looted railroad on their hands, he felt he was wreaking vengeance on Drew, Gould, and Fisk. But he reckoned without the satanic ingenuity of Gould.

Gould and Fisk thrust the aging and traitorous Drew aside. They made a prompt alliance with Tammany, put Bosses Tweed and Sweeney on the board of the Erie, and acquired the corrupt Judge Barnard as one of their own assets. They used him relentlessly, Fisk getting him to sign an injunction on one occasion at night in the boudoir of his mistress. The new headquarters of the railroad, with its opera house and a private passage between Fisk's private box and his offices, was called Castle Erie.

In the Castle, Fisk called himself the "Prince of Erie." Strutting aboard the flagship of his Albany fleet in an elaborate uniform, he called himself "Admiral." Marching at the head of a militia regiment that he commanded, he was styled "Colonel." He occasionally exhibited himself in a gaudy equipage drawn by six horses, three black on one side, three white on the other, embowered amidst a bevy of his strumpets. Yet this preposterous and malignant clown possessed an audacious cunning that when united with the acute and sinister genius of Gould made them a menace to investors, speculators, banks, and industry until Fisk was shot down by a jealous lover and Gould vanished from the scene, consumed in the fires of his own restless nature. They were to harass Vanderbilt almost to the end of his days. They carried on a traffic war, playing the Erie against the New York Central. When the old Commodore cut rates, Fisk went West, bought up vast herds of sheep—the most undesirable and unprofitable freight—and filled Vanderbilt's cars with them at destructive charges.

The Commodore was to encounter these bold raiders upon another scene. Gould's peculiar genius found its highest expression in plot and conspiracy for swift raiding adventures. In 1870 he perceived that the supplies of gold in the nation were quite limited. The government had a large gold reserve locked up in the Treasury vaults. And Gould saw that if he could manage to keep that locked up it would be possible to corner the floating supply. He managed to meet President Grant during a visit of the latter to New York. He then pointed out to the President that, as the movement of the crops was near, he was in a position to bring a great benefit to the farmers if he steadfastly refused under any circumstances to permit any of the government's gold reserve to be released. If the President did that it would tend to raise the price of gold on the gold market and this would depreciate the dollar in terms of gold. Foreign buyers of wheat must buy American dollars to pay for wheat. If gold were high these buyers could buy more dollars with their gold. Thus, wheat would be made cheaper for foreign buyers, which would stimulate buying of wheat here. This was essentially the same theory that the late Professor Warren sold to President Roosevelt in 1933 and that President Roosevelt naïvely swallowed with the same insouciance as Grant.

Gould exploited his conquest of the gullible Grant by exhibiting the President in Fisk's private box at the opera house in Castle Erie and aboard one of Fisk's Albany liners, entertained publicly by Fisk in his admiral's regalia. Then Gould bought seven million dollars worth of gold, sending the price up from 132 to 140. Thereafter he and Fisk, with certified checks issued from a bank they controlled, bought forty millions of the dwindling metal until they had driven the price up to 150. Gold became so scarce that business and banking were deranged. Speculators were ruined. Brokerage houses suspended. It was the greatest panic in

history on the Exchange. Then Gould got advance word that
Grant, disillusioned, was going to release government gold to ease
the panic. He secretly betrayed his partners in the conspiracy and
began to sell while they were still buying. Friday morning, pande-
monium broke loose in Wall Street and the Gold Room. Fisk was
buying frantically, pushing the price up to 162½, while his pal
was selling. When the government gold flooded into Wall Street,
the price of gold slipped back to 135. The whole market fell into
the worst panic it had ever known. Fisk and all the coconspirators,
including Gould, were caught in the decline. They had to force a
closing of the Gold Room through an order of their friend Judge
Barnard, to save themselves from ruin.

Once again the aging Commodore Vanderbilt was called in to
help the market with his wealth. He made loans of a million
dollars on that Black Friday to support the market. But it is not
true that his part in this crisis amounted to anything more or that
it played any major part in the crisis. After this, his battles with
the spider Gould and the peacock Fisk came to an end. Fisk himself some years later, arrayed in velvet and glittering with diamonds, was killed coming down the grand staircase of a New
York hotel to enter his ornate coach. His murderer was a rival
profligate named Stokes, suitor for the affections of Fisk's public
strumpet, Josie Mansfield. Old Daniel Drew, started on the road
to ruin by his two honor pupils in a bear raid on Erie which Drew
attempted only to be caught and squeezed out of a million by his
pals, was driven from Wall Street ultimately and died in poverty.

As for Vanderbilt, he became a legendary figure. He was easily
the first among the great money captains of the country. Greatest
among the industrial giants were the railway kings, and he was
the greatest railway king of all. He could not be compared in
intellectual gifts with Gould, who was, perhaps, one of the most
powerful minds among all our money barons. But Gould was
essentially a crook. His mind worked in crooked ways. He could
achieve only as a conspirator, a wrecker, a public enemy, medi-

tating and carrying out sorties and raids upon the public and private purse.

Vanderbilt was the richest man in America, worth a hundred million dollars. He remained more in seclusion. His very name was one to conjure with. He occupied such a position as only the elder Morgan attained a generation later.

———————————————— x ————————————————

Almost to the end Vanderbilt continued to give a general supervision to his vast interests. His son, William H. Vanderbilt—he of the long flowing Dundreary whiskers—assumed immediate charge of his railroad empire. But the foul-mouthed, blasphemous, and terrifying old barbarian held fast to the virility that had driven him forward. Men stood in awe of him. His son William never ceased to fidget uneasily in his presence. But he had more time to survey the infinite now, and his explorations brought him to the sanctum of Mrs. Tufts in Staten Island. The Fox sisters were still exciting the curiosity and wonder of the world since their discovery of the spirits thirty years before. And Mrs. Tufts was a practitioner of the dark art of communication between the Earth and the Beyond. The spectacle of this rowdy old pragmatist softened down to an evening at home with the shades of old Phoebe Hand and his departed son George titilated the risibilities of the hard-boiled gentlemen of Wall Street. But, after all, why snicker at Vanderbilt? For while he was fraternizing with the ghost of his grim and masterful old mother was not the far more astute and incredulous Sir William Crookes walking arm in arm with the spirit of a lovely female in his laboratories?

In the summer of 1868 Mrs. Vanderbilt died. The aged and bewildered former hostess of Bellona Hall received a state funeral worthy of a Chicago gangster. Horace Greeley and other notables attended, along with the thirty grandchildren of Sophia and the masterful mate she had never learned to stand up to.

About this time Vanderbilt's interest in spiritualism led him
into an affair with as odd a pair as ever set the gossips cackling in
that Age of Innocence. They were Woodhull and Clafin, brokers
and bankers, 44 Broad Street, actually Victoria Woodhull and
Tennie C. Clafin, two sisters who bore the names of husbands
who belonged to other chapters in their checkered lives. After
various shady adventures in other pastures they turned up, about
the time of the Erie wars, in Wall Street, where, despite their
complete ignorance of securities and money, they opened offices
as bankers and brokers. What is more, they made a howling success—$750,000 in profit the very first winter.

In the stodgy Manhattan of the 'sixties, when women still sim-
pered and fainted and obeyed their lords, these two handsome
and peppery ladies were feminists, suffragists, champions of the
single standard and of birth control, stockbrokers professing a
mild brand of socialism, and bankers functioning as leaders of
labor. They were vanguard persons. In the World of Yesterday
they became advance guards for the World of Tomorrow. Victoria
announced herself a candidate for the presidency and even
wore bobbed hair. Tennie C. was a section leader of the International Workers' Party and colonel of the Sixty-first Regiment,
which she equipped at her own expense and drilled. The sisters
published *Woodhull & Clafin's Magazine*, a weekly devoted to
sex, isms, and scandal. It got them into the toils of the law more
than once. But they were also spiritualists, and Victoria was a
medium. Since her third year she had specialized in visits from
the angels.

And, the old Commodore being a spiritualist and a perfect
reservoir of tips on the market, it would have been strange if he
had not made his appearance in the role of an angel in the drawing
room of the weird sisters in Great Jones Street. Indeed, he became
a constant visitor to both Great Jones Street and 44 Broad. The
huge earnings of these innocent girls were generally connected
with the Commodore's market clairvoyance. He was an intimate
of Tennie C., and rumor had it that no sooner was poor Sophia

cold in her splendid tomb than the amorous septuagenarian began making passes at Tennie. How far he got with that exploit must remain a subject of speculation. But he soon abandoned that chase and disappeared one day from his accustomed haunts. When he returned some days later it was to bring to No. 10 Washington Street, as its mistress, the young lady with whom he had eloped to Ottawa. She was Miss Frank C. Crawford, a tall, good-looking, and dignified Southern girl, about the age of his older grandchildren. It was a jolting blow to his family. But not one of them ever dared to lift so much as an eye in reproach to this imperious old householder on this or any other point. As for Victoria and Tennie C., they shook the dust of New York from their heels soon after. Well supplied with funds they went to England where, as might be supposed, they married men of wealth, Tennie C., now known as Tennessee, becoming Lady Cooke and Marchioness of Montserrat.

Commodore Vanderbilt died at No. 10 Washington Square on January 4, 1877, a little short of his eighty-third year. The great engine, subjected to excessive mileage, ran down. The deathbed scenario might have served for the passing of a bishop. The children and their spouses, the preacher, the doctors, and the new wife and grandchildren stood around and sang about old Daniel Drew's Lord. The Commodore's last words, so an admiring world was told, were: "I'll never let go my trust in Jesus."

During the later years of his life he had been profoundly concerned about one form of immortality—the immortality of the great name of Vanderbilt. He had erected a terminal station in lower Greenwich Village and adorned its façade with a $250,000 entablature—a bronze monstrosity of which the central figure was a statue of himself. He meditated deeply about his dynasty, and the empire of which the Central was the mother state. He was worth $105,000,000. He determined that this majestic pile of wealth should not be dissipated by his descendants whom the Commodore never rated very highly. William H. Vanderbilt, his son, who was managing his railroad properties, had won the old

man's respect. He therefore left to him property valued at
$90,000,000, while among all the others he divided the remaining
$15,000,000. To Cornelius, his wayward son, he left only the
interest on a $200,000 trust fund.

William H. Vanderbilt expanded this empire to a point where,
before his death, he confided to a friend that he was worth
$194,000,000. He, in his turn, but less severely than his father,
left half of that to two sons, William K. and Cornelius, and the
balance partly directly and partly tied up in a trust to his other
six children. The scions of William K. and Cornelius were numerous, but the chief heir was Alfred, who died in 1928, leaving a
hundred million. The combined wealth of all the Vanderbilts today
is probably as large as it ever was. But its domination of business
is far less. Numerous progeny have divided it. And the modern
technique of managing vast fortunes has tended toward diversification and diminution of control over any particular enterprise.
The Vanderbilt stock in the New York Central does not amount
to more than three per cent of the whole. Dynasties have hard
going against the erosion of progeny, laws, fate, and the times.
And in the Vanderbilt clan itself has arisen no one remotely
resembling that remarkable mixture of blood and nerve and
gristle and guts and audacity and intolerance, irreverence and
greed, who founded the fortune.

His was the golden era of capitalism. It began to wane a
decade before Vanderbilt died. What has followed since has been
a capitalist machine very highly complicated by speed mechanisms
and governors and brakes that hamper and foul it. Then there
was the free economic society—no government regulation, no
self-rule in business, no Sherman laws and ICC's and utility
commissions, on the one hand, and no trade-association dominance
and cartels, on the other. Competition reigned supreme. The age
of machinery had developed far, but manufacturing and farming
and commerce were still operated by comparatively small units.
There was an abundant mortality list and an equally abundant
birth rate in industry yearly. In farming, manufacture, and dis-

tribution, the production of wealth and utilities was carried on wholly by independent proprietors. The corporation, the chain store, the holding company, and the vast technological fermentations of the last fifty years had not yet been developed. A man got rich by producing goods and exacting for himself as large a share as he could by making laborers work as long as he could, paying wages as low as possible, and charging as high a price as the traffic would bear, usually powerfully limited by competition. His yield was pure profit, the difference between cost and price. The machine had enabled him to share in the product of a far larger number of men than during the simple handicraft age. But the wealth that individual men accumulated was moderate by present-day standards.

In railroading, the corporation had made its appearance, and there men like Vanderbilt and Gould and Fisk and Scott and, even before them, Daniel Drew were perfecting the mechanism of exploitation of properties through stock manipulations. This was a process that enabled the exploiter to make vast gains that did not come out of the property at all. It did not consist in making railroad profits and lopping off an unreasonable share. The object of the game came to be to lay hold of the savings of other men rather than their expenditures for goods and services, to entice them into stock buying, and by manipulation of the stocks to swindle them out of their savings. This was the technique John Law showed to the world and which came to be the characteristic of wealth getting in the age about to dawn. Daniel Drew did not calculate, as he would say, to grab the profits of the Erie. He was not concerned about the Erie making profits. And it made none. But he made millions just the same, not out of the people who bought passenger and freight service from the road, but out of the investors who tried to buy into its ownership through stocks.

This was a wholly new method of money-making. And when it was finally understood it became possible for men like William H. Vanderbilt, with little or no skill as a capitalist, to make fifty million dollars in a single operation or for Henry H. Rogers and William Rockefeller to make $39,000,000 in a few days in one flyer in Amalgamated Copper.

If there is anything in capitalism worth saving and if there were any who wished to save it, the time to have done so was in those early days when Drew and Gould and Vanderbilt began their experiments in corporate manipulation. From that time on the history of the system has been the invention of one device after another by exploiters to control it for the purpose of exploiting it, the struggle of one group after another to protect themselves from exploitation by further control devices, and the long battle of the government by still other controls to prevent or circumvent the controls of the private groups. The end is the encasement of the system in a framework and tether of constricting chains that are slowly destroying it and that have almost finished their job.

HETTY GREEN

CHAPTER VI

Hetty Green

THE MISER

— I —

EARLY IN 1833 a young man arrived in the town of New Bedford and went at once to the offices of Isaac Howland, Jr., & Company. His name was Edward Mott Robinson and thereafter he was the "Company" in that important firm of merchant-adventurers. He was a dashing figure, tall, erect, handsome, distinguished in his bearing.

On December 29 of that same year New Bedford learned why this romantic young stranger had been brought into the great house of Howland. On that day Edward Mott Robinson married Abby Slocum Howland, the daughter of Gideon Howland, Jr., who was practically head of the firm.

If ever this nation was money-mad it was in that decade of our history. Men talked about the Money Devil. The whole country was up in arms helping the redoubtable Andy Jackson smite that monster, who was supposed to be roosting then in the wicked United States Bank. But for all that, a French traveler observed that the "money devil may be found sitting in state upon his altars in all the towns of these states with large numbers of the population bowed down in adoration before him." Speculation ran wild. Men gambled their time, their fortunes, their lives in pursuit of quick riches. And then, as now, one of the most romantic of all the gambles was the oil business. But the oil business of that day was carried on not with the drill but with the harpoon. Men bored for oil not in the rocks but in the blubber of the whale. Whale oil was the light of the world. New Bedford was the Mecca of whale oil. And the Howlands were its prophets.

The house of Isaac Howland, Jr., & Company was formed in
1811. The Howlands had been in and around New Bedford since
1621. From the first they possessed the secret of making money.
By 1833 they had not merely acquired great wealth; they compelled an unquestioning recognition as the peak of the very upper
crust of New Bedford aristocracy. The Howlands were to New
Bedford what the Cabots were to Boston. Theirs was not a codfish
aristocracy. Their Brahminism was founded upon a bigger fish.
For fifty years they sent out a fleet of more than thirty fine whaling craft. For fifty years they wreaked upon the whale the vengeance of the faithful for its treatment of Jonah, and waxed fat.
And in 1833 when young Robinson entered the business and the
family, the Howlands were on the way to supplying America with
some of its first crop of millionaires.

Robinson himself was a patrician of unmistakable caliber. Like
the Howlands, he was a devout Quaker. He hailed from Providence. His grandfather had been a justice of the Supreme Court
of Rhode Island. His great-grandfather had been speaker of the
Colonial Assembly and deputy royal governor. He himself had a
fancy for commerce. And his subsequent career confirmed the
wisdom of this fancy. He became quickly a man of the first
importance in New Bedford.

A year later, upon a very windy November day, a horseman
galloped up to the counting room of Isaac Howland, Jr., & Company with a message for Mr. Robinson. He was to come home at
once. His lady had just been delivered of an infant. Boy or girl?
A girl, replied the messenger. A brief shade passed over the brow
of the new father. The house of Howland and the house of Robinson needed a son. Had this been a boy, Mr. Robinson would
have leaped upon his horse and hurried to his home. As it was
he arranged the papers on his desk very carefully, adjusted his
greatcoat with deliberation, put his high hat on his head at the
proper angle, looked it all over in the long wall mirror, and
trotted off to behold his daughter. In his wife's room he looked

with interest at the infant who had just entered this money-mad world. A girl! Well, there was no help for it. Better luck next time. Meantime this child must be named. And so they called her Hetty—Hetty Howland Robinson, to be known in later years to all the world as Hetty Green, the richest woman on earth, and the strangest.

In eighteen months the house of Robinson had better luck. A boy was born. And when this happened little Hetty was bundled off to the home of her grandfather, Gideon Howland, Jr., under the care of her maiden aunt, Sylvia Ann Howland. For some unknown reason, that continued to be her home. She went occasionally to her mother's and sometimes her mother visited her. But always Aunt Sylvia Ann was her mother in fact. Even after the baby brother died in infancy she continued under her aunt's roof. It is probable that her mother was an invalid and unequal to the task of rearing this strong, vigorous child. Then too there is some reason to believe that this frail Abby Slocum did not get along so well with her imperious spouse.

As Robinson grew older he became more immersed in his business and his investments. He got a kind of local reputation for greed—very genteel greed, of course, not dusty and squalid and ugly like Miss Hetty's in later life. But enough, all the same, to make someone say in New Bedford that he "squeezed a dollar until the eagle screamed." It is a local tradition that this was the origin of that famous phrase. Meantime Gideon Howland, Jr., was growing older. His eyesight was failing. He had difficulty reading his New York newspaper and its financial and trade news. And so each day he took his seat by the fireside and his little granddaughter Hetty would read to him all the business and financial news. In a little while she astonished friends by quoting prices on bonds and stocks and furnishing bits of business news in the shop talk that went on in Gideon's home.

It is an odd fact that financial geniuses display great precocity. John D. Rockefeller made an original discovery of interest on money at ten. He was a man of wealth at twenty-five. Russell Sage was a successful wholesaler at twenty-three. J. P. Morgan, Andrew Carnegie, Edward Harriman, all revealed their talents for profit at an early age.

One day a little girl of eight years walked into one of the banks in New Bedford. This was before the masses had been invited into the banks. The bank was the rendezvous for the dollars of the well to do and the adult. But this little girl was the daughter of Edward Mott Robinson, and so the bank president patted her benignly on the head and asked what she wanted. She wanted to open a bank account. And she did open it there and then. This she had done of her own accord and without consulting anyone at her home.

In the grim, relentless Hetty Green of mature life there was no suggestive remnant of the merry, handsome girl of those New Bedford years. At first she had a governess. Later she was sent to Eliza Wing's boarding school in Sandwich, where the prosperous Quakers sent their daughters. After that she went to Miss Lowell's select school in Boston. She loved singing and dancing and while in Boston lived as gaily as any girls in that period. But at home, under the severe eye of her pious Quaker aunt, she wore her plain gray frock and her leaden-colored bonnet.

It was because of the severity of this devout home that Hetty loved to go to New York. There she attended social functions at the homes of the Aspinwalls, the Rhinelanders, the Astors. Her father's growing wealth and social position made for her an easy entry into the most exclusive circles. Her own bright, vivacious conversation made her a companion much sought after. Moreover, she enjoyed the prospect of great wealth. Later many recalled her as a young woman of stately carriage, high color, and a wealth of glorious hair.

But already she was beginning to display those traits of personal economy—even parsimony—that characterized her later in life. Once, on a protracted visit to New York, her father sent her $1200 to buy clothes. When she returned to New Bedford she still had $1000 of it to put into her bank account.

In February, 1860, her mother died. This event brought Hetty her first money and her first serious family quarrel. Her mother had inherited $40,000 from her grandfather, Isaac Howland. This sum had been put in trust for her. When she died there arose the question of how the estate should be divided. A Boston lawyer wrestled with the problem and held that the personal property should go to the husband, Mr. Robinson, the real estate to the daughter, Hetty Robinson. But when the estate was inventoried it was found the personalty amounted to $120,000 and the realty to only $8000. Hetty and her Aunt Sylvia felt deeply aggrieved at this. It was the beginning of a coolness between Aunt Sylvia and Hetty's father.

The father decided to move to New York and its larger fields. Hetty remained with her aunt who compensated her for the loss of her inheritance by a present of $20,000 in stock. This was the beginning of her fortune. But in 1863 her father requested her to come to New York. She accordingly said good-by to Aunt Sylvia, her old home, her Quaker friends, and to New Bedford, now at the top of its prosperity as the center of the whaling industry. Henceforth her home was to be in the great city whose financial purlieus she was to haunt for the next half century.

II

On June 14, 1865, while the nation was still draped in black for the death of Abraham Lincoln, Edward Mott Robinson died in New York City. The next day, and while her father's body was still lying in its coffin, Miss Hetty Robinson sent the following note to the men in charge of his office:

GENTLEMEN: I have to request that you will answer any questions that Mr. E. H. Green may put to you on all matters about my father's business affairs. I wish you gentlemen to consult with Mr. Green on all matters of importance where advice is required.

HETTY H. ROBINSON

Behind this cold epistle lay a story that has never been fully explained. Early in June Mr. Robinson became ill. He feared death to be imminent and sent for his daughter, who was away at the time. When she arrived he demanded to see her alone.

"I have been murdered," he said. His life was ebbing fast and he spoke in quick, feeble gasps. "I have been poisoned by a band of conspirators. You will be next. Watch over yourself."

He added that she was to receive his entire fortune and that Edward H. Green and Henry Grinnell were to be his executors. He told her also, according to her story, all the details of the conspiracy against his life. Then he closed his eyes and died.

Was there any truth in this? Or was this just the fevered delusion of a dying man? Hetty Robinson believed it. Not only that, but to her dying day this weird revelation continued to exercise a powerful influence over her life.

In a few days Mr. Robinson's will was opened. Her father's fortune was indeed left to her. But to her amazement and chagrin only one million dollars was given to her outright. The balance, supposed to be about four million dollars, was put in a trust for her. Instead of Green and Grinnell, two others, employees in her father's office—clerks, she called them—were named as executors and trustees. Her acceptance of her father's dying accusations now became complete.

But she was now worth a million dollars. And as she escorted her father's body to New Bedford for burial beside her mother, her mind was torn between her plans for investing her new fortune and the terrors inspired by the tale of the plot her father had related.

Hardly had Miss Hetty returned to New York when she was shocked by the news of the death of her Aunt Sylvia Ann, just three weeks after her father's death. Sylvia Ann Howland was one of the richest women in America. Her fortune was not less than two million dollars. She had always declared she would leave her whole estate to her niece Hetty. Now Hetty hurried to New Bedford. She wondered if this could be another chapter in the plot first to concentrate her father's and her aunt's wealth in her person and then assassinate her.

At Sylvia Ann's funeral the relatives swarmed like the Chuzzlewits at the pretended deathbed of old Martin. The place was overrun with doctors and nurses and neighbors. Among them all Hetty Robinson, usually robust and full of color, presented a picture of consuming worry. She was haggard, pale, weary. The alarm that had eaten at her heart since her father's death was now intensified almost to consternation. One of her aunt's doctors, strangely deficient in tact, commented to her on her condition, which he attributed to grief.

"If you continue like this, Miss Robinson," he observed, "you will not live a year."

Some close relatives with their heads together in a little group talked of the dead woman's fortune and her will.

"We are to get everything when Hetty dies," one whispered. "When that happens we are going to add a greenhouse to this place."

Hetty, standing beside them unseen, heard this. That night she crept up to a storeroom of the old house, locked the door, piled the furniture around so as to conceal a bed on the floor, and slept there until morning. For days she repeated this. She refused to eat a morsel prepared for her by any other hand than her own.

When Sylvia Ann Howland's will was offered for probate Hetty Robinson's terror was changed in an instant to rage. Half of the good lady's fortune was given away to civic and charitable institutions and to numerous relatives. The other half was left to Hetty but, like her father's fortune, was tied up in a trust.

She immediately protested the probate of the testament. But the evidence of its authenticity was so complete that she withdrew her appearance and the will was admitted by the court. This, however, was but the beginning of this suit, one of the most famous will cases in the annals of the American courts. A month later Miss Robinson appeared with another will which she demanded should be put into effect. This rambling, half-illiterate document bequeathed all her property to her niece "as freely as my father gave it to me," all "except about $100,000 in presents to my friends and relations." Then it revoked all wills "made by me before or *after this one.*" The testator then declared that she gave this document to her niece so that she might show it in the event a will "appears made without notifying her and without returning her will to her as I have promised to do. I implore the judge to decide in favor of this will as nothing would induce me to make a will unfavorable to my niece; but being ill and afraid, if any of my caretakers insisted on my making a will, to refuse, as they might leave me or be angry."

Along with this document Hetty Robinson offered the following explanation. Her aunt was determined that Hetty's father, living at the time this will was made, should never receive any more of the Howland fortune. She therefore proposed to Hetty that she, Sylvia, would make a will leaving all to Hetty if Hetty would in turn make her will leaving all to Sylvia. Hetty agreed to this, whereupon the above testament was made. Hetty in turn gave a similar will to her aunt. She now asserted that this amounted to a contract and she called on the court to enforce performance of it.

The case presented some novel points of law that we need not notice. To the people of New Bedford it involved one all-engrossing question—did Hetty Robinson forge this document?

The case became a *cause célèbre*. It dragged along for two years. The testimony filled a thousand pages. It consumed $150,000 in costs. Among the expert witnesses called were Dr. Oliver Wendell Holmes, Professor Louis Agassiz, and Professor Benjamin Peirce, the celebrated mathematician. Handwriting experts were called on both sides. Some pronounced the newly discovered will an obvious forgery. Others declared the alleged signature of Miss Sylvia Ann Howland genuine.

Did Hetty Robinson forge that will? The court never answered the question. The case of Sylvia Ann Howland's remarkable will was disposed of on a purely technical point. But Hetty lost her suit. She never got over the defeat. It was the beginning of a lifelong hatred for lawyers. It was also the beginning of a long life of endless litigation about an infinite variety of things ranging from a two-dollar tax bill to suits involving millions. It served also to introduce her to the American newspaper-reading public, before whom she was to remain for another half century. She never forgave any of the parties to the suit.

In spite of her defeat, however, she was the possessor of a million dollars in cash from her father and several more millions in trust from her father's estate and her aunt's. Compared to the monumental fortune she reared on this foundation this was a modest start. But she was, in fact, already one of America's richest women.

Now began that remarkable career of investment and money-making which has been equalled by no other woman who ever lived and by few men. But also there took form in her heart that enduring and consuming bitterness that pervaded her whole life, that filled it at times with gloom, that led her into all sorts of strange meannesses and ruthless quests after revenge, and that in the end raised up in her mind a kind of mania of persecution. All her life she believed her father was murdered, that her aunt was murdered by the same hands, and that her relatives, bound together in a persistent plot, were resolved to murder her.

III

On the eve of Saint Valentine's Day in the year 1865, a gentleman named Edward H. Green, a bachelor of wealth, sat down in his apartment to write some letters. Among other things he put a valentine into an envelope. Then he made a check in payment for a suit of clothes—a very cheap suit of clothes, although this bachelor was a man of large means—and put that in another envelope. Then, getting his envelopes mixed, he addressed the one with the valentine to his tailor. The one containing the check he addressed to the lady of his heart—Miss Hetty Howland Robinson.

Mr. Green was weary of his lonely life. He was now forty-four years old. Only a short while before he had met Miss Robinson and he launched at once a violent attack upon her heart. She had hesitated at first, not from coyness. She was now thirty-one years old and her practical, unsentimental nature held her back from precipitate investment—unconsidered investment of any sort.

However, when the envelope containing the check intended for the tailor arrived, she was completely overcome. Here was a man worth a million dollars who was so careful of his money that he paid the very lowest price for his clothes. What woman's heart could be proof against such touching economy, thus so artlessly revealed? We do not know what the tailor thought when he got the valentine, but we do know that Miss Hetty there and then made up her mind to accept Mr. Green. When her father was dying he urged her to complete her intention and marry Green, who would be a responsible helpmate in the management of her fortune.

Throughout her life Hetty Green employed a rather crude system of investigation before making any investment. She herself went to persons she knew to be the enemies of the man or corporation seeking the funds. Thus she learned everything that could be said on the other side. Then she bluntly confronted the applicant for funds with all the criticisms and accusations against him and asked for a reply. But apparently she did not do this when Mr. Green proposed that she invest her life and happiness in marriage. Had she inquired she would have learned that the tailor's bill for the cheap suit was a poor indication to her lover's real character. She would have been told that he was already known as Spendthrift Green. He loved at times to play the grand seigneur, a role for which he was well equipped. He was a large, portly man, standing head and shoulders above his fellows. He carried himself erect, walked with a brisk, decisive step. He was worth a million dollars and he was already known in Wall Street as a daring and successful speculator.

What Miss Robinson did know, in addition to the delicate intimation conveyed in the misaddressed tailor's bill, was that her suitor had begun life as a poor boy, though of fine family, and had risen to wealth through his own exertions. He came of an excellent family with its beginnings in early Massachusetts days. His father had been a merchant in New York and Bellows Falls, and in the latter town Mr. Green was born. At eighteen, with no other assets than his pleasant, affable nature, he became a clerk in the firm of Russell, Sturgis & Company of New York. He was sent to the Philippine Islands. He must have been an attentive agent and a good businessman, for in five years he was a member of the firm. He was making money. He put other irons in the fire. He extended his operations to the port of Hong Kong and made more money. When he came back to New York he was a rich man.

When her father died Hetty was already plighted to Green, and he remained by her side throughout the great will case, counseling and encouraging her. Just before the decision against her the pair were married—on July 11, 1867—at the residence of Henry Grinnell in Bond Street, New Bedford.

If Miss Hetty did not investigate her fiancé's character and habits among his enemies, she did not fail to observe one precaution. She required him to sign a contract under which his wife's fortune would not be liable for his debts but at the same time stipulated that he would be liable for her support. How this arrangement turned out in the end we shall see.

Miss Robinson's newly acquired husband had spent most of his early business years in the Orient. With his headquarters at Manila, he had ranged about China, India, and Japan, with his eyes open for profits. Something of the rover lingered in his makeup. And now that he was married, the wanderlust flamed up in him anew. He steered his ship for England and persuaded his wife to agree upon this course.

Mrs. Green at this time was filled with disgust at the stupidity of American courts and the villainy of American lawyers. It is possible that this mood aided her husband in bringing her around to this revolutionary change in her life. At the time, he was a large, impressive, expansive man, with grizzled Jovian whiskers, the sort one sees on the substantial gentlemen in one of Bulwer-Lytton's novels. It is quite possible that he cast a feeble spell over her mind and that in her own hard, practical way she was fond of him. At all events, as soon as the business of the Sylvia Ann Howland estate was wound up, Mr. and Mrs. Edward H. Green took ship for England.

Here they were to remain for six or seven years. Here some thirteen months after the marriage their first child—a boy—was born at the Langham Hotel in London. He was adorned with all the ancestral tribal names—Edward Howland Robinson Green—every one of them a patron saint who had made his million. Three years later their second and only other child arrived. She was called after her mother and her Aunt Sylvia—two female millionaires.

In spite of these domestic events it was here in London that Mrs. Green definitely turned her attention to business. She had a million and a half in her own name, perhaps more. She had a million in her inheritance from her aunt in a trust fund. She had several million in her father's estate also in a trust fund. There was something ludicrous in this collection of trustees set up to protect this innocent female in her financial affairs. Even her husband had been urged upon her by her dying father as a kind of protector for her fortune. What all her guardians did with their funds and what she did with those under her own control will appear later. Now, however, she went resolutely about the business of pounds, shillings, and pence. Very naturally, her first investments had been in government bonds. She was reading about bonds to her grandfather at an age when most little girls are reading about the three bears. Before she had left America she had already revealed her feeling for profitable investment.

The end of the Civil War found the country's credit impaired. The war had eaten up huge quantities of money, more indeed than the government could supply. To make up the deficiency the Treasury had done what governments always do in the same situation—it turned to the printing press and began to print money as fast as it was required. These notes became famous or infamous as "greenbacks." They were worth fifty cents on the dollar in gold. They dragged the market value of government bonds down with them. Here was an excellent chance for any far-seeing person to pick up government securities at half their value. All it required was a little faith in the nation that had just demonstrated in a most extraordinary way its ability to come through a terrific civil war. Looking back at it now, the recovery of the country ought to have seemed a sure thing to any observer. The war had given an immense impetus to the resources of the continent—coal, iron, oil, copper, gold, and silver were just being discovered and developed. But for all that, the nation's credit was at low ebb and through 1865, 1866, and 1867 Hetty Robinson bought all the government bonds she could lay hold of. Some she got as low as forty cents on the dollar. She knew how to wait out the market and buy bonds on the declines that occurred every time a gust of bad news swept the country.

When she got settled in England she continued this course, adding, however, an interest in railroad securities, especially Rock Island bonds. She became well known in the financial district of London. Indeed, she associated herself with a group of financiers and organized two banks from which she made large profits. In one year in London she made more than a million and a quarter dollars. In a single day she cleared $200,000. "I have made more money than that on individual deals," she said in afteryears, "but that was the largest single day's earnings of my life."

She was already dropping into those personal idiosyncrasies that marked her among women in later years. The habits of thrift that had expressed themselves in her girlhood were now hardening into a state of mind bordering on parsimony and meanness. She might have been a handsome figure now, in the full tide of her womanhood. Her features were strong but well formed. Her skin was clear and suffused with a rosy glow that persisted late into life. Her deep-sunken eyes were large and luminous, even brilliant. Her beautiful hair, combed in a severe part on top, fell over her neck in a rich roll of abundance. But these charms were all lost through her excessively plain and even homely dress. Fashion passed her by. She had no interest in it. Indeed, it may be doubted if she had any mechanism for the perception of the beautiful. Her mind was now engrossed with her bonds and her banks and with the small boy who trudged at her side wherever she went.

It was while she still lived in London that Mrs. Green found herself at the fork of the roads in her domestic life. One road led off into Threadneedle Street, the other to the London clubs and Rotten Row. The wife took the trail that led to Threadneedle Street, the Exchange, and the banks. The husband took his way along the road that led to London club life. This was the beginning of those two trails that this ill-assorted pair traveled for so many years and that came together in the end under such pathetic circumstances. Mr. Green, of course, took an interest in his fortune. He was by no means a ne'er-do-well. But he was content to instruct his broker from a pleasant lounge in a London club. His wealth was large and he fully lived up to the prenuptial contract under which he was to meet all living expenses. His wife was able to devote herself to business under what must have seemed to her almost ideal conditions—making great profits and spending nothing. She ruled her own finances with an iron hand. But she was acutely aware of the differences in temper, in tastes, in aims, and in modes of life between herself and her husband. She grew to dislike England, and when her son was still under ten she demanded that the family return to the United States.

IV

A few years after their return to America the Greens began living in separate quarters. There was no scandal about it. There was no quarrel. There was no legal separation. They did not become estranged. They merely took up separate abodes.

Thereafter she took an office in the building of the Chemical National Bank and gave herself up wholly to building her great fortune. And as this fortune grew the fear of assassination took deeper hold of her mind. She intimated more than once that it was this fear that led her into all the penurious ways she adopted to conceal, perhaps, her identity and wealth. But on every hand, in every dark corner, she saw the assassin lurking. She declared that in a boardinghouse in Brooklyn she found ground glass in her food. She lived for a while at a house in Hempstead, Long Island. One night burglars broke in. Mrs. Green insisted they were not burglars but murderers come to kill her. As she walked along the street one day a shower of bricks fell from a building on the sidewalk around her. She was untouched. Again the mysterious scoundrels were at work. On another occasion a huge block of wood fell from a house in course of construction. It dropped at Mrs. Green's feet. Another miraculous escape. Certainly whoever these would-be assassins may have been they were sorry bunglers. But her soul grew darker and she managed to infuse this fear of assassination into the minds of her children.

Some years later her son's leg had to be amputated. This she attributed to an assault years before upon the boy by her own enemies. Dr. Lewis A. Sayre, of New York, however, told a different story. One day a shabbily dressed woman with a boy whose knee was badly infected entered the doctor's office. The boy had bruised it some years before, she said, while sliding down a hill. She herself had treated the injury which remained an open and troublesome sore. Finally she applied hot sand to it, causing the flesh to slough off. Dr. Sayre, supposing the woman to be in dire

poverty, took the boy to Bellevue as a charity patient. Because
the injury had certain interesting professional aspects the boy,
with the mother's consent, was used for a demonstration at which
the doctor lectured to the students. After this Dr. Sayre learned
his shabby patient was none other than Hetty Green. He there-
upon refused to treat the case further until she paid for his services
and in advance. This she refused to do and never returned. Some
years later this leg was taken off.

Another blow was now in store for her. In the year 1884 Mr.
Edward H. Green sat in an easy chair in the Union League Club,
his favorite lounging place, discussing the very lively political
campaign then in progress between James G. Blaine and Grover
Cleveland. Presently a messenger handed him a letter. Mr. Green
read it, passed his hand over his darkened brow, and went out
of the club hurriedly. That night when the evening papers arrived
his cronies learned why he had left so hurriedly in the afternoon.
The brokerage house of J. Cisco & Company had failed. Green
was deep in the market, and the prospect of a Democratic victory
had caused a slump. He was called on to make good his obligations
and could not do so. His securities were thrown on the market,
and when all the smoke had cleared away, his fortune, amounting
then to $800,000, was swept away. The husband of Hetty Green,
who had been commissioned to guard her fortune, was bankrupt.

She resolutely refused to aid him. There is reason to believe
that she did pay his debts, but she would give him no money to
recoup his losses. Thereafter he did not have a penny. He was
sixty-three years old and accustomed to indolence. His outlook
was hopeless indeed, save as a pensioner of his wife.

She was a warlike spirit, and life now furnished her with plenty
of battlefields. She crossed swords with some of the most astute
financiers of the day and never sheathed her blade in battle. One
day the little Houston & Texas Central Railroad swam into the
news as a bankrupt road. Collis P. Huntington, of the Southern
Pacific, bought the stock as low as $10 a share. He proceeded to
reorganize it. The bondholders were asked to turn in their bonds

and co-operate in the plans. All the bondholders did—save one. That one was Hetty Green who held a million dollars' worth of this paper. Huntington tried argument, coaxing, cajolery, and threats. All failed. She threw the road into the hands of a receiver, forced a public sale, and collected her bonds in full. Thereafter she added Collis P. Huntington to her list of hatreds.

Sometime later, she was found to be in the market, gathering in Louisville and Nashville stock. The market woke one day to find that Mrs. Green had almost driven this issue into a corner. Later still, she did actually succeed in cornering the market on Reading, and the humiliated he-operators of Wall Street had to come with their hats in their hands to the financial ogress in the Chemical National Bank.

V

One cherished dream of her life Mrs. Green now sees blossoming into perfect fruit. Her son, Edward H. Green, the apple of her eye, is fairly launched upon his business career. Though a Quaker, he has just been graduated from Fordham College, the school of the Jesuits in New York. He has now finished his course as a lawyer, is admitted to the bar, and is ready for business. He does not practice law, however. Doubtless Mrs. Green's long career as a litigant and her hatred of lawyers has led her to make this boy independent of the breed. He will go into business. He will be his own lawyer. And he will be the richest man in America. She has been preparing him to be what all his ancestors have been for two hundred years—good business managers. From his earliest years she has taught him the meaning and the value of money. She has lectured him about his way of life. When he was graduated she called him to her office one day. She handed him a package. "Ned," she said, "this package contains $250,000 in bonds. Take it to San Francisco and deliver it to the address on the outside. But be careful it is not lost or stolen."

The first night on the train Ned sat up watching that package.

For the rest of the trip he kept it in his hands night and day. Finally with relief and pride, he handed it safely to the bank official to whom it was addressed. The package contained some canceled insurance policies. Mrs. Green had given her son a lesson in caution.

Reporters asked him what religion he followed. "I was born a Quaker," he said, "raised a Protestant, educated a Catholic, and by business I am a Jew."

She kept him near her for a while, took him to Chicago on several large real-estate deals, and initiated him into all the methods she employed in the management of her millions. At first he went into the office of the Connecticut River Railroad. When he was just twenty-one he was elected a director of the Ohio & Mississippi Railroad. When he was twenty-four she sent him to Texas to foreclose on the Texas & Midland road, a mortgage being due her for $750,000. He did so and bought the road in for his mother at the sheriff's sale. Then she wired him: "The road is yours. See what you can do with it."

He assumed the presidency of this defunct concern. His mother's heart glowed with pride when she could say that her Ned was the youngest railroad president in the United States. So far he had done only what she made possible for him. But now the breed of the Howlands and the Robinsons shone out in him. He made his residence in Terrel, Texas, and set about the rehabilitation of the Midland. In a few years he had made it the model road of Texas.

His mother never took her eye off his operations and occasionally she intervened with one of her characteristic gestures. In those days railroad officials were constantly pestered by politicians for passes. Giving free rides on her railroad tortured the soul of Hetty Green. And so she had prepared a little card, and whenever a politician or anyone else asked for a pass he received one of these little cards. It read:

MONDAY: "Thou shalt not pass." Numbers XX, 18.
TUESDAY: "Suffer not a man to pass." Judges III, 28.
WEDNESDAY: "The wicked shall pass no more." Naham I, 15.

THURSDAY: "This generation shall not pass." Mark XIII, 30.
FRIDAY: "By a perpetual decree it shall not pass." Jeremiah V, 22.
SATURDAY: "None shall pass." Isaiah XXIV, 10.
SUNDAY: "So he paid the fare thereof and went." Jonah I, 2.

What is more, her son had made himself a figure in Texas public life. He possessed a fine commercial mind, like his mother's. But he had also the genial, kindly suavity of his father. And before long the country was interested to read that the son of the world's richest woman was running for governor of Texas on the Republican ticket. Of course a Republican nomination was merely a kind of laurel wreath of personal popularity or a key to unlock a rich man's pocketbook.

VI

One of the powerful emotions that controlled Mrs. Green's life was her hatred of lawyers. To her dying day she would talk with anyone by the hour about lawyers. Once she took out a permit for a pistol. It was really because of her fear of assassination. Someone asked why she had done this. "To protect myself from the lawyers," she answered. "I am not afraid of other kinds of burglars."

Her favorite joke, that she would tell upon the slightest provocation, went this way.

"Why," she would ask, "is a lawyer like a man who is restless in bed?"

When no answer was forthcoming she would answer her own question.

"Because both lie first on one side and then on the other."

This hatred of lawyers grew out of the long series of lawsuits that had begun following her aunt's death and that never ended until her death. She was in incessant legal controversies with all sorts of people about all sorts of things. In spite of her conviction that all lawyers and all judges were scoundrels, no one in America applied for the services of these gentlemen more than Hetty Green. But the greatest of all her lawsuits, next to the famous will case, was the one that grew out of charges against the trustees of her father's estate.

It will be recalled that during all these years her father's and aunt's estates remained intact. Trustees administered them for her benefit. There was something a little ludicrous in this woman, beyond doubt the most astute financial mind that her sex has ever produced, having her funds in the hands of guardians who were supposed to protect her.

At all events, in 1892 the sole surviving trustee of her father's estate, Henry A. Barling, applied to the New York courts to be discharged from his trust. He rendered an accounting. And this accounting Mrs. Green contested. She made many extravagant allegations. She declared her father left an estate of $9,000,000, that she received only $334,000 income from the trustees, that Barling had been just a clerk in her father's office, and that undue influence had been used by him to get control of the estate. She went through the accounting with a fine-tooth comb and made innumerable objections to all kinds of items. The whole subject was referred by the court to a referee and thereafter for a long time testimony was taken before him.

Nothing could give a better picture of this remarkable woman, her appearance, her habits, her manners, her aggressive and imperious nature, her swift wit, and her withering sarcasm, than an account of this trial. At the time, the newspapers made it a matter of daily extended reports and got all sorts of vivid and entertaining news from it.

The referee was a little, round, pink-faced lawyer of the mildest type, named Henry H. Anderson. He returned from luncheon each day looking a little rounder and pinker than before. And invariably within half an hour after resuming proceedings his head would droop forward a little and he would sink into a gentle doze.

Mrs. Green herself was always in attendance and very much in evidence. At this time she had perfected that appearance of shabbiness which marked her for the rest of her life. Her dress was of the poorest materials, black but already revealing tints of green such as one sees in an old umbrella. A cape of the cheapest fur covered the rents and patches. On her head she wore a little bonnet held on with a stringy ribbon tied under the chin. This bonnet she had worn for ten years and insisted she would wear it for another ten. Over her whole person, her dress, her cape, her bonnet, and over her face itself there seemed to have settled an ashen dust that completed the utter destitution of her appearance. Behind all this squalor, however, was a spirit of indomitable resolution. Her eyes, steel gray with just a glint of blue, burned with the brilliance of black eyes and looked out with the sharpness of two steel points. The skin itself was quite pink and her mouth thin, but large, firm, and resolute.

Against her and representing the executor was no less a personage than the distinguished Joseph H. Choate, later to achieve world renown as the American Ambassador to Great Britain. Choate was a masterful lawyer. But he was hardly a match for the terrible figure he now opposed. Mrs. Green would address him as "Choate" or "Joe Choate," very much to the impairment of his dignity. She had known him as a girl. One day in a recess she was fulminating against him.

"That's little Cupid Choate," she said with sneering laughter. "Why when I was a girl Joe used to call on me and whisper little love tales to me. He used to call on another girl too, named Kitty Wolf, and tell her the same tales. We used to meet every Friday and compare notes. We called him Cupid Choate. But now I call him Cherub, because he isn't exactly a cupid any longer. He is a reformer now and his wings have begun to sprout."

Hardly had the referee begun to doze, when Mrs. Green would say aloud: "Look at that man. I'm paying fifty dollars a day for him to sleep." Whereupon there would be a laugh and Mr. Anderson would awake with a start.

She changed lawyers so often that the proceedings were very much delayed. One day she dismissed one lawyer, William H. Stayton, in open court. Stayton was her husband's lawyer also. He got up to address the court. She waved him archly away and said: "I don't want any traffic with you. Charles W. Ogden is my lawyer now. My son sent him to me from Texas. He's a good lawyer, too. He can beat Choate. He's a regular Texas steer, but I don't know whether he'll be able to live through this thing."

The referee complained that Mrs. Green, as soon as a lawyer became familiar with her case, dismissed him.

"When they get hypnotized, don't I have to change them?" she said. "Choate hypnotizes them. He hypnotized Stayton."

Another day Referee Anderson attempted to rebuke her.

"Hear that," she exclaimed. "He's mad because I said he snored last Saturday. Well, the only difference between us is that Anderson snores and I get nightmares."

Mr. Anderson rapped sadly for order. What was mortal man to do with such a litigant? Then a question arose over the books of the estate.

"The books," said the executor's lawyer, "must be kept at the office. This is not a small estate—"

"But getting smaller every minute," shot out Mrs. Green.

The referee looked helplessly at her: "There's no use, Mrs. Green, adding more—"

"Except a little money," she put in. "I'd like to see a little more money."

Later her lawyer, cross-examining the executor on the witness stand, said: "Don't you know that your fellow executor, at the time that letter was signed, was in a lunatic asylum?"

"It was not a lunatic asylum," retorted Mr. Barling angrily. "I've been there myself—"

"Why not?" interrupted Mrs. Green with a loud laugh.

"Visiting," added the embarrassed witness, turning red.

A moment later Mr. Barling's lawyer went to the witness chair and to look over some papers the witness was examining. The heads of lawyer and witness were close together.

"Look at that," snapped the terrible Mrs. Green, "a two-headed witness. That ought to be in a dime museum."

For months this travesty went on, lawyers, witnesses, referee struggling to push ahead and riddled by the machine-gun fire of Mrs. Green's withering jibes, while all New York laughed. The utter frustration of her foes came, however, toward the end of the trial when the referee's report had been made against her and the matter was being argued before the court. Joseph H. Choate was addressing the judge. He was picturing the sufferings of the sorely tried executor who went on with his burdensome duties under the load of Mrs. Green's incessant criticism and obloquy. He grew eloquent. He was sailing aloft along an altitudinous level of forensic pathos. Suddenly the judge, the spectators, and the lawyers became aware of Mrs. Green drawing a huge yellow pillow slip from under her cape, putting it to her eyes, and bursting into a violent burlesque of weeping at Choate's heartbreaking eloquence. The scene was so lugubrious that judge, lawyers, all broke into violent laughter that continued in ceaseless titters for the balance of Choate's address. The great lawyer for once was utterly crushed.

If Mrs. Green hated lawyers before this suit, she regarded them with a deeper and blacker hatred forever after. She had scored brilliantly on the entertainment side, but in the end she lost this case as she did most others. Almost all great financial figures have managed to get themselves into court a great deal. John D. Rockefeller was in endless litigation. But Rockefeller always won his suits. Mrs. Green always lost hers.

VII

There is a little double flat in Hoboken in Bloomfield Street—a two-family house bearing the number 1309. In the parlor of the lower flat are three chairs, a table, a couch, and a rug somewhat the worse for wear. There is an old vase on the mantel holding aloft some artificial flowers. Over the mantel hangs an oil chrome, and there are a few other cheap framed prints on the other walls. This is the living room of Mrs. Hetty Green, the richest woman in the world. If, as the Germans say, "true wealth is to have everything you want," then Mrs. Green, in addition to her money, is rich indeed. For this is all she wants. She has another home at Bellows Falls, her husband's native village. She goes there for a few weeks each year. In Wall Street it is said she maintains this as her legal residence in order to escape New York taxation. But her home throughout most of the year is in Hoboken.

One might see her any morning at seven o'clock closing the door of this humble home behind her as she leaves for business in New York City. She says good-by to a little dog named Dewey. She calls the dog Cupid. His name is Cupid Dewey. In the little tin frame on the door under the electric push button is a soiled card on which is written what purports to be the name of the occupant of the flat. It is C. Dewey. This is a grim mixture of Mrs. Green's sardonic humor and her terror. She foolishly imagines she is hidden away in this remote tenement. Everyone knows where she lives. However, she has other reasons for dwelling amid the secluded fastnesses of Hoboken. "It is the cheapest place to live I know of," she once said of it.

As she goes to the ferry she is indescribably shabby. Her old clothes hang about her as if they were wet. This is part of her disguise. Yet on the ferry everyone recognizes her. "There is Hetty Green, the richest woman in the world," is said a score of times every morning.

Once in Manhattan, she goes to her office in the Chemical National Bank building. It is on the second floor of the bank—a large room with heaps of papers piled all around. There is no rug on the floor and an air of bareness and age about the whole place. In her office she changes her clothes. She puts off the raiment of the beggar and dons a less seedy costume. But it, too, is faded, worn, threadbare.

Here at this desk she transacts her business. Here come bankers, brokers, corporation presidents, church pastors, men of all sorts who want money. Over that desk millions flow every week. The most imposing and stately gentlemen in America—men who live in mansions, sail the seas in yachts, preside over vast industrial enterprises, operate vast railroads—all owe money to the squalid old woman who lives in the Bloomfield flat and whose only yacht is the Hoboken ferry.

The meanest forms of economy permeate all departments of this woman's life. Her business is transacted on the same basis. One day she was in Philadelphia and wanted to get to New York before the close of the Stock Exchange. It was necessary to have a special train. The railroad authorities quoted her a price for a locomotive and one car. The price staggered her. She tried to bargain with them but they informed her the price was standard and could not be lowered.

"All right," she said, "take the car off the train and five dollars off the price and I'll ride in the locomotive." And this she did.

At Bellows Falls one day she wanted to buy a horse. The owner asked $200 for it. He refused to lower his price. She went to a person who had been a lifelong enemy of the horse owner. She got all the particulars of his life, went back to him, and shocked him by revealing what she knew of his past. She offered him $60 and he took it. Afterward she laughed, saying she would have been willing to pay $100.

In New York she ate at cheap restaurants where she was known to waiters as the woman who never gave a tip. But at Bellows Falls she went each day to the town shops and bought in small quantities just what she needed for that day—a quarter pound of butter, a few crackers, a small quantity of sugar. She could never speak with patience of the extravagance of women. Whenever conditions were depressed in the country she blamed it on the extravagance of her own sex.

One day she went to a real-estate office on Fifth Avenue. The office had advertised for several caretakers to live in the basements of tenement houses belonging to the firm. All day long, forlorn old women had been coming in applying for the job. When Mrs. Green entered the young clerk flew at her and cried: "No more caretakers needed! No more caretakers today!" Mrs. Green was not in the least perturbed. She replied in her soft, smooth voice: "I am Hetty Green. I came here just to talk over a loan of half a million dollars your firm wishes to borrow from me."

She was wholly without that frailty which Saint Francis so abhorred—the sin of human respect. And above all things Mrs. Green hated a snob. On her place at Bellows Falls she had a cow. One day a very haughty English visitor crossed the lot and was promptly pursued by the cow. Much upset by his precipitate and graceless flight he went to Mrs. Green.

"Madam," he said, "your cow has chased me across the lot."

Mrs. Green surveyed him calmly but made no reply.

"Madam!" he fumed, drawing himself up in all his disheveled dignity. "Do you know who I am? I am the Honorable Vivian Westleigh of London."

"Go tell that to the cow," she said quietly.

------------------------------ VIII ------------------------------

At a comfortably late hour Mr. Edward H. Green rises in his apartments in the Cumberland Hotel. He is an old gentleman now some seventy-five years of age. He is still a tall, erect, distinguished-looking man, with a portly figure. He has his breakfast in his room and then looks carefully over his morning papers. He does not miss a page, scanning all the small items. Now he frowns darkly. He has come upon some little note about his wife. He is deeply displeased at this. But for all that he reaches for his shears, clips the item out, and puts it carefully in an envelope along with innumerable others.

No one but his most intimate friends are permitted to enter this room. But many try to reach him. Reporters occasionally present themselves at the clerk's desk of the Cumberland. There is a good deal of mystery about the husband of the world's richest woman, and reporters are forever trying to get to him for a little chat. The caller's card is taken away and in a moment the attendant returns to say that Mr. Green begs to be excused. The card has never reached him. The attendants at the hotel are liberally tipped by Mr. Green to protect him from all visitors save two or three who are known.

When he is through with his papers he amuses himself with a book until about one o'clock. Then he dresses and walks leisurely to the Union League Club where he spends the rest of the day. There he meets his familiar cronies who can be depended upon not to mention his wife. He plays a hand at cards, smokes a cigar or two, enjoys the conversation of friends, has his dinner, and remains into the night when he goes back to the Cumberland, save on those rare occasions when he goes to the theater.

He is now a man of leisure living on a pension allowed him by the wife who had forced him to sign a prenuptial contract that her funds would not be liable for his debts and that he would support her. The allowance was not a large one, but it enables him to live at a decent hotel and support by careful management the wants of a clubman. But he never attempts speculation again.

There is, however, one fly in the ointment. His wife exercises over him a surveillance which is most distressing at times. He becomes aware of her unseen presence through inquiries made by her in the most unexpected places. Thus one day Mr. Green went to the Bureau of Elections to register. He learned that his wife had been there before him to find out if he had made a change in his voting residence. These investigations of his wife are the chief reason for his careful arrangements to keep out all visitors. Perhaps this once wealthy man feels a little uneasy to be the guest of the Cumberland and the lounger at the Union League while the bills are paid by the shabby woman in the Hoboken flat.

Meanwhile, Mrs. Green's fortune is rising. Her business is money—making dollars into more dollars. She was not a builder. She projected no great productive industry. Her business was to stand on the side and take her toll from those who were producers and builders and needed her money. Most of the great millionaires of this country have been primarily creators of wealth, dreamers of great enterprises. Rockefeller organized the oil industry, Hill created a railroad empire and developed a vast region, Carnegie put together that amazing system of industries that became the foundation of the United States Steel Corporation, Ford raised up a great network of wealth-producing plants that employ hundreds of thousands of men. Hetty Green never created a dollar.

Of all American millionaires the one she resembled most was Russell Sage. Her investments were made largely in government bonds and real-estate mortgages. Her speculative profits were made in the call-money market and in buying high-grade securities when the market was low and selling when it was high. This simple process, which everybody pretends to understand but so few follow, she began in early life when she gathered in government securities after the war. In Wall Street they would tell you that Hetty Green made her money through luck. But there was no luck in it. It was in following the obvious principle that Wall Street preaches and then ignores. She always insisted she never speculated. (It is odd how everyone fights shy of that word.) As a matter of fact she seldom bought anything to hold.

"There is a price on everything I have," she once said. "When that price is offered I sell. I never buy anything just to hold it."

This was in striking contrast to the investing philosophy of George F. Baker. When asked what he considered the right time to sell stocks he replied: "I don't know; I never sell anything."

"About all that can be said of my investments," said Mrs. Green on another occasion, "is that they have been carefully chosen and have turned out well as a rule. A fortune cannot be built up around a fixed idea or in other words without the exercise of just plain common sense. I buy when things are low and nobody wants them. I keep them until they go up and people are anxious to buy."

Then she added: "I never speculate. Such stocks as belong to me were purchased simply as an investment, never on margin."

What she meant was that she never speculated unwisely. After the panic of 1907 she said: "I saw this thing coming. When it came some of the solidest men in Wall Street came to me and tried to unload all sorts of things, from palatial residences to automobiles. When the crash came I had money and I was one of the very few who had. The others had their securities and their values. I had the cash and they had to come to me."

Her real-estate holdings were vast. She owned or had mortgages on an endless number and variety of places—great business buildings, palatial city homes, theaters, factories, hotels, livery stables, country estates, farms, ranches, undeveloped acreage, churches, and cemeteries. Once she decided to make a personal tour of inspection of all her real-estate investments, and it required two years of constant traveling all over the country to visit them all.

What she was worth it would be difficult to say. She always preserved the greatest secrecy about her wealth. She was equally secret about what she bought. If she was asked what was a good business to invest in she would reply: "The other world." One estimate of her wealth placed her New York City realty investments at between 30 and 45 million dollars. She owned from 40 to 60 millions in industrial and mining securities. She had from 15 to 25 millions in railroad stocks and bonds, about 10 millions in farm and other tracts in the Southwest, and another 10 millions in Boston, Chicago, and St. Louis real estate. Around 1900 her wealth was not less than 60 million dollars. By the time she died it had certainly doubled.

IX

And now on the door of the small flat in Hoboken the name of C. Dewey is still in the little tin frame. But in the frame just above it is another name. It is that of E. Green. This is none other than the expansive and genial clubman and former millionaire, Edward H. Green. He is now past seventy-eight, ill, feeble, weary. At last he has been brought down to the dingy level of his wife. His old apartments at the Cumberland have been abandoned. He is done with the Union League Club. He is too old and broken to go on alone. Now he occupies the little flat above his wife's.

It is difficult to say precisely what were the feelings of this self-willed woman toward this fallen man. He was really never quite out of her thoughts. Even while away from her she exercised a ceaseless vigilance over him. She was a hard woman. She was never swayed in her actions by watery human sympathies. This man and this woman, brought together in their maturity, looked out upon life through eyes so different that what they saw constituted two wholly different worlds. She had no patience with the things that attracted him. His loss of a whole million dollars must have tormented her soul. And yet there is some reason to believe that now as she saw this once strong and handsome man brought so low she felt a glow of affection for him. Their daughter Sylvia remained in Hoboken to look after her father, and Mrs. Green proceeded, as was her way, to boss with an iron hand the job of nursing him.

After a while, perhaps early in 1902, the family, doubtless at the insistence of the children, moved him to his old home at Bellows Falls. He was now a man of eighty years and utterly without spirit. His daughter now remained with him altogether. Mrs. Green moved her office to Bellows Falls and tried to stay there too. But it was a most inopportune time for him to choose to die. That was a year of extraordinary prosperity. A new race of daring promoters was in the field—the Harrimans, the Gateses, the Rogerses, and their like. Also a new breed of dangerous and brilliant radicals were on the warpath. It was a time when people of vast wealth had to watch their stations with ceaseless vigilance. William J. Bryan, Eugene V. Debs, Tom Watson, all pointed their fingers frequently at Hetty Green as the symbol of useless and parasitic wealth. Besides, the call-money market was running wild. Rates were going high, and there was big money to be made by sitting close to Wall Street. Hetty Green had raised the towering structure of her fortune so high that she had to be patrolling it always to keep it from rust and loss.

And so while the indomitable wife labored night and day with her far-flung interests, the shadows gathered around the man who thirty-five years before had been chosen to guard her fortune. Now, utterly broken in spirit, Edward H. Green died on March 19, 1902.

———————————————————— x ————————————————

The Robinsons and the Howlands and the Greens had all been precocious in the making of money. But they had displayed no precocity in love. The elder Green had not married until he was forty-seven. His son, Edward, remained single until after his mother's death, until he was forty-seven—the age at which his father married. Mrs. Green was thirty-three before she married, and now her daughter at thirty-eight was still unwed. In 1909, however, Mr. Matthew Astor Wilks, a clubman of prominence and a grandson of John Jacob Astor, approached Mrs. Hetty Green and asked for the hand of her daughter Sylvia. Mr. Wilks had been paying court to the lady for some ten years. But he had been always painfully aware of Mrs. Green's opposition to his suit. And she was not a figure to be approached upon an unfavorable subject with impunity. However, early in February, 1909, Mr. Wilks presented himself to his future mother-in-law. He was plainly getting on in years. Really his proposal could hardly be deferred longer. When he laid the matter before Mrs. Green her answer was characteristic:

"You are sixty-five years old, Mr. Wilks," she said, "and you have got the gout, if you'll excuse my plain language. I think Sylvia ought to marry a younger man. I have no doubt you will treat her well. But, to speak plainly again, I'd like an heir to my estate, which will be Sylvia's when I am gone."

Nevertheless she relented when she found the young turtle doves quite determined. The wedding was fixed for February 23—just ten days away. Mrs. Green, with her wonted vigor, proceeded to boss that job, too. As arrangements progressed and she found herself superintending the purchase of the trousseau—spending money quite lavishly—she experienced a strange thrill in this extravagance. Despite much secrecy the news got out and promptly the Bloomfield Street flat was besieged by reporters. The day of the wedding they were camped in numbers outside the house. In some way, however, the family managed to escape unseen, get into a hack, and drive to Morristown, New Jersey. Soon after the reporters discovered they had been tricked, they commandeered cabs, carts, milk wagons, every species of vehicle and attempted pursuit but without success. At the church of St. Peter in Morristown, with but sixteen or eighteen relatives present, Hetty Sylvia Ann Howland Green gave her hand to Mr. Wilks. Perhaps for the first time in thirty years Mrs. Green put aside her shabby old clothes. She appeared, radiant, in a new black-silk dress and with a hat, rather than a bonnet, beaming with red flowers and an ostrich plume. And she gleamed with diamonds. Always she owned diamonds. She bought them as she bought stocks, to hold until someone wanted them at an advanced price. Now they came in handy to adorn her at the wedding.

By the time the Great War broke Mrs. Green's health had begun to fail. She was then eighty years of age. In spite of her regular habits she had driven herself with work. Besides, her fortune was now reaching gigantic proportions. She had always scorned those modern innovations in office management for the control of details. She trusted few employees. All the threads of her varied and widely scattered interests she held in her own strong hands. The hands were tired. But she held on firmly and refused to rest. Someone asked her if she thought of retiring. "Retire!" she exclaimed. "Why should I give up work? I was never more capable of managing my affairs. Besides business has become a habit after so many years."

But for all that she began to reach out for help. Her son had already been summoned back to New York gradually to take hold with her of the reins of her interests. He had many interests of his own by this time. He was a bachelor of wealth and culture. Unlike his mother he had a whole collection of hobbies. Chief among them was flowers. His mother still had her little artificial bouquet in the vase on her mantel. At Dallas he had a huge nursery. He was an enthusiastic fisherman and organized the Tarpon Club of Texas. He was a yachtsman and owned a palatial vessel. He took up aviation and formed an aviation club in Texas. A lover of life, he was now called from all this in Texas to associate himself with his grim mother. She had formed the Westminster Company, giving him half the stock to assist in the management of her business. Later she set up the Wyndham Corporation to take over her real-estate mortgages and interests.

But she continued to be the directing genius of her affairs. In 1915, in the excitement of the stock market when the European war began to stimulate business here, she loaned millions on call at twelve per cent. She began to take an interest in stocks new to her. She worked ceaselessly putting her fortune into such shape that it might be least affected by the tax gatherer.

On April 17, 1916, she was felled in her Hoboken flat by a para-lytic stroke. She was eighty-two years old. Nevertheless she rallied and, after being removed to her son's home at 7 West Ninetieth Street, recovered rapidly. Her old hatred of extravagance flamed up in her new surroundings. To provide her with two nurses her son had to introduce them into the household under the guise of seam-stresses. Daily she got reports upon her multitudinous affairs.

But she began for the first time to sense that her own end was near. She looked this grim fact in the face without fear.

"I am not worrying," she said. "I do not know what the next world is like. But I do know that a kindly light is leading me and that I shall be happy after I leave here."

One day, on returning from a ride in Central Park, toward the end of June, a second stroke laid her low. In spite of this, her unconquerable spirit flared up anew. But she knew that death stood at her elbow. And she was quite unperturbed. The glittering mass of her countless dollars drew dim. Her bonds, her buildings, her stocks, her beloved mortgages, all now seemed thin and unreal. On Monday, as the first flow of dawn came into her room, she showed signs of sinking. The doctor was sent for. The weary countenance and tired, half-closed eyes presaged death. But her pulse was strong. The iron engine inside refused to be stilled. The doctor felt her pulse. "She will live out the day," he said, and left.

In half an hour Hetty Green, rid of her millions, her old, black, faded dress, stripped even to the soul, had gone to some other world.

She was laid in the cemetery at Bellows Falls beside the man whose name she bore and whom she had known so little.

XI

Mrs. Green's death was the signal for one of the most extraordinary spectacles ever witnessed in a probate court. It will be recalled that Mrs. Green had inherited a portion of her Aunt Sylvia Ann Howland's estate amounting to a little over a million dollars. This sum, however, was not given to her outright. It was put into a trust fund with instructions that the income was to be paid to Mrs. Green during her life. After her death the whole amount was to be divided "among the lineal descendants of my grandfather, Gideon Howland." Gideon Howland had been dead for nearly a hundred years. And now Miss Sylvia's estate was released for distribution among all the descendants of the old whaling merchant, and they had been multiplying with extraordinary rapidity for a century.

The earth seemed to open and cast up heirs. They came pouring as if answering the trump of doom into the Valley of the Last Judgment. They came from the four corners of the globe. The terms of the will had always been known, and this horde of claimants had sat about waiting with growing impatience for the passing of the almost indestructible Hetty Green.

Mr. William M. Emery, an accomplished journalist and genealogist of New Bedford, has written a whole book about these heirs and this famous will. In 1918 he found living 1478 direct descendants of Gideon Howland. The lawyers set up a genealogical bureau to determine who were the rightful inheritors. When the work was concluded Miss Sylvia Ann Howland's estate was divided among some 438 rightful claimants. This came pretty close to a socialization of wealth. Some got minute fractions, one heir getting one seventh of one half of one thirty-second of one forty-fifth. The curious reader with a flare for mathematics may figure that out for himself.

No woman was ever more generously provided with guardians than Hetty Robinson in her young womanhood. Her father left most of his estate in the hands of trustees. Her aunt left all of Hetty's inheritance in the hands of trustees. Her husband was selected as a prudent businessman who would aid her in managing that part of her fortune which was put into her hands. It is interesting to contrast the work of the guardians provided for this innocent, unsophisticated woman by the wise men of her race. The aunt's estate after fifty years was hardly a dollar greater than it was at the start. The father's trustees had actually achieved a shrinkage in his trust fund. Poor Edward H. Green was allowed to furnish no guardianship to Hetty's own money and as to his own he became a bankrupt. Mrs. Green herself took her original million dollars and turned it into more than a hundred million—two hundred million, some have said. Her estate was divided between her son, Edward Green, and her daughter, Mrs. Matthew Astor Wilks.

Interlogue Two

MISERS

THERE CAN be little doubt that Hetty Green satisfied most of the elements in the definition of a miser. Whatever other ingredients this definition ought to contain, certainly a French version—literally translated—is not amiss: "The love excessive of the silver for it to accumulate."

Love of money is a spiritual malady that runs through almost all the persons who are the dubious heroes of these chapters. A common observation about men of wealth in which their eulogists indulge is that they "care nothing for money," that they are interested rather in the things—with the emphasis on the good things—they can do with money. Rockefeller said he looked upon himself as a trustee of his money—God's trustee. "God gave me my money," he exclaimed. His great aim was to use it according to God's will. Certainly much can be said for the wise use which Rockefeller, among all his multimillionaire contemporaries, made of his money. But one may well indulge in a mild surprise on learning that all the stratagems Mr. Rockefeller employed in gathering his riches had the complete approval of his Divine Partner.

The insistence that these rich men "do not love money" is probably made to counteract the impressions made by those misers of fiction and the stage who rub their hands and drool in obscene glee over the little heaps of gold coins—"my little shining darlings." The dramatists, from Plautus' Euclio to Molière's Harpagon and the trembling wretch in *The Chimes of Normandy*, have estab-

250

lished in the common mind a fixed pattern of what the expression "love of money" means.

As a matter of fact, few persons, save perhaps some who are mentally diseased, suffer from the sheer love of the metal we call money. Money itself is merely one form of property. And what these rich men have in varying degrees of virulence is the urge of acquisitiveness—the relentless and forever gnawing appetite to add more and more to what they already possess. And this urge arises, not out of any special affection for the physical possessions, but from certain special uses to which they hope to put these possessions. They want power. They want security. They want glamour. And mixed up with this they have a special talent for accumulation which, like all persons who have special and strong talents, they love to exercise. They find the same delight in the patient, ceaseless planning and execution to make a profit as others do in winning a game of tennis, achieving a low score at golf, or managing large bodies of men in military formations.

All sorts of men want power or want pleasure or want acclaim. But there are all sorts of ways of achieving power, getting pleasure, and winning acclaim. Acquisitive men want the kind of power, the sort of pleasures, and the brand of acclaim that can be purchased with riches. All of them, incidentally, do not have the same acquisitive abilities and, of course, all do not want the same thing. Many of them do not want much more than security. They start out in life with little, or at least some of them do, and acquire much, not through any great ability as producers, but by dint of incessant, patient, remorseless saving and stinting. The miser, therefore, may be said to be an acquisitive man who shrinks from spending. He is a getter, a saver, but not a spender.

Upon examination one is impressed with the fact that most misers are not to be found in any sort of industrial or commercial enterprise, but rather in some business that has to do with the handling of money. The talent for business is not a simple affair. One man is a good salesman, another a good merchandiser, another an excellent manager of men, another has a talent for finance. The misers are usually found among those who have this talent for finance. In some it is great. In others it is meager and, as a rule, at least so I conclude, the misers will be found among those whose talent in handling money is meager.

When we have the man or woman with the acquisitive urge but no special capacity for making money by producing wealth or managing large enterprise, with a bent for finance but not very much talent in that direction, and all this coupled with a powerful element of fear—fear of destitution—we have the authentic miser. For then he supplements his moderate power to earn by an abnormal passion to save, to deprive himself and his family of the necessities of life even, to say nothing of its decencies, in order to accumulate a fund against the day of want.

Some years ago police entered the home of a carpenter in Brooklyn. The children had gone without food for two days. They had no shoes. Investigating, the police found a thousand dollars in bills in a small tin box in a pocket of the father's coat. When asked why he did not give some money to his wife, he replied in amazement: "Oh, no! I'm saving that." Saving it, doubtless, against the day of want—a day of worse want than that which was then in his home. Lady Gregory, the writer on Irish folklore, touches, if whimsically yet closely, the germ of this. She tells of the "Man who went beyond the hope of God." He was a poor peasant who had forty-four potatoes and who could expect no replenishment of his supplies for forty-five days. He reasoned that since there would be one day without a potato he would do well to fast on the first day and thus be able to look forward to forty-four days of safety. But, alas, he starved the first day. The fear of destitution, which is a normal protective caution in all healthy minds, expands to abnormal proportions in the minds of men and women who are not equipped to combat it by successful accumulation of wealth. It expresses itself in intense and even degrading parsimony. And a person who has cultivated this habit of parsimony for many years finds it continuing to dominate the mind even after wealth has been accumulated either through grinding savings or inheritance.

Daniel Dancer, famous London miser, might well have been supposed to be relieved from the terror of destitution when he inherited an income of several thousand pounds a year. But he and his sister continued to live in squalor, to find their food in refuse, to pick up dead bodies of sheep for meat until she died from poisoning as a result. Even then he found a reason not to incur the expense of a doctor. That would be interfering with God's will, he explained. What did he want money for? Not power, not glory, not pleasure. Only the unconquerable fear of starvation in the end. He lived in his wretchedness to an old age and willed his whole estate to a wealthy noblewoman who visited him in his illness.

A somewhat different type of miser was Thomas Cooke of Islington, of the early eighteenth century. Cooke was a miser with no wealth until he married the widow of a wealthy brewer. But his niggardliness remained unaffected and the widow is said to have died of starvation not long after the marriage. Cooke took no part in the management of his beer making. He continued to assure his safety, not by earning more but by stinting on all things. But in this case, unlike Dancer, he was fond of the good things of life, particularly of good food. He laboriously cultivated many friends, visited them much, hinted that their children would be remembered in his will, and thus got many invitations to dinners and excellent attention. He would, upon occasion, fall down in a simulated fit in front of a good home, would be carried indoors, given good food, would later call to express his gratitude and his determination someday to reward his rescuers, thus getting more good meals. Obviously he could have provided himself with an endless succession of good meals had he had the talent to apply himself to productive business rather than to those humiliating and cheap schemes for getting what was so cheap in those days. He would, when ill, put on rags and call on some benevolent doctor for aid. This will recall Hetty Green's delivery of her son into the hands of a free clinic to be the subject of a lecture because of an infected leg, and her refusal to pay a doctor when the clinic physicians discovered who she was, the whole story ending with the loss of her son's leg. Cooke left a fortune of $650,000 entirely to charity when he died at the age of eighty-six.

Of course, these attributes of the miser assume different shades and degrees of meanness. Russell Sage of New York and John Elwes of Southwark, England, were not wholly unlike, save that Sage was probably softened somewhat by his unusual wife. Sage was a character who combined both avarice and parsimony. He was what Wall Street called a skinflint. Although at his death he left an estate of $66,000,000, he lived with the greatest frugality, haggled and bargained, never took a vacation, quarreled with the poor apple woman in Wall Street about the price of her apple, and angrily bargained like an Oriental peddler with the candy man near Trinity Church for a small reduction in price on a slightly soiled bar of chocolate.

He began as a wholesaler, made money as a youth, was elected an alderman of Troy and later to Congress. He made a lot of money as an alderman unloading a local railway on the city of Troy and later is said to have got for himself a large haul when as a banker he settled with his depositors in depreciated paper, taking the currency for himself. He went into Wall Street, which he haunted as a moneylender, speculator, and most of all as a dealer in puts and calls for many decades, about the same time that Hetty Green moved like a witch through its shadows.

Sage lived in a modest, yet decent home, was a devoted husband, and was undoubtedly rescued from more debasing meannesses through the influence of his wife. It is said that she even induced him on one occasion to make a gift of $100,000 to some school. He was coldly and cruelly avaricious. If he was not as miserly as the wretched Dancer or the shabby Cooke, it was because he did possess what they did not have, an extraordinary capacity for making money.

Elwes, in London, did not descend to the same coarse levels of meanness as Cooke because he, too, had never known poverty, having inherited a fortune from his father at the age of four. He came of a family of miserly folk and was congenitally grasping, mean, and stingy. Like Sage, he went into politics, being elected to Parliament for several terms. Like Sage, he could be guilty of an occasional generosity—he made a number of loans to needy colleagues in the House. But, though having an estate of over two million dollars, he lived in a small country seat, kept but a single servant, never traveled in a coach or entered a hotel, riding instead on horseback, detouring through muddy roads to escape the toll gate, slept by the roadside, and, when in London, occupied, instead of a hotel, whatever house or room he could find among his numerous properties, got up early in the morning to walk out a great distance to buy his meat cheap at the farms. When he died he left an estate of $4,000,000.

Such a man as the Duke of Marlborough had in him some of the ingredients of the miser, but they were restrained by certain other qualities, such as his enormous interest in military science and his ambition for power. He lived in a state befitting his rank, but both he and his wife were guilty of an endless number of petty meannesses that in the end lost for them practically every friend they had.

Hetty Green, unlike most misers, had an extraordinary genius for making money out of money, pursuing relentlessly the cruelest bargains, squeezing the highest interest rates through the devious methods of discounts and fees, watching the market with catlike patience for its high points and its low points—buying, as she said, low and selling high. But she took an almost fiendish delight in the power she acquired over men who called themselves rich and powerful and who strode about the world in grandeur while she lived in a dismal flat in Hoboken. But she was pursued by the haunting fear of murder and of losses all her life.

But none of these persons engaged in industrial enterprises as producers of the wealth they craved. They depended wholly upon the scheming management of money.

———————————————— II ————————————————

POVERTY

It is not possible to talk so much about wealth without thinking of the reverse of the shield—poverty. There is a widely held, if hazy, notion that poverty is not merely the reverse of wealth but its deformed child; that it is Dives who has created Lazarus. There is another popular conviction that poverty is the creature of the machine age; that this blessed miracle of skill and power, the machine, turns out not merely our prized gadgets but our disprized paupers.

Certainly poverty is no new phenomenon. It did not come in with the machine. In all ages, under all forms of government, in all economic systems there has been widespread poverty. So far as the machine is concerned, the worst indictment that can be brought against it is not that it created poverty, but that it has failed to abolish it.

After all, poverty is not a simple disease. There is the poverty that arises out of natural causes—droughts, famines, plagues. There is the chronic poverty that afflicts large areas of society even in the most favorable times.

Throughout history poverty has been produced by two causes— the convulsions of nature herself and man's ignorance of his world.

The story of man's long and agonizing struggle against nature is the most terrible chapter of human history. Almost all the countries in the Old World and most of those in the modern world have been afflicted so persistently by famine and disease that the effect upon their populations has been persistent, filling up the intervals between disasters with poverty. The University of Nanking has made a table showing that between 108 B. C. and A. D. 1911 there were 1828 famines in China—almost one a year somewhere in that unhappy empire. One can understand why a polite salutation on meeting a friend in parts of China is "Have you eaten?" These afflictions have continued in our time. In 1920-21 the drought slew half a million people and rendered twenty million destitute. In 1876-79 the area devastated was 300,000 square miles and the victims from nine to thirteen million human beings.

These famines were caused by droughts, floods, swarms of locusts. Concentrated wealth was not responsible, though it may have accentuated the suffering. Man did not know how to restrain the vengeful hand of cruel nature. His lack of knowledge of the forces against which he had to contend, the rudeness of the instruments with which he worked, his merciless superstitions, his unintelligent social organizations—in a word, his ignorance—accounted for his sufferings.

Concentrated wealth may indeed have aggravated human suffering. An old Sanskrit chronicle tells us that "the Jelham River [in India] was covered with corpses during the drought and the land became strewn with human bones like a burial ground. Yet the king's minister and guards became rich selling stores of rice at high prices."

Agra and Delhi were scourged by a severe famine. The governor was Hemu. Of him Badaoni, a contemporary historian, writes: "The people died with the word bread on the lips and yet Hemu valuing the lives of a hundred thousand men at no more than a barley corn, continued to feed 500 elephants upon rice and sugar and butter."

Abdul Hamid, a native chronicler, writes of a famine in central India in 1628-29: "Men devoured each other and the flesh of a son was preferred to his love. The powdered bones of the dead were mixed with flour." The Mogul emperor, Shah Jahan, fabulously wealthy, heard of these degrading agonies with ten million dollars of jewels hung around his neck. The curious insensibility of the wealthy rulers to the hunger pangs of their subjects deprived these societies of the aid of the only leadership that could ameliorate their condition. That condition appalls the mind as we read the dreadful record of human degradation under the pressure of hunger, men eating cats and dogs and their own children, waiting like vultures around the scaffold for the bodies of executed criminals.

Men suffered this poverty because they did not know how to prevent or arrest the floods, how to irrigate their lands, or escape from sun-baked prairies to which they were chained by religion, how to prevent the plagues which wiped out in western Europe a third of the population at a stroke and, in cities like Vienna and Bologna, two thirds. This poverty was the fruit of ignorance.

But there is another type of poverty that is chronic in societies and is more nearly related to wealth concentration, though it would be a great mistake to say that this is its chief cause. It inheres in all economic systems. In simpler economic groupings it arises out of men's weakness, struggling alone against nature to win subsistence from the soil. The isolated feudal social islets depending on the limited resources of their small demesnes and their inability to exchange goods upon any considerable scale with others made the condition of almost all in the community one bordering closely upon poverty. In Japan we find feudal colonies starving next door to other colonies enjoying for the moment at least relative abundance. Seldom able to produce enough for the current year, they were without any reserves when drought or floods or insects interrupted production.

It is found in the world today as in remote ages. Louis Adamic, describing a community in the Black Mountain, Montenegro, writes:

Tsernagora is the same today as it was . . . a hundred years ago. It is as poor as ever. Rocks, rocks, rocks. Sheep, goats, scrawny cattle snatch up every blade of grass as soon as it sticks its point above the stoney bleakness. On tiny patches, few larger than a city lot, and most considerably smaller . . . growing corn, tobacco, cabbage, and potatoes, subsist from one to ten families. But how can they? The cruel and simple answer is that their wants, restricted by centuries of lack and struggle, are extremely small. Thousands of families do not see the equivalent of five dollars throughout the year. . . . Thousands of persons, especially women, live on a meagre piece of crudely baked cornbread and a little sheep or goat cheese a day. Both men and women, if necessary, can go foodless from two days to a week without thinking they are starving.

In the Dalmatian Highlands, Adamic found what he called a land of perennial economic crisis, sugar and salt undreamed-of luxuries, kindling wood at night their only source of light. Toward the end of winter, when food runs short, adults, particularly men, all but entirely refrain from food, strapping flat, specially shaped rocks close to the abdomen to keep the stomach from growling.

The responsibility for this must rest in a variety of sources—the sterile soil, the strange earth tie that binds them to these unyielding hills, the venality and corruption at the center of government. But most of all, populations are impoverished by systems of land ownership that herd swarms of men upon patches of land while great tracts are reserved for the wealthy.

The exactions of the landlord in countries like Japan—not to speak of the United States—keep the tenant farmer poor when he cannot possibly harvest a crop sufficient to keep himself and his landlord. The poor farmer, after paying his rent, has not enough left for subsistence. His lot is hopeless. But we will do well to remember that this is not the consequence of vast fortunes merely. Most of the landlords are small capitalists and many of them are hardly raised above the level of poverty.

In the larger groupings in the populous cities where the more complicated money economy does its mysterious work upon society, there is an inherent flaw. It reveals itself in a process by which portions of the working population are rejected as unusable. We hear much of our early insurance against this defect. Unemployment was eradicated by draining off large numbers of families into what was called our "frontier." It was so in Athens. Pericles found a frontier in the islands of the Aegean. Rome did the same, parceling out the lands of Italy until they were all gone and then dividing up the lands of conquered provinces.

But in Rome, in Athens, as in the United States, as fast as the social organization was emptied of its excess working population, the system went promptly to work to produce a new surplus. To express it differently and more simply, that is the way capitalist money economy works. Imagine a population of a million workers. Aside from occasional spasms of boom, that society will discard a hundred thousand as useless. If the hundred thousand are moved utterly out of the society by immigration, the remaining nine hundred thousand will soon suffer another convulsion of rejection. Another hundred thousand or more will be found unusable. When they are removed by voluntary or forced exile, the purged society of eight hundred thousand workers will soon mark another ninety thousand or more for rejection. If the frontier is big enough and other forces do not intervene, it will drain away the whole population, after which it will, perhaps, feed them back to the old lands or to new ones if they can be found. The figures I have used are arbitrary and chosen merely to illustrate the point.

This phenomenon finds its origin in the central flaw of the money economy—that up to now no one has discovered how, by healthy means, a sufficient money income can be distributed to all of the workers to enable them to purchase the product of the producing machine.

The concentration of wealth has something to do with this state of affairs, though it is by no means the only cause. Nor are the great aggregations of capital the only concentrations which nourish this fatal defect. Small fortunes may well be as deleterious to the system as large ones.

Nor are all large fortunes equally unhealthy. A fortune like John D. Rockefeller's, acquired wholly in wealth-producing processes, is by no means as injurious as a fortune like Morgan's, acquired almost wholly in parasitic functions. The Rockefellers, the Carnegies, Armours, Fords, du Ponts are associated with the creation of wealth-producing machinery. One may very well argue that they have all drawn from the product more than either their ethical or economic share. But in the case of the finance fortunes, they have been acquired by pouncing upon wealth-creating machines already built and developed, capitalizing them for promotional and speculative purposes, reducing the ownership factor to liquid form, and running that liquid form through stock markets into the hands of investors as a means of withdrawing from those investors large gobs of their money savings. These parasitic promotional fortunes are, as a rule, almost wholly injurious and do, actually, play hob in the jamming of the economic system.

Today, in highly organized modern capitalist money economies, the cyclical disaster takes the place of the hurricane, the earthquake, the drought, and the plague. It produces those acute rashes of poverty that break out in our cities and farms when the economic machine breaks down. But the problem of chronic poverty remains; it hangs on in the midst of great booms. It is beyond a doubt associated with the problem of the distribution, not of wealth, but of income, in which problem the man of wealth is a serious factor.

CHAPTER VII

Mitsui

THE DYNAST

I

IN THE PRIVATE museum of the Mitsui family in Tokyo there is preserved an ancient sign. It is the sign which hung over the first Yedo store of that Mitsui who founded the family commercial empire. It was hung out in 1673. It reads: CASH PAYMENTS AND A SINGLE PRICE. Two hundred and fifty years before Woolworth and, for that matter, a hundred years before that London Bridge draper for whom Robert Owen worked, there in ancient Tokyo was a cash-and-carry, one-price store in the bickering, bargaining Orient.

This was the store of Hachirobei Mitsui. He began his career as a boy of fourteen in a little Tokyo shop. He ended as the leading merchant in the Japan of his day. He must have been a merchant of unusual talents. For in that distant day and in that uncommercial world, he is credited with having introduced a group of mercantile innovations that American business-office essayists are fond of extolling as the peculiar fruit of the McKinley-Coolidge cycle.

He opened branch stores, at least six of them, before he died. He established his own central warehouse. He inaugurated profit sharing among his higher employees. He housed his employees in large, airy dormitories, carefully supervised them, and introduced several hygienic regulations. He used double-entry bookkeeping. More surprising, he was a pioneer in advertising. On rainy days his spacious store in Suruga-cho, Tokyo, would lend to customers umbrellas flaunting on their roofs the name of Mitsui. He used billposters proclaiming the name of Mitsui in large block letters. He subsidized producers, playwrights, and actors to work the

HACHIROBEI MITSUI AND HIS WIFE

Mitsui name and store into the lines of the picaresque dramas so popular in that day, thus becoming a sponsor and by two hundred and fifty years anticipating the radio "commercial" of today.

These striking similarities in the commercial devices of Japan and Europe—cut off from each other by Japan's guarded isolation and the length of two continents—were not the only points of resemblance. When Hachirobei Mitsui opened his first small store Japan had a feudal society. And the rise of that society, its evolving pattern, its disasters and disorders, and its changing forms paralleled closely the origin, rise, development, and disintegration of feudalism in Germany and France. Thus men, pursued by the same fears and needs and crowded by the same pressures, hit upon the same escapes, yield to the same messiahs, embrace the same panaceas. The desperate Nipponese in flight from economic distress and bewilderment follows much the same economic road as the desperate Teuton or Briton—from despotism to feudalism, to guilds, to the money economy, to the dominion of the merchant, the entrance of money, the struggle between central power and feudal estate, until finally the two-sworded lord who had not a yen to his name had to fall back before the million-yenned merchant who had not a sword to his name, and needed none.

The Mitsuis, according to the family's own account, belonged to the "middle-class feudal gentry" and traced their ancestry to a statesman of the seventh century named Kamatari Fugiwara. One of his descendants settled in Omi province and took the name of Mitsui which means literally "three wells." The name is associated with some dim legend of how that first ancestor found fortune in three wells upon his arrival in Japan—presumably from heaven. There, though noble, the family became a vassal of the powerful Sasaki clan. And around the middle of the fifteenth century a son of the Sasaki clan was adopted by the Mitsuis. Probably virility was running low and this youth, Takahisa Sasaki, was brought in for glandular reasons. He built a formidable castle on the shores of Lake Biwa in Namazue, became a leader of the Sasaki clan, and was known as the Lord of Echigo.

This feudal society, like that of thirteenth-century Germany, let us say, was split up into a number of estates or baronies—little economic islets secluded from the rest of the world. Over these baronies presided a lord, who was called a daimio. He owned the barony and wielded the power of life and death over its people. Between these baronial islets little or no trade flowed. Instances are on record of men dying of hunger in one daimio's demesne while in the neighboring estate the land overflowed with Japanese abundance.

Over all was an emperor who was a deity and a name, but with no real power. The power was in the hands of a Shogun, but not in that absolute way in which the later Shoguns exercised it. It was quite futile against the local despotism of the daimio. And as regards central power, whatever central power the Shogun had was operated by first one and then another group of daimios who shouldered around that dignitary and dominated his functions.

Some of these daimios were very wealthy. Mayeda, the Lord of Kaga, is reported to have had an income of a million koku of rice a year (a koku had the value of about a pound). Others—a large number—had incomes of 10,000 or more koku of rice. Many were just small plantation owners. The Mitsuis in Omi were daimios and, after their alliance with the Sasaki clan, wealthy.

Then in the latter part of the sixteenth century there arose one of the great figures of Japanese history—Oda Nobunaga, a kind of Oriental combination of Louis XI and Garibaldi, an able warrior who set out to bring Japan under a strong central government. Nobunaga declared war upon the weak Ashikaga Shogunate. In his path to Kyoto lay the demesne of the Lord of Echigo—the Daimio Takayasu Mitsui (son of Takahisa). He was no match for the doughty Nobunaga who was bowling over the recalcitrant barons with regularity as he moved on Kyoto. He destroyed Mitsui's castle, drove him and his family from their demesne, and ultimately made himself the master of Japan. His work was completed and consolidated by two other figures scarcely less important than himself—his successors, Hydeyoshi and Ieyasu. The latter

installed himself as Shogun and became the founder of the Tokugawa Shogunate, which ruled Japan for two hundred and fifty
years during the long seclusion era that preceded the arrival of
Admiral Perry.

As for Takayasu Mitsui, the dispossessed Lord of Echigo, he
fled with his family to Ise province, probably as insolvent as a
Russian duke after Lenin. He was disgusted with arms and war.
He resolved never again to use the two swords which were the
mark of his rank. His son and successor, Sokubei Mitsui, was a
peace-loving soul from whose spirit every last drop of romantic
samurai nonsense about the heroism of arms had been drained.
It was this Sokubei who decided to throw away his two swords
and to enter the merchant class.

The plunge from noble to trader was a steep one. In this land
of caste, the court families occupied the top rank. Wasters and
idlers, they lived in Kyoto, without estates or incomes, around the
emperors, supported wholly by pensions from the state. Next in
order were the daimios, or feudal barons. Then came the samurai,
the gentlemen who monopolized the military functions of the society and supposed themselves alone to be fitted to fight battles,
until the peasant armies of the emperor after his restoration chased
the heaven-chartered warriors of the Satsuma clan into speedy
submission. They lived upon the estates and served as the warrior
knights of the daimios. And in the two hundred and fifty years of
peace after Ieyasu, they were a wholly unprofitable charge upon
the country. Below them were the farmers. The next layer were the
artisans and below them the merchants, only a step above the
handlers of dead bodies—the slaughterers, skinners, tanners, un-
dertakers. It was down through this six-storied social structure
that Sokubei plunged almost into the basement. "With remarkable
fortitude," says the Mitsui chronicle, "Sokubei abandoned his own
class and enlisted on a commercial career as a brewer of sake."
Sokubei's fortitude was doubtless reinforced by his appetite, like
the aristocratic *émigrés* of Russia who turned up as headwaiters
and *couturiers* in New York and London. He had left only his two

swords. The revenues of his rank were gone. Ieyasu Tokugawa
had them. There wasn't much else for Sokubei to do.

He married Shuho, daughter of a tradesman. She is today more
famed in the family annals than he. She was a sort of Japanese
Hetty Green, a yen pincher and born bargainer. Sokubei became
a brewer, which means he set up a little shop and made sake and
shoyu from the soybean. The redoubtable Shuho opened a little
bar with a pawnshop attached, an excellent combination, each
department fattening upon the other. Sokubei died in 1633. But
Shuho, his widow, survived him forty-seven years, ruled her small
shop and her family with an iron hand, and died at the age of
eighty-seven.

When Ieyasu Tokugawa became Shogun he established his capital at Edo, a small, almost negligible village, later called Yedo
and now the six-million-peopled metropolis of Tokyo. The new
Shogun built an imposing, rambling, fortified castle expressing the
might of his rule. The new capital quickly attracted numbers of
people, and Ieyasu invited merchants to come to Yedo and make
a market. Curiously it was the men of Ise province who went in
numbers and almost usurped the trade of the new town. Among
these was Saburozaemon, the oldest son of Sokubei. He opened a
small drygoods store. When his youngest brother, Hachirobei, was
fourteen, his mother sent him to Yedo to learn his trade in the shop
of Saburozaemon.

There Hachirobei remained fourteen years. When he was twenty-
eight he retired to his native Matsuzaka and set up as a moneylender on his own account. Matsuzaka was a small town, and how
much Hachirobei prospered is not reported. But he remained there
until he was fifty-two years old. Then he moved to Kyoto, the home
of the emperor, and established a drygoods store. This was in 1673.
And there this Hachirobei laid the foundation of the Mitsui
fortune. The Mitsui family in celebrating the three-hundredth
anniversary of the formation of their commercial house chose
Sokubei's shop opening as the date. In a sense this was historically
correct. But Sokubei was a mere village alky cooker and tavern-

keeper. The brother Saburozaemon seems to vanish quickly from all the old chronicles. It is Hachirobei who is really credited by the Mitsuis as the founder of their commercial structure.

After thirteen years of progress in Kyoto, Hachirobei opened a drygoods store in Yedo, which was now expanding as the new capital. There he put his famous sign—CASH PAYMENTS AND A SINGLE PRICE. The store grew; warehouse after warehouse was added until the store occupied a large space on both sides of the street Suruga-cho and employed many hundreds of clerks. It remained there, operated by the Mitsuis, until 1904. Then the Mitsui firm parted with it and it has since been owned by a separate corporation called Mitsukoshi, the largest department store east of Suez and in precisely the same spot in Suruga-cho as that first store. At first the store traded in silks and other textiles, the brocades of Nishyin being one of its specialties. But gradually other articles of merchandise were added. In 1708 we find it establishing buying agents at Nagasaki to buy woolens, tortoise-shell ware, sugar, chemicals from Dutch ships.

Man is a groping animal. He feels his way bungling, one step at a time. And it is an extraordinary observation upon his development in the commercial world that almost everywhere he has followed the same steps. The scenes, the costumes, the manners, the cast of characters differ in different countries. But men in the seventeenth century were turning with surprising inevitability to the same financial and commercial devices in Japan as their distant and unknown brethren in the Germany of Maximilian and the France of Francis I, getting into the same holes and out of them by the same devices and into still other, but similar holes. I have no doubt that, if one day we explore the moon and find it inhabited by men like ourselves, we shall find they have invented stores and money, bills of exchange, promissory notes, banks, double-entry bookkeeping, debasement of the coinage, national debts to keep the moon's economy afloat, corporations and brokers and all the paraphernalia of the earth's economic life.

The unit of production was the estate of the daimio. He collected from his vassals and feudal tenants his share of the produce in rice. The rice was sent to Osaka to be exchanged for money or for other goods. The daimio consigned his rice to a broker—a kakeya —who offered it publicly and sold it to the highest bidder. In time these brokers formed an exchange. The buyer of rice was required to pay ten per cent down and the balance in ten days. The broker himself remitted the money to his client monthly. Thus he got the use of it for thirty days without interest and could do a kind of banking business. The buyer of the rice did not have to accept delivery immediately. Great warehouses were built and warehouse receipts were issued against the rice. After a while the buyer could pay his ten per cent down and borrow the balance from a broker or other moneylender, giving the warehouse receipt for security. And thus he could speculate in rice futures. A brisk trade sprang up on the exchange in these rice futures. And thus there developed in Japan a system of marketing rice like that in vogue in the cotton market in New Orleans and the wheat pit in Chicago. Indeed, in time the speculation became so wild, so violent, so upsetting to lenders, daimios, and buyers generally that a great scandal ensued. The government stepped in, instituted an investigation, prosecuted many brokers, executed several, reorganized the exchange, abolished margin trading, licensed brokers, and subjected the whole business to government supervision.

Hachirobei Mitsui opened a bank in or next to his store in Yedo and there became a lender of money and, perhaps, accepted deposits. The evidence on this latter point, however, is a little unsatisfactory. But he did become a kakeya, represented a number of daimios, indeed was the broker for several whole provinces. This business gave him an insight into the possibilities of profit in the handling of other people's money. And sometime around 1690 he conceived an idea that men had already experimented with in Europe.

The Shogun collected no taxes in money. All was paid in rice. Each district had a minor deputy known as a daikan who collected rice from the daimios. He shipped it to Osaka and sold it for gold or silver. The metal he sent to Yedo to the Shogun's treasury. This was an expensive trip requiring many coolies, packing, and great danger of loss on the roads infested by brigands. Hachirobei had stores in Kyoto, Yedo, and Osaka. He went to the Shogun's officials and proposed that he contract to deliver the gold or silver in Yedo within sixty days without cost. He planned to have the gold turned over to him by the governor of Osaka. He could then buy goods with it, ship the goods to Yedo in fifteen days, sell them for cash within the sixty days, and deliver to the treasury funds collected right in Yedo, thus doing away with the need for so much transportation of metal. The officials approved his plan and later extended the period for delivery to one hundred and fifty days. Hachirobei then had a continuous flow of Shogunate funds pouring into his possession and open to his use for exploitation for five months. In other words, he got a five-month whack at the use of the government's taxes before he was required to deliver them up in Yedo.

This became the basis for the use of the bill of exchange in Japan, although singularly Hachirobei did not apparently take this next step. Other merchants saw that the same method could be applied to the transport of money for commercial as well as government purposes. There was a flow of payments from Osaka to the government at Yedo. But there was also a flow of payments from Yedo merchants to Osaka merchants. Brokers in Osaka found that they could collect money in Osaka and make delivery of metal to a creditor in Yedo without actually shipping silver save occasionally, by balancing credits in the two cities against each other.

---------------------------- II ----------------------------

After the Tokugawa Shogunate got under way that powerful social chemical—money—began its slow work. Very little at a time, but very surely, the old feudal system began to lose its vitality, indeed to lose its way. Little by little the money system and all that went with it—the capitalist system—began to trickle over Japanese society.

Gold and silver coins had begun to circulate around 1429—in the Muromachi period. Goto Mitsutsugu began to buy placer gold and gold bars and to mint them into coins. Daikakuya minted silver into coins about the same time. Both grew rich. Some others followed suit. Also Chinese copper coins circulated freely. But when Oda Nobunaga rose to power he put an end to the nondescript and miscellaneous issuance and circulation of coins and conferred upon Mitsutsugu and Daikakuya the monopoly privilege of coining gold and silver respectively, so that these men became among the richest in Japan. As in Europe, men who had goods or services to sell preferred to be paid in money. Money began to have an agio, or preference, over rice. By the middle of the Tokugawa Shogunate, a Japanese philosopher wrote:

> The possession of gold and silver means wealth. The foolish are held to be wise and the wicked good if only they are possessed of gold and silver. On the contrary one who has neither gold nor silver is held to be poor. However wise he may be he is dubbed a fool. A clever man with no money is regarded by the public as a dullard. And a good man so circumstanced is looked upon as a worthless person. As all things, life or death, success or failure, depend upon the possession of gold, all people irrespective of rank run after gold as the first requisite of existence.

Japan was a country of about 26 million workers, a few hundred thousand samurai, and a handful of daimios. The daimio, to be sure, performed a function. He was the agrarian entrepreneur. He managed the economic producing unit—the estate or barony or plantation. The wretched farmers under the daimios were levied upon "so that they should neither die nor live."[1] All above what was necessary to the most meager subsistence of the workers was taken by the daimio as his share. He used that to get the things he wished by barter and translated as much as possible into money. The Lord of Kaga had an income of over a million koku, which seems large. But he operated a barony with a population of 586,000 souls and he had to maintain not merely the economic machinery of this vast estate but supply all the functions

---

[1] *Social and Economic History of Japan* by Eijoro Honjo, p. 79.

of a highly independent local government as well. There were about forty-five daimios with incomes of 100,000 koku or over and 195 with incomes of 10,000 koku or more. There were many whose incomes were so small as to be unimportant.

But the samurai rendered literally no service whatever. He was a professional warrior with no battles to fight during the long Shogunate peace. He assumed a heaven-sent charter as soldier. Yet in the many agrarian revolts during the Shogunate against individuals and groups of daimios, the revolts were frequently successful. The divinely appointed warriors, encased in magnificent armor, fled swiftly to the castle and sent out envoys to negotiate peace. There were 350,000 of these parasites, each equipped with three hereditary servants who had also to be supported. They made up a swarm of over a million who toiled not, spun not, but lived upon hereditary, stipulated revenues paid them by the daimio out of the produce of the estate. As they were persons of exquisite fancy and cultivated appetites, they were among the first to discover the potency of coins to purchase the things they liked. And as gold, silver, and copper became more and more the coin of the growing cities and as daimios and samurai sought more and more to translate all their income into coin and as the merchants and bankers invented new ways to increase the amount of gold actually and potentially by increasing its velocity through credits and bills of exchange and clearances, money came more and more to dominate the daily operations of the walled-in island.

Inevitably this began to increase the importance of the merchants who were gradually accumulating all the money, for the daimios got hold of it only to spend it again with the merchants and bankers. It began to trouble the daimios and samurai who became borrowers, who learned how to spend this year the income of next year and to add to the other burdens of administration the burden of interest.

Some of these were thrifty gentlemen who knew how to adjust themselves to the new order of things. Thus it is recorded that the daimio Tsushima, who had a small barony with an income of only

20,000 koku, bought Korean ginseng and other articles at low prices, sold them at a good profit, and was better off than a daimio with 200,000 koku. In short, the noble gentleman became in effect a merchant. The daimio of Matsumae with an income of only 7000 koku sold the products of his own and another fief—Ezo—and lived equally to a daimio with an income of 50,000 koku, while another, Tsuwano, with 40,000 koku, turned manufacturer and made pasteboard, with a resulting income of 150,000 koku.

But many of the daimios went from debt to debt, living in a state of continual emergency. Samurai were most severely hit. For they were continually borrowing from the town moneylenders, pledging as security their stipends from the daimios. Ultimately they became hopelessly and helplessly involved in debt and reduced to a state of grave poverty. Many of them drifted into the towns and turned to manual chores for a living, while others, putting the high ethics of the knight under foot, turned to such forms of graft as their special and various connections made possible.

In this way the claims upon the income of the nation were being reshuffled. Before plowing and harvesting time came around, the daimio had a claim upon the product of the labor of every workman or feudal tenant who lived upon his land. The samurai had a claim upon a part of the daimio's share. And the government had a claim upon both. But now the merchant moneylender—the lowly *chonin* —was establishing claims upon the income of the daimio and the samurai who owed them money. And slowly the money supplies of the country were being drained off into the hands of these traders and moneylenders through the processes of interest and profit. The samurai were being ruined, many of them declassed. The daimios—most of them—were being impoverished. The workers beneath them all were being driven to desperation by the taxes and other exactions wrung from the fruits of their labor. The merchants were becoming wealthy. The Mitsui family was expanding. It had six branch stores, the largest at Yedo, before Hachirobei died. It was in every form of moneylending and handling.

But there were others richer than Mitsui. In Yedo were the wealthy and ornate Messrs. Kinokuniya-Bunzaemon and Naraya-Mozaemon, fabulously rich by the standards of the times and exhibiting their wealth in the most ostentatious manner. At Kyoto was the *nouveau riche* Naniwaya-Juemon, who is said to have made the people gape at his splendid residences, his gardens, his dinners, his raiment. Richest of all was the leading rice broker, the great kakeya—the J. Pierpont Morgan of Japan—Yodoya Saburoemon, whose new palace and fresh magnificence seemed almost imperial. He put on such a show that the Shogun confiscated all his property. What was gathered in this seizure gives an idea of what the possessions of a wealthy Osakan or Yedoan consisted. The bailiffs seized fifty pairs of gold screens, three toy ships made of jewelry, 360 carpets, 10,500 kin of liquid gold, 273 large precious stones and countless small ones, two chests of gold, 3000 large gold coins, 120,000 ryo of koban, 85,000 kwamme of silver, 75,000 kwamme of copper money, 150 boats, 730 storehouses, 12 storehouses of jewelry, 80 granaries, 80 storehouses of beans, 28 houses in Osaka, 64 in other places, claim to the rice stipend of one daimio amounting to 332 koku, and 150 chobu of cypress forest.

How large the houses, how roomy the storehouses, we do not know. But here was a considerable accumulation in a new regime and in a new economy.

These Park Avenue Osaka and Kyoto and Yedo exhibitionists brought down upon their heads the wrath of the Shogun because he deemed them to be disturbing to society. Disturbing indeed! These upstarts, freshly risen from the dung heap, who were compelled to kneel in the street as their bankrupt debtors passed them; these despised traders, class neighbors of the animal skinner and the gravediggers, to be giving themselves the airs of court nobles! It would be difficult to keep the starving artisan and the slaving farmer feeling himself the superior of these men in brocades. It upset completely the class arrangement. Therefore they must be reduced to their proper level, at least in appearance. Hence they were forbidden to indulge in displays. Then to add a touch of logic to the rule, they must be stripped of some of their wealth at least, by taxes, by confiscations, by *goyokin*—forced loans upon merchants—by currency devaluations, since thus funds were provided for their impecunious superiors. The debts of samurai were canceled at intervals.

In addition to these reactions upon the trader groups from the woes of the bewildered agrarian nobles, the cities were developing their own troubles. The various producing groups, in this land of scarcity, feared they were the helpless victims of competition and overproduction. They sought monopolies. And the Shoguns, hard-pressed for cash, granted them for a consideration. Traders, brokers, merchants formed themselves into associations to monopolize their trades. That is, guilds grew up in the towns. The fisherman coming home with his catch and the merchant to whom he sold it found themselves beset by all the real and imagined evils of competition.

An apostle of self-rule in business named Sukegoro of Yamato appeared with his cure. He formed the fishmongers into a trade association. He set up a code of practice. He enrolled 391 wholesalers and 246 brokers in his corporative code authority. It was a scheme to protect the middleman. The fisherman bought his boat and supplies and got credit from the wholesaler or broker and in return gave him exclusive right to his catch. The association fixed the prices the fisherman received. The wholesaler sold only to the retailer. The consumer could not buy from the fisherman or the wholesaler. Sukegoro built preserves to keep the fish alive until the market was ready for them. He did under the authority of the government what fishermen have many times sought to do in New York under the sponsorship and enforcement machinery of gangsters and what all sorts of producers attempted under authority of the NRA; what the building trades do in defiance of law. The excess production was kept off the market. The price was kept up. The number of competitors was kept down. Other trades were similarly organized. There were jurisdictional disputes between craftsmen. The sawyers complained that the carpenters were sawing up too much of the lumber in buildings at the job site. The Shogun sought continuously, by subsidies, by warehousing the surplus, by price decrees, to keep up the price of rice to protect the daimio whose staple was rice.

Apparently the Mitsuis steered as far as they were able out of these trade agreements. They seem to have contrived in every way open to them to evade these monopolistic arrangements, to buy in as large quantities as possible, and through efficient management to sell at lower prices in the interest of larger volume. Named as one of the ten bankmen to control the money market, they appear to have shied away from that combination.

Above all, under the direction of Hachirobei, as their money-lending affairs grew, the Mitsui house refused to lend money to the nobles—to court nobles, daimios, or samurai. They sought in every way to keep their finances extricated from the shaky finances of the ruling class. Hachirobei lectured his sons about this ceaselessly. The house was rewarded with immunity, therefore, from the disasters that in all ages have descended sooner or later upon the banking houses that became the creditors of princes. They escaped the fate of the Bardi and the Peruzzi of Italy, and eventually the Fuggers in Germany, and of the Mendelssohns in our own time. Takafusa Mitsui, in a manuscript containing his recollection of the observations of his father Hachirobei, records this advice to merchants:

Only a fool would believe that the feudal lords would permit the merchant to make unreasonable profit. These lords promise to send their rice to the merchant in Osaka, and on that security borrow money in advance. For the first year or two they appear to be willing to deposit more and more money with the merchants. Never will they pay back their debts by sending the promised amounts, but sending their rice to another quarter where they expect accommodation, they refuse the payment to the merchants from whom they already borrowed large sums.

Through these stratagems and through the bankruptcy of the lords innumerable merchants were ruined. Takafusa records the names of forty-eight merchants in Yedo alone who were wiped out through their unfortunate loans to the nobles. Of all the many houses of that day the House of Mitsui and the House of Kenoike alone survive to the present.

Hachirobei died in 1694. Before he died he had apparently meditated much upon the possible dissipation of his fortune. He had seen the solid substance of the great daimios melt away. He had seen rich merchants ruined. He saw the erosive power of successions to numerous heirs. In the *Chonin Koku Roku,* a manuscript privately circulated by his son, he is reported to have observed that "great fortunes will develop symptoms of decline when they reach the third generation." It was natural that in his world, where the family played so important a part, he should seek to devise some means of preventing the dispersion of his fortune. He therefore contrived to organize his business in the form of a family corporation. He had six sons—one in charge of each of the six branches. He established six family groups and allotted to each a proportion of the inheritance. But the inheritance—that is the business itself and the fortune—were to remain intact. A son might manage in each branch, but all the branches belonged to the family. The profits belonged to the business, and the family was to determine what each member of the family should receive as his share in any season. His will outlined a code of family ethics and a procedure of management. After his death his oldest son, Takahisa Mitsui, who succeeded as head of the house, reduced his precepts to a code which still governs the family. It follows:

1. The members of the House should deal with one another in close friendship and with kindness. Beware that contentions among the kin would in the end ruin the entire House.

2. Do not needlessly increase the number of families of the House. Everything has its limits. Know that overexpansion, which you may covet, will beget confusion and trouble.

3. Thrift enriches the House, while luxury ruins a man. Practice the former but avoid the latter. Thus lay a lasting foundation for the prosperity and perpetuation of our House.

4. In making marriages, incurring debts or underwriting others' debts, act always according to the advice of the Council of the Family.

5. Set aside a certain part of the annual income and divide it among the members of the House according to their portions.

6. The lifework of a man lasts as long as he lives. Therefore, do not, without reason, seek the luxury and ease of retirement.

7. Cause to be sent for auditing to the main office the financial reports from all branch houses; organize your finance and prevent disintegration.

8. The essential of a business enterprise is to employ men of great abilities and take advantage of their special talents. Replace those who are aged and decrepit with young men of promise.

9. Unless one concentrates, one fails. Our House has its own enterprises which are ample to provide for any man's life. Never touch another business.

10. He who does not know, cannot lead. Make your sons begin with the mean tasks of the apprentice, and, when they have gradually learned the secrets of the business, let them take a post in the branch houses to practice their knowledge.

11. Sound judgment is essential in all things, especially in business enterprises. Know that a small sacrifice today is preferable to a great loss tomorrow.

12. The members of the House should practice mutual caution and counsel lest they blunder. If there be among you any evildoer, deal with him accordingly at the Council of the Family.

13. You who have been born in the land of gods, worship your gods, revere your Emperor, love your country and do your duty as subjects.

Hachirobei saw that if successions could work dispersion and finally extinction of a fortune, holding intact the fortune through the years, accumulating its profits—plowing them back, in modern parlance—and uniting the combined wealth of an ever-growing number of heirs in a single continuing enterprise would progressively expand the fortune. This is what he attempted to do. Many great fortune builders have sought to do the same thing—the Medici, the Fuggers, the Rothschilds, and Cornelius Vanderbilt in our own time. But the Mitsuis succeeded where others failed.

The family has continued to be merely stockholders in a vast central enterprise. The enterprise, with its own special identity apart from the family, has grown in wealth and power until today it is one of the most potent commercial instruments in the world.

It was perhaps easier in Japan, with its strong national and religious emphasis upon the family and its long isolation in a feudal society, to keep alive this cohesive family enterprise. The family has been made, in accordance with the plan of old Hachirobei, a living, continuing, sacred institution. Each Mitsui, on coming of age, is required to take the following oath:

> In obedience to the precepts of our father and in order to strengthen the everlasting foundation of our House and to expand the enterprise bequeathed by our forefathers, I solemnly vow in the presence of the August Spirits of our ancestors, that as a member of the House of Mitsui, I will serve and follow the regulations handed down in the Constitution of our House, and that I will not wantonly seek to alter them. In witness whereof, I take the oath and affix my signature thereto in the presence of the August Spirits of our ancestors.

Because of the laws in Japan, where it is apparently possible to entail a fortune, the family, organized and acting like a state through recognized and all-powerful representatives, can enforce this oath, since it controls the combined and concentrated wealth of the family and the income of each member. The youthful neophyte finds that he preserves his fealty to the family, to the august spirits of his ancestors and his dividend check, all in the same act of faith.

III

In 1858, after Japan had abandoned her seclusion policy, the Emperor was restored to power over the Shogun, and the new era in Japan began. By this time the Mitsui family had become one of the three richest families in Japan. What this means we can only guess. There is a good deal of easy use of large figures in describing the wealth of old barons and the magnificence of princes, but it is difficult to avoid a pinch of salt as seasoning for these statistics.

When one reads that upon his accession to power the Emperor sent for the three leading banker-merchants and borrowed 1000 ryo each from them—the ryo being similar to, if not the same as, the yen—we catch a glimpse of the very diminutive figures in which they spoke.

For two hundred years, since that first little moneylending shop in Matsuzaka, the family had been, by persistent accretion and ruthless limitation upon withdrawals, creating a large bolus of wealth. It had, because of its inflexible policy, escaped the great losses that resulted from numerous debt repudiations by the barons. It must, of course, have suffered from the many ryo devaluations. It must also have been subjected to many troubled nights and suffered losses through its association with the finances of the Shogun's government. But apparently it found a means of steering amid the shoals and rocks of Shogunate finance.

But in the end the Mitsuis became weary of the tottering Shogunate. The Shogun lost his power and the Emperor regained his because the old social fabric of the feudal era had drifted upon evil days. It was hopelessly entangled in debt. The government itself was trapped in endless financial difficulties. The clash of energies between the old feudalism of the barons and the new money economy of the merchants was tearing the economic system apart. The barons had grown tired of it because, for reasons they did not understand, the wealth of the nation was passing into the hands of the lords of Main Street. The merchants were sick of it because they were the ready-to-hand victims of the bewildered Shogun's soak-the-rich policy. The government had to find funds to salvage failing daimios, to help the drifting samurai warriors, to appease the continually revolting farmers and the occasional town mobs. It taxed until the tax limit was reached; then it borrowed. Behold a treasury statement for the year 1830:

Expenditures	1,453,209 ryo
Revenues	925,099 "
Deficit	528,110 ryo

One finds this budget balanced by an item called "special revenue," which meant the profit on devaluing the currency. In the records of that Shogunate the deficit was increasing every year. Every year the budget was balanced by the device of devaluing the currency. In ten years the government created for itself 7,558,000 ryo of "special revenue" by devaluing the currency. There should be nothing unfamiliar in this picture for the American, Briton, Frenchman, German, or Italian of today.

When, after Admiral Perry landed in Japan with his fleet of United States ships and opened Japan to the world, the merchants, barons, farmers who bore most of the burden of this disintegrating regime, were happy to see it vanish. The Shogunate capitulated without a struggle and the Emperor went from Kyoto to Yedo, henceforth called Tokyo, to assume the government of the nation. When he went, Saburosuke Mitsui, then head of the family, went along with him as treasurer.

The new era meant opportunity upon a vast scale for the Mitsuis and for those who had the means of perceiving precisely what it was all about. For now feudalism was to be replaced almost in a trice by capitalism. It was almost as if the curtain were rung down upon one act and lifted presently upon another. Japan was to leap forward over a gulf that it had taken France, Germany, and England three centuries to traverse. It was a dizzy plunge from the Holy Roman Empire of Maximilian to the Germany of Bismarck in a few brief years.

The age of long, slow accretions had ended as far as the Mitsuis were concerned. Now they were to see what could be done with coins when they were really put in motion. Japan, exposed to the new capitalist world, yielded to the infection as to some savage and swift organism. All of a sudden she needed everything, all the highly developed instrumentalities of the capitalist world— machinery, corporations, modern deposit banks, banks of issue, the refinements of credit. Above all she needed capital. The opportunities were unlimited for those who were able to see. The Mitsuis sent a mission of five younger Mitsuis abroad to inspect this new world and its money-making inventions. They returned to Japan knowing what they should do among their twenty-six million countrymen who knew nothing of the wonders of the outer world.

When the new Emperor Mutsuhito—to be known as Meiji— found himself in power, he found himself also without funds. He summoned Saburosuke Mitsui, Ono-Zensuke, and Shimada Hachirozaemon and made a modest touch of a thousand ryo each. Later he repeated this favor. But this was chicken feed, as he soon found. He sent for the three leading Main Street merchants and money men and told them to prepare a list of a hundred merchants. The Emperor summoned these gentlemen and told them plainly that he needed three million ryo. Mitsui, Ono, and Shimada were called on to underwrite the loan. The money was forthcoming. Capitalism was marching on.

They were well rewarded. Mitsui, Ono, and Shimada were made exchequer agents of the crown. They collected all taxes and held possession of them for a while before remitting to the treasury. A Mitsui man was made director of the mint. Another was made head of the bureau of specie and currency and another governor of the bureau of commercial law.

After a while it became apparent that what the new Japan needed was a modern bank. The Emperor's finance minister, Inouye, whispered to the Mitsuis that they should organize one. It was then 1872. They sent their mission to America. After some difficulties and disappointments they opened for business their own bank, now known as the Mitsui Bank, Ltd. They had been a little embarrassed by a sort of enforced association with Ono and Shimada in another bank in the exchequer business. But a favorable circumstance in 1874 relieved them of that embarrassment. There was a brief recession in Japan. The three houses had been enjoying a boom. They collected the tax moneys of the Emperor. They held them on deposit. Rumors got around that these deposits were endangered. The finance minister called upon the three houses to produce the government funds. Ono and Shimada could not do it. Mitsui, by a tremendous effort, did. The other two houses were ruined, and the field was left clear to Mitsui. Then they launched their own bank and established thirty-one branches in Japan. Thus the Mitsuis extended thirty-one arms into all the corners of Japan and proceeded to draw in funds from every section. The bank grew swiftly. It had a capital of two million yen in 1876 and deposits of 11,369,000 yen. In 1932 it had a capital of 60 million yen and 687 million in deposits. It is and has been the core of the Mitsui development. Like those bank affiliates in America in the nineteen twenties, this reservoir of funds and creator of bank money drew into its treasury the savings of countless thousands that the Mitsuis could use to finance their numerous adventures.

Then came that proliferation of enterprises that characterizes the family today. With unlimited money resources open to them through their bank and their possession of government funds they began slowly to reach out in every direction, to tap all the new sources of profit. Inouye, finance minister in Ito's cabinet, left the ministry a rich man and set up a trading company called Senshu Kaisha to handle foreign trade. It prospered abundantly. The Mitsuis too, in 1875, organized a small company called Kokusan Kata (National Products Company). When Inouye went back to the cabinet in 1876 the Mitsuis took over his Senshu Kaisha, combined it with their Kokusan Kata, and organized a new concern called the Mitsui Bussan Kaisha. This became the holding company of numerous enterprises and is today the agency through which the Mitsui family carries on its great domestic and foreign commercial adventures.

When the Meiji ministry got down to business after the restoration, it began to encourage and to organize modern industries. The government owned the Oji Paper Works. It built a model silk mill. It organized and developed the Shibaura Engineering Works. It built the Kanegafuchi cotton mills. It owned the Miike mines—the richest coal treasure in Japan. After a while the Mitsuis began as tenderly and quietly as possible to lift these off the government's hands, buying out on the most favorable terms.

Thus it went into silk manufacture, imported silkworms from Italy, taught the peasants more modern methods of silk culture, and ultimately made itself the largest factor in the world silk industry. They took over the Oji paper business in 1872. Today the Oji Manufacturing Company controls about sixteen corporations which own forests, sawmills, paper-manufacturing companies, power companies, railways, security companies, and a newspaper —the *Mainichi*—in Osaka. They took over the Kanegafuchi cotton mills. They still operate them and have spread out as the greatest textile producers in Japan. They tapped the China cotton market, buying cotton there and sending back cloth to compete with the English traders. They acquired the Shibaura Engineering Works from the government. Then they fixed their eyes on the Miike mines.

These mines, the greatest coal deposit in Japan, they got through some clever management in the ministry, for 4,550,000 yen. In the first year of operation they made back the whole purchase price. In half a century they realized a profit of 450 million yen. Thus money, cotton, silk, coal, and, little by little, other products fell into the skillfully exploitive hands of the Mitsui family.

———————————— IV ————————————

Persons outside Japan, when they hear the term "Mitsui family," are apt to think of an extraordinary group of able and skillful Mitsuis managing the vast network of enterprises that make up their domain. It is more than doubtful if this extraordinary clan would today bulk so large in Japanese economic life if this were so. Even before the restoration, when Takahisa Mitsui was head of the business, the family had already learned to depend upon the administrative abilities of what the Japanese call *bantos*, or "head clerks." And it was one of these—Minomura—who piloted the business through the troubles and shifting movements of the restoration period.

Just when the family began using this method is not clear. But

always the family council and the heads of the family branches
were free to interfere and even to collaborate actively in management. However, around 1890, this numerous and wealthy family
organization had to submit to one of those processes that in our
corporate affairs we call "reorganization." And a wholly new technique of management suited to the new era was adopted. It came
about thus:

The Mitsuis collected government taxes. The taxes remained
on deposit with them. This was a source of great profit. But
Japan was growing up. In 1880 the government decided to collect
its own taxes and to establish the Bank of Japan. This was a
blow to the house. However, they still continued as local agents
to transfer taxes from the provinces to Tokyo. But capitalism in
Japan was developing all its familiar phenomena. Debt making
had proceeded merrily. The farm debt had risen from an insig-
nificant sum to 233 million yen. There were crop failures, unfavorable trade balances, losses on foreign exchange. There came,
in short, a first-class capitalist depression. Then rumor began to
whisper about the Mitsuis: their bank was in danger. There was
a run on the Kyoto branch. It spread to Tokyo. The powerful
Mitsuis, who had so many times found the government on its
knees begging for loans, now had to appeal to the government
for help.

Inouye, powerful finance minister and Mitsui ally, later to be
known as the Mitsui representative among the elder statesmen,
agreed to save the house but demanded that it should submit to
reorganization at his hands. It was in no position to resist. There-
upon the imperial finance minister set about studying its affairs,
its family code and laws, the constitution of similar European
families. He decided that the Mitsui *enterprises* had to be protected ruthlessly from the Mitsui *family.*

He therefore drew up a new constitution. It organized the
Mitsui business as a modern corporation, dominated, controlled,
administered by executive heads wholly separated from the family
council. It organized the family as a wholly separate entity. As

a result, the business was put in the hands of a giant, over-all holding company—the Mitsui Gomei Kaisha—which holds directly or indirectly through subsidiaries all of the numerous enterprises of the concern. It is managed not by the family, but by directors who may include family members. But at the head of the Mitsui Gomei Kaisha is a managing director—a *banto,* or head clerk— who functions precisely like the chairman of the board of the United States Steel Corporation, as well as through various series of executives.

The family, on the other hand, is merely the stockholder in this immense holding company. On its side it is organized, too. There is a family council. And when you hear of Baron Takakimi Mitsui as head of the family, it means head of this family council. He is, of course, nominal head of the business, too—the Mitsui Gomei Kaisha. But its actual head and manager is its reigning *banto,* its prime minister.

The family is a carefully organized tribal unit. It is an economic clan existing as a sort of social bolus within the state and functioning under a written constitution. There are, in fact, eleven Mitsui families—six main families and five branch families, all exactly defined under the constitution. These constituent stems are immutable. This family and its domestic provinces are ruled by a family council organized as a sort of constitutional monarchy of which it is the house of peers. This council consists of the eleven heads of each family plus the retired heads, if any, and such heirs apparent of the existing heads as may have arrived at their majority. But only the eleven heads have a vote. The president of this council, the tribal patriarch, with a veto on its judgments, is the head of the chief family. This council meets in secret once a month. It deals with family affairs—philanthropies, deaths, inheritances, marriages, family debts, troubles, assignments of family members to business enterprises, and plans of all sorts. The council determines how much each of the eleven family households shall be permitted to spend. It may impose punishments and invoke sanctions for its decrees. Within the framework of the civil society this autonomous aristocracy assumes to regulate the conduct of its members. All families do not share equally in the dividends of the Mitsui enterprises. The head branch takes 23 per cent of the yield of profits of the Mitsui Gomei Kaisha. The five other main branches take a total of 57.5 per cent, the five branch families take among them 19.5 per cent.

These *bantos* have been gentlemen of the most imposing importance in Japan, comparable to the board chairmen of such American institutions as General Motors or United States Steel. They have been, in fact, proportionately more important, because the House of Mitsui spreads over a far larger acreage of the economic life of Japan than any American or British corporation. The first of them, Rizaemon Minomura, piloted the family enterprises through the difficult, reformative days of the restoration and helped to shape the modern form and direction of the business. Unlike the Mitsuis themselves he began life as a candy maker and peddler who entered the service of Oguri, the last finance minister of the old Shogunate, became a banker with Oguri as his patron, and entered the Mitsui service to afford it the powerful friendship of the minister. He it was who saw the opportunities opening before the house in the new capitalist restoration period, saw that its beloved textile store at Suruga-cho was small potatoes in the new Japan, induced them to put it aside and turn to finance and promotion on the new model.

He died in 1877, and there followed a more direct family management that ended in the disaster of 1890 and the reorganization in 1900. By this time the Emperor's finance minister, Kaoru Inouye, was the imperial patron of the Mitsuis and through his influence Hikojiro Nakamigawa became the *banto*. He was an intellectual, who began as a teacher at Keio University, wrote articles for magazines, served an apprenticeship in the foreign office, edited brilliantly the newspaper, *Jiji Shimpo*, became president of a railway, and then, at Inouye's urging, went into the Mitsui bank, rose to its headship, becoming managing director of the Mitsui Gomei Kaisha. He played an important role in the reorganization of the existing industries and the acquiring of new ones. He drove the old Mitsui organization from the more leisurely ways of the old Japan to the faster tempo of the new. He was a bold, shouldering, self-reliant, and driving executive. He died in 1901 to be succeeded by Takasi Masuda.

Masuda had started life as a houseboy for Townsend Harris, first American minister to Japan. He then formed a connection with the powerful Inouye and became the head of his trading company. When the Mitsuis took it over and formed the Mitsui Bussan Kaisha, he became its first president and was largely responsible for the success of that institution which started with a loan of 50,000 yen from the Mitsui bank and in sixty years had an authorized capital of 100 million yen. He set the Mitsui foreign trading upon the course that has made it so powerful. He built up the cotton, silk, steel, and munitions business of the company.

When he died he was succeeded by Takuma Dan, a graduate of the Massachusetts Institute of Technology, who became the head of the Miike coal mines before the Mitsuis bought them. He built those into the tremendously profitable industry they became. He directed the affairs of the company during the Great War and developed the vast munitions interests of the Mitsuis. He was assassinated in 1932 to be succeeded by the aristocratic Seihin Ikeda, Harvard '95, a patrician who got a job with the Mitsuis in 1895 at thirty yen a month, became managing director of the Mitsui bank in 1909 and *banto* in 1933. He was finance minister in the cabinet of Prince Konoye, was for a while governor of the Bank of Japan, and was known as the Tiger of the Money Market. He retired from the headship of the Mitsui house, for the same reason that he retired from the finance ministry, because he was unpopular with the army.

The business organization is for all the world like one of our great American corporate giants held in the hands of a central master holding company, save that its interests are far more diversified. At the top is the holding company—Mitsui Gomei Kaisha. This in turn owns a controlling interest in nineteen other corporations, most of them subholding companies. There are two others which handle the Mitsui philanthropies.

Through this corporate pyramid the family carries on adventures in finance, trading (domestic and international), department stores, mining, engineering, cement, textiles, lumber, chemicals, coal, oil, sugar, cereals, fertilizers, and so on. The whole imposing web is too complicated to describe. The Mitsui Gomei Kaisha is capitalized at 300,000,000 yen.

The wealth of the family is indeed great—greater still measured against the standards of Japan. Mr. Oland D. Russell, in *The House of Mitsui,* says that the present head of the House, Baron Takakimi Mitsui, when he came into the estate of his father, took over a taxable inheritance of 166,400,000 yen, or $55,000,000, but adds that Mr. Shumpei Kanda, writing in *Shufunotomo,* estimated this private wealth at 450,000,000 yen, or about $130,000,000, and that archivists in the Mitsui library admitted this was "probably pretty accurate." The heads of the other ten families have fortunes as follows:

Takahisa Mitsui	170,000,000 yen
Geneyemon	200,000,000
Baron Takakiyo	230,000,000
Takanaga	140,000,000
Baron Toshitaro	150,000,000
Takamoto	60,000,000
Morinosuke	80,000,000
Takaakira	60,000,000
Benzo	60,000,000
Takateru	35,000,000

TOTAL including Baron Takakimi (450,000,000)   1,635,000,000 yen

This is the equivalent of $450,000,000.

These great fortunes in large measure were the product, of course, of wise management, shrewd organization, and family policies to protect the growing mountain from erosion. But also they were not made without well-arranged, carefully nurtured, and well-oiled contacts with the proper government authorities. The restoration turned out to be a paradise for the rich merchants and the acquisitive patriots. Such statesmen as Inouye, Ito, Okuma made fortunes out of their ministries. Inouye, once Minister of Public Works, built many miles of railroad track. When he resigned, the cost of construction was cut in half. The great liberal Okuma was closely allied with the Mitsubishi. He was premier during the Satsuma rebellion in 1876 and financed it with paper money. It is said that when it was over he hauled several cartloads of scrip to his home. It was not difficult to do business with politicians like this. Almost every leading statesman was backed by some banker or promoter. The Mitsuis helped finance the Seiyukai or conservative party of Ito and Inouye; the Mitsubishis supported the Minseito or liberal party. Inouye, powerful finance minister, was intimately associated with the Mitsuis as a sort of superconsultant—guide, philosopher, and friend. After his retirement a Japanese yearbook referred to him frankly as the Mitsui representative among the Elder Statesmen.

We need not rest this upon mere surmise. In June, 1910, Japan was about to contract for the building of the battleship *Kongo*. There was keen rivalry for the contract. The Mitsui Bussan Kaisha was agent for Vickers, the British armament firm. Takoto Sokai was agent for the Armstrongs. Both began to put pressure upon Admiral Matsumoto, Director of the Naval Stores Department. The Mitsui Bussan Kaisha engaged Matsuo Tsurutaro, a retired naval constructor-general, because of his intimacy with Matsumoto. He offered Matsumoto one third of Mitsui's commission from Vickers for the Admiral's assistance. Matsuo told one of the Mitsui directors of the arrangement. He consulted with the other directors. The Mitsui Bussan Kaisha advised Vickers and asked that their commission be increased to accommodate Admiral Matsumoto's demands. Vickers approved the deal and the commission was increased to 1,150,000 yen. Admiral Matsumoto was given 400,000 yen. And Mitsui-Vickers got the contract. The deal leaked out.

Similar corrupt deals between the German Siemens-Schuckert Company and Japanese admirals exposed in the Reichstag by Dr. Karl Liebknecht, the socialist leader, excited the suspicion of Diet members in Japan. They did some probing and exposed the whole ugly Japanese bribery plot. Seven Mitsui directors of Mitsui Bussan Kaisha were indicted, along with their agent Matsuo Tsurutaro and Admiral Matsumoto. All were convicted and given two years in prison, Matsumoto getting three years and a fine of 400,000 yen. A little later the Mitsui family set up a fund of 750,000 yen for the education and care of convicts.

We have no need to pursue the fortunes of this extraordinary dynastic family further. The Great War, of course, added enormously to their wealth. The Mitsuis have placed all their influence and power behind the imperialist adventures of Japan in China. They are up to their necks in that episode—and there are men, sinister men in Japan, radicals who hate Mitsui support of the military, and, strange as it may seem, military men too, for different reasons, who look at them with a threatening glance.

The Mitsui family possesses vast wealth. It controls 78 per cent of the paper industry in Japan, 17 per cent of all mining, 15 per cent of rayon, 17 per cent of cement, 11 per cent of coal and shipping, and an enormous amount of Japan's foreign trade. Its flag, with the Mitsui crest—the Japanese figure three enclosed in a square—may be seen stenciled upon boxes and bales on the docks of the whole world. It has subsidiaries, affiliates, branches everywhere. It operates in Germany as the Deutsche Bussan Aktiengesellschaft, in France as the Société Anonyme Française Bussan, in South Africa as Mitsui Bussan.

The five great family industries of Japan—Mitsui, Mitsubishi, Sumitomo, Yasuda, Okura—control, according to Mr. John Gunther, 62 per cent of the wealth of Japan, 70 per cent of its textiles, and 40 per cent of its bank deposits. This is not to say that these five groups stand united against Japan. On the contrary, there is keen and, in spots, bitter rivalry between them. The Mitsuis back the Seiyukai or conservative party while the Mitsubishis support the Minseito or liberal party. They are pre-eminent in different fields—Mitsui in foreign trade, textiles, paper; Mitsubishi in shipping and finance, insurance and trust companies; Sumitomo in engineering and the heavy industries; Yasuda in banking— owning the largest bank in Japan—and Okura, a newcomer, in trade and engineering. However, they are one at least in the support of those fundamental principles upon which their vast interests are based.

But all of them face trouble now. The foreign-newspaper reader sees Japan symbolized by a large-jawed, heavy-necked, cruel-looking little soldier with a bayonet. He is apt to think of all Japanese like that. But behind the Japan of the China adventure is a population of plain people deeply troubled and filled with all sorts of discordant elements. The Mitsuis have had one assassination—Takuma Dan, the great *banto*—in 1932. Today, strangely enough, the army, which it has so loyally supported, asks what service this immense family of traders is supplying in charging the government, which is the army, heavy prices for all that it supplies. Why could not the government take over these supply functions itself? The spirit of the military Fascist looks with unfriendly eyes upon its backers in Japan, as it has done in Germany. The Mitsuis speak softly in Tokyo. They spend moderately, fear to display their wealth. They have created a fund of 30 million yen for a foundation, not unlike the Rockefeller foundations, to purchase national good will. But the Mitsuis and all of the traders and bankers in Tokyo have been playing with fire. The flames leap about them and no one knows who or what they will consume.

This family is unique in the annals of vast wealth gathering. The conditions of their country have made it possible for their founder to succeed in holding it together for so long a time. Money is the greatest of all money-makers. Old Hachirobei knew that. And he knew that if he could hold the central capital of the family together indefinitely its capacity to re-create and expand itself would grow progressively. He was able to create this commercial family dynasty because he wrought in Japan and because his descendants had the wisdom to submit to the creation of a monarchical structure with a monarch holding power in theory and a prime minister, chosen for his brains, exercising it in fact.

CECIL RHODES

CHAPTER VIII

Cecil Rhodes

EMPIRE BUILDER

—————————————— I ——————————————

CECIL RHODES, empire builder and diamond monopolist, dreamer and money-maker, who made a million dollars while taking his bachelor's and master's degrees at Oxford, is unique among the great fortune builders of history.

Of him Spengler said: "He is the first man of the new age. He stands for the political style of a far-ranging, western, Teutonic and especially German future, and his phrase 'expansion is everything' is a Napoleonic reassertion of the indwelling tendency of every civilization that has fully ripened. . . . Rhodes is to be regarded as the first of a Western type of Caesar whose day is to come, though yet distant."

With some modifications, this is a just estimate. The Caesar ingredient in this powerful figure was large. He himself was pleased to be told that he looked like the Emperor Hadrian. He was an organizing and money-making genius of the first order with an overmastering hunger for that kind of power that can be had only with money. He conceived a design no less grandiose than the theft of a continent and, for a while at least, toyed with the idea of the theft of the whole world for the British crown. He amassed millions and spent them prodigally in pursuit of his passion of delivering the whole of Africa into the hands of the British Empire, as a prelude to making Britain mistress of the world.

Today, on a lofty peak that he named "World's View" in the Matopo Hills of Rhodesia, the immense colony he stole from

Lobengula and the Matabele people, the body of this mystic Caesar rests under a granite slab, brooding over the rich empire he coveted and took. He had conceived the dream of an African empire while preparing for his degree at Oxford. Later in Cape Town, when England controlled merely the Cape Colony and Natal, the young diamond digger put his hand on a map of Africa near the Cape of Good Hope and, sweeping his broad palm upward to the Mediterranean, said: "All this to be red—that is my dream." For this he plotted, intrigued, wrought throughout his life until he saw his own career close amid the flames of a cruel war that must forever remain a blot on England's name, but that marked an inevitable step in the march of the empire toward the goal of Rhodes.

Cecil John Rhodes was born July 5, 1853. His forebears for several generations had been successful farmers. They had the money gift—that flair for getting along that flowered in the true British pattern when his grandfather was able to set up in the manner of a squire on an estate in Essex. This gentleman's son, Francis William Rhodes, attended Harrow and Trinity College, took holy orders, became the vicar of Bishop Stortford in Hertfordshire, married, and produced eleven children. Seven of these were sons. Cecil was the seventh child and the fifth son.

The Reverend Francis Rhodes was not an impecunious parson. He enjoyed, in addition to the honorarium of his sacred office, a decent patrimony. Cecil was sent to the grammar school at Bishop Stortford, which his father refurbished with his own funds. There he remained until thirteen, when his father became his tutor. At sixteen he was ready for Oxford where he was registered. But his health was far from robust. What was probably tuberculosis induced the family physician to order a long sea voyage. Fate perhaps took a hand with the physician in this, for the voyage took young Rhodes to South Africa, where he was destined to remain throughout his life and play out a great role in the swelling drama of England's imperial theme.

Cecil's oldest brother, Herbert, had settled some years before in Natal as a planter of cotton. Cecil made his home with Herbert.

His health improved so rapidly in the healing air of Natal that he decided to remain indefinitely in South Africa. Very soon after, the two brothers went to the Komanzi Valley, south of Pieter-maritzburg, to try their hand at cotton raising. As things fell out, the chief labor of doing this rested with Cecil. Herbert left early in 1871 for the diamond fields. In spite of many hostile elements and general predictions of failure, Cecil produced two excellent cotton crops. And in after years, whenever admonished that he could not accomplish some difficult task, he was fond of saying: "Remember I made cotton grow in Komanzi."

II

When in 1870 Cecil Rhodes first set foot upon the soil of South Africa it had been but lightly touched by the European colony hunter. Think of a mere black-line outline of Africa. The holdings of European empires made but a few thin smudges at a few points along that outline. Great Britain held two small colonies at the very southern tip of the continent—the Cape and Natal. The Dutch farmers held the Transvaal and Orange Free State, independent republics, next to Cape Colony. North of them, through all the far reaches of mountain and jungle and desert, the land was inhabited by Negro, Semitic, and Arabian peoples in varying stages of savagery and civilization.

The Dutch settled at the Cape in 1652—a far outpost of the Dutch East India Company. The French seized the colony after conquering the Netherlands. The British took it from the French in 1795 and returned it to the Dutch farmers in 1803 under the Treaty of Amiens. But three years later a British squadron appeared off the coast, drove the Dutch away, and reseized the Cape. Eight years later the British paid the Dutch six million sterling for their loot.

The Dutch farmers settled in Natal in 1828 and fourteen years later the English seized Natal.

Six years later—in 1848—the British forcibly took possession of another Dutch settlement, Orange Free State. This last outrage excited so much indignation in the Cape and Natal and the Transvaal that the English, to allay feeling, recognized the independence of the Transvaal and the Orange Free State. These Boer farmers had suffered cruelly at the hands of the English and hatred of Britain became almost a part of the religion of these stern African evangelical Dutch.

Thus when Rhodes arrived in South Africa, the Transvaal and Orange Free State were independent republics, while the Cape and Natal were British colonies. Immediately north was a magnificent domain that had already begun to arouse the hunger of every sovereign in Europe. What riches slumbered in its mountains and jungles they could only surmise from an event that had just occurred near Natal, just a few hundred miles from the cotton plantation of Herbert Rhodes.

-------------------------------- III --------------------------------

One day in 1867 Farmer Chaik van Niekerk, visiting a friend in Orange Free State, observed his host's son playing marbles with an unusually brilliant stone. Niekerk's host presented him with the marble. The host, like Othello, was to learn he had thrown away a pearl richer than all his tribe, save that it was not a pearl. Van Niekerk showed it to a mineralogist at Cape Town who pronounced it a diamond. The Governor bought it for £500. What van Niekerk gave the boy who owned it is not recorded.

Two years later a witch doctor brought to this lucky van Niekerk another brilliant. The farmer gave the man of magic five hundred sheep, ten oxen, and a horse—all he possessed—for the stone. In turn he sold it to a Hope Town dealer for £11,000, who sold it to Lord Dudley for £25,000. His lordship called the diamond the Star of South Africa. It weighed eighty-three carats. These two stones, one discovered by a child and the other by a witch doctor, changed the whole course of history in South Africa.

The Star of South Africa spread its beam over the wide veldts and presently Dutch and English farmers and tradesmen swarmed along the Vaal River. Ten thousand diggers spread out along eighty miles of stream. They found diamonds—enough to keep alive interest in the new industry. Then, in 1870, diamonds were found in the yellow sands on the Dutoitspan farm—larger stones and in greater abundance. Some fifty-carat gems were found. The word "diamond" ran over South Africa, and even the world, as the words "oil" and "gold" had in California and Pennsylvania. The diggers poured in from all over the world by every ship. And it was in the midst of this excitement that a young student with a weak chest and seeking only health, with no suspicion of the acquisitive fire that burned in his bosom, set his foot upon the soil of South Africa. This young Cecil Rhodes was scarcely established on the new Komanzi farm to which he and his brother had moved before the restless Herbert left for Dutoitspan, leaving Cecil to tend the cotton. But, in 1871, Cecil, just eighteen, abandoned the cotton farm and, with some digging tools, some Greek classics, and a Greek lexicon, set off in an ox cart to travel four hundred miles to join his brother in the diamond fields.

There we may see the youthful prospector—half money-maker, half student—sitting, according to his own description, on an upturned bucket, sorting gravel on a small table, fishing in the gravel for gems, and at other times deep in his textbooks. All about him, over a field five miles in radius, spread the new settlement. White tents were all mixed up with the lime heaps where 10,000 men, whites and blacks, labored like beavers in pursuit of diamonds. Herbert Rhodes did not remain long. He went off to hunt wild game. But Cecil did well. He wrote home in 1872 that he was making £100 a week. And after a little while he took a partner—C. D. Rudd—who was to remain with him through life—a young man like himself who had a bad chest, a feverish appetite for profit, and a great talent for administration.

There were all manner of men on that dust heap. But these two boys were the most extraordinary of the lot. The prospector was limited to one claim. Soon one man was allowed ten claims. Rhodes bought up nine more. Later all limitation was abolished. Rhodes and Rudd went ahead getting possession of additional claims.

By 1873 the town of tents on the Dutoitspan farm had grown to a city named Kimberley that spread out over the Dutoitspan, Bultfontein, and De Beers farms. Rhodes, though yet in his teens, was among its richest citizens. He had grown in health and in physique.

He had never ceased to lament the loss of his course at Oxford. In 1872, for recreation, he made a trek by ox team through the wide veldt, among the mountains and streams of the Cape. He permitted himself the luxury of long hours lying on his back, camped at night looking up at the stars, drinking in the soft aseptic air of Africa and dreaming of the future—a time killer he indulged in all his life. He made up his mind to return to Oxford to take his degree. In 1873, leaving his partner Rudd to look after the business, he returned to England, and, having passed the entrance examinations, entered himself at Oriel College, Oxford. He studied at Oriel half the year and looked after his mining interests in Africa the other half, fleeing to the friendly airs of Kimberley in the English bad seasons. It took him eight years to finish the job at Oxford. But he left with his bachelor's and master's degrees taken together. He was twenty-five years old. And he was worth a million dollars.

--------------------------------- IV ---------------------------------

Rhodes, with his sheepskins, went back to Kimberley in a moment of destiny. The prestige of England in South Africa was at its lowest. But during those years, while he studied at Oxford and wrought at Kimberley, great events were taking place in the world. England's poets, professors, and preachers were inoculating her with the virus of world empire and Germany's Junkers were taking her people along new flights of militaristic preparation. Writers, statesmen, warriors, and promoters were industriously sowing the seeds of the Great War and the Age of Hitler in the far future.

So far as the masses of England and her public men were concerned, they had lost their appetite for imperialism. Gladstone was in power. When Disraeli conferred upon Victoria the title of Empress of India, Englishmen muttered, even protested, audibly. They did not want an empress. They had had too many and too bloody battles to put their sovereigns in their place. Having gone to long lengths to make the kingship less substantial they drew away from transforming their queen into an empress. Disraeli knew this and tried to put Victoria off. But she was eager for the title and never quite forgave her people for their resistance to her royal whim. It was necessary for Disraeli to assure the English that Victoria would be empress in India but only queen in England.

As for Africa, the English were sick of the game there. As early as 1854 the government had set its face against further expansion in South Africa. English forces were in Egypt but the occupation was looked upon as temporary. Gladstone had said that the whole South African problem with its racial divisions superimposed on the grave native problems was practically insoluble. But events and certain drifts in the mind stream of Britons as well as all Europe were running in another direction. More than one apostle of empire was putting the heady draught to the lips of Englishmen. As the young prospector-student, Rhodes, took up his seat at Oriel, John Ruskin was preaching the doctrine of power and national vigor. "This," he told Oxonians, and through them the youth of England, "is what England must do or perish. She must found colonies as fast and as far as she is able; seizing every rod of waste ground she can set her foot upon and then teaching these her colonies that their chief virtue is fidelity to their country and that their first aim is to advance the power of England by land and sea."

There was, of course, the dire implication of violence and war in these grandiose counsels. But war had its apologists. Carlyle had told his countrymen that "war was the supreme expression of the state as such." It was neither antireligious nor antisocial but "an evidence of the life of the state concentrated on an ideal end," that "manifestation of the world spirit," as Professor Cramb later inter-preted the Scottish philosopher, "hazarding all upon the fortunes of the stricken field."

It was this same Dr. J. A. Cramb, of Queens College, London, who gave the most robust expression to this dream of "imperial Britain," in frequent bursts of exhortatory rhetoric. "Imperialism is patriotism transfigured by a light from the aspirations of uni-versal humanity." War, the handmaiden of imperialism, he glori-fied "as a phase of the life effort of the state towards complete self-realization; a phase of the eternal nisus, the perpetual omnipresent strife of all beings toward self-fulfillment."

And while the warlike professor talked about England's mission to "updo the world, to establish there her peace, governing all in justice," as in Rome, nevertheless these academic Caesars had a supreme contempt for that peace that was to be the supreme flowering of their world conquest. "Universal peace," said the predatory doctor, "in the light of history, is less a dream than a nightmare."

At the root of such a philosophy, of course, could be but one logical basis and that the glorification of the race. And so we find Dr. Cramb informing us that in "a race dowered with the genius for empire as Rome was, as Britain is, imperialism is the supreme, the crowning form which, in the process of evolution, it attains." Exalted by his own rhetoric, the world-hungry doctor cried out: "If ever there came to any city, race or nation, clear through the twilight spaces across the abysses where the stars wander the call of Fate, it is *now.*"

Dr. John A. Hobson, writing critically of his countrymen, said: "The Englishman believes he is a more excellent type than any other man; he believes he is better able to assimilate any virtues they may have; he believes his character gives him a right to rule which no other can possess."

One by one, under the exhortations of teachers, philosophers, poets, and statesmen, one leader after another and soon the people slowly succumbed to the intoxicating draught until, by the time

Cecil Rhodes' race was run, all England, from the romanticists who played with the knight-errant motif to the prospectors who hunted gold and diamonds, was aflame with the delirium. Before she was done with this arrogant pursuit of the visions of Ruskin and Cramb, she had seized dominion over four and a half million square miles and a hundred million people in Africa and another empire of 700,000 square miles and twenty million people in Asia and she had isolated herself from the affection and esteem of the world.

It would be strange indeed if this evangel did not sink deeply into the soul of Rhodes. We find him saying in 1877, when he was twenty-four, after four years at Oxford: "We are the first race in the world and the more of the world we inhabit the better it is for the human race." Here is that mortal doctrine that Roman, Spaniard, Frenchman, Briton, and now Fascist and Nazi in their turn have proclaimed upon the European continent and that has drenched that continent in blood. The cultural promoters of Hitler boast that the German Aryan is not only superior to the African and the Slav but to the Englishman, just as one of Cecil Rhodes' most distinguished subalterns in the South Africa Company, Hubert Hervey, proclaimed through his literary ghost, Earl Grey, that "insofar as an Englishman differs from a Swede or a Belgian he believes he represents a more perfectly developed standard of general excellence. Yes—and even those nations like ourselves in mind and sentiment—German and Scandinavian—we regard as not so excellent as ourselves." And it is not sufficient that they should nourish their pride with the contemplation of this excellence, but "it is essential that each claimant to the first place should put forward his whole energy to prove his right. This is the moral justification of international strife and war." To strut and boast is not enough; they must "updo" the world.

Just before Rhodes had first gone to Cape Colony, as we have seen, diamonds were discovered in the Orange Free State, a Boer republic. At a later day Lord Salisbury had said that Britain "had been called to exercise an influence upon the character and progress of the world such as has been exercised by no other empire" and this call had "come from what he preferred to call the acts of Providence." The clarion call of the almighty God was trumpeted to what the Archbishop of Canterbury called Britain's "Imperial Christianity" from the yellow clay of the Griqualand diamond mines. Those mines were found north of the Orange River and it was that river beyond which England said she would have no further "territorial ambitions," using almost the same phrase Adolf Hitler used to Chamberlain at Munich.

The new treasure was found in what was known as Griqualand. This territory had always been considered as part of the Orange Free State. President Brand of the Free State promptly undertook to police the mines. Presently Waterboer, the Griqua chief, set up a claim to the diamond fields. The British government compelled the parties to submit to arbitration. President Brand and Waterboer agreed on Lieutenant Governor Keate of Natal. Keate, a British civil servant, awarded the fields to Waterboer. And immediately thereafter Waterboer appealed to the British to take over his country, which the British obligingly did, diamonds and all, annexing it to the empire as a lieutenant governorship and later incorporating it in Cape Colony. The Boers saw in this a scheme of deep perfidy that they never forgot. Their suspicions were confirmed when in 1876 Lord Carnarvon, Conservative Secretary for Foreign Affairs, tacitly admitted the wrong done the Free State when, as a solatium, he paid to it £96,000.

This was in 1876. In the following year England, despite her recognition of the Transvaal Boer republic in 1854, violated this agreement and seized that small nation without warning. The pretext was a Zulu uprising. The benevolent empire feared the Boers would not be able to cope with the warlike Zulus. Paul Kruger and General Joubert hurried to London to plead for their independence. They were told by a smiling Secretary of State that their people—the Dutch farmers—wanted the annexation. Kruger and Joubert hurried back to the Transvaal and readily produced a petition bearing the signatures of practically every voter in the Transvaal, protesting annexation. To mitigate the crime the British promised the Boers the fullest measure of local self-government. Instead the government set up was a military dictatorship. Gladstone denounced the whole proceeding. "If Cyprus and the Transvaal," he said, "were as valuable as they are valueless, I would repudiate them because they are obtained by means dishonorable to the character of the country." But when the great liberal premier came into power in 1880 he refused to restore Boer independence. Gold had appeared in the Transvaal—not a great store but enough to give the land a pleasant smell. The voice of the Lord calling the great imperial Christian empire to service was rumbling in the bowels of the Rand. In the end the Boers, under Kruger and Joubert, revolted and in four pitched battles beat the British, the last at Majuba Hill where General Sir G. Colby, in command, was killed. Thus the pretense that England must grab the Transvaal to save it from the Zulus was utterly exposed by the swiftness and decisiveness of the defeat which the Boers administered to their "saviors." Sir Garnet Wolseley warned that there was gold in the ground, that the time to finish the conquest was *now*. But Gladstone feared—with reason—that the revolt would spread to the Free State and the Cape Dutch and he again recognized the independence of the Transvaal.

This was in 1881. It was on the heels of Britain's disastrous raid upon the Transvaal that Rhodes ended his studies in Oxford and returned to Kimberley, twenty-eight years old and one of the richest men in the Cape.

He brought with him a compendium of ethical and political concepts which, if he did not invent, he assembled and edited and made into a philosophy of action. Rhodes was a thinking animal, but thinking was not a mere exercise in speculation. It was a practical instrument set for practical ends. Thus at Oxford he had read a small volume by Winwood Reade that had profoundly shaken his belief in God. The speculations of the Darwinians had added to his heresy. He kept Reade's book near him throughout his life and dipped into it again and again. But one of his biographers observes that Rhodes was not the sort of man to leave so important a question as the deity hanging in the air. He decided that it was a problem beyond his own powers or leisure to settle, but that, as matters stood, it was a fifty-fifty proposition that there was a God. He had to adopt some theory as a working proposition. And so he took God on a fifty-fifty chance.

It was part of his mental system that he had to have a basic charter of dogmas, if not intellectual principles, upon which to act. Many years later he told a gathering at Oxford that in his student years he came across Aristotle's definition of ethics as "the highest activity of the soul living for the highest object in a perfect life." And he chose there at Oxford that "highest object." It did not matter that he had misunderstood Aristotle who had spoken of "the highest principle of right" rather than the "highest object in a perfect life." The object he chose was the extension of the rule of the Anglo-Saxon race over the world. And this design he continued to follow through his life with a singleness of purpose and a disregard of the vulgar virtues in a manner to satisfy completely the specifications of Spengler, who adopted the dictum of Goethe that "the doer is always conscienceless."

In 1877, at the age of twenty-four, about the time that Disraeli seized the Transvaal, Rhodes, who saw in this a good beginning, made his first will. In it he planned a secret society, Jesuitical in its techniques, that would have as its mission the extension of British rule throughout the world; the occupation by Britain of the entire continent of Africa, the Holy Land, the valley of the Euphrates, Cyprus, Candia, all of South America, the islands of the Pacific, all of the Malay Archipelago, the seaboard of China and Japan, and the ultimate recovery of the United States of America.

Here was indeed a plan to updo the world; a dream of imperial expansion beside which the fire of Hitler is a pale and ineffectual flicker. But Rhodes throughout his life never lost sight of this goal.

V

Since Rhodes was an acquisitive dreamer, this is a proper point at which to clear up the details of his acquisitive program.

That hive of tents and lime hills that peppered the veldt and that was Kimberley gradually turned to a town of streets and buildings. Money flowed into its roistering population. And there Rhodes spent his time between semesters at Oxford.

The diamond industry, too, was taking form after the usual pattern of the pioneer mining rush. The promise of gold, diamonds, oil draws thousands of men with no other talent for growing rich save the urge of the wildcatter and the taste for wandering to far places. The diggers had but to lease claims and dig and if luck was with them the diamonds came quickly enough. But once the shovel had done its work a new talent was needed—the talent of the entrepreneur. From that point on the inevitable winnowing process began. When it became possible for one man to have as many claims as he could acquire Kimberley became the scene of the same comedy as the Pennsylvania oil regions. It became a battle for claims—for expansion—in which the weapons were money and business acumen.

At first the diamonds were found in the shallow yellow clay. Later it was necessary to excavate the deeper blue clay. The treasure was richer but the cost was greater. At this point the impractical, the extravagant, the impecunious diggers began to disappear. Men like Rhodes and his partner, Rudd, began to buy them out. Rhodes had an eye open for every source of profit. He and Rudd brought hydraulic pumping machinery from England to pump out flooded mines. They built an ice plant to supply the eager and profitable market on that blazing veldt. They made much money at both ventures. By the time Rhodes was done with his Oxford studies, he had almost complete mastery of one of the diamond fields.

There were two such fields—the De Beers and the Kimberley.

And just as Rhodes rose to the dominance of the De Beers digging, another equally colorful and extraordinary figure was widening his sway over the Kimberley mines.

In 1873, about the time that Rhodes was beginning his career as a student at Oxford, a very different person, named Barney Isaacs, was making his way to Kimberley. Isaacs, the grandson of a rabbi and the son of a Whitechapel shopkeeper, was a product of the London ghetto. He had some superficial schooling in the Jewish Free School until fourteen. After that he and his older brother, Harry, with a flair for the theater and the music hall, tried their hand at clowning, juggling, and acrobatics in some cheap music halls. Stories of diamonds in South Africa and quick riches interrupted this career. Harry Isaacs went to the Cape in 1871 and Barney in 1873. They had adopted the name of Barnato in their clowning acts and took that name to South Africa with them. Barney took forty boxes of cigars which he peddled to the miners at fancy prices, but his whole capital was swiftly exhausted. He tried his hand at boxing and clowning in Payne's circus. He worked in stores, began buying and selling any sort of merchandise, bartered old clothes and other trinkets with miners for the privilege of giving their dust a second sifting. When he had made enough money this way he appeared around the sorting tables of the mines with the little black satchel of a *kopje*-walloper—the buyers who moved around daily buying for ready cash the gems of the less thrifty diggers. Before long he had acquired a claim and in time he had extended this to four.

Unlike Rhodes, who was concerned with his education and played with grandiose visions of empire, Barnato devoted his energies with wholehearted singleness to making money and amusing himself. He diverted himself amidst the gay life of Kimberley and Cape Town, patronized the race tracks, frequented the bars, the restaurants, the gambling rooms, the theater, sponsored amateur performances of the drama and became himself one of the leading amateur actors. But all this merely gave him relaxation from the promotion of his fortune. He grew rich. He established a banking house in London—Barnato Brothers. He bought up Kimberley claims until, like Rhodes on De Beers, he became the chief influence in the Kimberley field.

By 1881 these two men—Rhodes and Barnato—dominated the diamond industry of South Africa. The acquisitive talent, like that of the artist and musician, is precocious. Rockefeller was a prosperous merchant at eighteen, Morgan was wealthy in his own right at twenty-one, Hetty Green could call off the stock quotations as a child, Fugger revealed his special genius in the twenties. Here, in South Africa, two precocious money getters were the leading figures in that art—Rhodes at twenty-eight, Barnato at twenty-four. It was inevitable that they would wage war. Neither would be content in his own province. Rhodes, indeed, had returned from England not only with a dream of imperial aggression for Britain but with a dream and a plan for industrial aggression for himself.

At twenty-eight Cecil Rhodes was thinking the same thoughts as the thirty-two-year-old Rockefeller twelve thousand miles away. Rhodes concluded that the rich rewards of the diamond industry could be drawn off only by a monopoly. Competition, production, prices must be controlled in the interest of "stabilization." There are enough swains in the world to spend on their brides and wives and mistresses four million pounds for diamonds a year. No matter how many stones were offered, that, he had calculated, was the fund available to buy them. The course of wisdom was to offer the smallest number of stones, get the largest prices for them, make the largest profit, and conserve the supply. This could be done only by monopoly control. He therefore decided, in the intervals of meditation upon the ethics of imperialism, the functions of the deity, and the perusal of the classics at Oriel, that he would capture the monopoly of South Africa's diamonds. He would proceed quite as the elder monopolist, Rockefeller—of whom perhaps he had never heard—had proceeded, covering himself with riches and odium.

He began his preparations before he was through with Oxford. In 1880 he formed the De Beers Mining Company, £200,000 capital. He induced many diggers who would not sell outright to him to go in for shares in De Beers. Barnato did the same. He formed the Barnato Mining Company with £115,000 capital. Barnato was no slight adversary. He was richer personally than Rhodes. Through his London house he had access to large capital resources. He was shrewd, quick-witted, audacious, with unlimited confidence in himself. He loved to gamble and boasted that he had never had an unsuccessful operation. He was lively, buoyant in spirits, pugnacious, and money hungry.

But he had one weak spot in his armor. His company owned most of the Kimberley mine fields. However, an important section was still held by a French concern—the Compagnie Française des Mines de Diamond du Cap—whereas Rhodes had all of the De Beers field. By 1885 Rhodes felt himself strong enough to begin his offensive against Barnato. And he began with the French company. He arranged a loan with the Rothschilds in London for £750,000 and through a Hamburg syndicate issued £750,000 in shares. With these funds he made an offer to buy the French company's holdings for £1,400,000. This deal was on the point of going through—had indeed been approved—when Barnato, getting wind of it, made an offer of £300,000 more. Rhodes went to Barnato. He told him with convincing frankness that De Beers would raise his bid no matter how much he offered. Then he offered to sell the French company to Barnato for £1,400,000, precisely what he proposed to pay for it. This looked like complete capitulation. But Rhodes insisted that Barnato pay him for the French company with shares in the Kimberley company. Rhodes reasoned that even though he got possession of the French company's shares, he would have to begin an aggressive fight to get into Kimberley. Furthermore, he saw that if Barnato got the French company, the complete control would be in Kimberley and if, at the same time, he got a foothold in Kimberley he would be on his way to getting possession of that whole diamond field. Barnato, apparently, did not bother about this. The French company holdings would complete his possession of Kimberley and he did not believe that Rhodes could

stretch his minority interest in Kimberley thus acquired to a controlling interest. He agreed.

Immediately Rhodes set about grasping Kimberley company
control. He began buying shares in Kimberley. Barnato, on his
part, set out to cripple De Beers by a diamond price war. Also
Barnato began to compete with Rhodes in buying Kimberley shares
as they came on the market. Thus two wars—a diamond price war
and a stock war—ensued. The price of diamonds went steadily
down. Barnato thought he could either break De Beers or force it
to surrender. But he was playing a desperate game against a master
general.

Once again Barnato played his hand wrong. He made the mistake of underrating Rhodes' financial resources. Rhodes had at his
side one of the most remarkable financial figures of South African
history—Alfred Beit, a Hamburg Jew who had started life as a
diamond merchant in Amsterdam and graduated into banking, a
shrewd, prudent, yet bold financier of great wealth, who had his
own banking house and rich connections in Amsterdam and Hamburg. He idolized Rhodes.

Moreover, in the stock war, Rhodes' buying was done by himself, Beit, and his colleagues acting as a unit and aiming at control.
When they bought Kimberley shares they kept them. Barnato,
however, was supported in his buying by friends who were not so
much interested in control as in speculation. They bought Kimberley shares. But when the market rose swiftly, they sold to take
the profit and, as they sold, Rhodes' agents were on hand to buy.
As the game got warm and Barnato perceived what was happening
he appealed to his friends to buy and hold. But now his price-war
stratagem smote him. He was asking men to hold on to shares from
the sale of which they could make a rich profit—shares in a company which, as the share prices rose, was losing money as the price
of diamonds declined. He awoke finally to see that Rhodes had got
a clear majority of Kimberley shares. There was nothing to do but
sue for terms.

Rhodes organized a new company—the De Beers Consolidated

Mines, Ltd., which took over the holdings of both the old De Beers and the Kimberley company. Barnato became one of the board of life governors with control completely in Rhodes' hands. Rhodes was to be general manager. The diamond industry was a complete monopoly under Rhodes' thumb and he had traversed the first stage in his ambitious plan. But he had another at the same moment.

In the course of negotiations, Rhodes had made upon Barnato the extraordinary demand that the resources of the De Beers company should be available for use in extending the dominions of Britain in South Africa. This ruffled the hackles of Barnato's business sense. He wanted no mixture of politics with the business of making money from diamonds. But Rhodes was obdurate. For eighteen hours the two men argued the settlement with this strange item in it. Rhodes threatened, reasoned, cajoled. In the end Barnato capitulated. He said later he always avoided Rhodes when he differed with him. "When you have been with him half an hour you not only agree with him but come to the belief that you have always held his opinion," Barnato said.

Nevertheless, it took eighteen hours of wrangling to bring Barnato around to Rhodes' imperial ingredient in the diamond corporation. Rhodes had to flatter him. Barnato, rich though he was, had never been able to crack the crust of the social shell that excluded him from polite Cape society. He had never got his foot inside the Kimberley Club. Rhodes took him there to luncheon, promised him membership. The once humble Whitechapel juggler softened in that solvent atmosphere. When the deal was concluded Rhodes said to Barnato: "You have had your whim. Now for mine. I have always wanted to see a bucketful of diamonds." Barnato produced them. Four hundred and thirty truckloads of blue clay in a year had to be washed to produce a bucket of diamonds. Rhodes ran his fingers through the precious brilliants, letting them sift through his fingers. At thirty-six he had fought an epic battle against his thirty-two-year-old adversary for one of the greatest prizes in the world. He was master of the diamond world. The sparkling fruit of that tree dripped through his fingers now like sand. It must have seemed easy. Beyond lay still other and more difficult worlds to which he looked. He lost no time in making the start.

VI

Rhodes, the businessman, with his dream of British empire, was drawn inevitably into politics. Griqualand West, the diamond country, was incorporated into the Cape in 1881. And Rhodes was named one of its first members in the Cape House from Barkeley West.

He was already a figure in the Cape. Millionaire, diamond digger, Oxford man—in that small world with the population, as he described it, of a third-rate English city such a one was not to be discounted. Tall, broad-shouldered, auburn-haired, a "fine, ruddy Englishman of the country squire type," as a contemporary described him, blunt of speech but friendly, giving himself no airs because of his success or education, he took his seat in 1881. Some older members made faces at his refusal to wear the conventional claw-hammer coat and high hat of the Cape statesman. "I am still in Oxford tweeds," he said, "and I think I can legislate in them as well as in sable clothing." He loved to mingle with politicians, men of affairs, and newsmen who gathered at the Civil Service Club and Poole's for lunch and reveled in the talk.

He took his seat as the Boer war fiasco approached its end in 1881. Rhodes was hot with anger at Gladstone's surrender. He opposed Boer independence. He would not be trampled upon by these Dutchmen. But the war was over; he was done with it. He spoke of it little. The man who had swept his hand over the map of Africa and said it must be all red now set about achieving that dream.

At the tip of Africa nestled the small Cape. Above it was Bechuanaland, a broad province of grass and desert. On one side of it— the west—lay German West Africa. On the other were the Orange

Free State and Transvaal. It was a broad corridor, a "Suez Canal" as Rhodes said, leading northward from the Cape to the interior of Africa. If England did not seize that, her pathway north as Rhodes planned it would be closed.

He proceeded at once to urge upon the Cape parliament the acquisition of Bechuanaland. There was no time to be lost, he said. Bismarck had only recently hoisted the German flag over German West Africa and was looking about for more. On the other side, the Transvaal Boers were ceaselessly seeking to push the dominion of their pastoral republic northward into the rich grazing lands of Bechuanaland. If the Boers took that country the Kaiser, Rhodes said, would find some pretext to attack and grab the Transvaal, thus commanding a stretch of territory running completely across South Africa above the Cape and locking Britain in.

By 1883 Rhodes succeeded in having a commission named to investigate certain Griqualand claims. Named on this commission, he expanded its functions to suit his ends. He went to Bechuanaland. He visited the native chief, Makorane, and induced him to appeal to the Cape to take over his land to protect him from other chiefs. The Boers had entered. Two small Boer republics were organized there—Stellaland and Land of Goshen. He induced the Stellaland president, van Niekerk, to accept a British protectorate. He did not have the same success at Goshen where van Pettius, a stubborn and resolute Boer, held out.

However, Rhodes, in February, 1884, induced Lord Derby to proclaim a protectorate over Bechuanaland. A commission was sent headed by a narrow and race-proud clergyman, John Mac-Kenzie, to organize the territory. He got into trouble with native chiefs and Boer leaders. He refused to recognize the pledges Rhodes had made to the Boers to respect their land titles and permit full measure of self-government.

At this point, Paul Kruger, President of the Transvaal republic, acted. He proclaimed Land of Goshen Transvaal territory and sent in some Boer troops to make it good.

Rhodes counseled swift action by the imperial government. An expeditionary force commanded by Sir Charles Warren with 4000 men marched into Goshen on Christmas, 1884. Kruger saw he had gone too far. He asked for a conference. The conference was held at Fourteen Streams in the Cape. There the two men who would impersonate the hostile forces in the rising crisis of South Africa—Paul Kruger and Cecil Rhodes—met for the first time.

Stephanus Johannes Paulus Kruger—later to be known as Oom Paul—President of the Transvaal, was then fifty-nine. Born in the Cape he had shared with his family and people the great northward trek out of the Cape beyond the Vaal River and the founding of the Transvaal republic. A magistrate at seventeen, military officer of his ward, he had engaged in the wars against the Matabeles, the Zulus, and the Basutos. He had risen through the grades of commandant general and vice-president to the presidency the preceding year. Patriarchal in appearance, iron-willed, nourishing a profound hatred of the British out of his memory of all the wrongs his people had suffered, deeply religious, preaching every Sunday in the church opposite the presidency the primitive evangelism of the Dopper branch of the Dutch Reformers, he looked upon himself as the chosen instrument of almighty God to lead his people.

These two men—Kruger and Rhodes—were driven along by the same design of expansion. Kruger dreamed of an independent Boer republic from the Orange River to the Zambezi. Rhodes dreamed of an imperial dominion of the British empire in that same land. For the next fifteen years the plans of these two men in their respective directions would shape the development of South Africa and lead in the end to a bloody and disastrous war. It is possible that if diamonds had not been discovered in the Free State and gold later in the Transvaal, Kruger would have had his dream. In later years Rhodes spoke of him as "that extraordinary man" and "one of the most remarkable in South Africa." But now as Kruger faced Rhodes for the first time at Fourteen Streams, the accumulating energies that flowed from the diamond mines, the still-small gold mines, and the growing half-braggart, half-com-

mercial imperialism of Britain were too much for him. He agreed
to withdraw from Land of Goshen. General Sir Charles Warren
and his 4000 regulars assumed the rule of Bechuanaland, with
Rhodes as a civil adviser.

Warren, inflexible militarist imperialist, proceeded to act the
role of Roman proconsul. He overran the country, quarreled with
everyone, repudiated all of England's pledges, and even arrested
van Niekerk on a preposterous charge of murder. He finally
quarreled with Rhodes, who wanted a moderate, ingratiating policy with the Boer settlers, while Warren thought in terms of force,
obedience, authority, hierarchy. He was the perfect fruit of that
principle of racial coxcombery that lies at the root of imperialism.
Rhodes quit his post in disgust, returned to Cape Town, resumed
his seat, and denounced Warren's methods. Warren had to be
recalled. Bechuanaland was then erected into a protectorate. But
Rhodes had completed the first step in that series of aggressions
by which England would become the overlord of most of Africa.

VII

After the Bechuanaland affair the prestige of Rhodes stood
high in the Cape. He had by his criticism of Warren conciliated
the Dutch. And he had practically doubled the land area of British
possessions in South Africa. His wealth had grown royal. His influence in parliament was vast. His expansive dream of empire
had become infectious. By 1889 he was acting treasurer general
and in 1890 he was elevated to the premiership of Cape Colony.

But before he became Prime Minister he set in motion that
project which was to be his chef-d'oeuvre. The conquest of Bechuanaland was merely the prelude to his ultimate aim which was,
as some began to phrase it, to make Africa "British from the Cape
to Cairo." His next step was to move northward yet again, this
time into the vast country of Lobengula—a province twice as
large as Texas, one day to be known as Rhodesia.

In 1887 Rhodes heard that Boers were meditating a northward

trek into Lobengula's country—the land of the Matabeles and the Mashonas. Though Rhodes held no office he made the Boers understand that if they went into Matabeleland they must go as British subjects. "There will be no more Boer republics permitted in South Africa," he said. Then he moved himself. And now we may see clearly the clever surgery of imperialism.

He had a mission sent to Lobengula which negotiated a treaty with him. It was agreed (1) that peace should continue forever between the British and the Matabeles; (2) that Lobengula would refrain from entering into any agreement or correspondence with any foreign state to alienate any part of his country without previous knowledge or sanction of the British High Commissioner of South Africa (February 11, 1888).

A second mission followed, managed by Rhodes' partner, Rudd. Lobengula was a huge, intelligent, but not very warlike chieftain. He had developed a keen talent for negotiation with white men. Rudd and his two companions, representing Rhodes and not the government, remained nine months amid the strong odors of the Matabele chief's kraal at Bulawayo fishing for an agreement. They wanted a concession. They sought an arrangement to permit them to hunt for and work metal mines in Matabeleland. Some gold had been found there by a German in 1864 and a promising gold belt by an Englishman in 1869, though little had been done about these discoveries.

Lobengula was wary of his visitors. He listened ceaselessly to the arguments of his suppliants. He wanted to be sure no infringement of his sovereignty was intended. He wanted no white settlers. Rhodes' agents told him: "All the white men want is for you to let them dig in the country of the Mashonas for gold."

Then one day Lobengula sent for the interpreter who accompanied the Rhodes party. "You are sure you are not coming for grass and ground?" he asked.

"King, no. It is minerals we want."

Thus assured, he put his mark to an agreement. This document gave Rhodes "complete and exclusive charge over all metals and

minerals in my kingdom" and to "do all things that they may deem
necessary to procure the same." Rhodes agreed to pay Lobengula
100 pounds a month, 1000 Martini-Henry breech-loading rifles,
100,000 rounds of ammunition, and a steamboat with guns to
patrol the Zambezi.

Lobengula always insisted that he had been duped. He wrote
a protest to the Queen later in which he declared: "Men asked
for peace to dig gold and said they would give me certain things.
A document was presented to me which they said contained my
words. I signed. Three months later I was told that I had given
away all minerals in my country."

The account of one member of Rhodes' own mission serves to
bear this out. But, even accepting the document on which Rhodes
relied, all he had was an instrument giving him an exclusive concession to work mineral deposits in Matabeleland. Yet the next
Lobengula knew of this transaction was when his warriors informed him that Rhodes' agents had entered Mashonaland with a
military force of 320 troops, escorting 180 settlers under command
of Sir John Willoughby, armed with a charter from the British
government that gave Rhodes the right to administer and govern
the country, to set up courts and administer justice even among
the natives.

If Rhodes had proceeded with consideration for the natives in
Bechuanaland, he unloaded those virtues now in Matabeleland.
Had he merely invaded the country he might have appealed to
the higher law of the superman and the superstate. But he first
made a solemn agreement with Lobengula, obtained upon palpably
false promises, and then violated the agreement the moment he
had obtained it.

As soon as he had his metal concession he hastened to London,
where he induced the government to give him a charter for a corporation called the British South Africa Company, after the model
of those old imperialistic trading companies under cover of which
Dutch and French and English trader-adventurers had seized
great portions of the world's surface. It conferred powers of gov-

ernment upon the British South Africa Company with a reservation that the British government might take over administration of the company on compensating Rhodes. These trading companies were the precursors, organizers, and missionaries of imperialism in the early capitalist era, often without any design on the part of the government. They spread their administrative authority over great areas as part of their commercial activities and gradually created colonial dominions that governments had to step in and administer. It was the Dutch East India Company that had first colonized South Africa, as the British East India Company had exploited India. And it was such a company that Rhodes now formed to seize and masticate Matabeleland as a prelude to its digestion by the crown. It had a special advantage for promoter and crown. Salisbury was now Prime Minister. Rhodes' dream of empire in Africa enjoyed high favor in London. The soil of South Africa was revealing rich reasons for the spread of Christian civilization on that continent. Diamonds in Griqualand were succeeded by gold in Witwatersrand. The good earth there looked good indeed to Downing Street. But the scramble for territory in Africa bristled with difficulties. The government could well leave the next stage of conquest to a trading corporation. It could disown the blunders of such a company. The company could withdraw from positions without compromising the prestige of the empress. As for Rhodes—to him the record of direct imperial government in Africa was a chronicle of blunders. He wanted no more Bechuanaland mistakes. If the penetration, confiscation, and organization of Matabeleland could be carried on by him, he could proceed without the hampering red tape of the Foreign Office.

He pulled strings to get his charter. He lured several noble gentlemen into the enterprise. He made the Duke of Abercorn president and the Duke of Fife vice-president of the chartered company. He issued a million shares at a pound a piece. The promoters took 90,000 founders' shares (founders' shares which American promoters were to discover with delight twenty years later). And these took fifty per cent of the profits. The ordinary

shares were sold to small investors. The meticulous old London
Times plugged them valiantly. The country of Lobengula was
"fabulously rich," a veritable "Land of Ophir," it repeated. The
shares were eagerly snapped up.

Having got his charter, Rhodes returned to South Africa and
organized that expedition of settlers and soldiers that had alarmed
the disillusioned Lobengula as it marched into Mashonaland in
July, 1890. The chieftain demanded that the column come to Bulawayo in order to reveal its intentions. It ignored this summons,
pushed into Mashonaland, built Fort Salisbury, hoisted the British
flag, and took possession of the country formally under the protection of the British crown.

By this time Rhodes had become Prime Minister of the Cape.
Entrenched in political power there and in absolute power at the
head of the chartered company, he was prepared to work his will
freely.

But the enterprise did not prosper. In two years it was in trouble.
Few settlers arrived. The company exacted fifty per cent of all
minerals recovered. Food had to be brought through a difficult
jungle. A police force of seven hundred was organized. The chartered company paid out £250,000 a year and got little return.
The settlers grumbled. Lobengula bided his time to smite the in-
vaders. The white settlers stole the natives' cattle, which was their
chief wealth. Finally Lobengula sent an army to Mashonaland on
pretext of chastising his serfs, the Mashonas. By this time Dr.
Jameson was administrator of the chartered company. He opened
fire on Lobengula's warriors and the first Matabele war was on.
Jameson with nine hundred men pursued Lobengula and in two
pitched battles defeated him. The king abandoned Bulawayo, his
capital. He was pursued but died of smallpox. The Matabeles surrendered. Rhodes won a costly victory, but in England the whole
episode was roundly denounced as a recrudescence of medieval
imperialism.

The trouble did not end here. Some years later, after the famous Jameson Raid had impaired Rhodes' power, there came a

second Matabele war. The natives revolted again. A British force was sent under General Sir Frederick Carrington to subdue them, but without success. They were finally subdued by Rhodes himself. And the manner in which he did it is the subject of one of those apocryphal fables that are built up around famous men—like the hatchet and Washington—which have more to do with forming popular judgment about them than the facts of history.

The legend represents Rhodes in the heroic mold. Carrington, in winter quarters, planned a spring offensive to cost £20,000,000. This meant bankruptcy for the chartered company. Rhodes decided upon a daring strike. Taking five companions he went to the Matopo Hills. The chiefs agreed to see Rhodes. They assembled in a natural amphitheater walled by the granite hills. Rhodes went to them alone where he found the surrounding cliffs and rocks swarming with the warriors in war paint. They advanced, forming a menacing circle around him. He addressed them; admitted some grievances, and then, his eyes blazing, he denounced them for their cruelties. He ended by crying: "Is it to be war or peace?" Overcome by this display of courage one old chief threw down his weapons at Rhodes' feet. "There is my rifle. There is my spear," he cried. And the war was over.

It is a pretty story, but untrue. Rhodes did go to the Matopo Hills. But Colonel Plumer was camped there with eight hundred men. He set up his own tent at a little distance, since he hated camps. He had several companions, among them a woman, Mrs. Colebrenner, and her husband. Instead of his going to the Matabele camp alone, one of the elder statesmen of the tribe, Babiaan, visited Rhodes' camp alone and remained as a guest for two weeks. He feasted on Rhodes' hospitality, returned to the Matabele settlement, and persuaded the chiefs to visit Rhodes, which they did and agreed to end the war. They then arranged a great peace meeting to which Rhodes went and partook of the great feast spread for him. At two or three meetings Rhodes concluded a treaty with them ending a war that was costing the British South Africa Company £4000 a day. It was a triumph of skillful negotiation but in no sense the heroic adventure narrated by some biographers. The account given here is that written by Rhodes' secretary who accompanied him on the trip.

It ended with Rhodes adding another magnificent domain of over 400,000 square miles to the British land loot of South Africa —a territory more than four times the extent of the United Kingdom itself. By 1890 this pragmatic dreamer of empire for Britain and riches for himself had, in nine years, acquired for himself undisputed control of the diamond monopoly of South Africa, a powerful claim upon the vast gold holdings of the Transvaal discovered in that time, and for Britain he had brought the territorial holdings up to nearly a million square miles, or one third the land surface of the United States.

VIII

By this time Rhodes had matured his political philosophy about South Africa and the British Empire. He held steadfastly to the view that there must be a union of the white states—the Cape, Natal, Transvaal, and Orange Free State. The Dutch statesmen nursed the same ambition. But as the Transvaal and Free State were all Dutch and the Cape and Natal heavily populated with Dutch, their objective was a unified Dutch republic. And Dutoit, of the Afrikander Bund, insisted that "the one hindrance to this was the British flag."

Rhodes, however, did not want a union run from London. He believed, as he put it himself, in a "government of South Africa, by the people of South Africa, with the imperial flag for defense."

Rhodes had been dwelling much upon this theme since he wrote that first will some fifteen years before in which he had planned a great Jesuitical society to bring the world under the domination of the British Empire. The Matopo Hills, which he had conquered, had become a sort of wild natural cloister for him to which he went alone to wander and to meditate. And there, his friend W. T. Stead said, Rhodes spent long hours in solitude weaving the details of his dream—working out his plans. He had begun to feel the urge of the Caesar in him. Stead speaks of the strange compound of hostile elements in this man, son of an old Roman emperor crossed with one of Oliver Cromwell's Ironsides and educated by Ignatius Loyola. He was an agnostic, but he said to Stead: "If there is a God I think he would like me to paint as much of the map of South Africa red as possible." Thus with a religious zeal he threw himself into the grandiose plan of carrying out the hypothetical design of an imaginary god in whom he did not believe, save to give some sort of spiritual authenticity and sanctity to his personal ambition. And in pursuance of this scheme he played with three ideas. One was the immediate object of bringing Africa as swiftly as possible under British rule. The other was the reduction of the whole world—or as much as possible—to this rule and as part of this the recovery of the United States for the British crown. The third was the creation of an empire which would resemble the Holy Roman Empire, a federation of self-governing nations or dominions united under an emperor. The United States was to be one of these dominions.

This recapture of America fascinated Rhodes' mind. And he believed it wholly feasible. "Fancy," he wrote to Stead, "the charm to young America, just coming on and dissatisfied, taking a share in a scheme to take the government of the world. Their President is dimly seeing it." World mastery as the basis of stable rule seemed essential to him. "It would have been better for Europe if Napoleon had carried out his idea of universal monarchy."

So essential did he look upon the inclusion of the United States in this scheme of things that he told Stead that if the young republic refused to come into the empire, England should apply for incorporation in the union of states. And so bent was he on establishing the principle of autonomous dominions within the empire that he contributed £10,000 to Charles Stuart Parnell's movement for a separate Irish parliament. He made as a condition of the gift that the Home Rulers, while demanding self-government for Ireland within Ireland, would also insist on representation in the

British Parliament. This he felt would be a beginning. For he believed the ultimate form of government would include local parliaments in each free nation, including England, and an imperial parliament that would control imperial affairs in which each dominion would be represented.

———————————————— IX ————————————————

In 1886 gold was found on a farm in the Witwatersrand in the Transvaal. Rhodes, Beit, and Rudd were among the first on the scene. They bought up farms. They struck rich veins. In a year they put their properties under the direction of a corporation formed by Rhodes called Gold Fields of South Africa. It began with £125,000 capital. In five years the capital grew to £1,250,000. The corporation, reorganized as Gold Fields Consolidated, Ltd., in 1892 paid ten per cent dividend, fifteen per cent in 1893 and fifty per cent in 1894.

The irrepressible Barney Barnato also, somewhat tardily, spread his operations to the Rand. He became the largest single property owner there. And as the new city of gold, Johannesburg, rose amid the mines, Barnato became the same sort of colorful figure there he was in Kimberley and the Cape.

By the middle 'nineties Rhodes' interests were vast and consuming. He was at once Prime Minister of the Cape, head of the Chartered Company of Rhodesia—a sort of proconsular despot— managing director of De Beers Diamond Mines, and master of Gold Fields Consolidated. To all these operations he gave the most exacting attention.

In addition to this he owned hundreds of thousands of shares in all sorts of enterprises. He looked upon himself, by reason of his position in government and business, as having a claim to a part in any enterprise in South Africa. There seemed no bounds to his acquisitiveness. He did not hesitate to express his disgust and annoyance at any promoter who floated an issue without cutting him in on the preferred list. In founding Gold Fields he, Beit, and Rudd had taken for themselves founders' shares—a sort of superpreferential security that gave them a first claim upon a large section of the company's profits before the ordinary shares. He was in continual quarrels with the shareholders about this. He bickered incessantly with the stockholders of De Beers and the Chartered Company about his share of profits. In the end he was forced to relinquish for ordinary shares his founders' shares in Gold Fields. As for his numerous stock investments, his secretary Jourdan, a by no means idolatrous apologist, says he did not go in for market speculations to make quick profits on the changes in stock prices. But he certainly kept a running account with Wernher, Beit & Company and bought and sold upon a large scale. During these years his income was frequently as high as a million pounds a year. But he spent it lavishly. It is a singular fact that a man with such large revenues should be overdrawn at his bank most of the time.

His mind dwelt incessantly on his vast schemes. He toyed with such projects as a railroad from the Cape to the Isthmus, with telegraph and telephone systems. His ceaseless pursuit of money was inextricably mixed up with his imperial ambitions for power for himself and for the empire. He was fond of attributing his acquisitiveness to his need for money for these designs. "No use," he would say, "having big ideas unless you have the money to carry them through."

He worked like a man who felt the shortness of life and the length and immensity of his purposes. He was an inveterate letter writer. He would dictate often as many as fifty or more a day. At table with his guests he would keep his secretary near to dictate a letter or notes as his mind jumped to the idea. He would go sometimes at any hour of the night in his pajamas to his secretary's room to dictate a telegram.

Rhodes lived for many years in small bachelor chambers with his friend Dr. Leander Starr Jameson in Kimberley and at his club in Cape Town. But in time he built a magnificent estate called Groote Schur at the foot of Table Mountain outside of Cape

Town. The house, a spacious castle, was in the Dutch style. The furnishings were the same. The rooms were filled with Dutch and Flemish antiques, tapestries, china, furniture. The walls were covered with trophies of the chase, native spears, guns, shields—relics of the Matabele wars. He was fond of collecting old oaken chests. The grounds were extensively landscaped. There was a menagerie in them of well-known African animals. He himself gave much attention to a large collection of roses he collected. He spent little on art treasures. There were paintings, but only one of importance—a canvas by Sir Joshua Reynolds.

Rhodes never married. At Groote Schur his sister, Edith Rhodes, ministered as his hostess. He was fond of guests. Groote Schur was a sort of open house where there were often throngs for dinner. Rhodes was a lusty Englishman who was fond of good food and drink and could account for large quantities of both. He took a mug of champagne and stout—what we now call black velvet—in the morning. At dinner he drank champagne. At night he permitted himself more potent libations. Some said he drank to excess. He did indeed consume quantities of liquor that would have been excessive in other men. His capacity was large. But he did not get drunk. He danced little but occasionally took part in the lancers. He was a good billiard player and was fond of cards. His favorite diversion was reading. Rhodes was too much the man of affairs and his mind was too generally occupied with large projects to have the time for attention to books that he would have liked. He had a large library and he spent as much time as he could with the volumes he preferred. He retained his early interest in the Greek and Roman classics. Many of these he had specially translated for him, carefully typed and handsomely bound. It was not surprising that he should be attracted by Gibbon and Carlyle, who supplied him with some choice philosophical supports for war and empire. He thought Rudyard Kipling the greatest living man. Indeed, he invited him to Groote Schur, built a bungalow for him at the base of Table Mountain, where Kipling regularly spent a part of each year.

Rhodes was a pleasant and thoughtful neighbor. But in the pursuit of his designs he was ruthless. He had an insatiable appetite for power, to which he brooked no challenge. There was a time when the imperialists in London began to fear that Rhodes was nourishing a plan to detach South Africa from the empire and make himself its master. It is hardly probable that he ever seriously toyed with the idea. He was known as the friend of the Dutch. He did indeed cultivate their good will and ultimately won it. But it was a part of his whole plan to unite South Africa, and the friendly support of the most numerous element there was essential to that design. He could be cruel to them as to the natives for whom, also, he sometimes stood up. He was one of those men who are more interested in omelets than in eggs. The omelet he was preparing was a great African empire. The eggs were nothing more than African Zulus and Kaffirs, Dutch burghers and English soldiers. He could not be too much concerned about cracking some of them.

Rhodes was in no sense a religious man. He was a Darwinian. Science, he thought, had pulverized the Bible. He was an agnostic. William T. Stead insisted he had a broad strain of religious feeling. He certainly was not a Christian. And his acceptance of God was largely for political and working purposes. He did have in him, however, an attraction for the external and dramatic elements of mysticism—some sort of spirit, some form of pagan divinity—which comprehended the glorification of power and the infusion of mystic forces into the trees, the rocks, the mountains. This perhaps is why Spengler classed him as a type of Teutonic Caesar. He loved to wander alone on the sides of Table Mountain or, better still, in the wide solitudes of the Matopos. There he could draw from the majestic bulk of its boulders and its peaks the spiritual support of his dreams. He chose a spot amid the rugged rocks on a lofty height in these Matopos which he called World's View. There he could see as in a vision the world he had set out to conquer in the name of his British blood. For above everything else he was a worshiper of race and the ruling urge of his life was that primitive and semibarbarous dream of blood dominion that moved the earliest kings and tribes upon the banks of the Nile, the Euphrates, and the Tiber.

———————————————————— x ————————————————————

Was it in the wild loneliness of the Matopos that Rhodes came at last to that fatal decision that would unhorse him in South Africa, drive him from the premiership to disgrace, force him out of the directorate of the Chartered Company of his beloved Rhodesia, bring his chief lieutenant and friend, Dr. Jameson, to a London cell for fifteen months and himself to the very gates of that same jail?

By 1895 his conquests seemed to have covered every immediate objective save one—the Dutch republic of the Transvaal. He was Prime Minister of Cape Colony. He dominated the diamond fields of the Cape and the gold mines of the Transvaal. He had added Bechuanaland and Matabeleland to the British Empire and pushed the Union Jack north as far as the Zambezi. The time had come to deal with his old enemy, Paul Kruger. And this he proceeded to do in the best traditions of empire building with the ancient weapons of conspiracy, theft, stealth, deceit, and violence. Not Clive hatching the destruction of Suraj-ud-Dowlah in Bengal nor Warren Hastings ousting Chait Singh drew more heavily upon the resources of perfidy than Rhodes in the ill-starred Jameson Raid. Clive and Hastings at least could claim that their crimes had been sanctified by success. Rhodes committed the crowning crime of failure that darkened the hue of all the other deeds preceding the disaster.

One of the most extraordinary characters in Cape history was Dr. Leander Starr Jameson. Born in Edinburgh, he studied medicine, but ill health forced him to the Cape to practice his profession. He became Rhodes' physician, friend, and fellow lodger and was induced later by Rhodes to give up his practice and take over the administration of the Chartered Company of Rhodesia. He commanded in the operations which destroyed Lobengula. He worshiped Rhodes and shared with him the passion for British world supremacy. In 1895 he was filling the post of head of the Chartered Company with much success. It was with Jameson that Rhodes entered upon the conspiracy to steal the Transvaal.

Just as Griqualand West excited the appetite of the imperial government when diamonds were discovered, so the discovery of gold in the Rand signaled the doom of the Boer republic. Prospectors had swarmed into the Transvaal. These adventurers had established Johannesburg. It was not long before they outnumbered the Boer farmers, owned half the property and most of the wealth of the country.

In time these newcomers—known as Uitlanders (Outlanders)—developed certain grievances against the Dutch republic. Some of them were not without foundation. They were heavily taxed. A tariff of thirty per cent was imposed on supplies, including food, coming in to them. Kruger established a government monopoly of dynamite, an essential commodity to the miners. He charged exorbitant prices. The miners said it imposed a tax of $3,000,000 a year in excess cost of blasting materials. It was the republic's method of drawing from the wealth found in its hills a share for the people, and it did not take from them nearly as much as, a little later, England took by an income tax from her own citizens. Despite these exactions the Uitlanders were practically excluded from citizenship by a provision that required fifteen years' residence as a condition precedent.

The other side of the story is that Kruger knew the English settlers in Johannesburg were not interested in citizenship in the Dutch republic merely to become part of it. He knew that across his boundary was a master organizer who was biding the day when he could swallow the Transvaal. He knew also that the English dwellers in the mine fields, many merely adventurers and camp followers, wanted citizenship in order to shape policy without any intention of transferring their allegiance and that to admit them

would be, in the parlance of today, to admit a great Fifth Columnist
and a prelude to the end of the republic.

In any case Kruger claimed for his country nothing more than
every nation asserts—the right to determine the conditions of citizenship. And many nations, including the United States, have
exercised that right to exclude altogether not merely from citizenship but actual entry other nationals not wanted for one reason or
another.

The grievances of the Uitlanders were being industriously employed by the imperialists to foment irritations that might become
the prologue to a seizure of the Boer republic.

A Reform Committee was organized in Johannesburg to demand
a redress of grievances. Rhodes was invited to join. He named first
his brother Ernest and later his brother Frank Rhodes to represent him. While this committee was engaged in agitation to force
concessions from Kruger, Rhodes saw in it the opportunity for an
act of outright aggression against the Boers. He prepared his plans
for seizure of the Transvaal for the British crown. In all that followed he kept far behind the scenes; so far, in fact, that few suspected that he had a hand in the tragedy.

The plan proceeded as follows. The Uitlanders were to be
whipped into a state of hysterical wrath over Kruger's inevitable
refusal of their demands. The citizens of Johannesburg would revolt. The ensuing disorder would be used by Rhodes, as Prime
Minister of the neighboring Cape, to send troops into the Transvaal
to protect British subjects and to restore order. In the end the republic would be extinguished and the Transvaal follow the fate
of Griqualand, Bechuanaland, and Matabeleland.

Preparations in Johannesburg for the internal uprising were
entrusted to Colonel Frank Rhodes. Arrangements for the external
military force to invade the republic were put in the hands of Dr.
Leander Starr Jameson, then head of the Chartered Company in
Rhodesia.

Sometime in November the Johannesburg Railroad was to be
seized by the rebels. Jameson, camped near the border with troops,

was, upon an appeal for help, to march into the Transvaal. Arms were sent from the Chartered Company offices in London both to Jameson and Colonel Frank Rhodes in Johannesburg. Drafts for the expenses were honored by that company and by Rhodes and Beit. Rhodes honored drafts for £60,000; Beit for £200,000.

Jameson assembled a large force and stationed it within striking distance of the republic. He added 350 men to the Rhodesian police. A military force was also organized, made up of cavalry, engineers, and artillery commanded by Sir John Willoughby. The real purpose of this was concealed behind rumors given out that native uprisings were feared. The whole force was marched by Jameson outside of Rhodesia into Bechuanaland to a village—Pitsani— three and a half miles from the Transvaal border. So secretly was all this managed that Sir Hercules Robinson, British High Commissioner, did not know of it. Rhodes' own secretary suspected nothing.

Rhodes made all this possible. To do so he had to abuse a series of trusts. As head of the Chartered Company he had to use its funds and staff for an act of war without knowledge of its directors. He mobilized the police of Rhodesia for an invasion of a neighboring state. As Prime Minister he permitted the use of the territory of Bechuanaland by the Rhodesian troops to march on the Transvaal. And all this he had plotted in spite of the pledges of friendship and confidence with which he had won the support and good will of the Dutch citizens of the Cape, whose allegiance made it possible for him to be premier. He had, in fact, upon his own authority, without the knowledge of his parliament, the British High Commissioner, or the English government, prepared a war upon a friendly state. And to add to the perfidy of the plan a touch of Machiavellian ethics, Jameson was provided with a telegram written in advance of action, signed by five members of the Reform Association, which read: "Women and children at mercy of aroused Boers." The date was left blank to be filled in.

But when all was ready difficulties began to hamper the adventure. There being no open strong leadership, the conspirators in

Johannesburg quarreled over details. Rhodes' agents insisted that
the rebels should hoist the Union Jack. Others insisted the Boer
flag should be used. The Uitlanders could not agree. Rhodes' whole
design was not in all their minds. Thus the time wore on. Then
December 2 7 was fixed for the uprising. When the time arrived it
seemed impossible because the English were busy with the races
and the Boers with *nachtmaal,* their Christmas communion. The
blow was put off to January 6.

But Jameson and Willoughby were growing restless at Pitsani.
Jameson decided to wait no longer. He wired Rhodes for authority
to move. "Unless I hear definitely to the contrary shall leave tomorrow and carry into effect my second telegram to you," he said.
Rhodes saw with terrifying clarity the difference between marching
into Johannesburg to quell an uprising and going in without any
provocation. He felt the revolt in Johannesburg had petered out
"like a damp squib." He tried to stop Jameson with two wires.
Neither reached him.

The impetuous doctor crossed the Transvaal border. He was met
almost immediately by a force under Generals Piet Joubert and
Louis Botha. By this time his rash act was known at the Cape. At
Elan's River an order reached him from Sir Hercules Robinson,
High Commissioner, to turn back. He disobeyed. He attacked and
a running battle was fought to within ten miles of Johannesburg.
Next day a wire reached Jameson from Robinson proclaiming him
an outlaw. Another dispatch told him the Reform Committee would
send no help. The *kopjes* all around him bristled with Boer bayo-
nets. He was trapped. He hoisted the white flag, surrendered to
General P. A. Kronje, and was marched off to jail.

Up to the very last minute Rhodes denied all knowledge of the
adventure. The news of Jameson's mad dash came to him as he sat
at table with guests. He immediately left them. A Dutch leader,
Schreiner, called next day and found him like a caged lion, his eyes
fevered, dark circles framing them, his hair grayer. He knew all
was up with him. Without further ado he resigned as premier.

Jameson and his fellow officers were tried by a Boer court.

Jameson, Lionel Phillips, Frank Rhodes, and the American John
Hays Hammond were sentenced to death; others to prison or fines.
Kruger commuted the death sentence, but forced the prisoners to
pay £25,000 each in fines. Jameson and certain colleagues in the
fiasco were taken to England and tried for violating the Enlistments
Act. The doctor was sentenced to fifteen months in prison; others
to lesser terms. Frank Rhodes was forced to resign his commission
in the army.

Rhodes paid all the expenses of the prisoners, including the
£100,000 in fines assessed against Jameson, Rhodes, and others.
He and Beit together assumed all the other expenses of that fatal
expedition—thus relieving the Chartered Company. The whole
amount exceeded a million dollars.

Two parliamentary investigations of the raid were made—one
by the Cape parliament in 1896 and the other by the British South
Africa Committee of the British Commons in 1897. The Cape
committee held Rhodes guiltless of giving the final order to Jameson
to march, but also found that he had been concerned in the previous
arrangements for the raid. When this investigation was made
Rhodes was in the Matopo Hills settling the second Matabele war.
His part in that event made a powerful appeal to the English in
South Africa. That part was embroidered in the telling with several
heroic details that did not conform to history but that made good
publicity. This much overshadowed the findings of the Cape committee as Rhodes prepared to go to London in 1897 to "face the
music" before the House committee. As he made his way to Cape
Town to sail he was met at every station by crowds which acclaimed
him.

Rhodes himself was troubled by one feature of the Raid. He
realized that as Prime Minister he had been guilty of a breach of
trust in plotting secretly an attack on a friendly neighbor. He said
so privately. And in that kind of exultant repentance that welled up
in his heart under the stimulus of the friendly demonstrations, he
made up his mind to make his apology publicly in an address at
Cape Town before sailing. He intended to say that he made a grave

error in not resigning the premiership before he engaged in the arrangements for the Raid. But as he began, applause interrupted him and rose to a roar. He stopped midway in his purpose and never uttered that apology.

In London he faced a committee with some notable enemies on it. They wanted to brand Rhodes but they were after bigger game, too. They wanted to show that Joseph Chamberlain had been in the conspiracy "up to his neck." The committee never succeeded in doing that. In the end it censured Rhodes for being implicated in the arrangements but acquitted him of having given the signal to Jameson to make his dash. Generally the committee's report was taken as a whitewash. And Chamberlain himself applied a second coat immediately afterward by saying that Rhodes had done nothing inconsistent with his personal honor. The most that can be said for Rhodes was that Jameson marched before he had given him the cue. It must, of course, be said for him that he himself assumed full responsibility for what happened and, to his latest breath, never blamed Jameson.

Jameson's health broke in prison. He had been released and moved to a nursing home when Rhodes got to London to testify. Later Rhodes induced him to return to South Africa. And it is a singular commentary upon the attitude of the Cape population toward the Raid that this man, who had committed so grievous a folly, was eight years after the date of that folly premier of Cape Colony.

The judgment of the English public was merciful. Rhodes indeed had done nothing that most Englishmen would not have been happy to see a success. The interest of England in South Africa was high at the time. Gladstone had given way to Rosebery and then Salisbury. The imperialist philosophers and poets were singing lustily. And the cry of "Buy Kaffirs!" on the London Exchange was mingled with the jingles of Kipling and the clamor of God himself to England through his agents in the Church of England to press forward the cause of "imperialist Christianity." The irrepressible Barney Barnato was in London through 1895 launching stock issue after stock issue. His Consolidated Mines, Ltd., rose five hundred per cent in the City in a few months. The fever of speculation ran high. It blew up in September, a few months before the raid, and poor Barney lost three million pounds. But the market collapse did not extinguish the fires of empire. Incidentally, the disaster did not bankrupt Barnato by any means. But shortly after this his mind began to give way. He fell into fits of gloom. And while going with the South Africa contingent to the Queen's jubilee, he leaped overboard and was drowned.

Rhodes went back to South Africa. He gave most of his attention to Rhodesia and in this period settled the second Matabele war already described. Lord Milner was made High Commissioner. Lawyer, politician, bureaucrat, he devoted himself assiduously to promoting the final crisis that ended in the Boer War. England was spiritually ready for the crime. In 1899 Rhodes, returning to South Africa from England, was received with acclaim everywhere. Crowds gathered at railroad stations to greet him. "The people of England," he said, "have found out that trade follows the flag and they have all become expansionists. . . . Bygone ideas of nebulous republics are past."

Gladstone, shrewdly peering into the future at the inevitable consequences of England's first steps in South Africa, had said in the 'seventies: "Our first site, acquired in Egypt, will be the almost certain egg of a North African empire that will grow and grow till we finally join hands across the equator with Natal and Cape Colony, to say nothing of the Transvaal and South Africa Free State in the South or Abyssinia in the North to be swallowed by way of viaticum on our journey."

Now in 1899 Rhodes said: "When I began this business of annexation both sides were timid. They would ask one to stop at Kimberley. Then they asked one to stop at Khama's country. . . . Now they won't stop anywhere. *They have found out that the world is not quite big enough for British trade and the British flag.*"

He had stood for his old seat of Barkeley West in the elections of 1898 and been returned. He was in parliament when the preliminary scenes of the Boer War were being enacted. That dark chapter in British imperial history opened in October, 1899. Rhodes was right. Britain would not stop anywhere—not until she was stopped. The end of that disastrous victory was to give to Britain almost all of South Africa.

Rhodes had no part in the active direction of the Boer War. It was Milner's war, he felt. Moreover, early in the war he had gone to Kimberley and been trapped there in the siege. He bore his share in supporting the rigors and problems of that long ordeal. He raised and equipped at his expense the Kimberley Light Horse, three hundred strong.

When the siege of Kimberley was ended, he went to London, made a visit to the Nile, and returned to London during the latter part of 1901, while the Boer War dragged on to its end. Here one last episode rose to plague him. For a number of years a lady charmer, the Princess Catherine Radziwill, had been a source of incessant irritation to him. She was an adventuress who edited a small journal in Cape Town. She thrust herself upon him, dined with him often, until she wore out her welcome as a visitor to Groote Schur. Finally she succeeded in creating the impression that Rhodes was a frequent clandestine visitor to her apartment and even that they were secretly engaged. There is literally no evidence to support either of these stories and very much to refute them. While Rhodes was in England he was informed that the Princess had been hawking about several promissory notes purporting to be given to her by him and amounting to around £20,000. Rhodes authorized his bankers to repudiate them. The Princess was arrested and Rhodes urged to return to the Cape to testify against her.

He was a sick man. His heart was gravely impaired. He had been enjoying an occasional hunt and rides in Hyde Park. He went often to the offices of the Chartered Company, to whose directorate he had been restored. Dr. Jameson, who was with him, protested against his return to Cape Town because of his health. But Rhodes felt he should go. He feared what might be inferred from his absence at the trial. No one, he said, could predict what such a woman might say if he were not there to deny it. The trip to South Africa was a difficult one. He contracted a severe cold. A violent storm made the passage difficult. He was twice thrown from his berth. He arrived in a greatly weakened condition. But he testified against the Princess at the hearing before the committing magistrate. She was bound over to the higher court where she was convicted of forgery and sentenced to eighteen months in prison, nine of which she served. She was released because of ill health and lived to write a bitter memoir of Rhodes fifteen years later.

However, before her final trial Rhodes was taken ill at Muizenberg, near Cape Town. There he died on March 26, 1902. The Boer War, which was to seal the claim of England on South Africa, ended two months later—May 31, 1902. That end was in sight as Rhodes died. But his vision was on the later and wider details of his immense ambitions. As he died, according to his friend W. T. Stead, his last words were: "So much to do! So little done!" The final stages in his dream of a British imperial domain in Africa from the Cape to Cairo would not come until sixteen years later. The Boer War, fought frankly as an imperialist war, universally condemned in America, gave Britain a complete dominion in South Africa. The Great War, fought to make the world safe for democracy, gave her the balance. And this time America fought at her side.

In his will Rhodes had written:

> I admire the grandeur and loneliness of the Matopos in Rhodesia. And therefore I desire to be buried in the Matopos on the hill which I used to visit and which I called the "View of the World," in a square to be cut in the rock on the top of the hill covered with a plain brass plate with these words thereon—"Here lie the remains of Cecil John Rhodes."

Like the imperial Jacob Fugger who built a royal tomb for himself, Rhodes designed this mortuary chapel to acquire a grandeur from nature beyond the power of any architect and, unlike the boastful Fugger, he left an epitaph which derived its eloquence not from a collection of vain words, but from the panegyric implied in the noble surroundings and the implications in the masterful understatement of the legend itself. This majestic spot Rhodes designed as the Westminster Abbey of South Africa. And there, as he planned, his body was placed as the first of its immortals.

Rhodes did not propose that his lifelong effort to bring the English-speaking people together as closely as possible to advance the designs of a world-encircling British empire should die with his death. He left a will establishing the Rhodes Scholarships, which was the final form which that early dream of a world fellowship on the model of Loyola assumed. He bequeathed an estate valued at around thirty million pounds, which he made over to his trustees, to be used in perpetuity to support scholarships at his old alma mater, Oxford. Young men were to be chosen from all the British colonies and dominions, plus thirty-eight from our American states, who would spend three years in graduate work at Oxford. Students were to be chosen according to their abilities and with an eye open for young men interested in literary and public affairs—the sort who might reasonably be expected to become leaders, at least vocal leaders of thought. Exposed to the genial British atmosphere of Oxford for three years, while associating with their fellow Rhodes beneficiaries from every British state and colony, they might be expected to develop an empire consciousness. In time a great society of Rhodes scholars, with its members all over the world, including America, might well be counted on as a powerful nucleus of pro-British and empire feeling, particularly in moments of crisis. In the United States in 1938 there were 755 scholars, a number which now approaches 1000. One third of them were teachers, 155 authors of books, 167 authors of articles and pamphlets, while many are college presidents and editors and preachers and radio announcers and commentators in this country. It is out of these inheritors of the great imperialist tradition of the master that so many of those plans for the union of the American republic and the British empire are born. The spirit of the great imperialist planner is not dead.

F.P.G.

BASIL ZAHAROFF

CHAPTER IX

Basil Zaharoff

THE WARMAKER

— I —

IF THE Lord God Jehovah had not created Basil Zaharoff, some novelist sooner or later would certainly have got around to the job. Indeed, it is by no means certain that Zaharoff, as we have him, is not the joint product of God and the fiction writers.

Lieutenant Colonel Walter Guinness, member for Bury St. Edmonds, committed the blunder against history of referring to Zaharoff in the House of Commons in 1921 as the "Mystery Man of Europe." Having fixed upon him that fascinating label, the figure of Zaharoff became thereafter a costumer's dummy upon which the news caricaturists of Europe draped whatever garments would vindicate his reputation.

Mysterious indeed he is and still more mysterious he became at the hands of the sensational news portrait painters. The mystery begins with his birth. A French biographer, Roger Menevée, records that he was born in Moughliou, or Mugla, on the Anatolian coast. But a German, Robert Neumann, asserts that Zaharoff, testifying in a London court as a young man, said he was born in the Tatavla or poor section of Constantinople, and he notes that the Mugla nativity is attested by an affidavit of a Greek priest made forty-two years after the event and was based upon memory.

It was never known with complete certainty to what country he owed allegiance. He was a Greek, born in Turkey, who lived in Paris. His right to the ribbon of the Grand Cross of the Legion of Honor was questioned in the Chamber of Deputies and M.

Clemenceau had to assure the Chamber that "M. Zaharoff is a Frenchman." But also he was throughout his life the guiding genius of a great British armament concern, acted as a British agent, was a Knight of the Bath, known in England as Sir Basil Zaharoff.

Journalists said he spoke fluently fourteen languages—which is probably an extravagant exaggeration. They reported how he had confided to a written record the story of his life, filling fifty-eight volumes which he ordered to be burned at his death, while others told how he had himself destroyed the record, two days being consumed in reducing it to ashes in the furnace of his Paris home. Extravagant tales were told of his habits, his amours, his dinners, and the exotic dishes brought fresh by plane from immense distances for his table. But, in fact, the reporters and the historians have produced but little about the personal life and affairs of the man. Searching the extensive but empty records, one fails to discover any documents or letters or speeches or records or meetings or conferences or instances in which the man is actually present. Always one hears that he is somewhere in the background, off in the shadows, pulling the strings, supplying the stratagems and the money.

Yet it is certain that he remains the most considerable figure in that feverish world of the munitions makers that has had so much advertisement since the Great War. Only a few names take first rank among this dubious company—old Alfred Krupp, the cannon king of Essen, the Schneiders of Creusot, Thomas Vickers, the English gun maker of Sheffield, Skoda, du Pont de Nemours, the American powder king, Colt and Winchester and Remington and Maxim. They were all, as Messrs. Englebrecht and Hanighen have called them, "Merchants of Death." But the mightiest "merchant" among them, the man who played the largest role in the "merchandising" of munitions, the greatest market maker, was Basil Zaharoff.

It was his melancholy good fortune to come upon the scene when the world went in for arms on an unprecedented scale and it was he who, more than any other man, developed the international market for arms. He did not invent it, to be sure. Old Alfred Krupp had played off Turkish orders against his native Prussia when Zaharoff was a mere fireman in Tatavla. And long before either of them—centuries before—old Andries Bicker, Burgomaster of Amsterdam, had built and supplied and provisioned and even financed a complete navy for Spain when the Spanish king was waging war upon Holland. He then explained to the outraged Dutch that if Holland had not armed the Spanish enemy, the Danes would have done it and reaped the profit.

But Zaharoff played a leading, if not the leading, role in that strange world comedy of the arms makers leading the double life of chauvinists and internationalists. They gave us the spectacle of Boers mowing down English regiments with Vickers' pom-poms, Prussian surgeons picking out of Prussian wounded Austrian shrapnel fired by Krupp's cannon, French poilus massacred by shot poured out of guns made in Le Creusot, English Tommies killed by weapons produced by Armstrong and Vickers, and American ships sent to the bottom by U-boats built on models supplied by American submarine builders. Zaharoff was the master of what one biographer has called the "principle of incitement," under which war scares were managed, enemies created for nations, airplanes sold to one nation and antiaircraft guns to her neighbors, submarines to one and destroyers to another. He did what the cigarette people did, what the liquor industry, the beauty industry did—created a demand for his merchandise. The armament industry became a game of international politics, the arms salesman a diplomatic provocateur, the munitions magnates of all nations partners in cartels, combines, consolidations; exchanging plans, secrets, patents. He was the greatest of all the salesmen of death, and, as one commentator has observed, if you would see his monument, look about you at the military graveyards of Europe.

------------------------------ II ------------------------------

Zacharias Basileios Zacharias—later to be known as Basil Zaharoff—was born October 6, 1849, apparently in Mugla, near the Turkish capital of Angora. His people were Greeks who had lived in Constantinople, fled to Odessa during the Turkish persecutions in 1821, returned to Mugla, and then, when Basileios was three years old, took up their home again in the Tatavla or poor district of Constantinople. The boy went to school until he was sixteen, when some disaster to his father forced him to go to work. He worked, we are told, as a fireman, a guide, a money-changer. There is more than a hint that these early years were passed amid rough surroundings and that this impulsive and somewhat lawless boy—like one of our prominent labor racketeers, to use his own explanation of his twisted ethics—suffered from lack of "bringing-up."

When he was twenty-one he found work with an uncle in Constantinople who had some sort of mercantile business. One day Basileios disappeared, taking with him money from the cash drawer. The infuriated uncle traced him to London where he was arrested. How or why he was arrested in London for a crime committed in Turkey is not made clear. It was perhaps a stage in the process of extradition. In any event Zaharoff pleaded that he was a partner, not an employee, of his uncle, producing a paper attesting that fact—a paper he had miraculously discovered in his trouser pocket on his way to the courthouse—and was let off. This episode is by no means clear. But what there is of it reveals the more or less dark cloud in which he began his career.

As in all things relating to Zaharoff, there are other versions of this flight. Robert Neumann, who spent some time investigating the story, but unfortunately envelopes all that he writes in a cloud of luminous smoky words, insists that it was not money, but goods that Zaharoff stole and not from an uncle but from a Mr. Hiphentides; and, having converted the merchandise into money, fled to London where he was arrested on the complaint of Mr. Hiphentides, after which he was not acquitted but let off with a reprimand on his promise to make amends.

Zaharoff, after this narrow escape, went to Greece, Turkey being "no thoroughfare" to him. In Athens he made his Basileios Zacharias into Basil Zaharoff. He remained in Athens from 1873 to 1877, living by odd jobs of all sorts. Somehow stories of Zaharoff's unsavory past leaked out in Athens. The atmosphere chilled for him among the youthful compatriots with whom he fraternized. Apparently Athens became too unpleasant, and the harassed youth moved on. A singular piece of good fortune overtook him at this point. Shortly after his disappearance a brief newspaper story told how a prisoner, Basileios Zaharoff, in an attempt to escape from the old prison of Garbola in Athens, had been shot and killed by a sentry. Zaharoff had made one friend in Athens— Stephen Skouloudis, later the compliant premier of King Constantine in his attempt to put Greece on the side of Germany, and then well on his way to riches. He had taken a fancy to Zaharoff and he was shocked at this story of his death.

Skouloudis went to Garbola, got a description of the prisoner who had been killed, had the body exhumed, and satisfied himself that it was not his maligned young friend. He traced the incident farther and learned that the shameful calumny had been printed by a reporter who hated Zaharoff. Having fled to England once more—this time to Manchester—Zaharoff returned to Athens as soon as he heard of Skouloudis' vindication of him to take advantage of the sympathy created for him by this shocking injustice. This seemingly happened in 1877. He needed work and Skouloudis added another claim upon his gratitude by recommending him to the representative of a Swedish gun maker, who was leaving Greece and looking for a successor. Zaharoff got that job, rushed in a frenzy of gratitude to Skouloudis' home, fell upon his knees, covered his hands with kisses and tears, and swore eternal friendship. Thus the first phase of the career of this young Monte Cristo ended. Strangely, one does not hear of further contact with Skouloudis until 1915, when Skouloudis was made Prime Minister of King Constantine and Zaharoff was the brains and moneybag behind the conspiracy of France and Britain to dethrone Constantine and bring the Greeks in on the side of the Allies.

------------------------------ III ------------------------------

Zaharoff—twenty-eight years old—was now in the munitions industry in which he spent the remainder of his eventful life. Torsten Vilhelm Nordenfeldt, a small Swedish manufacturer, commissioned Zaharoff as his agent for the whole Balkan territory at a salary of five pounds a week, later augmented by commissions. It was a small beginning, but in a most opportune time. The whole face of the munitions industry was changing—due to the pressure of inventors, politicians, and merchants.

There was, of course, nothing new about the arms industry. It was not invented before the World War or by the German junkers. It is a business, like any other. Man, in his discussions with other men about questions of religion, statecraft, geography, trade, has always reached a point in the discussion where it has seemed wise to reply to his opponent by disemboweling him or knocking his brains out. The demand for instruments of discussion of this type, from the day of the leathern armor and the flint spear, has always, quite naturally, inspired thrifty entrepreneurs to provide them for profit. It is a business like law or prostitution or hanging or banking or making shoes. Before the conqueror can lift his sword the armorer must make one for him in his forge. Before armies can march there must be men—thousands, hundreds of thousands of them—who will make guns and cannon and tanks and trucks and uniforms and shoes and food. It is a business and must be run as such. It must have a producing department and a finance department and a sales department. And as it is the function of the production department to develop and produce better and

deadlier means of slaughter, it is the function of the sales department to find buyers, nay more, to stimulate consumer demand.

And so behind every great warrior and war has loomed the
figure of the sutler, perhaps just a poor peddler following the
troops with rum, or some magnificent gentleman in his countinghouse doing business not with the private in the field, but with
the chief of staff in his bureau. Behind Pericles was the shield
maker Cleon. Behind Caesar was the banker Crassus and the war
contractors of Rome. Behind Maximilian was Jacob Fugger and
his rich copper mines in the Tirol. Behind Jeanne d'Arc was
Jacques Coeur, who, like a true patriot, supplied the Maid with
arms and funds, and, like a true munitioneer, sold arms, against
the law of God Himself, to the infidel and was stripped of his
wealth and clothed in sackcloth and made to murmur on his knees
that he "had wickedly sent armor and arms to the Sultan, enemy
of the Christian faith and of the King." Cromwell had to have his
army provisioner, the pious Thomas Papillon. Behind Louis XIV
was Sam Bernard the banker and the Brothers Pâris de Montmartel; behind Napoleon stood Ouvrard.

It is a strange business, indeed a little weird. Like any other
business it calls for a special kind of man with a special kind of
talent and a special kind of ethics. It is, indeed, in the words of an
American agent of a large submarine manufacturer, "a hell of a
business, where you have always to be hoping for trouble in order
to prosper."

I do not pretend to fathom the depths of its ethics. Let someone
unriddle for me this human enigma: M. de Wendel, Frenchman,
built a great blast furnace in Briey. Briey lies on the German
frontier; on the other side, in Germany, is Thionville with its huge
German blast furnaces. There they are on either side of the frontier
—Briey in France, Thionville in Germany. Briey belongs to M.
de Wendel; Thionville to the Germans. The Great War begins.
The French do not attack Thionville; they do not defend Briey.
They withdraw their lines and permit Briey to fall into the hands

of the Germans. Then throughout the war Briey and Thionville are operated as one huge war production unit by the Germans. They turn out iron and steel that is hurled in huge Big Berthas and little German machine guns at French poilus who are mowed down by the hundreds of thousands. First one officer and then another asks why France does not attack and silence Briey and Thionville. General Malleterre demanded an attack. M. Pierre Étienne Flandin, one day to be premier, an officer then, urged it at the front. Bombardment was begun by General Guillaumat, but stopped instantly by headquarters. Deputies clamored for its destruction. A committee of the Senate urged it. Even the Cabinet asked why Briey and Thionville were not stopped. But nothing was done. They went ahead pumping out materials for Krupp's throughout the whole war. When the war was over Briey was handed back to M. de Wendel unscathed. Who is M. de Wendel? What manner of man is he? What goes on underneath his vest? What goes on inside the heads of the men, the officers, the politicians who protect "property" that is flooding its iron and steel to Krupp's to slaughter French boys in a war for the very life of France? Are they monsters? Are they demons? Unfortunately they are not. And that is what makes it all so mysterious and so difficult to deal with.

It was into this strange business that Basil Zaharoff stepped, carrying with him an almost ideal spiritual equipment for the job. It was not then a huge industry. Best known perhaps was Alfred Krupp, the cannon maker of Essen. At ten he inherited a modest iron foundry from old Frederick Krupp who had started it in 1823. At fourteen Alfred went into the business and slowly took over its direction. Cannon were made of copper. Alfred perfected a solid crucible steel block from which he made cannon. But he had not yet perfected any projectile capable of penetrating the intransigent mentality of military bureaucrats. Cannon were made of copper, had always been, must always be! Herr Krupp learned from the start that the way to sell cannon to the Prussian king was to sell them also to Prussia's neighbors and enemies. He made his first sales to Egypt, then to Austria. When the Austro-Prussian War began, both armies fired Krupp's cannon balls at each other, and his guns would have been working in both armies in the Franco-Prussian War but for Napoleon III's refusal to buy them. Krupp's cannon made Bismarck's swift victory possible. After that Krupp made and sold his cannon everywhere in 1877 when Zaharoff entered the arms field.

In England Thomas Vickers developed the little engineering plant of his late father into first a prosperous iron foundry making car wheels, cast-steel blocks and cylinders. He then turned to making gun barrels and armor plate and finally a growing line of weapons.

In France, Joseph Eugène Schneider, a small banker, bought Le Creusot, an iron foundry and arms plant that had made weapons for France since Louis XIV. Schneider was on the verge of bankruptcy when Napoleon III's adventures saved him, rehabilitated him, and made him rich. Schneider was trying desperately to break into the international arms business but was meeting determined and successful resistance from Krupp.

Over in America, the du Ponts, Colts, Winchesters, and Remington were prospering as a result of the impetus from the Civil War. Eleuthère Irénée du Pont, son of the famous French radical, Pierre du Pont, emigrated to America, found the powder for hunting quite poor, established a powder mill patronized by Napoleon, and supplied most of the powder used in the War of 1812. He was the friend of Jefferson, suffered the inevitable after-the-war slump, and got aid in France from Madame de Staël and Talleyrand. He then found rich markets in Spain and in South America when dictators and revolutionists fought it out, refused to sell to Cuba during our Mexican War because he feared his powder would go to Santa Anna (though he hated that war), grew rich when railroads and frontiersmen needed dynamite to blast the Western prairies and mountains and forests, sold all he could make to England, France, and Turkey during the Crimean War, and was the mainspring of the Union in the war between the states. In 1877 the du Ponts were already the dominating figures in the powder combinations being formed in America, and by 1897 they were powerful enough to enter into an international arrangement by which the powder makers of America and Europe divided the world among themselves.

Colt made revolvers, sold them to the soldiers and frontiersmen who conquered the Texas plains, failed, but grew rich through the Crimean and Civil Wars.

Remington made a fortune with his guns in the Civil War but was ruined by the peace. But Remington recovered from the Civil War by diversifying his products, going into typewriters and sewing machines, and in 1877 he again had his agents in Europe contending for the business of the armies there.

Winchester, whose guns had created a sensation at the London Fair in 1851, made a sensational repeating rifle during the Civil War, had thirty-eight establishments making small guns, when Zaharoff became a munitioneer, and had in the field one of the first of the world's arms salesmen extraordinary, Colonel Tom Addis, who equipped Juarez in Mexico and whose guns sealed the fate of Maximilian.

There were other smaller firms. But taken as a whole the munitions industry was not a vast affair. The men who made fortunes out of arms in earlier times—the Brothers Pâris, Châtelain, Ouvrard, Rothschild, Bicker, Jacques Coeur—were not producers of arms or powder and ball. These things had always until the first half of the nineteenth century been made in small shops, by individual craftsmen, in little foundries, the largest of which hired only a few hundred men at most. The fortunes were made by contractors, middlemen, and brokers who assumed the function of collecting weapons, food, grain, clothing for the armies. But with the growth of Krupp and Schneider and Vickers and du Pont and the others, the business of producing weapons and explosives had taken on larger shape.

All the drifts in the world were moving in the direction of the magic business into which young Mr. Zaharoff had stumbled.

The customer of the munitions maker is the soldier. And Europe was learning how to produce many customers for him. France had begun it—republican France—with her mass conscription during the Revolution. But the practice had died out when, after 1815, liberalism once more swept over Europe, until, with Napoleon III, the whole dark movement of militarism took on life once more. Bismarck made almost every German a soldier. And after the Franco-Prussian War, every monarch in Europe was eager to copy the junker model. Then the nation did not wait for a war to raise an army, a small mercenary army. In every country armies were formed during peacetime, far outnumbering any that had ever fought in war. In short, every able-bodied man in Europe was a customer for the gun makers, and peace became as flourishing a period for them as ever war had been. Europe became an armed camp, and the Krupps and Schneiders and Vickers did not have to wait for war to do big business. France, sullen, mourning her "lost provinces"; Italy, nourishing the dream of "Italia Irridenta"; Germany, preparing against France's effort for revenge, Russia, with her pan-Slavic dreams, the Balkans, waiting for the day to free her enslaved peoples from Austria, Turkey, Germany— all made a perfect climate for the trade of the sellers of rifles and cannon and powder.

Moreover, the manufacturers of death did not sit still. New and more terrible weapons were being fabricated. Smokeless powder, small-bore magazine rifles for accuracy and distance, rifling of gun bores, the French mitrailleuse blossoming into the machine gun, Krupp's breach-loading monoblock guns, recoil appliances, the armored warship that began with the *Merrimac* and *Monitor* and the submarine—all these gave to the arms drummers a line of goods that introduced into armament the stimulating element of style and quality obsolescence and kept the ordnance departments busy junking old weapons and buying new ones.

This last element was one that told heavily on the side of the new arms salesman in Athens—Nordenfeldt's new Balkan drummer. For Nordenfeldt, though small, had an attractive collection of lethal gadgets. He had the eccentric screw breach, the mechanical time fuse, an excellent quick-firing gun, and, wonder of wonders, a submarine that he had invented.

Zaharoff had to look for business in the Balkans. The Turko-Russian War had just ended. Greece saw herself left out of the division of loot and she determined to arm. She planned an army of 100,000 instead of 20,000—100,000 customers for the young arms drummer instead of 20,000. Of course, Zaharoff had to meet the competition of Krupp and others. But he was a Greek and, by this time, we may be sure, burning with patriotism and sales pressure.

But he did not sell a submarine until 1885 when he planted one in the Greek navy. Having done this, the Greek patriot went to Greece's enemy, Turkey, and sold two. By this time Hiram Maxim, the American, was running away with the business in quick-firing guns, for his Maxim machine gun outdistanced all rivals. He was going about Europe demonstrating it himself and getting orders. This was a serious matter for Nordenfeldt and his man Zaharoff. Just how it came about and who managed it, no one knows, but in 1886 Maxim and Nordenfeldt joined forces. But Zaharoff now held a substantial interest in the Nordenfeldt firm.

With this development, Zaharoff began to range over a territory wider than the Balkans. He had established relations with many of the most influential persons in European war departments, ministries, and noble social circles. He was the dominating sales force of the Nordenfeldt-Maxim combination. Gradually Nordenfeldt vanished out of the business, Zaharoff took his place as Maxim's partner, and the firm took the name of the Maxim Guns and Ammunition Company, Ltd. It is a singular fact that Hiram Maxim in his autobiography makes no reference to Zaharoff.

The next step was another combination with Vickers, Thomas Vickers—the second largest English manufacturer of arms.—Maxim became a member of the Vickers board of directors.

Zaharoff's name did not figure in the organization at all. But he and Maxim, in some proportion unknown to history, got for their company from Vickers £1,353,334, or over six and a half million dollars, partly in cash and partly in stock in the Vickers company. Zaharoff thus became a substantial stockholder in Vickers and would one day be the largest of all. He also became the chief salesman of Vickers which, unlike Krupp and Schneider, had remained up to this point out of the international market. But Zaharoff showed the way into this bountiful field, and thereafter he moved about Europe with a card announcing him as the delegate of Thomas Vickers & Sons.

But Vickers was in no sense a great business. Its principal function had been supplying guns for the British navy. It was prosperous and imposing after the modest standards of that day. Its great growth dates from the absorption of the Nordenfeldt company, with Nordenfeldt's submarine, Maxim's machine gun, and the shrewd, dynamic salesmanship of Zaharoff.

------------------------------ IV ------------------------------

Nothing was wanting but romance now to complete the equipment of Basil Zaharoff for the principal role in a Dumas novel. And this he supplied upon a pattern perfectly in keeping with his character. In 1889, while he was ranging Europe—particularly Russia—for orders, he met Maria del Pilar Antonia Angela Patiocinio Simona de Muguiro y Berute, the Duchess of Villafranca. She was the wife of a young man closely connected with the royal family of Spain. She proved useful to Zaharoff in arranging connections in Spain that enabled him to sell many millions of dollars of arms to the war department. But Zaharoff fell in love with her and urged her to divorce her husband, who was ill and on the verge of dementia. The Duchess, a good Catholic, would not consider divorce, but she became Zaharoff's mistress, confident that her husband was destined for a speedy death. His mind failed completely, he was put into an insane asylum, and proceeded to disappoint the Duchess and her lover by continuing to live for another thirty-five years. She continued as Zaharoff's mistress; he remained attached to her with singular devotion and in 1924, when her husband died, the two lovers—then aged and near the end of their lives, he seventy-five and she over sixty— were married in a little town outside Paris. They had had two daughters. The Duchess, however, survived this marriage by only eighteen months and her death left the aged bridegroom inconsolable.

About the time he met the Duchess, Zaharoff established a home in Paris. He was rich and a man of striking, distinguished appearance; a small mustache and imperial and drooping eyelids added an expression of inscrutability to his grave countenance. He cultivated the habit of silence. He avoided displays, public appearances. He took up his place in that foggy, ill-lighted world so fascinating to the readers of newspapers—the world of Behind the Scenes. He had acquaintances, if not friends, among the most important people in Europe. He was now a part owner, sales delegate, guiding spirit of a growing British armament firm, but with his home in France. He spoke Turkish, Greek, French, Italian, German, and probably various Balkan dialects. And the world was unfolding auspiciously if not beautifully before him in the grim business in which he flourished.

As for Vickers, it now began to expand upon an impressive scale. By 1890 England set out upon a more ambitious naval program than ever. Vickers, which had been a builder of guns, now went into naval construction, as did Krupp in Germany. It acquired a controlling interest in Beardmore's great shipbuilding firm in Glasgow. It took over the Naval Armaments Company with its dockyards, the Woolsey Tool & Motor Company and the Electric & Ordnance Accessories Company. It became a great department store of lethal weapons and could supply its customers with anything from a rifle to a battleship. Sir Vincent Caillard became its financial genius as Zaharoff was its sales genius. They made an excellent team. Caillard knew how to mix the hard, cruel functions of gun-making finance with the more delicate and spiritual values of versemaking, like another and earlier munitioneer, Bonnier de la Mosson, who accumulated a fortune as an army contractor in the time of Louis XV and exercised his leisure by writing verses so bad that Voltaire said they ought to be crowned by the Academy. Sir Vincent made music too and he found time amidst the dark sophistications of munitions finance to set to music Blake's *Songs of Innocence.*

Events favored them—the Spanish-American War, the Chinese-Japanese War, the English-Boer War, in which the Tommies, armed with Vickers rifles, were scientifically mowed down with Maxim's pom-pom, or quick-firing cannon, supplied to the Boers by M. Zaharoff of Vickers. But the greatest opportunity was the Russo-Japanese War. When it ended all Europe's war ministries awoke. The war had been a great proving ground for guns and ships—a laboratory for militarists. Above all, Russia had to start at the bottom and completely rebuild her shattered armies. The Czar provided over $620,000,000 for rearming. All the armament makers in the world flocked to St. Petersburg. Zaharoff, representing Vickers, arrived first on the scene. He spoke Russian fluently. He was a member of the Orthodox Greek Church. He had spent much time in Russia. He knew his way around.

The Schneider-Creusot firm felt it had a special claim on Russian business. Was not Russia France's ally? Were not French bankers financing Russia? There developed swiftly a struggle between Schneider and Vickers out of which Zaharoff emerged with the largest share of the booty. Indeed, this particular episode established him definitely as the great master arms merchant of the world.

This fight centered upon two projects—the Putilov munitions works and a plan to erect a new and comprehensive artillery plant somewhere in Russia.

The contest became somewhat complicated, as all armament contests in Europe are. Behind Schneider was the Banque de l'Union Parisienne, in which he held a large interest. Oddly enough,

allied with Vickers was another French bank—the Société
Générale.

The Putilov works had been heavily financed by Schneider with
l'Union Parisienne funds. But Putilov needed more funds. And
to make matters worse, Putilov was out of favor. Schneider, de-
spairing of continuing successfully to find an outlet for French
arms through Putilov, conceived the idea of building for Russia
an entirely new plant in the Urals. But Zaharoff was at work on
the same idea, got the inside track, and came off with an arrangement to build for Russia the huge arsenal of Zarizyn at a cost
of $12,500,000—the largest in Russia. Besides that, Zaharoff and
certain English interests with whom he was working got large
contracts through the St. Petersburg Iron Works and the Franco-
Russian Company. With the Russian Shipbuilding Company he
got contracts to build two battleships, while Beardmore, Vickers'
subsidiary, got a dockyard and a cannon factory. This was a
severe blow to Schneider. And all the time that Zaharoff was working for this he had a paper in Paris, *Excelsior,* which was pumping
out propaganda continuously for more French loans to Russia—
French loans that Russia could spend with Vickers.

Schneider now turned his attention again to salvaging the Putilov works and strengthening his hold upon it. He could get no
more financing from l'Union Parisienne, because it already had
too much tied up in Putilov and frozen in Balkan investments.
He appealed in desperation to the Société Générale, which was
secretly allied with Zaharoff and the English, though a French
bank. He was, of course, refused. Indeed the Société Générale
took advantage of Schneider's embarrassment, doubtless assisted
by Zaharoff, to force Schneider out of Putilov altogether. It became a fight between two French banks and a French munitions
magnate for Russian business. But at this point Mr. Schneider
executed one of those tactical movements we encounter in an
Oppenheim international mystery novel.

One day Paris read in the *Echo de Paris* a brief dispatch, date-
lined in St. Petersburg. "There is a rumor," it reported, "that the

Putilov factories at St. Petersburg will be bought by Krupp. If this information is well founded, it will cause great concern in France. It is known indeed that Russia has adopted French types of guns and munitions for her naval artillery and coast defenses. *The greater part of the material* produced at this time by Putilov was made in collaboration with the Creusot factories and the technical staff which the latter sent to the spot."

Here was a provocative item packed away in this little paragraph. Putilov made French guns from French plans. Krupp would get Putilov. Into the German hands would fall all the French ordnance secrets. This was the alarming message in that dispatch. Most disturbing of all, France's great secret gun—her carefully guarded 75-millimeter—would now come into the possession of Krupp's engineers. The little item swelled rapidly to a press sensation. Krupp denied the story. Vickers, also linked with the sale in some papers, denied it. France must not suffer this disaster. Russia wanted a loan of $25,000,000 for railway rehabilitation. The ministry appealed to patriotic Frenchmen to band together to make the Russian loan and as a condition perpetuate Schneider's hold on Putilov. The pressure was too great to withstand. The loan was made. Schneider got his financing for Putilov. Even the Société Générale had to help Schneider.

It was some years before France learned that the whole dispatch incident was a hoax. Mr. Albert Thomas, director of the International Labor Office in Geneva, in 1921 made a speech there describing how French industrialists boasted to him that they had forged the St. Petersburg dispatch in the office of *Echo* one night at ten o'clock, and how they had done it not because Putilov was threatened by Krupp but by another French group. They did not hesitate, in this contest for control of a Russian plant, to stir up public opinion against Germany, to set the old chauvinist pot to boiling.

Zaharoff had failed in his maneuvers to drive the French out of Russia altogether, but he captured for Vickers and other English arms makers the largest share of Russia's munitions millions.

—————————————— V ——————————————

Thus the arms makers drove Europe along up to 1914. The airplane had arrived, and Vickers added airplane production to its growing interests. In Paris M. Zaharoff endowed a chair of aviation at the Sorbonne. Indeed, M. Zaharoff, for all his pains to elude the spotlight, found that revealing beam playing upon him at intervals and to his discomfiture. Who is this M. Zaharoff? What is he? To what country does he owe allegiance? He was born in Turkey. He is a Greek. He is a French citizen. He is an English businessman. But what country does he serve? And what sort of game is he playing in France? These were not pleasant questions for one who, indeed, had what Mr. Roosevelt calls a passion for anonymity. Hence the endowed chair at the Sorbonne. And then a home for French soldiers. His name appeared upon subscription lists for all good French causes. And then the French ministry conferred upon him the rosette of an officer of the Legion of Honor—a reward for the chair at the Sorbonne.

Vickers grew, spread out—plants in Britain, Canada, Italy, Africa, Greece, Turkey, Russia, New Zealand, Ireland, Holland; banks, steelworks, cannon factories, dockyards, plane factories, subsidiaries of all sorts; an arms empire. It had share capital larger than Krupp's and had more extensive connections and possessions than Krupp's. And this growth was chiefly the work of the French citizen of Greek blood who, acting the role of ambassador-salesman, had planted the Vickers standard all over the world, from Ireland to Japan and from the North Sea to the Antipodes.

It was done with the aid of British-government backing and pressure, the immense financial resources of British finance; by means of bribery and chicanery, by the purchase of military and naval authorities and the press wherever newspapers could be bought. It is a dark, sordid story of ruthless money getting without regard for honor, morals, and either national or humane

considerations, while the Europe which they upset with their conspiracies and terrorized with their war scares, and to which they
sold hatred as the indispensable condition of marketing guns, slid
along with the certainty of doom into the chasm of fire and death
in 1914.

On March 18, 1914, on the very brink of the coming disaster,
Philip Snowden, disease-wracked, crippled socialist labor leader
rose in Commons to make a speech. When he had done, he had
rocked the British Empire with his disclosures. For two years
a young Quaker socialist named Walton Newbold had been tracing with infinite pains the tortuous trail of the international arms
makers. And Philip Snowden had in his possession the fruits of
that long quest when he rose to speak. One by one he pointed out
cabinet ministers, members of the House, and named high-rank-
ing officials in army and navy circles, persons of royal position,
who were large holders of shares in Vickers and Armstrong, in
John Brown and Beardmore, shipbuilders.

The profits of Vickers and Armstrong had been enormous, and
the most powerful persons in the state and the church and the
nobility had bought into them to share in the profits. Vickers had
among its directors two dukes, two marquesses, and family members of fifty earls, fifteen baronets, and five knights, twenty-one
naval officers, two naval government architects, and many journalists. Armstrong had even more—sixty earls or their wives,
fifteen baronets, twenty knights, and twenty military or naval
architects and officers, while there were thirteen members of the
House of Commons on the directorates of Vickers, Armstrong, or
John Brown. "It would be impossible," said Snowden, "to throw
a handful of pebbles anywhere upon the opposition benches without hitting members interested in these arms firms."

Ministers, officers, technical experts moved out of the government, out of the cabinet, the navy, the army, the war office, the admiralty, into the employ of the munitions manufacturers.

Snowden quoted Lord Welby, head of the Civil Service, who only
a few weeks before had denounced the arms conspirators. "We are

in the hands of an organization of crooks," said Lord Welby. "They are politicians, generals, manufacturers of armaments and journalists. All of them are anxious for unlimited expenditure, and go on inventing scares to terrify the public and to terrify the Ministers of the Crown."

Every business attracts to itself men who have the taste, talent, and the morals suited to its special requirements. This armament world of Europe was a behind-the-scenes world of intrigue, chicanery, hypocrisy, and corruption. It involved a weird marriage between burning patriotism and cold, ruthless realism. And the men who rose to leadership in it were men who combined the vices of the spy, the bribe giver, the corruptionist. They played with an explosive far more volatile and dangerous than anything made in their laboratories—chauvinism—and they did it with ruthless realism. There was, indeed, something singularly brutal about their realism.

The trail of that vast armament effort between 1877 and 1914 is stained by a record of bribery of admirals and generals, civil servants of all degrees ranging from cabinet ministers to messengers. One German armament maker said that "Krupp employs hundreds of officers on leave or withdrawal at high salaries for doing nothing much at all. For some families Krupp factories are a great sinecure where nephews and poor relations of officials whose influence in war is great find themselves jobs."

In 1913, a year before Snowden's exposures in the House of Commons, Dr. Karl Liebknecht, socialist leader in the Reichstag, made a series of grave charges against German armament leaders that resulted in the trial and conviction of the secretary-superintendent of the Ministry of War, four arsenal officials, and four lieutenants and others, including Brandt, the Berlin agent of Krupp. A year later, about the time that Snowden was shocking his colleagues in Parliament, Liebknecht again brought a series of charges against the corruption of Japanese officials by Siemens-Schuckert, another German arms concern. This led to the scandal unearthed by the Japanese Diet and showing that M. Zaharoff's firm of Vickers, along with the Mitsui Bussan Kaisha, had paid out $565,000 in bribes to Japanese officials to clinch the contract for the building of the battleship *Kongo*. Of course no espionage could follow the numerous and devious trails of the arms makers. It is strange that even so much of their corruption came to light. But what was exposed can be taken as no more than samples of the manner in which their business was conducted.

The whole excuse of this industry was national defense. Yet these enterprises were as busy supplying the armies of their enemies as the armies of their own countries. Up to the time of Alfred Krupp's death in 1887 he had made 24,576 cannon of which only 10,666, or less than half, were sold to the fatherland for national defense. The rest went to Germany's enemies and neighbors. Some of them —Austria and China—were supposed to be her allies. But Austria's Krupp cannons sent death through German ranks in the Austro-Prussian War, and when, in the Boxer rebellion, a German warship attacked a Chinese fort, the cannons Krupp sold to Li Hung Chang dealt death and destruction to German sailors. When Italy and Turkey fought in 1911 Turkey used a fleet largely supplied by Italy. And when Italy and Germany fought in the World War, Italy had a fleet of seventeen vessels built in German shipyards. Zaharoff had got from Turkey contracts for two dreadnaughts and a fleet of destroyers to patrol the Dardanelles, which were conveniently on hand when the British soldiers were landed in 1915 to attempt to carry that stronghold. Earlier still, British Tommies in South Africa were mowed down by Maxim's quick-firing cannon —the pom-poms—which Zaharoff for Vickers had sold to the Boers. The story is an endless one. It includes even the sinking of the *Lusitania*, which played so large a part in bringing America into the war. For this was the feat of a German submarine built upon plans supplied before the war to Austria by the Electric Boat Company, American submarine builders.

VI

The fame of Krupp—the part he, Alfred, and his son Fritz played in the development of the junker regime in Germany—gives to the name Krupp a kind of premiership among the Merchants of Death. And while Krupp never attained the size and expansion of the Vickers firm that Zaharoff built, and particularly of the Vickers-Armstrong firm, when these two were combined after the war, yet a special notice ought to be taken here of this vast German arms machine. Old Alfred Krupp, high-handed, overbearing, ruthless pursuer of wealth, died in 1887. The little steel plant at Essen had only about thirty employees when he began work in it. When Zaharoff entered the arms industry in Greece it had grown to a great enterprise employing over 16,000 men. Old Alfred went to his death a wretched, isolated misanthrope. He left as his heir his son Fritz, thirty-three, delicate, shy, sensitive, unpromising, who had filled various posts in the business since he was twenty in preparation for his destiny.

Fritz Krupp immediately embarked upon a policy of expansion, making armor plate, buying up shipyards at Kiel to be ready for the era of naval expansion that the youthful von Tirpitz was even then brewing.

Bismarck was let out, the last brake upon unrestrained militarism was removed, young Kaiser Wilhelm became a close friend and frequent visitor and hunting companion of Fritz Krupp. Von Tirpitz was made Secretary of the Admiralty, the first naval act was passed to spend 150 million marks on ships, and Krupp got the lion's share. The German Navy League was called into being. With the aid of large subsidies from Krupp and Stumm and other arms patriots, it unloosed upon the German people a flood of high-powered patriotic propaganda, backed by the Kaiser. The junker age was now in full career. Wilhelm ordered that half of all armament contracts be awarded to Krupp and the rest divided among the other German munitioneers. Germany kept her arms contracts at home. Krupp's mills, shipyards, and docks became indispensable to Germany, not only for war purposes but for peace. It was a vast industry that employed many men and provided still more employment among all the raw-material industries upon which it drew. When the Hague conference was discussed in Germany, looking toward disarmament, the militarist ministers asked what would become of Krupp's business if Germany disarmed. They put that in writing, and the Kaiser wrote upon the memorandum the question, "How will Krupp pay his men?" Armament had become a cornerstone of the German internal economic policy.

Fritz Krupp grew ever richer, worth 119 million marks in 1895, 187 million marks when he died in 1902. He had an income of seven million marks in 1895 and twenty-one million in 1902. He had put aside the severe manner of life of the crusty old Alfred. He had become an industrial monarch. He dwelt in three great German castles—Hugel on the Ruhr, Sayneck in the Rhine Valley, and Meineck in Baden-Baden—and was a member of the Prussian State Council, of the federal House of Lords, a Privy Councilor, surrounded by flatterers and parasites.

He was destined to a melancholy end. A man of strange tastes and mystifying behavior, he kept his wife in an insane asylum and acquired a place at Capri, the Hermitage of Fra Felicia, which he called the Holy Grotto. He had attendants clad in the gowns of Franciscan monks. He formed an "order"—an association of men, the members of which had keys to the Holy Grotto. There gargantuan feasts were spread. There the Cannon King II held wassail until the dawn sometimes—orgies, these feasts were called by the islanders. Presently Neapolitan papers printed stories about them. One German paper, the *Vorwärts,* retold the tales, more than insinuating that this was a homosexual "abbey." Fritz Krupp sued the *Vorwärts.* Socialist deputies flew to the charge, the episode became a national scandal in which the Kaiser felt called upon to intervene.

Then on the night of November 21, 1902, when the prosecution of the *Vorwärts* was being prepared, Fritz Krupp died alone in his bedroom. Whether he died of a stroke or killed himself remained a subject of violent controversy in Germany for many years. Certainly, contradictory reports about his manner of death were issued. The Kaiser went to Essen and walked on foot behind the corpse to silence scandal. The prosecution of the *Vorwärts* was dropped. And the widow, until Fritz' death held as an unbalanced person, assumed command of the vast enterprises and administered them for a while with drive and vigor.

VII

When the war broke over Europe the moment of paradise for the arms makers was at hand. At first glance it may appear singular that the activities of Zaharoff during the war remain so obscure. But if ever there was a time when Europe needed no munitions salesmen it was after 1914. The salesman's work was done. The war —modern war, the greatest, most insatiable customer of the munitioneers—had come into the market. Generals and admirals clamored for more and ever more arms and explosives. The work of the salesmen of death was over, for the moment, anyway. Therefore Zaharoff's industry did not need his peculiar abilities.

But the moment came when Britain and France desired Greece as an active ally in the war. This was when England launched her attack upon the Dardanelles. The Greek government was divided. The pan-Hellenic Venizelos, his majority in the chamber, and the National Council favored joining the Allies. Constantine, King, brother-in-law of the Kaiser, pro-German, favored neutrality. He was popular in Greece because of the recent Balkan victories. The King dismissed Venizelos. In June the voters returned Venizelos to power. The chief objective of the Allies at the moment was to keep Bulgaria out of the war, hence the threat of Greek participation on the Allied side. Bulgaria mobilized in September, 1915. Venizelos ordered a countermobilization. The King permitted it until he heard that Venizelos proposed to go to the aid of Serbia. Then he dismissed the Premier again.

At this juncture Zaharoff's offices were enlisted. When Venizelos was dismissed, Constantine named Skouloudis, Zaharoff's old friend and benefactor, as Premier. Perhaps this may have accounted for Zaharoff's interest. Perhaps he would be able to work the miracle with Skouloudis. But there was another reason. The Greek problem now literally assumed the form of a conspiracy to dethrone the King and drive him out of Athens. This was a business into which France and England could not very well enter officially. They dared not supply funds for the purpose. After all, Greece was neutral and on terms of friendly intercourse with France. Briand, therefore, drew away from having any direct part in managing or financing a plan to upset the monarchy in Greece. But Zaharoff, a private citizen, could do this, particularly if he supplied his own money. Just before Christmas, 1915, therefore, Zaharoff had a conference with Briand and agreed to assume the job of bringing Greece in on the side of the Allies or of ousting Constantine. Briand notified Venizelos of this good fortune. And Zaharoff set about his task.

Just how much he did personally, what steps he actually originated, and what pressures he organized and directed are not known. The money for the campaign is supposed to have been supplied by him and it is also reported to have run into many millions. Whether it was furnished by him or Vickers or various other interests is also not known. The propaganda in Greece, handled by a French naval attaché, had been execrable. He was relieved of his clumsy performances, and an instrument called the Agence Radio was set up to go to work upon the Grecian mind. It resorted to all the familiar devices of international propaganda. It subsidized newspapers, bribed editors, issued pamphlets, financed meetings, and generally managed all the standard techniques of underground activity. For one thing it played heavily upon Allied successes. In Europe every small country wanted to be on the winning side. And Zaharoff's Agence Radio pumped up such endless whoppers about French and English victories that the Russian minister in Athens protested that it was absurd.

Zaharoff, if he tried to do anything with his old friend Skouloudis, failed, for the Premier stuck to the King and worked incessantly for neutrality. But Constantine was growing weaker and Venizelos stronger. Finally, when the time was ripe, Venizelos went to Salonika, where the Allies had landed, and organized a revolutionary government which resulted in the abdication of Constantine in June, 1917. Greece joined the Allies and the following year threw 250,000 men into the great Macedonian offensive that forced the surrender of Bulgaria.

This was an important service, for the defeat of Bulgaria, with which Greece's participation had much to do, was the first great crack in the enemy front. Zaharoff was busy in other directions. He endowed a chair of aviation at the University of St. Petersburg and made $125,000 available in England for the study of aviation problems. He subscribed 200,000 francs for a war hospital at Biarritz. Mr. Lewinsohn, his most industrious biographer, credits him, upon the authority of the Paris *Temps*, with contributing not less than 50 million francs (about $10,000,000 at prewar value) to the cause of England and France during the war.

But Zaharoff was not done with Greece. The armistice did not end the dreams of that relentless Cretan patriot, Venizelos, for the realization of his pan-Hellenic dreams. Zaharoff met Venizelos for the first time in 1918. And at Zaharoff's villa the two Greeks planned great gains for Greece out of the victory about to be won. The story, much oversimplified, runs about as follows. Zaharoff, Greek to the core despite his many other national encrustations, proposed to finance Venizelos in the realization of his dreams of expansion in Asia Minor. In May, 1919, Venizelos won from the allied statesmen their consent to occupy Smyrna. In August, 1920, the Treaty of Sevres gave to Greece Smyrna, its hinterland and a large territory in Asia Minor. With Zaharoff's funds Venizelos began to occupy these territories. Lloyd George, British premier, supported Venizelos completely in these adventures.

But quickly a series of misfortunes overtook the great Greek statesman. First, France lost interest in her Greek ally. Then unrest spread rapidly through Greece against Venizelos. The repre-

hensible behavior of his subordinates in Athens, while he worked
with the powers in Paris, produced profound dissatisfaction, which
the agents of the absent Constantine skillfully exploited. However,
Constantine's son, Alexander, was King and Venizelos seemed secure with him. Then suddenly, young Alexander, bitten by a monkey, died of the infection, and the whole Greek political situation
was thrown into chaos. Venizelos, absent so much at the Paris conferences, had lost control and in an election forced in November,
1920, his ministry was defeated. Within a month Constantine returned to power, Venizelos was an exile, and Zaharoff's plans were
in the fire.

But the end was not yet. Constantine pressed on with Venizelos'
grandiose plans, launched an ambitious Greek offensive in July,
1921, suffered a decisive defeat at Sakaria, and in September was
driven from Smyrna by a revamped and refurbished Turkish army
under Kemal Pasha, which burned that hapless city to the ground
in one of the great disasters of history. Constantine was forced
again to retire. By this time Lloyd George was being bitterly assailed in England for accepting the advice of Zaharoff, and, in the
end, the ministry of Lloyd George was wrecked upon the rock of
the Grecian debacle. Zaharoff, we are assured, lost an immense slice
of his fortune in this daring and ambitious design to create a great
Hellenic empire in Asia Minor.

But this scarcely tells the whole story. Lord Beaverbrook had
said that "the destinies of nations are Zaharoff's sport." It was not
all sport. It was the kind of sport—gamble is the better word—in
which the wily old schemer played for high stakes. As early as 1918
Zaharoff began to plan for certain undisclosed adventures. While
the armies of the world strained on to the last scene of the war,
Zaharoff laid plans for the coming peace. He bought a bank in Paris
—the Banque Mayer Frères—renamed it the Banque de la Seine,
reorganized it, capitalized it at 12 million francs, and very quickly
increased this to 30 million. This was about the time he met Venizelos and concocted with him the Grecian program.

Later, in 1920, the Greeks had occupied Smyrna and the Allies were in possession of Constantinople. At that time, as the Greeks prepared for their offensive in Asia Minor, he founded a new bank in Constantinople—the Banque Commerciale de la Méditerranée. Had not Beaverbrook said, "In the wake of war this mysterious figure moves over tortured Europe." This bank was capitalized at 30 million francs, its ownership resting in the Banque de la Seine. It set up for business in the quarters of the Deutsche Orientbank. Next he organized the Société Française des Docks et Ateliers de Constructions Navales and planned to take over the docks of the Société Ottoman. For whom? All these companies were French in name at least—there was no smell of the hated Briton anywhere. But this would have given Zaharoff control of the most important naval docks in Turkey. Could it be for Vickers? For whom else? But the Turks refused to let M. Zaharoff have these valuable properties. And when this occurred did not the British government demand that Kemal Pasha turn them over to Vickers and Armstrong?

There was something more than Greek patriotism in Zaharoff's league with Venizelos. Beaverbrook said: "The movement of armies and the affairs of governments are his special delight." He had inspired the movements of the Greek armies. He had insinuated himself as the adviser of Lloyd George in Asia Minor. The British Prime Minister had made Zaharoff's plans part of his policy. Zaharoff had spent, it was said, four million pounds—$20,000,000—on the Greek campaign. But there is really no evidence of this. So far as I can find, the statement rests upon a single question, by a member of the British Commons, Mr. Aubrey Herbert in 1921, during an interpolation—a question which Mr. Bonar Law parried. How much Zaharoff spent and whether it was his money or that of the English armament firms under his leadership, who were using the disturbed state of eastern Europe to get possession of valuable properties there, remain completely unriddled. Their plans did not turn out well. The collapse of what is called M. Zaharoff's personal war with Turkey—the Greco-Turkish War of 1920-22—the disastrous defeat of the Greeks, the awful tragedy of Smyrna, and the execution of most of the Greek cabinet ruined all Zaharoff's plans and brought him the loss of millions.

But long before the disaster the name of Zaharoff was being whispered around the clubs in London as the author of Lloyd George's highly unpopular policy in Greece and Turkey. Mr. Walter Guinness attacked the Prime Minister in the House on this score in August, 1920, when the Turks started their vigorous counterattack. The next year Lloyd George was again assailed in Commons with greater effect by Mr. Aubrey Herbert. And when the great catastrophe at Smyrna shocked Europe, Lloyd George found himself at the end of his rope and resigned.

These Turkish enterprises were not the only fields into which Zaharoff's Banque de la Seine ventured. Very quietly, without fuss or trumpets, the Banque de la Seine became the owner of a company called the Société Navale de l'Ouest—a shipping company equipped to transport oil. Then another company appeared—the Société Générale des Huiles de Pétrole. Fifty-five per cent of its stock belonged to the Société Navale de l'Ouest, the Banque de la Seine, and Zaharoff, and forty-five per cent to the British government-owned Anglo-Persian Oil Company. This Société Générale was no small affair. Its capital in 1922 came to 227 million francs. It took over or formed other corporations with refineries, so that by 1922 Zaharoff had organized in France a British-owned integrated oil industry.

These projects were typical of the Zaharoff technique. In both cases he was acting as a Frenchman, a citizen of France, organizing what seemed to be French companies—one group to exploit the armament possibilities of Turkey and Greece for Vickers, the other group to exploit French territory for the Anglo-Persian oil interests of the British government. Always a large part of the working machinery and certainly the meaning of Zaharoff projects were underground. He was the mysterious entrepreneur, the schemer moving in the dark, playing with behind-the-door intrigues, twisting silently along tortuous routes for undisclosed agents. Various writers have woven different surmises out of all these performances. But unfortunately most of the factors in the problem of Zaharoff's designs remain unknown. The most that can be said with assurance of certainty is that he, accepted as a citizen of France, honored by the ministry, and enjoying the confidence of her most powerful ministers, used France—as indeed he had always done—as a base for managing an English trade offensive, trade in arms and in oil in France and the Near East, in direct conflict at many points with the French government's own objectives.

He is credited with immense losses in the fatal Greco-Turkish War. Doubtless he lost heavily, but doubtless also, his losses were shared by his colleagues in Vickers. He is also credited with being able to offset these losses with his new profitable oil investments. What these investments were worth to him must also remain a mystery. In the end his Banque de la Seine fell upon troubled days and he let it go. After a brief effort to adjust it to the new conditions, he saw, doubtless with complacence, others take it over. It is an extraordinary feature of these Grecian and Turkish and Anglo-Persian oil transactions that, though they form part of the history of the period that has been raked over by historians, and though Zaharoff beyond doubt was the field marshal directing them in France, his personal movements throughout remain in complete obscurity. No major figure has succeeded so completely in cloaking his movements as this master-intriguer.

VIII

Zaharoff suffered losses, staggering ones. Seemingly the war had brought a magnificent harvest for the war profiteers. In America firms like Calumet and Hecla Copper had had, at the peak, as much as 800 per cent profit on their capital stock. In the two years of 1916 and 1917 the United States Steel Corporation showed a profit of $1,100,000,000. The Bethlehem Steel Company averaged profits of $48,000,000 a year during the four years of the war. In the year before the war Vickers had a profit of roughly $5,000,000.

During the war, of course, it drove forward in a hot frenzy of production. It delivered to the armies and navies 100,000 machine guns, 2528 naval and field guns, thousands of tons of armor plate, built four battleships, three armored cruisers, fifty-three submarines, three subsidiary vessels, and sixty-two smaller boats. Under a British act its earnings could not exceed by more than twenty per cent the average of the two years preceding the war. But its capital was greater and its production was greater and earnings were calculated proportionately on production.

A day came, however, when all those thousands of guns that Vickers and Armstrong and Krupp and the rest had made for the warmakers went terribly silent. The greatest disaster of all had fallen upon the arms makers—the disaster of peace. As one writer has put it, Krupp's immense tangle of machines in Essen "stopped with an audible jerk." Suddenly there was nothing for the 165,000 employees of Essen to do. It was the same in Sheffield. It took the men who ruled these great mills a little time to realize what had happened to them. The great expansion of plant during the war was now no longer needed. And, for that matter, the expansion that preceded the war was, for the moment, excessive.

But apparently Vickers believed it could survive. How far Zaharoff's counsels ruled in this error no one has told. He was the driving spirit of expansion always. He was directing in France the extension of operations into the Near East. He went to Rumania to bargain with the government. Representing Vickers, he offered a loan of three million pounds to save Rumania from a currency collapse, asking in return a mortgage upon the Rumanian railroad revenues. This has a bearing upon his attitude toward the expansionist policy of Vickers after the war. A new arms concern was started in Poland in combination with Schneider, a shipyard was built on the Baltic, munitions factories were taken over in Rumania, the British Westinghouse Company was absorbed, the company went into the production of railroad equipment. It actually increased its investment in new plants by $85,000,000.

Doubtless they believed there was life in the old militarist carcass yet. There were the new nations just formed which had to have weapons. Then their greatest competitor was literally wiped out. Krupp was required by the Allies to destroy 801,000 tools and appliances, 157,000 cubic yards of concrete and earthworks, 9300 machines of all sorts, 379 installations, and 159 experimental guns, and was forbidden to manufacture arms. Krupp became a huge warehouse and miscellaneous fabricator of all sorts of things. And so Vickers and doubtless Zaharoff believed there would be plenty of orders again when the world settled down to its routine of business, diplomacy, intrigue, treaty violations, ancient hatreds and new ones again. And they were right. But it would not come in time. For the time being the game was up.

Vickers went from loss to loss and from crisis to crisis. A committee had to be named to look into its affairs. The report was a dark one. It called for drastic reorganization, shrinkage, liquidation of stock. The alternative was bankruptcy. The reorganization was effected. Two thirds of the stock was wiped out. Douglas Vickers was eliminated. Sir Herbert Lawrence became its head. Zaharoff, sustaining a huge stock loss, doubtless slid quietly out of any important place in the control thereafter. This was in 1925. A little after this, Armstrong was in even worse trouble. It suffered reorganization which ended in a combination with Vickers, and Vickers took the lion's share. The firm became Vickers-Armstrong. This was in 1927, just fifty years after Basil Zaharoff in Athens had become a five-pound-a-week salesman for Nordenfeldt, later to be merged with Vickers. And so Vickers' directors met and presented to Sir Basil Zaharoff a cup on the completion of his half century of service with the firm and "as a mark of their great appreciation of the valuable work he has done for them and of their sincere gratitude and concern."

———————————————————— IX ————————————————————

The frowns of Sir Basil's war god, however, did not leave him destitute. He had lost a few hundred million francs. But there were many millions left. What he had lost, of course, was his place at the center in the great game of moving armies, gambling statesmen, scheming gun peddlers. He lived in his mansion in the Rue Hoche in Paris for some months each year, then in his Château Balincourt on the Riviera and the Hôtel de Paris in Monte Carlo in the severe winter months. He had been an old patron of the beautiful Blue Coast. The Casino in Monte Carlo, after the war, was in trouble. Its old owner, Camille Blanc, somehow had lost touch with the changed world, particularly the changed world of money. The Prince of Monaco, in whose domain the great Casino nestled, wanted to get rid of Blanc, to bring in a business management of the institution that supplied him with his revenue and his small principality with its support. He approached Zaharoff and, for some reason, the aging munitioneer was interested. He got hold of the shares and, with the aid of the Prince, shouldered Blanc out of the place and became its master. The Casino was a natural money-maker. It called not for any special magic but merely for money and a thorough business administration. This Zaharoff supplied. He did not manage it himself. He put in his own men. And it paid him golden dividends.

It was not altogether an unbecoming spot to end his strange career—this singular little nation of twenty thousand souls, living on a rock in the Mediterranean, a Prince ruling the tiny entity with his little army of a hundred and twenty men, a single business enterprise, the Casino, paying all the bills, supporting most of the population. There they ruled, two old nabobs—one the civil despot, the other the economic despot, owning the economic fountain out of which all the taxes and wages of the place came; the Prince of Monaco and Sir Basil Zaharoff, twin rulers in a comic-opera state that lived by gambling. Zaharoff's wise administration brought him rich profits, and when he had made enough and was weary of the business—and perhaps of all business—he sold out at a great profit.

Meantime on September 22, 1924, in the little village of Arronville outside Paris, he and the Duchess of Villafranca, who had been his unwedded consort for nearly forty years, were married. And then eighteen months later, in 1926, his new wife, his affinity of forty years, died at Balincourt. And this was the end of Zaharoff. The tedious business of straightening out the affairs of Vickers had to be got through with. This was done the next year.

After that Sir Basil Zaharoff continued to grow older, but did not die until 1936. There came a time when he grew feeble and had to be wheeled around Nice and Monte Carlo in a chair. What does such a man think, sitting feebly in a chair, pushed around like an infant, as he surveys the days of his power when he strode the earth like a titan, had his hand on the wires in the ministries of Europe, and felt a hundred hills shake in the roar of his cannon. Zaharoff's world was done, at least for the time being. The armament makers had proved, beyond all peradventure of doubt, the futility of their weapons and the folly of the regimes upon which they flourished. Their whole crazy world had come down in fragments around their ears. But then, after a brief interval of remorse and penitence, as the old gun man grew grayer and feebler, the dark industry he had helped to build got back its wind and its energy and grew bigger and mightier than ever. In the year that he died, the gun mills were grinding faster and more furiously than they were in 1913, the nations that had slaughtered each other with the guns of Zaharoff and company were preparing to repeat the crime with other and deadlier weapons.

The munitions industry, of course, was and is nothing more than another way of making money. Its techniques differ only in that its direct customers are governments and its sales practices are adapted to that necessity. Its dark sins have been in the region of selling. But even in this, it has resembled many of those other industries that must find their clients among public officials. It used bribery of officers, penetration of cabinets and bureaus, intimacy with the powerful. All these weapons Zaharoff knew how to employ with consummate skill. We find him on terms of intimate collaboration at one time or another with the most powerful men in the state—with Clemenceau in France and Lloyd George in Britain, with Briand, foreign minister, and, of course, with war and navy ministers everywhere, with Venizelos in Greece and his opponent Skouloudis, with Bratianu in Rumania, where also we find him entertained by the Queen, who actually intercedes with him to assist the tottering throne of Greece upon which her daughter sits as consort. Such a man as Lord Sandhurst, Undersecretary of State for War in England, is trustee for Vickers bonds, and Arthur Balfour is trustee for the bonds of Vickers' affiliate, Beardmore. In Paris, Zaharoff is a director of the Bank of France.

It is this side of the munitions business that brings it into disfavor. For it is not content to corrupt officials as public contractors do, but mixes up in state policy to create disturbance. It flourishes only in a world where hatreds and controversies, dynastic and economic and racial and religious differences between peoples flourish. Hence it has spared no pains to keep these mortal quarrels alive, to alarm peoples and ministers with war scares, to breed suspicion and distrust. First among all the practitioners of this dark art was Zaharoff. There is little doubt that he loved the game. He was the troublemaker feeding upon trouble—the neighborhood provocateur raised to the dubious dignity of free-lance statesman. Beaverbrook was right—"The destinies of nations were his sport; the movement of armies and the affairs of government his special delight. In the wake of war this mysterious figure moved over tortured Europe."

He cared nothing for acclaim, apparently, or if he did he realized it did not run well with his business. He did not advertise himself with magnificence like Morgan or Krupp; he did not go in for pageantry like William H. Vanderbilt or Fugger. He hired no shirt stuffers to blow up his fame like the Rothschilds and Rockefeller. But he did find it necessary to establish credentials of respectability and power. The name Zaharoff was passed around coated with odium in more than one critical period. And so he contrived at the proper moments to have put upon him the hallmark of governments. In 1908 he was made a Knight of the Legion of Honor in France. In 1913 he was promoted to be an Officer of the Legion of Honor, having endowed a chair of aviation at the Sorbonne. The next year, at the very hour when Paris police were thrown about his house to guard him against the possible anger of the radical groups because of the assassination of Jaurès and when his lifework was about to flower into the most murderous of all wars, he was raised to be a Commander of the Legion of Honor. Then in 1918, before the war ended, and doubtless to advance the ill-starred campaign he was organizing in Asia Minor, he was awarded the Grand Cross of the Order of the British Empire and became a Knight of the Bath—Sir Basil Zaharoff. A little later France again elevated him to the dignity of Grand Officer of the Legion. She was not done with her eminent citizen. In 1919 he was given the Grand Cross of the Legion, the highest decoration the republic had to offer. Thus, two crosses gleamed upon his breast—the cross of Britain and the cross of France—and, incidentally, the cross of Christ, the Prince of Peace, upon the bosom of this angel of war and blood.

Benefactions, nicely placed, preceded these honors—a chair of French literature named for Marshal Foch at Oxford, a chair of English literature named for Marshal Haig at the Sorbonne. And, of course, Oxford made him a doctor of civil law, though his specialty was the highly uncivil law of war. He gave 200,000 francs to enable the French athletes to participate in the Antwerp Olympics, endowed the Prix de Balzac—a literary prize—established the Pasteur Institute in Athens, and put 25,000 pounds at the disposal of the clinic for poor children there, provided a becoming Greek-legation building in Paris, and showed some other evidences of an interest in his native Greece. These benefactions need not be exaggerated. A twenty-five-thousand-pound contribution by a man into whose pockets countless millions are rolling is no more than a dollar bill that the ordinary Christian tosses into the plate on Sunday or the ten-dollar donation to the Salvation Army at Christmas. The good Sir Basil never pinched himself or denied himself anything to aid any cause. On the contrary, most of his gifts were investments in good will when good will was sorely needed.

Interlogue Three

HUGO STINNES

ONE CANNOT speak of Krupp before the Great War without thinking of Hugo Stinnes after the war. For one brief, dizzy moment Stinnes was, perhaps, and in a sense, the richest man in the world. In the hot cauldron of inflation the modern ideal of liquidity reached its craziest perfection—liquidity of ownership, the ownership of everything in Germany reduced to complete fluidity, running like a turbulent wild river through the markets. The ownership of office buildings, hotels, apartments changed hands half a dozen times a day like wildcat shares on an exchange. In that amazing epilogue of war, Stinnes, in a delirium of acquisitiveness, poured into his holding companies banks and factories, railroads and power plants, mines and oil companies, steamships, hotels, building blocks, estates by the hundreds. Germans, taught by their war-makers to adore the colossal, opened their eyes and looked with awe at this supercolossal industrial miracle. German business seemed to be divided into two parts—one part belonging to Stinnes, the other distributed among the other millions of Germans.

The vast extent of his possessions in Germany may be imagined from a simple list of some of the odds and ends that dropped into his bag outside Germany as a sort of by-product of his internal acquisitions. He found himself in 1923 controlling 20 coal companies, 11 iron mines, four oil fields and refineries, 16 earthen, stone, and ceramic works, 29 smelting works, 20 metal, machine, wagon, and locomotive works, three telegraph companies, four shipyards, 80 electric plants, eight paper, chemical, and sugar plants, four shoe factories, 47 electric and gas plants, nine shipping companies, 14 newspapers and print works, three cotton and coconut plantations, ten banks and holding companies, 204 selling agencies.

For all this, his fortune, vast for an instant and sensational, possessed no lasting importance. What it was worth is difficult to say. Had the whole tangle of steel and copper mines and mills, factories, banks, hotels, stores, buildings been reduced to marks—billions of billions of marks—and converted into the currency of America or England, they would have fetched just about enough pennies to buy an evening's bus ride. The whole thing represented a tumescent boiling up of the blood of German industry in a fever of inflation, in the course of which this monstrous growth broke out. It was part of the nightmare of buying when everybody in Germany was running around frantically trying to get rid of their money as if it were a plague. Stinnes understood the crazy game better than others, but not well enough to see it through to the end. He was like a gambler sitting at a table piling up before him mountains of chips which were good for cash in a casino which was bankrupt and on fire in the midst of an earthquake. He began his mad game toward the end of the war. In five years he was dead, and his weird empire was scattered.

Hugo Stinnes, however, must not be dismissed as a mere gambler. He was a leading businessman of prewar Germany. His grandfather, Matthis Stinnes, made a fortune in shipping and coal. Hugo Stinnes was born in 1870, as Bismarck prepared to incite the Franco-Prussian War. At twenty-two he formed his own firm but also took a part in managing the family mining interests. His own business grew enormously, until by 1914 it comprised coal and iron mines, steel mills, railroads, ships, shipbuilding, banking, trading companies. He loomed large in the Ruhr.

He was the leading exponent of vertical combination in Germany. The German pattern of combination was horizontal, beginning with cartels as early as the days of Jacob Fugger. Stinnes was fascinated by the vertical type in which all the stages of production and even distribution, from the raw materials to the finished product, are brought under a central control. In America this had gone far—Carnegie and later Gary and Gates and still later Morgan brought it to full flower in the United States Steel Corporation. The war suddenly gave a swift boost to this type of combination, and Stinnes began to avail himself of the permissions and opportunities of the war. Owning steel and coal industries, he needed lumber for the mine pits. Hence he acquired forests. Having forests for lumber he could use it to make paper. Having paper he could use it in printing plants. Having printing plants he could publish newspapers. And so the endless chain of acquisition went in every conceivable direction. He helped plan the war management of Belgian industry. He spread his control into Belgium and Luxembourg. He took a leading part in the direction of Ruhr industries and used that position to his advantage. He was expanding all through the war.

His method was to acquire mere minority rights in companies. He banked on his personal force to make that dominant. Not tall, but thick-set, erect, heavy-featured, with close-cropped hair, well-trimmed beard, yellow complexion, eyes oblique but shifting and yet penetrating, cool, a calculating machine, talking but little and then in a weary whisper, he nevertheless radiated that mysterious personal force which reduced other men to obedience.

When the war ended and his Belgian and many other semiwar possessions were confiscated, his companies were compensated by the German government, putting him into possession of large amounts of cash. Then, as the inflation got under way, he could, through his own banks and credit agencies, borrow marks to buy shares, which marks he could repay in a few weeks with greatly depreciated currency. And as this process went on Stinnes, coolly calculating the chances, the velocity of inflation, the human elements at work, borrowed and bought and paid his credits until he seemed to be swallowing all Germany, and the whole world looked daily at the mounting expansion of his interests. He seemed to be getting everything—chemical plants, lighting plants, explosives, cellulose, newspapers, publishing houses, brass and copper mills, automobile factories, film companies, shipping lines, big banks, banks with branches all over Germany, mortgage companies, insurance companies, companies of all sorts in Russia, Austria, Czechoslovakia, Poland, Rumania, Switzerland, South America. A cyclone seemed to be sweeping everything in Germany into his hands. Then came the stabilization of the mark. All the tremendous forces that had been driving everything his way suddenly ceased. And Stinnes, too. Only fifty-five, he seemed to cease with the storm. He died on April 10, 1924. His two sons quarreled over the unmanageable loot. They were utterly unequal to the task, and so, in all likelihood, was Stinnes himself. In 1925 the whole thing broke down. When the brothers and other parties interested finished there was left a few coal mines, two iron- and steelworks, four metal-trading firms, four shipping companies, and a few miscellaneous items.

---- II ----

LAND FORTUNES

Those fabulous fortunes of the great feudal princes of the East naturally invite the imagination of those who are interested in the subject of wealth accumulations. And the same observation goes for the great land fortunes of England, many of which still exist.

It cannot be said that they are without economic significance, since they perhaps control the economic life of the regions where they exist. But they are certainly without significance for us here. They are no part of the pattern of the modern world. They hang on as a remnant of a world that is dead in most places and dying everywhere. Not only do they belong to the type of fortune of the Middle Ages but a few of them are actually those very fortunes. They are either feudal or semifeudal, and there is no essential difference between them whether they be found on the banks of the Ganges or Sweet Avon. Essentially they involve the ownership of the land as the indispensable condition of controlling the product of the dweller upon it. In earlier times or in more backward countries their ownership of the land was accompanied by political rights of the most despotic character over the lives and bodies of the tenants. In more modern and civilized areas these political rights have been either greatly reduced or wholly extinguished.

One hears of those storybook or cinemalike Indian maharajas who are invariably represented as possessing fabulous stores of gold and precious stones and sources of income that are mysterious but abundant. First of all, there is a good deal of exaggeration about them all, a very considerable lack of precise information. But aside from that, they are anachronisms in the world's economy.

Most often reported among these Oriental princes and unfailingly described as the richest man in the world is the Nizam of Hyderabad. Hyderabad is an Indian state about the size of Idaho, with a population of about 12,500,000, and lying on the boundaries of Madras and Bombay. The Nizam is the principal Mohammedan ruler of India, and the state itself has a lot of good agricultural land, and some coal, copper, iron, diamonds, and gold. But none of these resources has been very vigorously worked. Doubtless the Nizam enjoys an immense income. But we are asked to believe that he has $500,000,000 of gold stored away in a strong room, part of his personal fortune, and another $2,000,000,000 in jewels.

This is a huge amount of gold in a country that operates on the silver standard, and, of course, it is gross exaggeration. But exaggerations pursue one remorselessly through the mazes of Indian fortunes. One hears about Akbar, first of the Great Moguls in the sixteenth century, who had an income of $200,000,000 a year and who on festival days weighed himself against gold coins and gave his weight in gold to the poor. Then there was Shah Jahan who built the Taj Mahal, whose peacock throne cost $32,000,000, and who enjoyed an income from his land alone of $22,000,000. But neither raked in so rich an income as the later Mogul Aurangzeb who collected $385,000,000 a year. These utterly fictitious statistics, so general when dealing with Indian fortunes, leave one quite lost as to the facts, which, of course, do not remotely approximate these figures.

The English land fortunes, of course, are for the most part almost wholly hereditary fortunes running back over periods of varying length. Few if any of them extend back to the Middle Ages. In 1911 when a new *Domesday Book* was compiled, but one landed estate turned up which had been included in the original *Domesday Book* compiled in 1086. It was a small estate of 2000 acres in Somerset that had cost eleven pounds in the eleventh century and was valued at 27,000 pounds in 1911, with an income of 1400 pounds. It remained in 1911 in the name of the same family that had owned it in the year 1086.

As a matter of interest I need but mention a few of the larger estates that remained intact in 1883. I give below thirteen of the largest:

NAME	RENT-ROLL
Norfolk, Duke of	£269,698
Bute, Marquis	186,155
Northumberland, Duke of	182,557
Ramsden, Sir J. W.	166,681
Derby, Earl of	163,326
Devonshire, Duke of	145,860
Bedford, Duke of	141,549
Tredegar, Lord	124,598
Calthorpe, Lord	122,628
Dudley, Earl of	120,442
Haldon, Lord	109,275
Anglesey, Marquis of	107,361
Cleveland, Duke of	100,485

The largest in area was that of the Duke of Northumberland, which embraced 191,480 acres. The largest rent-roll, however, was that of the Duke of Norfolk who then collected 269,698 pounds a year from his tenants, though he had far fewer acres. But some of them were located in the choice districts of London.

Some of these estates embrace a good deal of worthless lands;

others include whole towns and valuable timber and mineral rights. But they are not characteristic of the existing economic system and under the impact of income and inheritance taxes are being very seriously reduced and in some cases broken up.

————————————— III ——————————————

DYNASTIC FORTUNES

The dream of the rich man, particularly the parvenu of other days, as soon as he looks about him and surveys his glory, is to perpetuate it in a dynasty. This was not so difficult in the feudal era when wealth rested upon the indestructible land and men could entail their fortunes through the practice of primogeniture. But when the laws against entails were passed, the days of the dynast became somewhat more difficult. Nevertheless, aristocratic families in England and Germany and Spain and other Continental countries have found ways of transmitting their wealth from one generation to another with a good deal of success.

But in America, where the land has got pretty generally distributed, where fortunes are invested rather in industrial and commercial enterprises, the fear of the dynast has been much diluted. One of the oldest fortunes is that of John Jacob Astor. Its founder died in 1825, leaving $25,000,000. When his son died in 1890 there were a hundred millions to divide. This went to two sons—$50,000,000 to each. It grew in their hands. One left $150,-000,000, the other $75,000,000. The owner of the $150,000,000 took himself off to England where whatever of dynastic energy is left is a rash upon England's limbs, not ours. The brother with the $75,000,000 died in America leaving his fortune among numerous heirs. The bulk of the American Astor fortune is in the hands of William Vincent Astor—$87,000,000. There are a few stray millions scattered about, but it is far under the $250,000,000 it was twenty years ago. And it continues to wane under certain new pressures while its owners have ceased to be dominating factors in any important business.

These pressures are several. They are the logical development of the whole system. One of them is the inheritance tax. New social philosophies are now powerful. But state necessities are even more imperative. Governments need so much taxes that ways have to be found to get them. The inheritance tax is the one that generates the least effective resistance. During life, income taxes now weaken the power of the fortune to accumulate, and, at death, the government steps in to take the lion's share.

The Vanderbilt fortune is one in point. Until his death old Commodore Vanderbilt strode the country like a colossus with his hundred million. His son William H. made it two hundred millions. He owned the New York Central Railroad as a man owns his corner store. But he found it wasn't healthy for one man to control a great railroad. He found it to his advantage to sell a lot of his control. When he died he left eight children. Eight children subject a fortune to a very enfeebling division. But his sons, Cornelius and William K. got $50,000,000 each. Cornelius' fortune at his death went to several children, but Alfred got the bulk, $80,000,000. When he died it had shrunk to $35,000,000. It was split $5,000,000 to his son William, $8,000,000 to the widow, and the balance to two sons of his second wife. William K. left $100,000,000. It went to two children, Consuelo and William Harold. The former withdrew her fortune to a ducal dynasty in England. Among the various heirs, a good slice drifted into the hands of Frederick W. Vanderbilt. He died in June, 1938. His estate, valued at $72,588,000, was liquidated in 1939, and the Federal government and state of New York took $41,272,000 of it in taxes.

Andrew Carnegie was worth at one time $300,000,000. He gave away most of it to the Carnegie Corporation for libraries and education. When he died his estate showed $23,000,000 left. His partner, Henry Clay Frick, left an estate valued at $150,000,000. $117,000,000 went to public benefactions. His children got $25,-

000,000, and this was subject to heavy inheritance taxes that reduced it by forty per cent.

The Gould fortune was a great bolus of wealth. When Jay Gould died it had swollen to about a hundred million. He tried to entail his estate with a trust for his son, George J. When George died after many financial disasters he left $30,000,000 in another trust, but much split up: $10,000,000 in trust for seven children by his first wife, $4,000,000 for the three children of his second wife, and the balance in trust for both broods.

Even in England many noble gentlemen with immense estates have found them too costly to keep up after the income-tax gatherer had got through with them, and the inheritance-tax office has been doing its deadly work upon what is left.

The Mitsui fortune has endured because of the peculiar social system under which it exists. It has been possible to organize a family there with sanctions behind its decrees that would not be possible in America, France, or England, or, for that matter, in any large modern state. Then, by separating the family organization and the business organization and putting the business into the corporate form, the whole structure has been given a quality of permanence.

But the very corporate form that has served the Mitsuis so well is actually tending to break up family control of business in this country. The corporate form makes it possible for men to distribute their investments over a wide range of industries. Modern investment studies have convinced owners of immense fortunes that the greatest safety lies in diversification rather than control of an industry. Therefore the fortunes of very wealthy men will be found spread around in the stocks and bonds of scores, and in some cases of hundreds, of corporations. The result is that they hold a dominating interest in none and exercise over industrial policies, save in a few cases, but very little influence.

A third element now enters. The uncertainties of the world, the wars, depressions, and political irritations, have induced many men to take refuge in government bonds. They do this for another reason—to escape the income taxes. All these influences tend first to minimize the power of dynastic families over the industries founded by their ancestors and second to break up those fortunes, first through income and inheritance taxes, second through family distributions, and third through the erosion of the last dozen years.

If we will go back one hundred years we will find that the largest fortunes in America were the following:

John Jacob Astor	$25,000,000
Stephen Van Rensselaer	10,000,000
Stephen Girard	7,500,000
Peter C. Brooks	6,500,000
William B. Astor	5,000,000
Amos and Abbot Lawrence	5,000,000
Peter G. Stuyvesant	4,000,000
James Lennox	3,000,000
Peter Schermerhorn	2,500,000
John P. Cushing	2,500,000
William B. Crosby	1,500,000
Isaac Bronson	1,500,000
Thomas H. Perkins	1,500,000
John Bolen	1,250,000
Henry Brevoort	1,000,000
Gouverneur Morris	1,000,000
John Mason	1,000,000
Jonathan Hunt	1,000,000
Samuel Appleton	1,000,000
Robert G. Shaw	1,000,000

Some of these, of course, are merely good guesses at the fortunes of these men, but they serve to show us how few are left today. There were a few others whose fortunes cannot be even guessed at —David Sears, millionaire stockholder; Jacob Little, security speculator; August Belmont, representative of the Rothschilds.

In the world of today the way of the dynast is a hard one.

MARK HANNA

CHAPTER X

Mark Hanna

THE POLITICO

———————————— I ————————————

MARK HANNA was born in the same year as J. Pierpont Morgan and two years before John D. Rockefeller. The shadows of these men, merged into one monstrous silhouette, brooded over the American scene for more than half a century. As Morgan dominated the financial life of the nation and Rockefeller gave direction to its industrial life, Hanna became the molder of those political forms proper to the age of Big Business.

The political control that took its rise with the rise of these men came to a pause—a dark, disordered, and even terrifying pause— in 1933. Hanna's assumption of national boss-ship in 1896 constituted a kind of initial invasion, in which big business broke into the government. The businessman in politics was, of course, always a familiar figure. If there were Carnegies and Fricks and Elkins and Keans and Blisses in the Republican Party, there were no lack of Belmonts and Whitneys and Paynes among their Democratic opponents. But up to the time of McKinley these businessmen were applicants at the hands of the politicians. Rich men might seek juicy favors from the state, but always they were supposed to send someone a check.

From the day of the United States Bank down to the wholesale traffic in congressmen by Oakes Ames and the Crédit Mobilier, businessmen had bought Senators and congressmen, legislators and aldermen. The technique that governed the relations of businessman and politician was that of corruption, bribery, and flattery. Always there have been statesmen like Disraeli in England and

McKinley in America who knew how to varnish over the acceptance of benefices at the hands of some rich Maecenas. Thus these bankers and industrialists exercised great influence in the state, but they did not master it. There had been plenty of Albert B. Falls but no Andrew Mellons. Of course the businessman in politics was not new. There have been businessmen holding positions of power since Nicias in Athens and Crassus in Rome. It went farther in England than anywhere. She had had the rich textile manufacturer, Sir Robert Peel, as premier, and Cobbett had referred with scorn to the large number of seats in Parliament purchased by county bankers. But it had not proceeded to that point in America.

With the advent of Mark Hanna came a change. Grover Cleveland's first Cabinet contained Thomas F. Bayard, a great Senator, as Secretary of State; Lucius Q. C. Lamar, a professor of mathematics and economics, as Secretary of the Interior; William Crowninshield Endicott, a justice of the Massachusetts Supreme Court, as Secretary of War; William F. Vilas, a professor of law, as Postmaster General; Augustus H. Garland, a statesman or politician rather than corporation lawyer, as Attorney General; John G. Carlisle, former Speaker of the House, as Secretary of the Treasury. William C. Whitney, millionaire lawyer and agent of powerful New York banking and utility interests, in the Navy Department, was a solitary exception.

McKinley's first Cabinet, on the other hand, included Russell A. Alger, an enormously wealthy lumberman; Lyman J. Gage, president of the First National Bank of Chicago; James A. Gary, a rich textile manufacturer; and Cornelius N. Bliss, New York banker. Wealthy manufacturers and merchants and *rentiers* were slowly to replace in the Senate, the Cabinet, and diplomatic service, and finally in the presidency itself, the professional politicians. And this was to go on until, on March 4, 1929, as this confused era moved into its latest stage, a millionaire businessman President, surrounded by a Cabinet of millionaire businessmen, took over immediately and directly the reins of the government, with a commercial banker at the Court of St. James, an investment banker in

Italy, a utility magnate in Berlin, an advertising man in Paris, a steelmaker in Spain, and millionaire businessmen in almost all the capitals of the world.

The process was completed when in October, 1929, we heard Gabriel over Wall Street and the President, as that fateful premonitory shiver ran through our economic structure, summoned around him the College of Captains. At that moment, every phase of our life was in the hands of businessmen. The test for their power was at hand and, led by a great engineer and great industrial ministers of state, these bankers and manufacturers and utility magnates were to seize the depression in its infancy and crush it. In that hour the Great God Business might be said to have become supreme, even though the very earth shook under the images of the idol.

It was Herbert Hoover's melancholy destiny to be the last inheritor of the scepter that Mark Hanna forged. For it was this wholesale grocer and iron and coal merchant, street-railway baron and banker of Cleveland, who was the first masterful instrument of usurpation by business, self-righteous and unquestioning, with ample cash and a profound respect for its power to keep the cinders pouring from the smokestacks of God and the seats of the mighty filled with men who could understand a smokestack. He drifted into politics in almost the same way business drifted into politics. And he became almost overnight the very symbol of big business ruling the government. The cartoonist, Davenport, seized upon his countenance and figure, decked him out in dollar-marked plaids and made him the type of the lawless baron crushing the lowly. But if Davenport had not done this, some other artist would have adopted that round, lusty face, with its strong jaws and low gable and the whole strong, portly figure. And to this day the caricaturist, aiming a shot at arrogant and despotic business, will, almost without realizing it, move his pencil into the lines of Davenport's devastating cartoon.

Hanna moved into power at the moment when big business put to work for its own purposes the cherished doctrine of individualism. Certain aggressive men had begun to expand their power out of all proportion to their natural endowment. They learned how to arm themselves with machines, to absorb the combined resources of many individuals through the corporate form, and thus to become, beside their lesser rivals, almost monstrous beings. Few men could hope to assume such armaments. But there were plenty of pious and complacent statesmen like the McKinleys and Hays and Roots to remind the people who cried out against these half-understood giants that any attempt to disarm the monsters would be a blow at the hardy cult of individualism. It was a merry invention to which Hanna gave his fullest assent. As the years wore on even many conservative observers of the swelling spectacle of big business began to see there was something askew in this notion of individualism, until Herbert Hoover arrived on the scene, and with the authority of the presidency behind him, invoked once more this discarded fetish and blessed it with the name of Rugged. The journals of apology took it up eagerly and proceeded to explain to little Jack that the Giant was an individual just like himself—though perhaps a trifle more rugged.

In every age the rich businessman has had a collection of weapons or tools with which to work. From earliest times men had been fashioning these tools. They got down to serious business in the development of this arsenal in the days of the Florentine bankers and the Augsburg merchants. In the chapter on Robert Owen we saw that as early as 1837 most of the weapons of that thing called "finance capitalism," for want of a better name, had been in use at least in rudimentary forms in Boston and Lowell. But now they were far more clearly understood by some men. Men like Rockefeller and Morgan could not use those weapons fully and freely save by friendly collaboration with the state, by legal authorizations, and by the creation of a benevolent legal and public mood upon which they could float safely. Hanna it was, more than anyone, who organized the political shell within which this new capitalism could function safely. And this he was able to do because he had first made himself rich and then, through the leisure that fortune gave him, dedicated his large abilities to political life.

Hanna held fast to the theory of prosperity by percolation. That, of course, was no new conception. The feudal lord enabled the elements of his strength to sift down to his vassals and their villeins. The Southern slave owner believed he was the divinely appointed wide end of the funnel through which blessings flowed down to his Negro hands, just as the haughty coal baron, George Baer, believed that God appointed the anthracite mine owners as the generators of the favors that dripped down upon the half-starved coal miners of Pennsylvania. Had Hanna been President when the depression arrived he would have convoked the College of Captains; he would have summoned the employers to be good to their workers and not to cut wages; he would have organized the Reconstruction Finance Corporation; and as the structure continued to crumble despite all these braces built around the roof, he would have wondered what evil and mysterious mischance defeated all these perfectly obvious and wise measures.

II

Mark Hanna was born September 24, 1837, in New Lisbon, Ohio. At the time, his grandfather, Robert Hanna, with his tall, industrious sons, were the rich men of New Lisbon, where they ruled a wholesale and retail grocery business. It was a strong breed —Virginia Hicksite Quakers and Vermont Presbyterians—bent on getting along, worshiping law, hating slavery, liquor, and disorder, keeping out of public affairs, minding strictly their own business.

Mark Hanna's education was of the most immature sort. As a lusty, rosy-cheeked boy he attended the public grammar school in the basement of the Presbyterian Church in New Lisbon. When the family moved to Cleveland he attended grammar school and then the Central High, where John D. Rockefeller was one of his classmates. Neither shone at school. Hanna, in particular, was twenty years old before he struggled to the end of the simple course of Central High with boys two to four years his junior. Then he went to Western Reserve College, only to be ejected after a few months for some harmless prank. After this he obeyed his own desires and put on a pair of overalls as a roustabout on the River Street docks in his father's prosperous grocery business.

After a brief novitiate as a roustabout, Hanna moved up to a clerkship in the grocery business of Hanna, Garretson & Company, then as a purser on one of its lake steamers, then as a traveling salesman, and then as a part of the general management of the enterprise. The world of affairs in Cleveland first became aware of this robust youth when in his twenties he became a familiar figure in River Street—a stocky, thick-chested, large-shouldered, virile young man, with huge, alert brown eyes and a heavy bush of matted beard along the edges of his powerful jaw. The upper lip was clean-shaven after the manner of the time.

When the war came, like the Rockefellers and Morgans and Wanamakers and other sensible businessmen of the time, he knew the Union was safe as long as the supply of common labor held out for drafting. At the close of the war he was drafted into service for a few brief months as a second lieutenant to help repel General Jubal Early's raid upon the Capital. It must be said for him, however, that after the war he did not join the G.A.R. and exhibit himself at campfires until near the end of his life, when the pressure of politics and the power of the American Legion of that day forced him in.

The remainder of his business career is soon told. From the grocery business he went into oil and then into the development of steamships on the lake. Then he married the daughter of Daniel Rhodes, a pioneer in coal and iron business on the Lakes. Soon after he was in his father-in-law's firm, and when the old man died Hanna dominated it and changed its name to M. A. Hanna & Company, with his brothers as partners. They became large miners and dealers in coal, iron ore, and pig iron, owners of a fleet of steamers, and finally builders of ships. Thus he amassed a fortune and when he died left an estate valued at seven million dollars.

There were two interesting features in his business career. One was the variety of his interests. Unlike Rockefeller, who stuck with dogged singleness of purpose to his last, Hanna had to have his irons in many fires. He bought and ran a newspaper, owned a theater, organized and headed a bank, and became one of the two leading street-railway magnates of Cleveland. The other point of interest lay in this little-considered fact: while he was regarded as the representative of big business and great corporations, Hanna himself did not commit his own fortunes to the corporate form. His business was and remained until after his death a partnership. And while it grew and spread to many allied lines—ships and railroads and coke and blast furnaces—some of which were actually incorporated, they were old-fashioned corporations, closely held, really incorporated partnerships. Hanna, like Rockefeller, and unlike Morgan and Rogers and Gould and many other contemporaries, never used other people's money. He was a builder and developer— a sound and able businessman, who accumulated a large fortune and ended by losing interest altogether in acquiring any more.

--------------------------- III ---------------------------

In 1896 after McKinley's nomination, when the convention rose and called for Hanna, the "kingmaker," and the thick-chested, rugged, smiling Clevelander mounted the platform, the newspapers hailed him as a newcomer in politics and as the businessman who had turned boss and routed the veterans Platt and Quay and Reed. The dramatization pleased the press, but Hanna was no tyro. He was a political leader at least as experienced as any man in the convention.

He began his career as a businessman. Until he was forty he took little active interest in politics. As it fell out, in the middle 'seventies an important phenomenon was shaping itself in American political life, the effects of which survive to this day. The party of Lincoln, fresh from the exalted evangel against human slavery, was being made into the party of that new thing, Big Business. This was the work of chance. The war had made the Republican party supreme in the North. Big Business was stretching out and challenging all sorts of old-fashioned rights. The railroads were in continual collusion with state governments. Oil, sugar, iron, coal corporations were moving ruthlessly back and forth across state frontiers. Gas companies and street-railway corporations had to appeal to city governments for the use of the streets. All the businessmen behind these enterprises, like practical managers, made their peace with the political party that was in power. And this chanced to be the Republican party. When the Democratic party returned to power in the South and some of the great cities of the East, the same elements could be found collaborating with their Democratic allies. Hanna's own interest in politics had been for years quite casual. He could be found around the polls on Election Day and at ward meetings with the "better element," throwing his weight on the side of "good government."

It was not until 1878 that he found a good personal business reason for moving actively in politics. At this time business and politics were two separate estates. Their edges touched. Some members in each estate flowed freely over the other's boundaries and sometimes it was a little difficult to tell whether this one was a businessman in politics or a politician in business. One of the best-known highways between these two states of business and politics was the little old-fashioned horsecar railway. And it was on this line that Mark Hanna rode finally into the world of the politicians.

Hanna's father-in-law, Daniel Rhodes, was part owner of a little fifteen-mile horsecar line in Cleveland that ran over the viaduct to the Public Square. It was managed by Rhodes' partner, Elias Sims, a hard-bitten old steamboatman, who was president of the company. Of course, old Elias Sims quarreled continually with the city authorities. Aldermen had learned early how to grant competing franchises to political friends to be sold out to the existing roads. Of course, old Sims had to keep *en rapport* with the Cleveland fathers. "All councilmen want," he complained, "is money. Have to go round with my pocketbook in my hand all the time."

When Daniel Rhodes died in 1875, Hanna assumed the management of his wife's interests. And immediately his interest in politics bristled. But it was not until 1879 that he became a director of the road and collaborated directly with Sims in its management.

Immediately Hanna confronted a new figure rising in Cleveland —a figure destined to make a generous contribution to the gaiety of the city. This was Tom L. Johnson. Johnson had begun almost as a youth with a single horsecar and had built up a prosperous streetcar line. He and Sims were in continual warfare. And Hanna was quickly drawn in. Between Hanna and Johnson there was an impassable gulf. Johnson was a huge, portly but powerful, dynamic, generous-minded man, quite as full of combat as Hanna. Both started in business and ended in politics. But Hanna was always the businessman in politics; Johnson, the politician in business. Hanna was profoundly satisfied with the world as he found it. Johnson was no less profoundly dissatisfied. Johnson became the leader in Cleveland's street railways. But in the midst of his success, a copy of Henry George's *Progress and Poverty* fell into his hands. When he had read it he rose up as completely converted as Saul of Tarsus. Henceforth he became a valiant warrior for George's single-tax theory and for other popular reforms in government. In the end he sold out his railway interests, went to Congress, became Mayor of Cleveland, and achieved fame by his celebrated crusade for municipal ownership and the three-cent fare.

He soon came to embody the spirit of revolt against control by the corrupt utility interests, while Mark Hanna became no less the symbol of that control. These two men fought for over two decades in Cleveland and Ohio. And this long warfare began as Hanna joined Sims in the direction of the little horsecar line. Johnson and Sims went through one of their numerous battles over a franchise. Johnson won and Hanna, who hated defeat, was furious. He hurried to old Sims and, glowering at him with his huge brown eyes and shaking his long chin whiskers, demanded that Sims buy him out or sell. Sims sold and Hanna became sole ruler of the little line.

Before long Hanna found himself facing the pushing Johnson in another fight. The river cut Cleveland in two sections. Johnson's line ran on one side of the river. He proposed to acquire a line on the other side, unite the two, and give a continuous ride across town for a nickel. He needed a new franchise for this, and before the council he found Hanna bitterly contesting the plan. All his life Mark Hanna stood against any cuts in the revenues of business. Years later his first battle in the Senate was to protect the steel trust's efforts to squeeze an extortionate price out of the government for armor plate. This Hanna-Johnson fight waxed hot. At every session of the council, the squat, square-shouldered, burly figure of the coal, iron, banker, and utility magnate could be seen in the chamber, buttonholing members, hammering his cane on the floor, expostulating violently with them. Two days before the final vote Johnson got a summons from old Elias Sims to visit him. Sims told Johnson he controlled two votes in the council and that these would be delivered to Johnson. "Why?" asked the astonished Johnson. "It takes mor'n a fool to beat Hanna," muttered Sims. "If you beat Hanna nobody can say any damned fool can beat Sims. You beat me. I want you to beat Hanna." With Sims' two votes Johnson did beat Hanna with but a single vote to spare.

Hanna denounced Johnson's plan to give "two rides" for a single fare. The service would cost five cents. The line would run at a loss. As it turned out the new line proved Johnson's most prosperous venture.

But Hanna could beat Johnson too. These two men rose to riches, electrified their lines, built them into powerful properties. Consolidation followed consolidation until two companies dominated the city—the Big Consolidated (Johnson's line) and the Little Consolidated (Hanna's line). Finally the two lines merged and Johnson sold out. Hanna hated Johnson. He hated everything the man stood for. He would grow red in the face and pound his stick as he denounced him as a radical, a Socialist, a destroyer of society.

As Mayor, Johnson attempted to run trolleys for three cents a ride. To Hanna this was hardly less than treason. Johnson forced the council to grant the necessary franchises to the city. Hanna promptly induced the attorney-general, Joseph Sheets, to bring an action declaring the city government of Cleveland unconstitutional. This was the same Joseph Sheets who later would dismiss the injunctions against the Standard Oil Company. The court sustained Hanna's contention. City governments all over Ohio were thrown into confusion by the decision. The governor called a special session of the legislature to reconstruct municipal governments. Hanna went to Columbus to sponsor a bill to permit granting perpetual franchises to his own company. The legislature adopted the new city government code but Hanna's perpetual franchise was a little too much even for that corporation-controlled body to swallow.

These battles raged for years. Cleveland belonged to its iron, oil, gas, electric, and streetcar interests, its banks and real-estate promoters, and Hanna became their recognized spokesman. They began to look to him to defend them. Thus led into politics by his railway company, he came to like it. He was a man of restless energy and loved combat and power. His own business was soundly organized and prosperous and he found he could take more and more time for his excursions into political strife. By the late 'eighties he was a familiar figure in Cleveland, with his round ruddy face, his long narrow beard streaming down over his chin, his portly body, his heavy square shoulders, his flat-topped bowler hat. His fellow citizens saw him driving along Euclid Avenue, sitting in his private box at his own theater, moving about the neighborhood of the Public Square, stopping to converse vigorously, often angrily, with acquaintances, pounding his stick on the pavement. Though only a local celebrity he was a figure of importance and power.

---------------------------------- IV ----------------------------------

Hanna will always be remembered as the man who made McKinley President. Hanna's ambition to be a President-maker had been formed before he became intimate with McKinley. He had, in fact, first come to know the latter when he was engaged, a dozen years before, in an effort to make John Sherman the Republican nominee for President. Hanna was named one of Ohio's big four in 1884.

It was at the convention of 1884 that he first found himself in contact with McKinley and Foraker, who were also delegates-at-large. Hanna supported Sherman, but Foraker and McKinley threw their strength to Blaine, who was nominated. Thereafter Hanna maintained friendly relations with both men but saw little of McKinley, then in Congress. In the next Republican convention Hanna took the lead as the campaign manager for old Senator John Sherman, who was thought to have a fighting chance for the presidency. The Ohio delegation was pledged to Sherman. McKinley was then a commanding figure in Congress; Foraker was the dashing Governor of Ohio. And in this convention Hanna formed his devoted friendship with McKinley and began his lifelong feud with Foraker.

McKinley's name first came into notice as a presidential candidate in that 1888 convention. Hanna, convinced that Sherman's star had set, decided to switch to McKinley because, as he told a friend, he "was going to stop riding the wrong horse." His real friendship for McKinley came after he had settled on that gentleman as his next entry for the presidency.

These three men—Hanna, McKinley, Foraker—formed a striking group. Each was to rise as a presidential possibility. Each represented a wholly different type in American politics. If we add to the group William Jennings Bryan, Theodore Roosevelt, and Matthew Stanley Quay, we have a gallery of indigenous leaders which could be duplicated on a small scale in every state and village of the country. McKinley, the pious, respectable patriot, the cautious opportunist speaking the language of courage, of strength; Foraker, the strong, able, audacious, and unscrupulous demagogue; Roosevelt and Bryan, both high-minded idealists, one a confirmed chauvinist and jingo with an immense store of practical political skill, the other an uncompromising crusader for fixed causes; Hanna and Quay—bosses—Quay openly corrupt and deriving his power from his dominion over an unspeakably rotten state machine, Hanna getting his power from the stores of money which he could command from the combined forces of business organizations interested in public privileges of all sorts. He was the businessman turned politician, with very low standards of public principles, but standing resolutely by them.

Of these, the most important in Hanna's career was McKinley. The Major, as he was known, was in 1888 just forty-five years old. He had already served six terms in Congress, where he had attained fame as a militant protectionist. When President, he said of Theodore Roosevelt that "he was always in such a state of mind." This described a temper precisely the opposite of McKinley's. The Major never tilted at abuses. Mark Hanna was not more satisfied with the world as he found it than McKinley, whose name is identified with no effort in any direction to enlarge or improve the condition of his fellow men.

He was a type peculiarly useful to stronger men in our boss- and business-ridden system. The busy, practical purveyors of privilege and collectors of graft who rule the machines must have well-favored men who can be thrust out in front to give a good appearance to their ranks. McKinley was peculiarly fitted for this role. He was a pious soul, eminently respectable, handsome, distinguished in appearance, an able speaker, and greatly admired for his domestic virtues. He staged himself elaborately and remained always in character. He was a man who looked learned and yet who possessed very limited information of history or economics or law. He was never a student or reader of books though he came to be looked upon as a model of wisdom. His range of ideas was, like Mark Hanna's, limited. He took up the philosophy, the mood, the character of the generation in which he was born and held fast to it.

A kind of legend grew up around the sweetness and patience of his home life. His wife was an epileptic. As a result she was a whimpering, querulous creature who spent her life in the contemplation and nourishment of her own sufferings. McKinley was deeply devoted to her. He yielded to this complaining and difficult woman a romantic and chivalrous attention that made Mark Hanna exclaim, "McKinley is a saint." Hanna, like Joe Cannon and other contemporaries, liked the society of men, enjoyed a rubber of whist and an evening of chat. He was a simple soul and easily mistook McKinley's lack of fondness for these perfectly normal masculine enjoyments for a kind of sainthood.

McKinley had an easy, unruffled amiability that never permitted him to quarrel with anyone. In his very first meeting with Hanna— which Hanna incidentally never remembered—the Major as a young attorney was engaged to defend a group of miners who were tried on a charge of damaging one of the Hanna company mines during a strike. Mark Hanna represented the operators in that fight and was present at the trial. One of Hanna's biographers refers feelingly to the pleasant impression that the attorney who defended the miners made upon the wealthy operators present by his kindly recognition of the fact that in prosecuting his clients they were merely doing their duty as they saw it. McKinley saved every acquaintance, good and bad, for a rainy day.

His critics accused him of weakness. He was certainly not a strong figure. He could yield and trim and change and backslap and smile with all manner of men on all sides of all questions. But when the issue reached that line where the career of the Major was at stake he could reveal sudden and unsuspected resources of iron.

He was far craftier than the forthright Hanna. He was a man of endless caution. He seldom committed his views to writing or his political thoughts to letters. He had a fondness, which his associates noticed, for messengers. When he did write, it was often for the purpose of putting himself on record, a precaution he did not fail to use with his most devoted friends. He had one faculty that he employed with great success—his ability to varnish over any sort of cause, however dubious, with pious platitudes. When Dewey took Manila, McKinley could cable him to report immediately which was the richest and most desirable of the islands and then turn to the nation with a ringing defense of annexation as "benevolent assimilation."

Foraker was a very different man—strong in his own right, an able debater, a powerful figure on the hustings or in a convention.

He ruled an effective machine. When he went to the Senate he became a loud, warlike, ready champion of every form of corporate activity until William Randolph Hearst drove him from public life by exposing his acceptance of money from the Standard Oil Company.

For many years these two—Hanna and Foraker—battled for supremacy in Ohio. At that 1888 convention already referred to, Hanna assumed the leadership of John Sherman's drive for the nomination. Foraker was Governor, a rising figure, enormously ambitious, and with an eye on the presidency himself. One day before the convention assembled Foraker walked into Sherman headquarters and saw the ruddy-faced Hanna, now bereft of his whiskers, surrounded by Southern delegates. His fingers were filled with currency and he was handing it out freely to his Negro guests. "Far from home and short of cash," as Foraker described them, these delegates were selling their tickets for the convention gallery seats to Hanna and throwing in their souls for good measure. Of course, Hanna did not want the tickets. As a matter of fact, he turned the batch over to an associate who had them in a trunk many years later.

Foraker, who understood the dramatic values of opportune indignation, pretended to be shocked at this wholesale direct cash bribery. He denounced it. Hanna defended it as necessary since other candidates were doing it.

Hanna's candidate, Sherman, was decisively defeated. Harrison was named to oppose Grover Cleveland but the man who left that convention with the largest dividend was William McKinley.

The two men were thrown together intimately during the convention. Hanna was astonished at the shrewdness and sagacity of McKinley. His surprise was mixed with pleasure because McKinley's talent was beautifully garnished with a show of high-minded sentiments. Hanna himself was a more or less artless creature. He was blunt, outspoken, direct, utterly without guile. He moved always by the shortest route to his objective. He rested upon an almost childlike faith in the right of his class—business—to have its way, to make its profit, and the bigger the profit the better for the country. Workmen were protégés who should be dealt with benevolently. Loyalty to friends, right or wrong; a profound respect for the power of money to achieve its ends, and a willingness to use it as well as all the other recognized implements of political warfare, made up the balance of his creed. Hanna was not always a cautious man. He could explode with wrath at inopportune moments. McKinley was the soul of caution. Moreover he resolved every action into one of high moral ingredients. If he refrained from doing anything because it was inexpedient he could give his omission the appearance of a personal sacrifice. Hanna came to be very fond of McKinley and this deepened soon after into a genuine affection for the rising congressman.

Hanna was sure now that John Sherman could never be named. He was also convinced that McKinley could have been named with a proper drive behind the effort. He had no notion of relinquishing his one ambition—to name a President—and he resolved to devote himself henceforth to bringing about the nomination of McKinley.

Harrison was elected by a narrow squeak, the popular majority going against him. And immediately the Cleveland coal and iron man went doggedly about pushing the interests of his new candidate. He went to Washington to promote McKinley's race for Speaker. But Thomas B. Reed, a stronger man than the Major, could not be beaten. Reed named McKinley chairman of the Ways and Means Committee and thus his name was given to the ill-starred tariff measure that would bring defeat to his party, sweep him from Congress, but in the end force McKinley to the top as the logical candidate of the Republicans in 1896.

Framing the McKinley bill made one of the most disgraceful chapters in the history of national legislation. McKinley called in the various special interests to be favored and told them to write out their own schedules. Advice was asked of no one else. Even so orthodox a protectionist as Blaine drew back from the surrender. He warned his party in Congress. But there was no favor which Big Business could ask that seemed exorbitant. When the next elec-

tion rolled around, the Republican collectors presented themselves
for their checks. But the checks did no good. Hanna was amazed
and dismayed at the blast which came back from the country. The
people had a score to settle and at the ensuing Congressional elections the Republicans were swept out of office. McKinley himself
met defeat partly because of a skillful gerrymander. But the country
at large knew merely that he had been defeated. The effect upon
his fortunes was most discouraging. His own spirits sank, but he
soon learned that he had a manager who could not be turned back.

Hanna's problem was very difficult. The clouds were gathering
over the nation's business. The government was grappling with
fiscal difficulties beyond its strength. A hostile Congress offered to
Harrison endless possibilities of trouble. There was no lack of woe
in Ohio. Following Harrison's election, Hanna set out to elect Mc-
Kinley Governor of Ohio and to remove Foraker from McKinley's
path.

He took personal charge of the fight and, when the legislature
met to select Sherman's successor in the Senate, Hanna went to
Columbus and spent his time, his money, his personal influence to
defeat Foraker. He succeeded. The election of McKinley and the
defeat of Foraker now made Hanna the most powerful political
figure in Ohio. Moreover it was widely accepted that he had a genuine presidential candidate on his hands.

Thus by his bold management, by his frank recognition of Mc-
Kinley's predicament and his fearless acceptance of the difficult
chance of defeat for his candidate in a year when the tide was running strongly against his party, Hanna completely removed all the
untoward effects of McKinley's last defeat. Moreover, by Mc-
Kinley's election as Governor in a Democratic year, he thrust the
Major forward again as a formidable contender for the presidency.

In this fight Hanna collected good political dividends from his
many years of liberal contributions to the war chests of the party.
Not only the state and city party machines, but numerous individual
candidates had made frequent drafts upon the rich banker's open
wallet. After the local campaign of 1897, Hanna dropped into Re-

publican headquarters to find the committee sitting about in lugubrious gloom. When he was told that a deficit of $1250 caused all
their sorrow, he laughed, wrote a check for the amount, and handed
it over without being asked. McKinley himself was one of those
politicians who was in occasional need of money and did not hesitate to borrow from Hanna. Hanna paid his personal campaign expenses in 1891. On one occasion he contributed $1200 to the
campaign of a county treasurer, then collected a group of friends to
sign the treasurer's bond for a million, and, thereafter, got a large
share of the county funds for his bank.

As the troubled contest of 1892 approached, Hanna perceived
that McKinley's moment had not yet arrived. President Harrison
had the usual commanding call on a renomination. Moreover the
drift was away from the Republicans. But Hanna had kept his
man well to the front. Throughout the campaign, while Harrison
was running for President in 1892, McKinley was running for
President in 1896, managed by Mark Hanna. And as the waves
closed over the head of the unpopular Benjamin Harrison, William
McKinley rose up above the waters as the unquestioned leader in
the race four years later.

Mark Hanna, now in collaboration with that peculiar series of
events that were referred to as the fruit of Major McKinley's destiny, went to work to nail down the prize. The Cleveland administration struck rock after rock—silver, Morgan's bonds, the Wilson
tariff bill, the income-tax fiasco, the railroad strikes and Cleveland's
suppression of them with Federal troops. The Democrats were
doomed. McKinley was triumphantly elected Governor of Ohio.
Hanna saw a cartoon one day in the *Cleveland Leader* depicting
McKinley's beaming countenance rising like the sun over the pros-
trate land and Uncle Sam pointing toward him as the Rising Sun of
Prosperity. Hanna saw instantly the value of that idea. He immediately dubbed McKinley the "Advance Agent of Prosperity."
Thus Hanna managed to put a label on the Republican party that it
was to wear successfully until it peeled off in the damp of the deluge
under Hoover. The theory that prosperity is inextricably tied up

with the domination of government by business was thus won-
drously stamped upon the public mind. And this was one of the
notions Hanna believed in with a consuming conviction.

It was in these years that Hanna moved into that position of
power that brought him closer to the role of national political boss
than any other man, before or since, has occupied without actually
being President. So far as McKinley was concerned his strategy
was to keep McKinley free of all entanglements and free from association with any issue save the good old Republican standby of the
tariff. In a campaign noted for its single-mindedness, its sheer per-
sistence, its ample treasury, and its freedom from errors, Hanna
pushed forward the fortunes of his smiling, handsome, and crafty
candidate until he was nominated and elected president of the
United States.

But this drive was interrupted by one strange mischance in which
it seemed as if all the friendly fairies had quit the entourage of the
Major. In 1893 Hanna had been summoned to New York by the
untoward effect of the panic on his own business. A wire came from
Myron T. Herrick, Cleveland banker, announcing that a man
named Robert L. Walker, a tin-can manufacturer of Youngstown,
Ohio, was in business difficulties and that McKinley was caught
on some $100,000 of his notes. Herrick and others were trying to
raise sufficient funds to bail the Major out and needed aid from
Hanna. Hanna hurried back to Cleveland only to find that the blow
had fallen, that Walker had gone into bankruptcy, that McKinley,
crushed by the news, had lost his nerve, was threatening to resign
as Governor, withdraw from political life, go into bankruptcy, and
devote the rest of his days to repaying his debts. A stranger fate
never overtook a presidential candidate.

The whole story of this odd episode has apparently never been
fully told. But enough has come to light to reveal the ease with
which the Major all his life could accept the bounty of other men.
McKinley in his youth had borrowed some $5000 from Walker to
pay his way through his law studies. This small item McKinley
never troubled himself to repay. When he became Governor,

Walker, then in the tin-can business, got McKinley to endorse his notes. One day one of these notes made its way to Herrick's bank. It produced some apprehension and Herrick went to the Governor, who with something less than candor explained that he owed Walker $5000. Herrick got that sum from a rich admirer of the Major and sent it to Walker. But the Walker notes with McKinley endorsements continued to appear in various banks. The sum totaled $130,000. Then Herrick notified Hanna. Before they could arrange the necessary funds Walker's business was devoured by the depression. He was adjudged a bankrupt, and the news got out.

Hanna and Herrick then hurriedly collected the necessary $130,000 from a select list of Republicans to pay the Major's way to solvency. Some gave, as John Hay's biographer informs us, "because they admired McKinley, some because he had served them in Congress, some because they wanted to save the party from unedifying criticisms." The subscribers to the ransom fund were Hanna and Herrick, Carnegie, Frick, Samuel Mather, and other big businessmen of Cleveland, John Hay, Philander C. Knox, H. H. Kohlsaat, and some others. McKinley's biographers relate that he deeded all his and his wife's property to three trustees, leaving to him only his business block in Canton in which he had an equity of $50,000.

Did McKinley ever repay these sums? His biographer and Mark Hanna's are singularly silent on that point. McKinley himself had a habit of making up the record for himself and so, although throughout this distressing episode he remained under the shelter of Herrick's home, there is extant a letter written by him to Herrick, recording his sentiments in grandiloquent terms. He described the transaction as the "collection of wildly scattered paper of his into a few hands." He "insisted that this paper be bought dollar for dollar," as if he were supplying the cash to his fiscal agents. This paper was to be held as an "obligation against me." Then with an almost Pickwickian gesture he declared he would have to decline the payment of his debts by his friends on any other terms.

Myron T. Herrick's biographer, a peculiarly inaccurate chronicler, declares that McKinley thereafter sent money which he saved from his salary. Herrick never appears to have disbursed any of it. Instead he invested it, and McKinley referred to "these little investments" in a letter to Herrick a few months before his death. After McKinley's death Herrick turned these investments over to the President's widow.

— V —

As the Republican convention assembled at St. Louis late in June, 1896, the nation faced a new war of the sections, this time between the West and the East, that took a very old form. Always in periods of depression the value of money rises and always the debtor class clamors for currency inflation in some form. Then it was expressed in the demand for the remonetization of silver. Hanna's strategy was designed to suppress the silver issue as McKinley's history on that point was bad. He had been a bimetallist. He had voted to override Hayes' veto of the Bland-Allison Silver Act and he had voted for the Sherman Silver Purchase Act. But now he sealed his lips on the silver issue.

Many men supposed him to be still an ardent bimetallist. The California delegation came to the convention instructed for McKinley and Free Silver. The West was for bimetallism. But the powerful East, which was Republican, and which would have to supply the sinews of war, was for gold. The syndicate that had bailed McKinley out of bankruptcy, as Tom Reed sneeringly described it, would never stand for a silver platform. Hence at St. Louis the position on the money question of almost every man present was known save that of McKinley, the aspirant for leadership. Newspapermen prodded Hanna to know where McKinley stood. Hanna replied that the convention, not the candidate, made the platform, ignoring the apparently unimportant fact that the candidate would have to stand on it. Old Senator Teller of Colorado headed a militant silver group unalterably opposed to gold. Henry Cabot Lodge and Tom Reed led the Eastern host equally set against silver. Hanna wanted the votes of all groups. He brought to St. Louis a money plank artfully phrased to satisfy the gold people and fool the silver wing. But it encountered in the Resolutions Committee Hanna's old foe, Joseph B. Foraker, who as chairman of the Committee forced through an unequivocal gold plank.

Even after his nomination McKinley refused to take the money plank seriously. "I am a tariff man standing on a tariff platform," he insisted. "This money matter is too prominent. In thirty days you won't hear anything about it." "In thirty days," replied his friend, Judge William R. Day, "you won't hear of anything else." At first McKinley tried to dodge the money question. He fell back upon obscure phrases like "sound money" and "an honest dollar." But Bryan had been named by the Democrats and had the country aflame with his holy war for silver. And so in the end McKinley, the bimetallist, was forced to unload his old faith and come out openly for the gold standard. This was characteristic of McKinley. No man could slip from under an issue more smoothly than he. He did no bleeding for unpopular causes. He chose with discrimination causes which called for no blood.

McKinley, of course, was nominated by an overwhelming majority. His nomination, indeed, was a foregone conclusion when the convention assembled—had been, in fact, ever since the Illinois convention in April which instructed for him. And when the convention adjourned his election seemed equally secure.

————————————————— VI —————————————————

It is the custom of conservative historians to describe the following of Bryan—the silver Democrats and their Populist allies—as a horde of maddened, class-crazed, violent agitators threatening the foundations of constitutional government. As a matter of fact, nothing could exceed the violence of the Eastern supporters of McKinley. They exhausted the resources of denunciation and abuse and stormed against Bryan and his "mob of repudiators," as the sober *New York Evening Post* called them, with incredible fury.

Theodore Roosevelt, who really knew no more about the money question than any cornfield soapbox orator in the West, flayed what he loved to call the "Popocrats" who would bring the country to social revolution. These dangerous nihilists demanded a graduated income tax, postal savings banks, recognition of Cuban independence, home rule in the territories and the District of Columbia, ballot reform, popular election of Senators and the President, the initiative and referendum, a program of public works during periods of depression, government ownership of railroads and telegraphs, and bimetallism. Most of these things have since been introduced into our system, and Roosevelt himself would one day out-Popocrat the Popocrats by damning with the same violence those who opposed these things.

The fashionable preachers of New York broke into full cry against the enemies of the Lord. Dr. Robert S. McArthur of Calvary Baptist Church and the celebrated Dr. Parkhurst poured out the vials of their wrath upon Bryan, and Dr. Courtland Meyer, in Henry Ward Beecher's old church, dramatically proclaimed: "I love the bloodstained banner of the cross and it is in danger." The *New York Tribune* bitterly assailed Bryan as the rival "of Benedict Arnold, Aaron Burr and Jefferson Davis in deliberate wickedness and treason to the republic." The *Evening Post* saw in the proceedings of the Chicago convention that named Bryan a duplication of the opening scenes of the French Revolution. The abuse and billingsgate heaped on Bryan was so savage that Dr. Albert Shaw, the conservative editor of the *Review of Reviews*, took his friends to task: "The editors, university professors, and Eastern bankers who are calling all the leaders of the West and South anarchists and demagogues are making the situation more difficult by their mischievous folly." When the contest was over, the *Tribune* rejoiced in the victory which had come because "God is God and right is right," while Cornelius Bliss and Jacob Schiff and Isaac Seligman and other great bankers sat around the festive board with the triumphant leader of the victorious gold hosts and "thanked God for Mark Hanna."

The fury of the other side was loosed chiefly against Hanna. Davenport's savage cartoon furnished an anthropomorphic devil upon which the hatred of the masses could vent itself. Those famous caricatures, representing Hanna leading McKinley, a diminutive Napoleon, crushing workers, bowling over women and children, piling up money bags, and fraternizing with the trusts, cut deeply into Mark Hanna's hide. "These hurt," he complained bitterly to Senator Dolliver.

VII

There was a deep-rooted reason for these violent emotions. A whole new era, a powerful congeries of new interests, the whole developing adventure of corporate capitalism or, as it has come to be a little obscurely called, finance capitalism, was at the crossroads. For a number of years these new interests under all sorts of industrial "captains" and commercial "kings" had been accumulating strength, creating and improving the new instruments of wealth getting, bowling ahead with the assistance of growing public approval—a kind of hesitant but growing admiration of their prowess—and the corrupt collaboration of lawmakers and public officials.

But for several years—particularly since 1893—the nation had been plunging into a deep and stubborn depression. The clamor of the farmers, the Western small businessmen, the workingmen in the Western cities for inflation in the form of free silver threatened the investments of the great bankers and their clients in the East. The rising anger at men like Rockefeller, Morgan, Gates, Harriman, and all the railroad buccaneers, the packers, the trust magnates reached a critical energy and fervor in the fiery evangel of Bryan and threatened the stability and security of that whole great corporate machine that they had fashioned for the production and concentration of wealth. The election of 1896 was a sort of crucial battleground that might well determine the course American development would take in the coming years. Certainly the highly excited partisans of the period felt it to be so. And this fanned their partisanship into the flames that made that whole campaign one of the most heated in American political history. At this particular moment Mark Hanna became the field marshal of the hosts of property in one of the great decisive battles of our own history.

He segregated and organized big business on the side of the political philosophy that was essential to its existence and he made it pay the bills for the warfare he was waging.

Hanna's name will always be associated with the perfection of that important art popularly known as "frying the fat," which is only a picturesque way of describing the process of rendering into campaign cash some of the suet which rich men are enabled to accumulate through political favors. It was not at all a new business. As business grew bigger and fatter and more at the mercy of government, politicians soon learned how to make the prosperous ones pay for immunity. William E. Chandler had learned how to draw generous sums from men like Roach and Gould. Carter, who managed Harrison's campaign, got $400,000 from the shipbuilder, George Cramp. In the preceding struggle between Blaine and Cleveland, Blaine's spectacular campaign was brought to an end with that famous Royal Feast of Belshazzar when Gould and Sage, Astor, Flagler, Mills, Carnegie, and some two hundred "money kings" sat down to terrapin, duck, and champagne at what the New York *World* called the "boodle banquet." Stephen B. Elkins needed more money for the last big Blaine effort and the money kings were brought together for the frying.

All this was just a loose way of doing what Hanna would do in an orderly manner and on a large scale in 1896. He told corporation executives bluntly that they got plenty of service from the Republican party and ought not to hesitate to pay for it. He levied an outright assessment on every bank. Later he denied a charge in the Senate by Senator Teller that he had done this. But his official biographer concedes that the assessment was one quarter of one per cent. The Standard Oil gave $250,000. Other corporations contributed in proportion. How much he actually collected and spent no one can say. His biographer admits it was $3,500,000 while Senator Foraker, who had opportunity to know, says it was not less than $7,000,000.

The dollar marks on Hanna's suit, put there by the cartoonist Davenport, were intended to represent not Mark Hanna's own personal creed, but the policy of using the money of corporate magnates to buy whatever they wanted in public life. And Hanna understood perfectly what the money was paid for. He hammered at contributors. "I know you people will do the fair thing," he wrote to Archbold, paymaster of Standard Oil, "and I want the state committee to get a liberal subscription from you this time. . . . This whole fight is against the corporations and me as their champion." When Archbold wanted service he called on Hanna and wrote him "to enlist your aid" to defeat two antitrust bills in the Ohio legislature. He wrote again to urge Hanna to be active to defeat Smith W. Bennett for attorney-general of Ohio because he assisted Frank Monnett in prosecuting Standard Oil.

There is a popular notion that the Civil War wrecked the Democratic party; that after that vast upheaval the population of the country became Republican as it had been Democratic before. This of course is not true. It was Mark Hanna and the full dinner pail and the legend of prosperity that wrecked the Democratic party.

Obviously Lincoln's second election, in the midst of the war, and Grant's two elections, with Federal troops in possession of all the Democratic states, cover a period of abnormal conditions in which, of course, the Democratic party ceased to function. But if we examine the elections from 1876—following the return of the wayward sisters—down to 1892, the result is a little surprising. In that time there were five presidential elections and in four out of five of them the Democrats obtained the undisputed popular majorities. Tilden and Cleveland three times obtained more votes than their Republican opponents. It must also be obvious now that they also obtained majorities in the Electoral College in three out of the five elections, since Hayes was declared elected only by giving him the votes of

Louisiana, Florida, and South Carolina which no man in his senses now believes represented the political sentiment of those states.

In that same period ten Congressional elections were held and the Democrats enjoyed majorities in six out of the ten. It was not until the election of 1896 and the strange combination of circumstances that followed, which established the Republicans as the guardians and conservators of prosperity, that Democratic defeat became almost a habit with the voters. Since then, out of nine presidential elections until 1932, Republican candidates have been victorious in seven and they controlled the House in thirteen out of twenty Congressional elections. It took the economic cataclysm of 1932 to shake them from power.

The full dinner pail did what a civil war could not do. Hanna promised prosperity if McKinley was elected. McKinley was elected. Prosperity came. The overwhelming demonstration was too much for a people who had been hungry too long. Of course, Hanna and McKinley and their tariff promises and their reluctant gold dosage had no more to do with the revival of business than the incantations of a ring of witch doctors have to do with the recovery of a tubercular savage.

The depression had been forming for years. It came when the orgy of reckless railroad building and industrial expansion and wild speculation, all on borrowed money, ended because no more money could be borrowed. Construction of all sorts ceased completely, as it has today. Conquest of the depression was possible only by reviving construction—short, of course, of an accident. No one seemed to know this save the despised Populists who clamored for a program of public works.

Just before the election the Indian wheat crop failed. This made an unexpected market for our own wheat which promptly went up to ninety-five cents and beyond all doubt settled the election of McKinley. But after the election, prosperity continued to lurk stubbornly around its corner. Stocks rose with the great news of Republican victory but fell back again just as they did in 1933. Seven hundred manufacturing establishments lit their fires but put them out again in thirty days. Failures increased and bank clearings were lower in the first seven months after the election than in the seven months before.

Hanna was deeply troubled. He did not know that the cure had already really set in from wholly uncontrolled sources. First, vast new supplies of gold were uncovered and the new cyanide process greatly increased the yield from the old mines. In 1904 Leroy Beaulieu pointed out that half the gold then in the world's central banks and treasuries had been accumulated since 1890. But even more important, France was swept by a drought, which cut her wheat yield by 93 million bushels. The Russian crop was damaged by rains, reducing it by 80 million bushels, while storms in the Danube Valley destroyed over 127 million bushels of its wheat. Moreover the good prices of wheat in the preceding fall had encouraged American farmers to plant more, so that now, with a tremendous shortage of grain in Europe, our farmers had an increased supply. Wheat went to a dollar on the Chicago Board of Trade. Our ships hurried over the seas laden with grain and returned with gold. As a result the gold reserve which was $44,000,000 in 1896 was swelled to $245,-000,000 in 1898. The Gold Standard Act was not passed until 1899. It required a gold reserve of $150,000,000 and this would not have been possible without these two accidental circumstances.

With this powerful stimulus business started up. We rushed forward again into an era of building electric streetcar lines, electric-light plants, and skyscrapers; of remaking our run-down railroads and creating new industries. Capital construction with borrowed money began again. Income expanded. Prosperity returned. And all this without the Grand Old Party moving its fingers, though it did move its jaws lustily to proclaim the magic.

———————————————— VIII ————————————————

There was a logical and poetic fitness in Mark Hanna's rise to leadership at this moment. He embodied the strength and the weakness of the people—their perfect attachment to getting along, their tolerance of the current art of getting along, their practical organizing power, their admiration of the adventurers they were pleased to look upon as Titans and whom they called, half affectionately, Captains and Kings of Industry.

Changes were in progress very deep under the surface. Our economic life had been undergoing a revolution. But Hanna himself understood little of its meaning. He believed an employer ought to be generous to his employees. Hanna always denounced those employers who refused to treat with their workers. His own record was above reproach on that score. In 1894 when Cleveland sent soldiers to Chicago to quell the Pullman strikers, Hanna, standing in the Union Club in Cleveland, created an uproar by denouncing Pullman. "Goddamn the man who won't deal with his men," he thundered, until Myron Herrick led him out. That there might be a flaw hidden away somewhere in the system itself never occurred to him.

Of course, this new economic order had to have a philosophy. And accordingly a confusion of apologists came forward. Americans who knew little of Nietzsche and Zarathustra began to hear much of the superman. Privately they would concede that you could not hold these great doers to the same ethical limitations that applied to corner grocers. Others who were reading for the first time the magazine articles about Darwin and Huxley, which were having a great popular vogue, explained that we were merely passing through a slightly accelerated phase of the evolutionary process, in which those strong men were hurrying a little the process of survival. The growing economics departments of the older colleges were, for the most part, provided with men like John Bates Clark at Yale who laid on lustily at the labor movement, and Professor J. Laurence Laughlin of Harvard and later Chicago University who could be depended on to explain all current phenomena in satisfactory terms, to say nothing of hirelings like Professor George Gunton who wrote monthly diatribes against the enemies of the trusts and pocketed the checks of Mr. John D. Archbold. Of course, pulpits everywhere, taking their cues from the Reverend DeWitt Talmage and their benefactions from their rich communicants, managed to compose the hostile properties of Nietzsche, Darwin, Mammon, and Jesus into a new and comforting theological goulash.

In such a society, agitated at the time by a profound depression, Mark Hanna assumed the direction of the political machine that would support and protect the ruling elements while they consolidated their control of the economic machine. He organized Big Business as a cohesive political entity.

As McKinley's inauguration approached, Hanna planned to take a house in Washington and prepared to assume the role of general superintendent of that machine. He had cherished, not an ambition, but a kind of remote wish for a place in the Senate. Hanna, despite his arrogance, knew his limitations and had a kind of blunt modesty and he never dreamed this wish could be fulfilled. Now, however, he was being dined and feted and thrust forward and called on for speeches. He found himself rubbing elbows with many so-called statesmen and became aware that he was not so far behind them. Thus the notion was born.

There was no vacancy from Ohio. Sherman had two years to serve. Foraker had just been elected. However, Hanna and McKinley talked it over and concerted a plan. McKinley would appoint John Sherman Secretary of State. The Governor of Ohio could then name Hanna to the Senate vacancy. But Bushnell, the Governor, hated Hanna. Hanna went to his old enemy, Foraker, and asked him to urge Bushnell to appoint him. The idea of Hanna in the Senate amazed Foraker. It seemed incongruous. Foraker regarded Hanna as inarticulate and ignorant. Moreover, Foraker did not like the appointment of Sherman as Secretary of State. He had observed at the last Zanesville convention, when Sherman presided, that the old Senator's memory was seriously impaired. He was an aged man incapable of coping with the now greatly enlarged duties of the State Department. But Hanna's mind was made up. Foraker went to McKinley and sought to dissuade him. McKinley backed Hanna. Foraker brought the proposal to Bushnell, who drew away from it. But, after all, McKinley was President. He was able to apply the necessary pressure.

In the end Bushnell had to yield—a triumph, thought Foraker, of impudence and gall. Sherman was named Secretary of State. But Bushnell kept Hanna on the griddle and did not hand the Senate commission to him until inauguration day, only a few moments before the Senate convened. As for Sherman, his infirmities soon asserted themselves. The old man saw very soon that the President was passing him over, summoning to the White House the assistant secretary, Judge William Day. When war with Spain was declared he resigned and retired to nurse his hatred of both McKinley and Hanna for having pushed him out of both Senate and Cabinet.

The Senate into which Hanna moved was now in process of being recast. There were plenty of the old school there—notably Senator George Hoar of Massachusetts and Senator Morgan of Alabama. But the wealthy utility and railroad men and their counsel had begun to make their appearance and before long Mark Hanna found himself the dominant figure in a ring of lawgivers he could thoroughly understand. There were Chauncey Depew, president of the New York Central, and Tom Platt from New York; Matt Quay and Boies Penrose, two of the most frankly corrupt politicians ever to sit in that body; Stephen B. Elkins, multimillionaire utility magnate, and Scott of West Virginia; Philander C. Knox, Carnegie's attorney, and Nelson W. Aldrich, another rich utility owner; Keane of New Jersey, holder of many gas millions. Of course it was never necessary to hand out money to these men, as it was to chaps like Foraker and Bailey, to get things done for big business. They *were* big business and they formed under Hanna's leadership the advance guard of that wave of big-business leaders who would swarm over the government, seize complete dominion of its machinery, and end by plunging it into one of the most crushing depressions in history.

Hanna had his seat by appointment. He had now to make it good by election. He promptly announced his candidacy and, at sixty years of age, with fear and trembling for the first time in his life, had to go out upon the hustings to support his claim. He quickly made good as an able, effective, rough-and-tumble political speaker, making two-hour speeches without any notes, flinging back sharp replies to the crowds, laying on his opponents with ungloved hands. He succeeded in getting a safe Republican majority elected to the Ohio legislature and when that body assembled he had no opponent. But a hostile coalition soon appeared. The Democrats agreed to support a Republican to defeat Hanna. The Republican insurgents and Democrats settled on Mayor McKisson of Cleveland and a riotous contest soon developed.

Wild excitement reigned in Columbus. The opposing factions provided bodyguards to protect weak-kneed followers from seizure. One Hanna legislator was kidnaped and locked in McKisson headquarters, until Hanna men recaptured him and spirited him back to their own camp where he was put under lock and key. When the final decisive vote was due Hanna had a majority of one. One backslider could upset everything. His supporters were marched to the legislature under guard. Armed men patrolled every entrance. Then came the bombshell. J. C. Otis, a silver Republican, rose in the House and charged that a man named Shayne, in the presence of Otis' counsel, had offered him a bribe of $1750 if he would vote for Hanna and Otis electrified the House by producing the $1750. This produced a sensation but did not prevent Hanna's election. The House named a committee to investigate. Its members, save one, were unfriendly to Hanna. But that lofty gentleman refused to offer any testimony.

The committee heard a number of witnesses, reported their findings, and the House voted to send the testimony and report to the United States Senate with a demand for an investigation. The Senate received the demand, sent it to a committee, and that body, over a minority protest, reported unfavorably on an investigation. Both majority and minority conceded that Otis' charge seemed to be sustained. But the majority insisted this did not cloud Hanna's title. The testimony submitted to the Senate is still extant and no fair-minded man can read it without admitting it establishes at least a prima-facie case justifying further inquiry. Hanna's contention that Shayne, a New York furrier, unknown to his supporters, traveled all the way to Columbus without any interest in the election save that of a mere busybody and bought a vote for Hanna with $1750 in cash is, to say the least, a little thin. Hanna and his friends blocked an investigation and his name must continue to rest under the odium of that act.

IX

Hanna's career as Senator lasted just seven years. The man was undoubtedly ill at ease at first. He never opened his mouth for the first two years. Thereafter his contributions to the debates of the Senate were limited to five occasions and four subjects, all of the type that would readily suggest themselves to the mind. He sought to force the Navy Department to adopt the Guthman torpedo, he defended the steelmakers in their extortionate price for armor plate, he led the battle for the shipping subsidies and also led the fight for the Panama Canal route against the Nicaraguan route. He was successful in his canal fight because he was able to unite with the forceful and dynamic Roosevelt. But in none of these did he exhibit more than the most ordinary capacities as a debater.

At first, of course, the problems of patronage consumed his time. Office seekers swarmed to his offices and his home so that, it was said, he took refuge in his dentist's chair. He was the most observed man in Washington. Visitors to the Senate gallery invariably asked to have Hanna pointed out to them first. His mail was the heaviest of any man in Washington outside the President's and he required a secretariat to handle it.

The time came, however, when he could devote more attention to his senatorial duties, which he always took with great seriousness. He attended sessions faithfully and could be seen with his large dark eyes fastened intently upon any Senator who addressed the Senate. He took almost no public part in the discussions of the Spanish war problems. Indeed for two years he followed faithfully the course of perfect regularity in his votes.

His first important entry into the debates occurred in 1899 when an attempt was made to resist the exactions of the steelmakers on armor plate. The Senate proposed to limit the price to $445 a ton and if that price were not met it proposed to instruct the Secretary of the Navy to build the government's own armor-plate factory. The steelmakers had been charging $545 a ton. With this attack on one of the greatest trusts, Elkins of West Virginia and Hanna broke their silence in the Senate and leaped to the defense. The going got hard for Hanna. When he found himself confronted by the formidable Senator Ben Tillman of South Carolina he begged for mercy. "I appeal to the Senator—I am a tyro here—to give me a chance." He had then sat in the Senate for three years. Hanna declared that $445 a ton was a low price. The Illinois Steel Company had offered to furnish plate for $240 a ton. Hanna called that a bluff. Former Secretary of the Navy Herbert declared it could be made for $192. "I think I know as much about it as Secretary Herbert," Hanna replied.

He first assumed leadership in the ill-starred ship-subsidy bill, that strange measure which, as the stanch Republican editor, Dr. Albert Shaw, observed, seemed to have a most mysterious origin. The driving power behind this measure, as it came out later, when the Archbold letters were printed, was the Standard Oil crowd, and chiefly Henry H. Rogers, whose company would be one of its chief beneficiaries. Chauncey Depew wrote an elaborate speech for the bill and sent it to Archbold for approval before its delivery. Hanna took the lead and made a vigorous fight for it at two sessions. The Democrats talked it to death the first time. The second time Hanna forced it to a favorable vote. But such stalwart Republicans as Spooner, Allison, Dolliver, and Proctor voted against it.

The time came, however, after McKinley's assassination, when Hanna became one of the most active members of the Senate. His activity consisted, however, chiefly in the influence he exercised over that body, through his political power rather than because of his senatorial talents. He won his most noteworthy success in the passage of the Panama Canal bill. Hanna always favored the isthmian canal. So did McKinley. But McKinley was won from the Nicaraguan route by the arguments of William Nelson Cromwell, the

American lawyer lobbyist for the French company at Panama. Hanna's two speeches for the ship-subsidy bills revealed no grasp of that subject. They were quite unimportant efforts. His speech for the Panama Canal, however, exhibited him at the highest mark he could reach. It was a good, clear, and able presentation of a subject which he had really studied, perhaps the first one in his life.

———————————————— x ————————————————

The assassination of William McKinley in 1901 suddenly wrenched from Hanna's grasp the principal lever with which he controlled the powerful Republican machine. The "madman" he feared most was thrust into the White House. Yet in the midst of the McKinley funeral arrangements, Hanna went to the house in Buffalo where the new President was sworn in and pledged his support. But he frankly made it clear that this did not involve standing behind Roosevelt for renomination. Until the end he stood squarely on that pledge. Roosevelt consulted him on every important point of policy and Hanna was a frequent visitor at the White House.

Curiously, Hanna's power in the Senate did not diminish. His prestige with the country, indeed, seemed to reach its highest point during these years. But all the same the great Boss was now in process of disintegration. He was still the foremost figure on the Hill. His mail continued to be greater than that of all the other Senators put together. To see visitors he did not use the marble lobby where other Senators talked to their constituents. He used the room of the Vice-President. If he wished to see a Cabinet officer he sent for him. He called on no one but the President. He was still chairman of the Republican National Committee. He still held the purse-strings of the party. He was still the Big Boss.

Hanna always indignantly denied he was a boss. He hated the word. He resented being bracketed with Quay and Platt and Croker and Cox and Abe Ruef and those other immortal rascals of the day. He was indeed much unlike these men. They were a sorry lot, excrescences thrown off by the blood diseases of the people, and Quay was the worst. If Roosevelt could be described as "pure act," Quay might be described as "pure corruption." Platt was different. He was the complete feline—not at all lacking in the essential virtue of dishonesty but veneering it, as Quay did not, with a thin coat of urbanity and piety. He wrote a book of hymns. He was "pure craft." Dick Croker, on the other hand, was pure force—a plug-hatted ruffian, beating down rivals with the sheer power of his blackguard spirit as he had once done with his fists. Hanna, with less education than all these men save Croker, was, however, a more civilized being. He paid out his money and never took any. He represented an idea—a bad idea—but one which a well-fed minister of the Lord could openly defend in his carved-wood pulpit. But all the same it was an evil thing destined to curse this rich land with poverty and chaos. He stood for the unrestrained sway of the acquisitive man, the power of money emancipated from ethical and social law, to buy men and to rule them.

But at this moment Mark Hanna, for the first time in his life, faced a situation he did not know how to deal with. He faced a man who was as audacious, as direct as himself and swifter in action. The weapon Hanna understood best was the club; his strategy was the frontal attack. His ammunition was cash. These things he could not use now and he knew no other way.

Like all successful men, good luck had played heavily on his side. He had hammered away for twelve years at making a President. He continued hammering until the day came when the cards fell his way, with the Democrats in power with a ravaging depression on their hands. That party was hopelessly divided, and Hanna had the perfect candidate in his possession. He promised prosperity and prosperity came. That the causes were different didn't matter. He had unlimited funds to use against a bankrupt opposition.

But now the tide moved not with but against him. He was at sea. And he was sick. And out there across his path stood a young antagonist, aflame with energy and ambition, who also understood the frontal attack, who knew precisely what he wanted, and who did not hang back from striking at the critical moment at the puzzled and vacillating Hanna. Such a blow he struck in 1903 when the Republican convention met in Ohio.

The rise of Hanna as a presidential possibility came first, feebly, after McKinley's second election and then more actively after his assassination. Newspapers referred to it continually. Important business groups talked about it. He himself said nothing save an occasional assurance to friends that he did not wish the nomination.

As the year 1903 wore on, the drive to nominate Hanna gathered force. It was engineered almost wholly by a group of powerful industrialists and financiers from Wall Street. They organized a committee and raised $100,000, with a promise of $250,000 for the campaign. They felt sure of New York, of Ohio, and of the colored brethren in the South. Quay stood aloof. John D. Archbold of the Standard Oil Company tried to bring Quay into the fold. But the shrewd Pennsylvania boss remembered how Hanna had run out on him when his seat in the Senate was threatened. There is no doubt that Wall Street determined to defeat Roosevelt. But Hanna refused to give his consent. Colonel Oliver H. Payne, of Standard Oil, went to Cleveland in the fall to urge Hanna to come out for the nomination. But he refused to do so. He wrote Scott that he would refuse to say anything more about it.

There is no doubt that Hanna was at sea. He of course would have been willing to be pressed into the White House. But he had no wish to be defeated for the nomination by Roosevelt. What he wanted most at the moment was washing clean his name. He chaffed under the stain of his first election to the Senate. He wanted re-election by a decisive majority. He had to run for the Senate that year. He had to meet again his ancient enemy, Tom Johnson. Johnson was a candidate for governor. The Democrats had a highly respectable candidate for the Senate. Johnson swept over Ohio with a big circus tent, denouncing Hanna as the agent of Big Business and demanding the single tax, free trade, war on the trusts. Hanna followed him, with Myron T. Herrick running for governor and Warren G. Harding for lieutenant governor—the Three-H Ticket. Johnson's attacks lashed Hanna, despite his failing strength, to apoplectic spasms of retaliation. He had his own tent, his own brass band. He called Johnson a carpetbagger, a faker, an anarchist, a blatherskite, and—worst of all—a Socialist. But Hanna won and got his re-election to the Senate by an enormous majority.

But he knew the weary engine was running down. After the Ohio campaign he found himself exhausted. His wife, his doctor, his friends all urged him to rest. But rest was impossible to Mark Hanna. His life was in pressing along. And he continued to press along until the worn and tired body fell under the pressure. He fell ill in December, fought against the growing weakness, got up several times and resumed his duties. But in the end an enemy appeared he could no longer ignore, typhoid. And while the papers continued to debate whether he would be a candidate, he lay dying in the Arlington Hotel. The end came February 15, 1904. Thus Roosevelt, whose first term was made possible by the death of McKinley, found his road cleared for a second term by the death of Hanna. After Hanna no leader remained to oppose him.

It is a popular fallacy that Hanna grew as he met new and wider horizons in public life. This is not so. He stood on labor precisely where he stood as a young employer. On other subjects he never altered his views. In the last half-dozen years he remained the same uncompromising tory he had been in the beginning. He had nothing but praise for the scoundrels who poisoned the army in the Spanish war. He stoutly denied there was a single trust in the United States. He went to Ohio in his last years to wring from the legislature perpetual franchises for his utility companies. He wrote and received the famous Archbold letters. In the last months of his life he stood by the notorious Rathbone and Perry Heath, who had been thrown out of the Post Office Department for the frauds unearthed by Bristow.

Hanna, the iron man, justified the extortionate armor-plate prices of the steel trust. Hanna, the shipbuilder, supported shipping subsidies. In the last days as in the first he was the symbol of the power of money to buy its way wherever it wished to go. The new rulers of our great industrial empire felt that their privileges were threatened, not by Socialists, but by what they called the populist element in politics. These men required for their adventures a collection of tools—banks, affiliates, corporation laws, securities, monopoly practices—all of which were impossible without the protection of the government. They felt that control of the government was essential. They feared Roosevelt and Bryan and they believed their security lay in making Hanna President. But they were mistaken. After the victory in 1896—the election of McKinley—they needed no more protection. Their system, their ethics, their ideals were hopelessly embedded in the system. The way was clear no matter who held office for the adventures that were to follow.

CHAPTER XI

John D. Rockefeller

THE BUILDER

———————————————— I ————————————————

THE APPEARANCE of John D. Rockefeller marks the beginning of that historic struggle between the government and organized business for the control of our economic life, which now moves to its final phase. One may doubt whether anything can be done to turn aside the stream of inevitable logical sequence. These powerful movements in society intrude themselves at first like a small trickle that, ignored too long, becomes the invincible force of a vast erosion. The Civil War might have been prevented when the first boatload of African slaves landed on these shores. After that it was too late. Perhaps the time to have checked the rise of Fascism in America was when that first group of promoters set up the industrial town of Lowell with the seeds of all the growth of finance capitalism in their small corporate structure. And yet it seems that perhaps the critical point is to be found in the 'seventies, when Rockefeller and his contemporaries began to use with understanding those weapons that now, in their perfected form, make up the arsenal of the modern corporate chieftain.

It was at this period that men began to tinker with the idea of controlling the economic society. They talked affectionately—as they still do—of that thing they call free enterprise. But they went feverishly about restraining the freedoms at every point. They were so far from wishing the society to be free that they forged all sorts of devices for limiting, even destroying, its freedoms. It was not the economic society they wished to be free. *They* wanted to be free themselves, which is quite another matter. They wanted to be

Davis and Sanford

JOHN D. ROCKEFELLER

free to subject the workers, consumers, and their competitors to such limitations and laws—affecting price, production, and terms of competition—as suited their objective, which was profit.

For seventy years this development would go forward. And during sixty-four of those seventy years the government would fight this development. The thing that organized business called "government interference in business" was not interference at all. Rather it was an attempt to prevent interference in business. These promoters, magnates, trade combines, cartels, trade associations were all attempting to interfere in the business activities and enterprises of businessmen generally—to make laws, regulations, agreements—to control business. The whole aim of the government, so far as it was pursued, was to keep free enterprise free—free from the intrusions and restrictions of organized business groups. In practice, however, the government was hopelessly defeated in this objective. Its attacks were halfhearted because its lawmakers, its executives, its judges were either the agents of organized business or at least men whose whole philosophy ran along with it. So that after sixty years of this gradual disintegration of the freedoms of free enterprise, culminating in an epochal depression, the liberal groups that had always fought the development surrendered and became the chief apostles of control.

The little war that we shall witness in the oil regions of Pennsylvania in 1872 was the first battle in a long struggle that ended in the strange episode of 1933, as Franklin Roosevelt came into power, known as the National Recovery Administration—the NRA. This was the complete adoption of the principle that the economic provinces of society and society itself must be subjected to rigid controls by the representatives of the producing groups under the general supervision of the government. It was just one of the concluding phases of the march toward the Fascist society, of which the corporative system is the economic expression. The NRA was the high point in the latest phase of this development toward the corporative state. The early projects of John D. Rockefeller in the 'seventies marked the serious beginning.

—————————————————— II ——————————————————

John D. Rockefeller was born July 8, 1839, in a small farmhouse just outside the then thriving village of Richford, New York. It was a farm without a farmer—for his father was a mysterious, roving peddler of medicines who appeared at the farmhouse only in the intervals between his long journeys over the country. Forced by the uncertain adventures of the elder Rockefeller to move frequently, the family lived first near Owego, then in Moravia, in Cayuga County, then back to a small farmhouse near Owego again, and then, when old Bill Rockefeller was indicted for some irregularities with some rustic wench, across the state and into New Connecticut in Ohio. The family settled in Strongville and later in Cleveland. And slowly the lusty old journeyman-pill-salesman drifted out of their lives.

Young John D.'s education consisted of the usual first years at the village school near Owego, then to Owego Academy, a small institution apparently partaking of the qualities of a junior high school, and finally to Central High School in Cleveland. When he finished there he took a course in B. S. Folsom's Commercial College, from which he was graduated in 1855 at the age of sixteen. As things went in those early days it was about as good an education as was afforded to all but that small number of youths who were privileged to go to college. It was very different from the education that the lordly young J. Pierpont Morgan was absorbing at the same time in select schools in Boston, Switzerland, and Germany.

At these schools Rockefeller met at least three people who were to play important roles in his life. Thomas C. Platt, the "Easy Boss" of New York, was at Owego Academy. At Central High in Cleveland one schoolmate was Mark Hanna and another was Laura Celestia Spelman, who was to become his wife.

His first job was as a clerk in the office of Hewitt & Tuttle, commission merchants, near the docks in Cleveland. He was paid $400 the first year, a little more the second, was offered $700 the third year, but demanded $800, and quit to launch his own business as a commission merchant with Maurice B. Clark as a partner, under the name of Clark & Rockefeller, along River Street. Thus, at eighteen, the precocious enterpriser was his own master. His firm cleared $4400 the first year and $17,000 the second year. When he was twenty, Rockefeller was a successful businessman and recognized as such in Cleveland. He was a quiet, handsome, dignified, serious, earnest young man, utterly absorbed in the important business of getting along. He had joined the church—the old Erie Street Baptist Church. He went to no plays, played no games, took part in no movements, acted on no committees, but resolutely "minded his own business." His diversions were found wholly at the Erie Street Church, where he acted as usher, took up collections, taught Sunday school, and religiously attended all the picnics and church affairs. He was in all things the model young Christian businessman.

On August 21, 1859, Col. Edwin L. Drake struck oil at Titusville on Oil Creek in Pennsylvania, an event that was to have more far-reaching consequences than the discovery of gold in California ten years earlier.

This discovery made no immediate sensation in Cleveland. A few businessmen ventured a timid investment in the new industry. Some merchants along River Street commissioned young Rockefeller to look over the prospects in oil. He did so, made up his mind that the refining end was the only department worth considering, but advised against going into that.

The oil towns along the Allegheny River grew in activity, turbulence, and the mad and disorderly pursuit of new riches on the pattern of the mining towns of the West. The whole business partook of the nature of a gamble. Oil fetched twenty dollars a barrel at the well until 1860. Then it slipped to twelve dollars. Wells multiplied. Oil flooded the valley. The price went to seven dollars, to two dollars. No one knew when these wells might run dry and the whole adventure come to an end. When the Civil War broke over the country, petroleum sank to ten cents a barrel.

It was at this point that Rockefeller decided to go into oil. He was twenty-two. Lincoln was calling for men. But Rockefeller, like young J. P. Morgan, had his own business to consider. He went on no committees, joined no movements, got mixed up in no wars. There would be no wars in the world if the John D. Rockefellers and the J. P. Morgans had to fight them.

Walworth Run, near Rockefeller's commission house, reeked with the smell of oil. Many little refineries making kerosene for lamps flourished there. One was operated by Samuel Andrews, a practical mechanic, who had been a maker of candles and was then a maker of lamp oil. He needed capital, which meant a partner. He also needed management, needed it worse than he knew. Rockefeller and his partner Clark became silent partners of Andrews. After two years both silent partners saw the golden profits in oil. Rockefeller made up his mind he was done with vegetables. He sold his interest in the commission business to Clark. He bought Clark's interest in the oil business for $72,500 and paid for it in cash. That was in 1865. The circumstance that decided Rockefeller was the discovery of oil at Pithole. That revealed to him that there was plenty of oil in the ground. The new firm became Rockefeller & Andrews. The year before Rockefeller had formed another partnership—he had married his old schoolmate, Miss Laura Spelman. His amazing career was soundly launched.

------------------------------ III ------------------------------

The commercial world thinks of the oil industry—or indeed any industry—as the product of certain groups of able enterprisers of the Rockefeller type. The oil industry, like the electrical industry, resulted from a long series of discoveries, experiments, inventions, adventures. Men active in those fields enabled the oil industry to become a source of wealth. The enterprisers swarmed over the oil industry after the real pioneers had created it.

Because America wanted better light than candles gave, lamps had been invented. They burned whale oil in New England, lard oil in the West, cotton-seed oil in Virginia, camphine distilled from turpentine along the Gulf Coast. Then coal oil was distilled from shale. All these were costly or limited in supply. Back in 1833 Professor Benjamin Silliman of Yale found that a luminant oil could be distilled from petroleum. Others explored that idea in the late 'fifties. Dr. Samuel Kier, who sold petroleum taken from salt wells, distilled kerosene from the crude oil, invented a lamp, and did some business. The commercial possibilities of kerosene were apparent. Only the supply of petroleum was lacking. That is why some men had their eyes peeled for it.

Along the Allegheny River in Pennsylvania, Dr. H. F. Brewer saw oil floating on the surface of Oil Creek. He sent a sample to Professor Crosby at Dartmouth who refined it and pronounced it a practical luminant. Crosby showed it to George H. Bissell, New York lawyer, with a promoter's instinct, who went to Venango County, Pennsylvania, and bought 103 acres. He took a partner, Jonathan G. Eveleth, organized the Rock Oil Company, which collected oil from the surface of the streams. But the supply thus gathered was negligible. The idea of drilling for oil—an idea that was worth billions to a generation of oilmen—originated with Eveleth. Salt wells were worked by drilling. Salt wells yielded some oil. Why not drill deeper and, perhaps, find more oil? Eveleth organized the Seneca Oil Company and induced Edwin L. Drake, a conductor on the New York, New Haven & Hartford Railroad, to undertake the drilling on a royalty basis. After innumerable discouragements and difficulties, Drake's drilling was crowned with success on August 21, 1859. These were the pioneers—Silliman who distilled petroleum in 1833, Kier and another named Ferris who saw the commercial possibilities in kerosene and produced a suitable lamp, Brewer who surmised that Oil Creek would yield enough oil, Crosby who confirmed the luminant properties of the Oil Creek product, Bissell who made the first effort to get oil there, Eveleth who conceived the idea of drilling, Drake who did the drilling and found that ocean of liquid gold that would change the living habits of the world. I need hardly say that none of these men made very much money out of their contributions to the industry. Drake died in poverty and would have starved save for charity.

It was so with the men who contributed the various devices and techniques of production and distribution after the industry was established—the men who originated the tank cars and pipelines and the process of manufacture. For example, Samuel Van Syckel, who invented the pipelines, became involved in ruinous litigation with the Standard Oil Company over patents and processes and died with but a small money reward for his services.

After the Civil War the industry revived, as Rockefeller had foreseen. New cities and towns sprang up along the Allegheny River, new and foolish fortunes flowered, hotels flimsy but gaudy, opera houses, dance halls, gambling joints, houses of prostitution, chambers of commerce, streets of mud, politicians, pettyfoggers, quacks of every description flourished.

The impact of Rockefeller on the industry became very quickly its great central fact. His growth was extraordinary. In 1867 he induced his brother William to join the firm of Rockefeller & Andrews. A separate firm was established in New York—William Rockefeller & Company—to handle the export business.

Rockefeller's ceaseless need was money. Money was got in those days by borrowing at the bank, taking a partner, or getting credit from dealers. Rockefeller solved his early money problems by taking in partners. One of the first was Henry M. Flagler, who had married a daughter of Stephen V. Harkness, wealthy whisky manufacturer. Harkness put $70,000 into the Rockefeller business, became a silent partner, and made his son-in-law Flagler an active one. Harkness died worth countless millions as a result of that happy gamble. The firm became Rockefeller, Flagler & Andrews.

In 1870 Rockefeller turned his business into the corporate form —the Standard Oil Company. He could refine 1500 barrels a day— largest capacity in the world. Cleveland became the largest refining center. He employed about 300 men in his refineries; 600 more were busy making barrels for him and operating 20 teams. He employed about a million dollars in the business and had outstanding bank loans as high as $350,000. In the Standard, Rockefeller held 2667 shares; William Rockefeller, Flagler and Andrews and Harkness, 133 shares each; O. B. Jennings, 1000 shares. There were thirty refiners in Cleveland with a capacity of from two to 1500 barrels a day.

Rockefeller's next move was to buy up nearly all his competitors in Cleveland, absorbing them into a single concern—the Standard. From this point on his course was one of gradual absorption. First, he acquired all the brains of the industry—rivals like Pratt and Rogers and Archbold and Vandergrift; second, he took over all his competitors without distinction, paying them in cash or Standard Oil stock. Those who took Standard stock and held it died rich. This process continued until the Standard Oil Company became as near to a complete monopoly as any such business in modern history, while the business itself produced a flock of fabulous multimillionaires whose names became household words in the realm of finance and industry for the next two generations.

— IV —

Behind this very simple chronological account of Rockefeller's personal rise to fortune lies the whole story of the rise of American big business. The entire tale can be told in the life of this man.

What happened in the oil regions is one of the great epic stories of American life and growth. It surpassed in drama, in importance, and in the outpouring of riches the great gold saga of California.

The story is more or less embedded in the American mind as a dramatic struggle between great numbers of noble little businessmen fighting to preserve the ways of free enterprise against a great and ruthless giant who sought to strangle not only them but the American system of free opportunity. What follows is a very great oversimplification of that story.

It was, in fact, a logical development of the forces that were at work, which few understood, and that were forcing men with the invisible but irresistible motion of a glacier.

Three sets of influences had been operating in America. One was the discovery and development of our vast natural resources, hitherto undreamed of. Another was the widening of the markets in which men could work and sell, a process made possible by the development of the railroads and the flood of immigration. The other was the development of machine methods that was but a lengthening and quickening of the industrial revolution.

The new age of big business was really beginning. Of course, for many years an increasing number of larger plants had been erected, but as yet there were few very large concerns. The pattern of industry was not greatly altered as yet save in spots. Every village had, in addition to its merchant, its barber, its saloonkeeper and hotel man, a group of small industries that supplied its own people —the shoemaker, the tailor, the tinsmith, the blacksmith, who made simple farm equipment and other materials, the wheelwright who built wagons, the gunsmith, the sawmill, the whisky still, the apothecary, the tobacconist who made cigars and cigarettes, the dressmaker. Mostly raw materials and a few standard articles came in from outside, but foods were prepared almost wholly in the homes.

The city reflected this manufacturing self-sufficiency. Cleveland, when Rockefeller went into business, had twenty-one flour mills, twenty-seven clothes factories, seventeen boot and shoe factories, thirteen furniture factories, seventeen machine shops, and fifty lumber mills. They supplied their local markets. There were a few large industries, of course. The textile mills were among them, located largely in New England, employing thousands of workers. The sewing-machine companies were operating large plants and selling everywhere, with gaudy showrooms. McCormick was making reapers, Case threshing machines, Studebaker wagons, Deere plows. At Chicopee Falls, Ames Brothers employed a thousand men. The arms factory of Colt was a modern plant. The machines were tooled, handwork abolished, platforms provided with jigs and cranes instead of men. E. K. Root, superintendent of the Colt arms factory, was the mass-production god in that machine. He got the fabulous salary of $25,000 a year. And so we see that while production and distribution was in the hands of small businessmen, the large production unit had made its appearance, and while production was carried on chiefly in localities, there were already a number of industries in which men produced for a national market. In short, the notion that Henry Ford or even Rockefeller originated mass production is wholly unfounded.

The development of machinery has taken two forms—first, the development of power and, second, the development of processing tools. All production involves an expenditure of power. Much of that power has always been provided by men, but for many ages an immense amount of the sheer power was taken from animals. For many years various mechanical devices have also been used to convert the power of men and animals to higher potentialities. The lever, gravity, pulleys enormously multiplied the power of men. But with the invention of the steam engine and the later invention of electrical power, the power at the command of man has been extraordinarily increased. How much, it is difficult to say. Mr. Carl Snyder, in his book *Capitalism the Creator,* makes the startling statement that the electrical industry now supplies an output of kilowatt energy that equals the product of 500 million men a year.

But the productive capacity of a nation supplied with the vast resources of power we now have must very clearly indicate one of the reasons for the greater production of wealth compared with an earlier age when power was so much smaller.

The other phase of mechanical development has been in processing machines, power tools that perform a multitude of operations. These require very little human power but demand great human skill. The linotype machine offers one example. This has gone on until it reaches terrifying heights—witness the great automobile-frame plant of A. O. Smith in Milwaukee. We have heard with awe of the Ford assembly line where the Ford car starts out as a mere embryonic frame, then moves along, pausing for a few seconds at intervals between long lines of men. Each man at his stop puts on a bolt, a screw, a piece of steel, a spring, until at the end of the line a complete car emerges. But in the A. O. Smith plant all this goes on with a difference. Instead of men adding a gadget here and a bolt there, little upright mechanical figures move toward the frame as it stops, insert a rivet, hammer it, or perform some other one of those cumulative acts that produce a finished frame at the end—literally a factory without men.

This development, therefore, passed through these phases—first power, then processing, then scientific management—which has had a startling effect upon our immense power productivity in the last fifty years.

The other factor, of course, was the extension of the market. Business establishments remained small for the very obvious reason that they produced for a small market—for the town, the neighborhood, or the state in which they were located. And this was due to the great expense of transportation. Transportation of heavy articles by stagecoach was altogether too expensive. Where a factory could reach a new market by means of water it could expand its sales, and many did so. But even here serious obstacles arose. The transportation problem involved not merely delivering the finished product but getting the raw materials. American producers actually found it cheaper to bring timber and iron across the ocean from Europe than to transport them by horse-drawn vehicles. Hence many of our natural resources long remained undeveloped. But the railroads were already changing this. A man in Cleveland could now produce goods and look for his market not merely in Cleveland and along its wagon trails, but wherever a railroad went, and railroads were going everywhere as the miles of new track multiplied yearly. It cost from twenty to sixty cents a ton mile to send flour from Pittsburgh to Philadelphia by horsepower; the same shipment could be made by railroad for three cents.

There was the development and discovery of America's natural resources, especially fuel and iron, the very heart and bones of the machine age. It is a singular thing that rich as America was in almost all the essential raw materials up to a decade or so before the Civil War, it did not realize these possibilities but depended for many materials—iron, copper, gold, silver—upon Europe. It was in the fifteen years before the Civil War that men began to find those precious deposits of coal, iron, copper, silver, gold, and oil that opened up a world of riches to those who were there to use them—not merely the mining prospectors who found the wealth, but the producers of locomotives, rails, engines.

These tools, therefore, were at the service of the businessman of Rockefeller's era. It had become possible for any able businessman to make far more money because machines, power, and the railroads enabled him to operate upon a far larger scale. The producer commanded not merely the increasing resources of the country and a great population of customers; he also possessed an immensely broadened technological endowment—an endowment from the brains of countless scientists, physicists, and inventors over several centuries. This mass of knowledge lay waiting like a huge mountain of gold. A man had only to dig in and use it, either by mastering its principles himself or hiring with money those who had mastered them.

But this is not the whole story. Large-scale operations required far larger sums of money. And the means of bringing together the necessary money resources for operation were not as yet very highly developed. These money resources involved savings, in the first place, and the means of tapping them, in the second place.

There were banks, but as yet neither the savings bank nor the insurance company was very widely exploited. Most banking resources remained in commercial banks, while the masses themselves possessed a very large part of their own savings. Even countless small businessmen kept their money reserves in their shops or cashboxes.

The techniques of gathering large amounts of money through the machinery of the investment bankers were, of course, known. They had been developing since the days of Fugger and Medici. But they had been applied chiefly to the money wants of states. The bonds of governments and municipalities were issued and sold and dealt in freely. There had also been operations in the securities of a few large-scale enterprises such as the stocks of the great trading corporations of Holland, France, England, and Belgium. And in America, railroad stocks had already been sold to large numbers of people. Nevertheless, the businessman's access to money for the larger scale operations of the new order was limited. Generally the man who wanted additional money went to a commercial bank, took in a silent partner or two who had amassed wealth, or else increased the number of his active partners. This is what Rockefeller did—taking in men like Harkness, Paine, Pratt, and others and borrowing incessantly at the banks. The corporation enabled partners to come into an adventure without assuming liability for more than the amount of their stock subscription.

The selling of stock in industrial enterprises was coming modestly into use. Most corporations were merely incorporated partnerships with a handful of stockholders. But the possibility of expanding the corporation was growing. National resources, machinery, power, savings—these were the instruments in the tool kit of the modern enterpriser.

------------------------------------ V ------------------------------------

We may now see with some clearness what took place in the oil regions—that historic struggle between Rockefeller and his smaller rivals. And in looking at it and at the wealth-getting techniques involved, we may see in camera the whole picture of modern American business. We see also the growth of that destructive force that intruded itself into the capitalistic system as money intruded itself into the feudal system and destroyed it.

The story has been confused and disordered and obscured under the forms of the hero-villain theory of human conduct, with Rockefeller as the villain and the little men of the regions as the oppressed.

What took place in the oil regions duplicated precisely what was taking place in other regions and industries and for that matter in other countries. In a sense, it was merely an extension of what had been taking place for many centuries. Competition between pro-

ducers has always been disorderly. In its nature—since each competitor is a little despot in his own domain—it can be nothing else.
It produces disturbances, personal, social, economic. All competitors are not equally competent or equally scrupulous, nor do
they have equal resources. In the nature of competition they contend for business. It is a continuous contest. It generates quarrels,
hatreds, controversies, injustices, unfair dealings, wastes, losses.
Wherever competition has existed its defects have been apparent.
And men have always attempted to do something about them. There
were the ancient guilds—organizations of tradesmen, craftsmen,
merchants to make rules among themselves to regulate their rival-
ries, soften the asperities of the commercial contest, protect them
from the operation of economic laws. As the capitalist system advanced the merchants formed pools and cartels among themselves
—they can be found in the fifteenth century. State monopolies were
established to increase profits. Other merchants sought to bring
their economic provinces under control through the medium of
outright monopolies, as in the case of Fugger's copper monopoly
in Hungary.

All down through the years businessmen have made various attempts to avert the dislocations, losses, consequences of many men
making the same goods, without the necessity of making agreements among themselves.

All this was true during the years when the producer found his
competitors right in his own town or even neighborhood, could see
him, chat with him occasionally, keep an eye on him, match his
stratagems swiftly. Also the conditions of competition were more
even. Given the same abilities, one man could summon to his
assistance only a very limited number of artificial aids. And there
was also a more or less natural limitation upon the individual's
power to absorb business.

This was why there were twenty-one flour mills in Cleveland
and seventeen boot and shoe factories.

But all this was changing rapidly. The artificial aids were being
rapidly multiplied. Machines were being installed with greatly aug-

mented producing power, thus limiting the number that could enter a given field because of the large capital investment required. Then there was, quite as important, the widening of the market so that the boot and shoe man could compete not merely for the trade of Cleveland but for the trade of cities hundreds of miles away. All the boot and shoe factories of all the cities were hurled into competition with each other, and competition with more powerful machines, so that competition became more violent for the same reason that war became more violent, because it included more combatants over a wider battlefield, using more terrible weapons. The advantage of the bigger and richer units in this struggle became obvious. The advantage to the better generals became greater. A higher quality of ability was needed, rarer abilities were called for. The very size of the field and of the combatants added to the fury, the disorder, and the fatalities of the combat.

In the midst of this something was causing trouble. Some strange force smote all this machinery for abundance. In simpler times the people had fewer resources to draw on; they had to work with simpler tools; they had less money and hence were satisfied with less. But here was all this flood of riches—gold from California, oil from Pennsylvania, coal from Pennsylvania, Virginia, Illinois, iron from Michigan, forests illimitable, grain without limit, and new machines to multiply the product of every man's labor. Nevertheless, poverty lingered on, men starved, crises appeared, depressions followed on each other's heels.

What could be the explanation? Well, it was obvious, quickly enough. It was so obvious men thought that they did not have to think about it. It was overproduction, they said. Too many people went into every business. Too many people bored for oil, dug coal, made iron or sugar or hemp or cord. We simply produced more than our people could buy. And when we piled up the surplus in the factories, the factories closed down until they could dispose of it. So there it was, as plain as a pikestaff—the thing to do was to control production and to limit competition and to keep prices up so there would be a profit for all.

This was not new, although the simple man, including Rockefeller, who labored in the oil regions, supposed it was. It is more or less clear from certain remarks dropped in later life that Rockefeller believed himself to be one of those misunderstood pioneers who had got hold of a great new idea, for which he was despised by his own generation until time had proved his wisdom and canonized him for it. But all this had happened before. The control of competition has been attempted throughout the ages. The old guilds did it. Jacob Fugger and his contemporaries tried their hands at cartels. Fugger went farther and built monopolies in the copper industry in order to control prices and production. The Fugger-Thurzo Company in sixteenth-century Hungary was a forerunner of Standard Oil in the nineteenth.

Indeed, history reveals that the little fellows in the oil regions saw this and acted upon it even before Rockefeller did. For these oil-well men got the notion that the earth gave up its black wealth for their benefit. Although the newcomers who flocked into the oil regions were a horde of strangers, they very quickly developed the illusion that they had some kind of God-given claim upon these riches; therefore, they had a right to govern the flow of oil, to decide how much would be permitted to flow, what price oil would sell for and to whom. They said: we ought to get five dollars a barrel for it, but we do not get that because too many bore for oil. We must unite against the rest of the world to limit the flow. And they came to have a sort of conviction that there was something immoral about places like Cleveland or Pittsburgh or New York harboring refiners to compete with them.

This is the producer's complex. It accounts for that series of legal, economic, social, and ethical concepts that grow out of the habits that men have of looking upon themselves as producers primarily, and forming their philosophies upon the basis of their interests as producers. Therefore, they organize as producers to get as much as they can for their product, and then, as they step into the market place with their earnings to spend, find themselves, as consumers, helpless and at the mercy of all the other producer groups organized against them.

The real force that was smiting the machine, slowing it down, fouling it, and at intervals halting it was something altogether different. This force arises out of a flaw in the money economy. No man can possess himself of food or clothing or anything he needs save by having money to buy it. And no man who produces anything can use it to get what he wants, rather than what he produces, save by selling what he produces for money. The thing that men use to buy what they want is money. And this money they obtain from their so-called money income.

In order to buy what we need we must convert into money the goods we produce or the services we render. Each year the nation produces a vast mountain of goods. Each year it pours out into the hands of its people a vast stream of money income. It is that money income that the people use to buy that vast mountain of goods. We have apparently solved the problem of how to produce a mountain of goods. We could produce twice as much if we wished. What we have not solved is how to make that stream of income—money income—flow out in *sufficient* volume, properly timed, to enable the people to buy that great heap of goods.

The problem lies there. The businessmen have supposed that it lies elsewhere—that it all comes from producing too much goods in that mountain. They bend all their efforts therefore to producing less. They overlook the fact that the goods are produced in our factories and business enterprises and that our income is produced in the same place. In other words, there goes out of all our business enterprises every day a great stream of goods into the market place and another great stream of money—payments for wages, rent, interest, and other services. These naïve gentlemen imagine that the way to make it possible for them to sell all they produce is to produce less—to cut down the size of the goods stream to the size of the income stream. What they do not realize is that when they cut down the size of the goods stream they also cut down the size of the income stream. Shut down a factory and you stop producing goods, but you also stop producing income. Curtail production and you curtail production of both goods and income. Reduce production in order to raise prices and by the very act of raising prices you reduce money income—by reducing its purchasing power.

American businessmen in the late 'sixties and early 'seventies began to play on an ever-increasing scale with this idea of limiting production upon the theory that overproduction was our curse. This notion persists to this day and has guided all organized business policies so far as they have been deliberate. It gradually penetrated government policies until finally, under the New Deal, we beheld the strange spectacle of the planners for abundance uniting with the business leaders to organize the most comprehensive and ruthless machine for producing scarcity in the interest of high prices and profits. The movement in America that culminated in the NRA had its organized beginnings on a large scale in the oil regions in the early 'seventies.

In those regions the competition took on several aspects. First, there was the competition between the producers themselves—the men who drilled for and produced the crude oil, wells being furiously put down, newcomers arriving daily, the derricks spreading out over all the surrounding hills and farms.

Then there was the competition between the refiners as such. There was the warfare between the producers and the refiners. There was the warfare between the various refining centers—city against city, Cleveland, Pittsburgh, Buffalo, Erie, New York, and others, and the regions against all of them. Oil has been the child and mother of war. Finally, there was the warfare between the railroads for the traffic and later between the railroads and the pipelines.

As early as 1866 the producers discussed a "combine for the purpose of attempting to make better terms with the refiners in the price of the crude product." The jobbers were also discussing a combination with a million dollars to build tanks and store oil to hold it off the market to raise prices. The refiners in the regions formed into a combination—a league as they called it—and boasted in the streets of Oil City that "they were determined to wipe Cleveland out as with a sponge." In 1870 the producers met in Oil City in Library Hall and agreed to stop the drill for three months to raise prices. The men in the oil regions were determined to make a monopoly out of their oil for the benefit of those in the regions. This happened before Rockefeller made any attempt at combination.

It was at this point that Rockefeller decided upon his course. He saw clearly enough his general objective. But it was only after several experiments that he hit upon the final plan that would bring him to a virtual monopoly of the oil industry and make him, perhaps, the richest man that ever lived.

Generally Rockefeller's objective was to do away, in the oil industry, with the evil effects of competition and to bring the oil industry as such under some kind of central government. Control of the economic province of oil was what he wanted. Rockefeller looked upon the small oil producer and refiner first as a shockingly wasteful and inefficient businessman. Second, he regarded him as upsetting the whole industry. Next, he felt that the industry as a whole could be operated upon a more secure and efficient basis if the small producer were eliminated. And finally he disliked, was indeed horrified at, the losses suffered by these little men and the losses of profits suffered in consequence by the larger producers.

His march toward his plan took the form of a series of stratagems. And this series may be said to mark the course of most of the other large industries.

First came the general spread of the idea of controlling prices, production, and such, by association, such as the small oil producers attempted in 1866.

The second phase was the cartel system—a sales cartel, used first by the salt-well men along the Saginaw River in Michigan in 1868. Then came, in 1871, Rockefeller's organization of the South Improvement Company. Under this plan Rockefeller in Cleveland and the leading refiners in each of the great refining centers—Pittsburgh, New York, Erie, the regions—would attempt to form local combinations. That is, Rockefeller would attempt (1) to take into his company the leading refiners of Cleveland; (2) to buy out the balance, and (3) to crush those who refused to surrender. The other leaders would do the same thing in their regions. Then these leaders would unite in a combination called the South Improvement Company, which would control the refining industry and dictate to the producers of crude oil and the consumers of kerosene. This South Improvement Company scheme was advanced by the use of railroad rebates and certain other favorable devices. But the plan became known before it went into effect. It produced a sensation and a storm of denunciation in the oil regions and was killed before it got under way.

Rockefeller's next attempt was still through association. It was a combination of the large refiners in all the regions. Its plan was to put the selling of refined and the buying of crude oil in the hands of a committee headed by Rockefeller. It too was a cartel. The country was divided into districts, each permitted to refine a certain amount. It was called the National Refiners' Association, with John D. Rockefeller as president.

It didn't work because the members refused to live up to the restrictions. The Association had no means of enforcing compliance. This is, of course, the weakness of these cartel agreements in democratic states. Individualists will not obey the rules; the democratic state cannot enforce them. Rockefeller in six months decided this would not work and dissolved it in June, 1873. It was not an exclusive combination. It was to admit every existing refiner. Price schedules were fixed. The Association made a contract with the producers. They agreed to stop the drill. The Association fixed a schedule of oil buying with them. The producers did not live up to their agreement. So Rockefeller broke it and they denounced him. The Producers' Association failed and the Refiners' Association was dissolved.

Rockefeller, however, did not abandon his plan that oil must be controlled. He merely decided that this could not be done in a voluntary combination. The only means was the outright corporate monopoly.

He had an absolute monopoly in Cleveland. He would extend that to the nation. He went to the leading refiners in all the large centers with a new proposition. It was not that they would join an association, but that they would merge their companies with his Standard Oil. He proposed they turn their plants over to the Standard, receive Standard Oil stock instead of their own stock, and become corporate partners with him, taking their places on the directorate of the Standard. Thus he brought in Warden and Lockhart of Philadelphia. He persuaded Pratt of New York, Archbold of the regions, Henry H. Rogers, Vandergrift, and others. Before long, all the important refiners in the industry were Rockefeller's partners in a corporate organization. When Rockefeller sat down with them now it was not as a member of an association but of a corporation of which they were complete masters.

They then set out to crush all competition so that they could make laws for the oil industry in their board rooms with no one to question them save their employees. They succeeded in this—in building the nearest approach to outright monopoly yet known in America.

In all this Rockefeller and his associates encountered grave difficulties, savage opposition. State and national governments pursued them. Legislatures investigated them. Courts prosecuted them. Laws were enacted to frustrate them. To evade the antimonopoly laws the trust was invented by Rockefeller's lawyer, S. C. T. Dodd. When this was declared illegal, the holding company made its appearance. The corporation to own corporations was adopted as the means of creating a monopoly without violating the Sherman Antitrust Laws. But this too was outlawed in 1911. But by this time the work had been done. The dominance of the Standard was everywhere recognized. Rockefeller's fortune was the greatest in history. And he himself was retired. And then, singularly, the automobile and its voracious appetite for gasoline was driving the horse from the streets and creating the immense new industry of gasoline production, from which Rockefeller would make far more money in retirement than he ever made in all the years of exhausting industry during his busy life.

These men, however, were making the pattern of the future America. The long, eloquent, bitter battles of liberals and radicals against the monopolistic practices of the great corporations and the trade associations would gradually lose their virility. Little by little great and powerful groups—including labor—would drop into the way of thinking that our economic society needed direction and control on the trade-association model—the plan used by Rockefeller first and discarded as unworkable. This is the central idea of the corporative system, which is the economic core of Fascism. It would not work for Rockefeller in 1872 because there was no means of enforcing compliance. It would not work for Franklin D. Roosevelt in 1933 because the government of a democratic society cannot possibly possess the ruthless powers that are necessary to enforcement. The corporative system can be made to work only under a dictatorship. It is in the direction of the Fascists' corporative system that our whole society tends. That tendency is based on the principle upon which Rockefeller worked in 1872—the principle of control by either monopoly or agreement of the economic factors in society in the interest of profit.

—————————————————— VI ——————————————————

What we have seen is the chart of the economic phase of the Rockefeller history. But mixed up with these economic threads were other strands that arose out of the struggle itself. These strands represented moral and ethical issues. They had to do with the methods Rockefeller used in pursuit of his objectives. And it was these that provoked those storms of protest and abuse that harried him for forty years.

Rockefeller was remorseless in following out his plans. He knew he was in a war and that the little men in the oil regions would rend him apart unless he extinguished them. Whether or not Rockefeller was a cruel man we cannot say. But certainly he had that quality of the great commander engaged on large enterprises of surveying the necessities of his task with high intelligence and appraising the suffering of his victims in its proper proportion to the scene. He did not shrink from measures because smaller men were hurt. He told rivals whose refineries he coveted that they could have cash or Standard stock for their properties, that if they were wise they would take the Standard stock, that if they did they would be rich, but that if they refused to surrender they would be crushed, and he crushed them. He undersold them. He intrigued to cut their credit. He put obstacles in their way. He made profit impossible to them. And he did it without a flutter of the spirit as he knelt in the Euclid Avenue Baptist Church on Sunday.

He used—though he did not invent—the system of rebates to crush rivals. That is, he made arrangements with the railroads to pay the published freight rates but got back secretly a large rebate on his freight bills, receiving as high as fifty per cent from some roads. The man who had to pay a dollar a barrel freight on his shipments could not contend with a competitor who shipped to the same point for fifty cents a barrel. What this meant to Rockefeller may be surmised from a report revealing that in the six months preceding March, 1879, the Standard shipped 18,556,000 barrels of oil on which it got an average rebate of over fifty-five cents, amounting to something over $10,000,000. Rockefeller defended the rebate on the principle of the quantity discount. Shipping in huge quantities, requiring whole trains at times, and ensuring regular runs and economical handling of loading, the roads could perform the service for him more cheaply. The defense would be more valid if the quantity discount had been open to others who had large shipments. They were not, save in a few isolated instances.

Far worse than the rebate was the drawback—an instrument of competitive cruelty almost unparalleled in industry. It amounted to this: the road allowed Rockefeller a rebate on his own shipments and paid him also a similar sum on his competitors' shipments. The railroad paid rebates on competitor shipments but the rebate went to Rockefeller and not to the shipper. Thus, on every barrel a rival shipped, Rockefeller made a profit. In March, 1878, H. C. Ohlen shipped 29,876 barrels of oil to New York. Ohlen paid $1.20 a barrel freight. Rockefeller collected from the road twenty cents on each of these barrels—a squeeze of $5975 out of one rival in a single month.

Rockefeller's competitors long felt that some cruel and mortal force was killing them, but did not know what it was. When they discovered it, words cannot describe the fury of their hatred.

A volume would be insufficient to outline the cases of men who ascribed their ruin to Rockefeller. Every incompetent who failed named Rockefeller as the cause of his failure. Ugly stories got wide currency. One example was that of Mrs. Backus, widow of an oil-man who told how she had appealed for assistance when her husband died and how Rockefeller had taken away her oil refinery at a third of its value. Miss Ida Tarbell gave much space to this case. No one can examine the facts without putting Mrs. Backus out of court.

Another was the much-advertised case of the Merritts, who claimed they had been swindled out of the priceless ore fields on the Mesabi Range. There is plenty of evidence on this case since it dragged through the courts. It is not possible to scrutinize that evidence without conceding that Rockefeller's conduct was without blemish throughout. The truth is that Rockefeller did not engage in what might be called personal perfidy. He was a patient, ruthless rival in business. He did not rob either his stockholders, his partners, or those with whom he dealt in personal relations. Those who came within the orbit of his competitive warfare got the full measure of the devices he had fabricated for their destruction.

Having set out to corner the refining industry, he came after a while to the conclusion that he must control the pipelines, which were slowly supplanting the railroads as carriers of petroleum. Also he went into the distributing field as well. One of the most dramatic and critical battles of his career, in which he revealed the full measure of his genius as a commercial chieftain, was his struggle with the Empire Pipe Line backed by the powerful Pennsylvania Railroad. After Rockefeller had forced the Pennsylvania to surrender, his prestige was so great that there was little energy left in the opposition to him.

Having got the pipelines and the large distribution units, he used them effectively to knock out ambitious rivals. George Rice made a lifelong fight against the Standard. That story broke into the newspapers at regular intervals as a stain on Rockefeller's name. Rice built a refinery at Macksburg, Ohio. Later he owned some wells there. Rockefeller hit him on the distribution front. The grocers were the retail outlets for kerosene. Grocers who carried Standard Oil were supplied with groceries at low prices in order to undersell those who dared to buy from Rice. Rice paid fifty cents a barrel freight to the railroad on his oil, the Standard paid twenty-five cents. On another road Rice paid thirty-five cents a barrel, the Standard paid twenty-five cents and collected ten cents on every barrel Rice shipped. Rockefeller ruined Rice, and in this case the evidence is complete against him.

John D. Archbold, Henry H. Rogers, and the Standard's local representative were indicted in Buffalo for blowing up the refinery of a competitor, Matthews. This was a grave charge indeed. Rogers and Archbold were acquitted. But the local manager was convicted and subjected to a grotesque fine of $250. Matthews sued the Standard and got a settlement of $85,000. But that sum was consumed in lawyers' fees and other costs. And Matthews was effectively ruined despite his settlement.

Bribery of public officials and the press was part of the equipment of the great company as it rose to power. State and national laws, city ordinances stood in its way. It must march through them. It would buy up the mayor and common council of Bayonne as readily as the members of the New Jersey legislature or some of the most important statesmen in Washington. The Ohio legislature was bought up to defeat an early antitrust bill with such a display of cash that it went into Ohio history as the Coal Oil Legislature. The Standard backed Henry B. Payne for United States Senator from

Ohio, and his son, Oliver H. Payne, treasurer of the Standard, sat at a desk in a Columbus hotel with stacks of bills in front of him, paying for votes on delivery.

The company bought space and good will in newspapers. One investigation revealed at least 110 Ohio papers had signed contracts to print editorials and news supplied by a Standard-supported agency in return for advertising. Some of the "copy" thus furnished makes strange reading today.

Standard officials, including Rockefeller, did not hesitate to mount the witness stand and lie gallantly in defense of their projects. In the Hepburn investigation Archbold denied on the stand that Standard controlled the Acme. Henry H. Rogers swore as a witness in court that he did not know who controlled the United Pipe Lines, though, of course, he knew the Standard did so. Rockefeller himself swore that he was not interested in gas and copper, though the Standard owned a dozen subsidiary corporations that produced natural gas, while Rogers and Stillman and William Rockefeller gathered up dozens of gas companies that bought their oil from Standard. When they could not lie with safety they took refuge in refusals to answer, which led to the most grotesque performances. Jabez Bostwick refused to state his name on the witness stand on the ground that it "might incriminate him."

Most famous—or infamous—of the corrupt performances of Standard Oil was carried on in an episode that became notorious as the "Archbold letters." William Randolph Hearst got possession of a packet of letters and copies of letters stolen by an office messenger from Archbold's files. They revealed Archbold as the arch-corruptionist of the company, sending checks and certificates of deposit to various Congressmen and judges and to such distinguished Senators as Joseph B. Foraker of Ohio and Joseph Bailey of Texas and to Matthew Stanley Quay. This made a long and shocking story when it broke upon the country as a sensation and ruined all of the public men it touched. Actual proof that the Standard vice-president sent a series of checks ranging from $5000 to $15,000 and totaling $44,000 in six months to a great Senate leader shocked the public. These revelations quickened the pace at which state legislatures, public prosecutors, political groups, and the national government pursued the Standard. Investigation followed investigation. Subpoena servers shadowed Rockefeller. In the end, at the direction of Theodore Roosevelt, the Attorney General brought suit to dissolve the Standard Oil holding company as a monopoly. This suit ended in the famous dissolution decree of 1911, which did break up the company into its component corporations, while at the same time the decision contained elements—the famous "rule of reason"—that so weakened the antitrust laws that they were effectively reduced as a fortress against the onward march of corporate restraints on trade.

When the Standard holding company was dissolved it owned thirty-three corporations, and John D. Rockefeller personally owned something more than one fourth of all the stock. What it was worth, it is difficult to say. The shares when first sold on the market immediately following the dissolution were valued at $663,000,000. Four months later they had risen to $885,000,000. They were probably worth still more. For the Standard had never made any effort to inflate its values. Whatever may be said of Rockefeller's fortune it was never made in stock adventures in Standard shares. The shares of that company were never peddled about. They formed the subject of no market operations. Rockefeller issued no bales of stock to be listed on the exchange, manipulated to higher levels, and then unloaded on the public. This was the method that Morgan employed and that later became the curse of American corporate business. No stockholder ever had any reason to complain against Rockefeller. As for consumers, he did strive to make the best oil and to furnish unequaled service. He was the best employer of his time, instituting hospitalization and retirement pensions. He paid the best wages in the industry. His sins were the sins of the industrial warrior, the sins of the ruthless competitor. His offenses were leveled against those who dared to sell oil in an oil world that this great monopolist had marked for his own.

When he retired, the Standard Oil Company was the greatest industrial corporation in the world. Its tanks were to be seen not only at every railroad station in America but along the Ganges, the Yangtze, and the Amazon, wherever boats or pipes or railroads or wagon wheels could carry his oil.

The precise period of Rockefeller's retirement always remained a mystery. As a matter of fact, it is of more than passing interest that this man, reputed the most omnivorous money getter in history, retired from active business when he was fifty-four. Stories of his broken health fascinated the public mind. People hated him cordially and told stories of priceless irony about the world's richest man who had snatched the bread from the mouths of his little competitors only to find himself unable to eat a square meal. It was said he had a standing offer of a million dollars to any doctor who could heal his inhospitable stomach. Rockefeller himself always denied the stories of his illness. The truth seems to be that his stomach had become seriously affected by the long, cruel strain that business, the pursuit of the law, and public odium had put upon it. His physician demanded that he relax his labors. In 1896 he complied. He remained president of the company, but withdrew from any daily or direct supervision of its affairs. He was worth, at this point, probably $200,000,000. But as he withdrew into the leisure of Tarrytown, patents were being taken out on the first simple automobile designs that, perfected later, changed the oil business from a kerosene to a gasoline industry, multiplying many times over the operations and profits of his companies. There did come a time, doubtless, when Rockefeller's fortune could have been estimated at a billion dollars.

After 1896 he planned to devote himself chiefly to the recovery of his health and the administration of his fortune in the interest of his philanthropies. And this he did until 1911, after the dissolution decree, when he separated himself entirely from all further connection with the immense industry.

Rockefeller must be recognized as perhaps the most constructive philanthropist in the history of America at least. How far this was

Rockefeller's own conception and how far it was the plan of his almoner, Dr. Frederick T. Gates, who acted as the director of his charities for many years, it is not possible to say. Rockefeller had begun his benefactions by donations for churches, hospitals, schools, seemingly good causes that came to his attention. But in time he developed a theory of giving to which he adhered to the end. This is best expressed by saying that Rockefeller became interested in agencies to study and prevent disease rather than in hospitals to treat its victims. He came to feel that human pity was a very active agent and could be relied on to provide hospitals after suffering men and women were stricken, but that it was of infinitely greater importance to find the seeds of disease and keep the patients out of the hospitals. This idea ran through all his subsequent philanthropies, whether in the field of science, business, or education.

When he founded the University of Chicago he was still the zealous Baptist. Before he was through he gave altogether $45,-000,000 to that institution. By 1928 the total of his gifts was as follows:

Rockefeller Foundation and Laura Spelman Memorial	$256,580,081.87
General Education Board	129,197,900
Medical Institute	59,778,141.14
University of Chicago	45,000,000
Miscellaneous	18,365,000
by John D. Rockefeller, Jr.	65,234,606.29
TOTAL	$574,155,729.30

This, of course, does not represent what the public has received from his gifts. Thus, he gave the Rockefeller Foundation $182,000,-000, but that Foundation out of its yearly revenues gave the public $141,000,000 in gifts between 1922 and 1928.

———————————— VII ————————————

Rockefeller must be accepted as the greatest business administrator America has produced. His immense wealth was the product of intense application to the business of accumulation, to the habit of planning with infinite patience and then executing these plans with indomitable fortitude, cautiously and slowly when possible, with militarylike swiftness when necessary. Unlike Morgan, he was in no sense the scowling autocrat. Rockefeller possessed an extraordinary capacity for acting with others. He made it a rule never to adopt a decision on any important matter unless he had the unanimous consent of his partners. He could spend years trying to convince them when his simple word would have been law. His fortune belongs in the group of the Carnegies, the Henry Fords—enterprisers who were producers and who got their fortunes by creating wealth and retaining for themselves as large a share of it as they could. They were wholly different from the group that included Morgan, Gould, and Henry H. Rogers, Rockefeller's partner. These were primarily speculators and gamblers, who insinuated themselves into industries created by other men, converted the ownership of those industries into liquid securities, and made money from the market changes in those securities. Rockefeller, Carnegie, Vanderbilt, many of the old railroad builders—whatever their other faults might be—left behind them great industries and great railroad empires.

Perhaps one of the most interesting features of Rockefeller's career was the length of his life. It was a planned life—in all things down to the last detail. When his stomach became affected in the 'nineties and the alarm became obvious, he proceeded to devote to the business of living the same meticulous planning he had brought to bear on the business of getting. Rockefeller, older than most of his colleagues, marked for the grave in mid-life by a public that hated him, actually outlived them all. He died on May 23, 1937, at the age of ninety-eight. The great fortune had been put either into the huge endowments already named or made over in some way to his family, chiefly his son, who administers it largely as a philanthropic enterprise. That portion retained by Rockefeller himself until his death amounted to $26,273,845.25. It included only one share of Standard Oil stock, valued at $43.94.

CHAPTER XII

J. Pierpont Morgan

THE PROMOTER

— I —

THERE CAN BE no doubt that the two most considerable figures in the world of business in their time, if not in any time, were John D. Rockefeller and J. Pierpont Morgan. Rockefeller was pre-eminently the richest man of his day. Morgan would have to be left out of this volume if the size of his fortune alone were considered. There were many men during his life, as well as before and after, who were worth more than twice as much. But no man, either before or since, left upon the great art of money getting so important an influence.

These two business titans were essentially different. They were alike only in that both loved to sing hymns, both turned in their righteousness to the God of Zion, both loved to keep books, and both loved money. But they were wholly different in all things else. Morgan was the splendid Christian potentate; Rockefeller the humble parochial Sunday-school teacher. One was the pious, abstemious Baptist; the other the zestful user of all that the Giver of All Good Things bestowed upon his chosen people of the Episcopalian persuasion. Morgan was the brusque, irascible, arrogant, and terrifying autocrat; Rockefeller the most patient of collaborators. Rockefeller husbanded with miserly prudence the last ounce of health according to the best scientific counsel; Morgan, like another great citizen of Hartford, Mark Twain, attained to the age of seventy-six by violating all the laws of health. But at that Rockefeller, who outstripped him in wealth by many hundreds of millions, outlived him by twenty years. Most important, of course,

452

Steichen

J. P. MORGAN

Rockefeller was a creator of industries, a producer of wealth, and, beyond doubt, the most constructive philanthropist in our history. Morgan created no industries, produced very little wealth. He fastened himself upon the industries that other men created and learned the trick of sharing their wealth with other men. How much Rockefeller advanced or impaired the development of a sound eco‑ nomic life remains yet a subject of debate. But it is probable that no man in our history inflicted upon our economic system a deeper and more destructive wound than J. Pierpont Morgan.

It is not easy to disentangle the Morgan of flesh and blood from the Morgan of the biographers. According to one, he was an example of moral excellence, singing the old hymns his mother taught him, fraternizing with bishops, forgiving his enemies, loving those who hated him, visiting sick friends and going sorrowfully to their fu‑ nerals, bouncing his grandchildren on his knees, and molding his numerous corporate reorganizations for the good of the country. Another sees him as the embodiment of all the seven deadly sins save sloth, alternating his episcopal confabs with visits to his mis‑ tresses, building parish houses for the dominies and theaters for the ladies, wrecking his rivals ruthlessly, and grasping with unex‑ ampled arrogance after money and power.

The man was magnificently endowed to play the role of financial imperator. There was the necessary bulk of bone and flesh. He was six feet tall, weighed two hundred pounds. Standing with feet apart, looking forward, he seemed poised to make a formidable advance. His head was large, craglike, well poised on his broad shoulders, his countenance rough-hewn. The upper lip, even as a boy, was heavy, and as he grew older, hidden behind his unruly mustache, it gave to his face an aspect of cruelty. His powerful jaws and rugged brow were drawn down in an imperious scowl. His bulbous nose accentuated the dark aspect of his visage. His large, wide-opened hazel eyes bent upon a visitor or suppliant with terrifying attentive‑ ness and made him a formidable man in conference. Whoever met him came away to talk about the impression of energy and power. He possessed what might be called psychic power and majesty—

those ectoplasmic tentacles that grappled people and held them helpless in his presence. Charles Mellen, New Haven railroad president, a Morgan satrap, confessed to a Senate committee that he stood in awe of Morgan, that when Morgan told him he was wrong, so vast was his respect for Morgan that he knew Morgan was right nine times out of ten. Morgan did not have by any means the intellectual endowment of the small ratlike Gould or the astute and realistic Harriman. But he had what none of them had, the Jovian mood, the principle of personal force, the imperial bearing that overawed and quelled opponents.

He was never a scholar. He collected first editions and manuscripts but read few of them. For years they were put away in a basement room so filled with such treasures that one could scarcely get in or out or find anything. But he was a wizard at figures. As a boy in high school his teacher said he was little short of a prodigy and could solve mentally problems in cubic root and numerous decimals. He could speak French and German because he had spent two years in a French school in Switzerland and two at the University of Göttingen. But he had no use for the classics. He could express himself in written English in a clear, direct, and vigorous style. Furthermore, even as a youth, he could put these excellent sentences down in a hand of great neatness and symmetry.

He had little understanding of music. He never went to a concert if he could avoid it. He occasionally attended an opera—he had a box—usually on the first night, thus beginning and ending the opera season. His taste in music did not rise above the hymns he had learned as a boy. He loved to sing them. His family insisted he could not follow any tune, even *Yankee Doodle*, but this judgment he indignantly protested.

His favorite hymn was *Blessed Be the Tie that Binds,* not an inappropriate sentiment for the master combiner. But he liked others —*Jesus, Lover of My Soul* and *I Need Thee Every Hour*—a phrase that became famous as a trade slogan of one of the pre-Volstead whiskies. He liked that one so much that he persuaded the moguls of Episcopalian music to admit it to their polite hymnal. He tried also to force in some old nonconformist Scottish religious ballad he liked, but even the great Pierpont Morgan could not get this barbarian religious folk song into the hymnal of God's elite.

Throughout his life Morgan was an inveterate churchgoer. Rockefeller himself was not more faithful. He went to church at least once on Sundays and frequently twice. On shipboard he never missed divine service. He was a vestryman of St. George's Church, where, on Sunday, God enjoyed the inexpressible privilege of beholding many proud millionaire heads bowed in humility and prayer. He was also a vestryman of the little church near Cragston, his country estate—the Highland Falls Church of the Innocents. Its name, of course, had no relation to the swarms of investors who bought the stream of securities that issued from the offices at Broad and Wall. He was a faithful and active participant in the temporal affairs of both institutions.

He had a fondness for bishops, who, indeed, were among his hobbies. In his youth one of his first adventures in collecting was bishops' autographs—Episcopal bishops only, of course. In later life he collected the bishops themselves. Bishops of the Episcopal Church are good company. They are cultivated men with a fondness for the good life. They do not eschew vintage wines and French viands like so many of the evangelical brethren. He counted many friends among them. He was for years a lay delegate to the triennial conventions of the Episcopal Church.

At those gatherings he appeared surrounded by that magnificence that followed him everywhere and that recalls the appearance of the great banker he resembled most—Jacob Fugger—at the Congress of Vienna. At Minneapolis he leased a large residence and sent Louis Sherry, the famous caterer, ahead, with a flock of waiters, to prepare the entertainment for the bishops. At San Francisco he leased the Crocker mansion; the inevitable Louis Sherry assumed command of the arrangements, and all trains between New York and San Francisco were sidetracked to permit the Morgan special and its cargo of bishops to whiz to the coast without stop. At Richmond he took over the Rutherford House, added an additional bathroom, recarpeted the stairs, organized it under Sherry as major-domo for several weeks, and housed a flock of Episcopal guests and their wives.

These Morgan headquarters were referred to half humorously, half critically as Syndicate House. These triennial gatherings, which usually included a number of multimillionaires among the lay delegates, were sumptuary displays. A hotel proprietor, after one of these conventions, said that, though he had entertained business, sporting, and social gatherings of many sorts, he had never seen men spend so much money or women flaunt so much jewelry as these Episcopal delegates and their consorts.

In 1875 Morgan appeared as one of the sponsors of a Moody and Sankey revival. It was held in the old New York, New Haven & Hartford depot. Morgan took his family frequently to the meetings, sat on the platform, and joined lustily in the hymn singing. At the other end of the religious spectrum he served for a dozen years as the treasurer of the Cathedral of St. John the Divine and took an active part in organizing and managing its finances.

Morgan was orthodox in everything. The world he lived in was suited to his tastes, particularly after he had fixed it over upon its industrial front. He would doubtless have answered as his bosom friend, George F. Baker, did when asked by a Senatorial inquisitor if he did not think the world was all right as it was, and replied, "Pretty nearly." God was a part of it; had always been; served a most useful purpose, helped to answer a lot of questions he had neither the time nor the taste to bother with. And so he accepted God as he did the institution of property and money and the church his parents had reared him in where he found the very best people. He was a believer in order and was deeply convinced that sin was a luxury that the poor could not be entrusted with. He was one of a group of righteous men like himself who sponsored that mighty policeman of the Lord, Anthony Comstock, in the organization of the Society for the Suppression of Vice.

He was superlatively choosy about his friends. Even as a boy in school he mixed with but few. But he was deeply devoted to them as well as to his family—his parents particularly. From the time he returned to America from school at Göttingen in 1857 to 1890, when his father died in Europe, he never let a ship leave for England without writing him a letter. Often he had to write these letters late at night after the rush of the day's work. His father preserved them in a series of books in his library. Twenty years after his father died, Morgan, looking through them, put them into the furnace. That was in 1911, a year of magnate hunting. He was growing old, and these letters were full of news, comments, opinions on the events and men of his time.

During his business life he was never a student. He turned for relaxation to his hobbies of which he had many. During the horse and buggy era he liked a pair of trotters. He was fond of dogs—at least of breeding dogs. His collies were famous. He kept about fifty at Cragston. He would go for a horseback ride over the country with fifty scampering, yelping animals at his heels—a spectacle to make the peasants stare. It was the Morgan version of taking the dog around the block. But most of all he loved boats. There was a succession of *Corsairs*, which expanded their length and beam as Mr. Morgan's beam as a banker broadened—first a small launch, then *Corsair I*, a long, low-hung rakish schooner, then *Corsair II*, a handsome ocean-going yacht that was taken over by the government as the *U.S.S. Gloucester* in the Spanish-American War; then *Corsair III*, a magnificent two-hundred-foot vessel upon which he sailed the seven seas and aboard which, tied up at port for long stretches, he would live and entertain. He was Commodore of the New York Yacht Club, and, in 1901, built the *Columbia* which raced against Thomas Lipton's first *Shamrock* for the America's Cup.

But most splendid of his hobbies was the collection of almost everything under the sun. He was a congenital collector. As a boy in school and in college he began by collecting pieces of broken stained glass, picked up around old European church ruins. When he left Göttingen for America he brought with him a couple of barrels of glass fragments which he later used to make a window or two in his beautiful library. He collected paintings—many of the greatest ever created—statuary, wood, bronze, stone antiquities, miniatures, cameos, etchings, first editions, original manuscripts, tapestries, brocades, cuniform tablets, ancient coins, medallions, vestments. Nobody has brought together such an accumulation of the original manuscripts of the great writers of all time as Mr. Morgan. In his later years he amused himself making catalogues of these treasures. The catalogues alone, magnificently illustrated in colors, cost a fortune. The size and importance of these collections may be seen from the fact that one catalogue of mere odds and ends ran to 157 pages.

Morgan gathered up these things because he liked collecting. But beyond a doubt the hobby contributed to the nourishment of his ego. It was part of another trait tucked away neatly amidst his other psychological equipment. It was one of his own partners who said:

> Mr. Morgan is not a conscious advertiser, but he has a conscious genius for advertising, that is for getting on the first pages of newspapers. Many other men buy pictures and horses and keep yachts and go into public enterprises; but when he buys, it is always prize-winning horses or dogs or celebrated pictures and he has the finest steam yacht afloat and solely and individually owns the cup defender. He starts the building of the New York cathedral—the biggest church in the country. He heads the syndicate that built the largest and most beautiful covered arena (Madison Square Garden), the largest and finest opera (the Metropolitan) and the best situated and most beautiful club house (the Metropolitan Club) and makes the first subscription to every public object.[1]

Certainly he set the scenes amid which he moved for his stupendous act. His home at 219 Madison Avenue, his town house in London—Prince's Gate—were filled with priceless treasures. He had a fine estate at Cragston in upper New York and another on Long Island. He inherited from his father his country home in England, Dover House. He had two shooting lodges, a fishing camp, a winter resort on Jekyl Island, while *Corsair II* was a sort of floating home that connected all the others. The world was filled with the fame of his wealth, his art treasures, his power. Monarchs received

---

[1] *J. Pierpont Morgan, an Intimate Portrait,* by Herbert L. Satterlee, Macmillan, 1939.

him with delight and even their flunkies looked at him with awe. Leopold of Belgium consulted him upon his personal investment problems. Edward VII visited him at Prince's Gate and Dover House. Kaiser Wilhelm II came aboard his *Corsair* and lunched with him. The Pope honored him.

Everywhere crowds fought for a peep at him. In New York during the 1907 crisis, when he sat like an archangel in the midst of the whirlwind, directing the storm, people ran along beside his cab or brougham to look in at him. In Rome crowds gathered outside the Grand Hotel to see the American "King" to whom the art dealers flocked with the masterpieces of Europe. In London, where he had tried to grab the bus lines and finance a subway, peddlers sold upon the streets little discs to be worn on the coat bearing the legend LICENSE TO STAY ON THE EARTH, and signed J. P. MORGAN. Admiring bishops conferred upon him the title of J. Pierpontifex Maximus. In Rome he was called The Magnificent.

Self-sufficient, arrogant by nature, all this power and acclaim, we may be sure, did not diminish his arrogance. One of his biographers, infected with what Macaulay called the *Leus Boswelliana*, or disease of admiration, has described how he walked through crowded Wall Street. He did not dodge or zigzag or slacken his pace to accommodate himself to the presence of others. He barged along, as if he were the only man on the street, the embodiment of power and purpose. Thus he moved through the world. He walked as if he owned its highways. If there were others blocking his path and designs, he moved as if he were preceded by Roark Bradford's Gabriel crying: "Make way! Make way, for the Lord God Jehovah!"

— II —

Morgan, being a royal figure, it has seemed necessary to his biographers to provide him with an aristocratic lineage. The first Morgan to arrive on this continent from England was Miles, who landed at Boston and shortly afterward went to some unclaimed

acres on the site of what was one day to be Springfield, Massachusetts. "He spent a large part of his life," says a member of the Morgan family in his life of the great man, "serving the community in
which he lived and took his share of fighting. His services in helping
lay the foundations of the Massachusetts Commonwealth *were publicly recognized in 1879 when a statue was erected to his memory
in Court Square, Springfield,* where it stands today to be seen by all
who motor by." [2]

The implication—nay the assertion—is that the people of Springfield thus honored the services of one of their founding fathers.
There in Court Square, sure enough, stands Miles in bronze. But
there also upon the pedestal is chiseled the information that the
statue was erected, not by the public, but "one of his descendants of
the fifth generation"—probably J. P.'s father.

Farmer Miles was succeeded by three generations of Josephs.
Joseph Morgan Number One was a weaver. Number Two was a
farmer. Number Three was a tavernkeeper. All were doubtless
thrifty and honest peasants—though Joseph Number Two served
as a captain in the Revolutionary army. Number Three was the
grandfather of J. Pierpont Morgan. He moved to Hartford and
opened the Exchange Coffee House. But he expanded in time into
something more than a dispenser of grog and victuals. He became a
hotelkeeper; owned the City Hotel in Hartford and the New Haven
House in New Haven. He accumulated a moderate fortune as a
moneylender and real-estate investor and became interested in and
a director of the then small Aetna Fire Insurance Company. Here
was a stream of good, decent blood, but this series of ancestors
hardly answers to the definition of aristocracy which means in its
broadest connotation a "class of persons pre-eminent by reason of
birth, wealth, and culture."

Junius Morgan was the son of this last Joseph. He was born in
Hartford in 1809, worked on his father's farm, went to a good
boarding school, and with his father's aid became a partner in a
wholesale drygoods store in Hartford—Howe, Mather & Co. Later

---

[2] *J. Pierpont Morgan, an Intimate Portrait.*

he moved to Boston to become a partner in a larger firm of merchants, J. M. Beebe, Morgan & Company. This Junius Morgan was a man of great ability, who later moved to London as a partner of the famous George Peabody, the American who became a leading English banker. And when Peabody retired, Junius Morgan established his own banking house in London, where he continued to live and grow wealthy for the rest of his life. This was the father of J. Pierpont Morgan.

There was another ancestor of a very different breed—Morgan's maternal grandfather, John Pierpont. What schoolboy has not recited Warren's address:

> *Stand! The ground is yours my braves;*
> *Will ye give it up to slaves?*

John Pierpont, poet, preacher, reformer, friend of William Lloyd Garrison, wrote this recitation. He thundered against slavery. He was so far different from Junius Morgan and his father Joseph that, in his own words, his interest "was in the great breathing mass of humanity."

In the old Hollis Congregationalist Church in Boston John Pierpont struck at so many kinds of human injustice that he irked the fastidious members of his congregation. Offended by his abolitionist views, some of them took advantage of his use of the word "whore" to brand him as immoral and call for his resignation. He resisted, demanded a trial, got one, was vindicated, and then resigned. He died at the age of eighty, the occupant of a small government office in Washington.

Here, united in the great banker Pierpont was good blood, but what different streams—the cold, Yankee, money-loving blood of the Morgans and the hot, rebellious blood of the old patriot reformer. There is, however, nothing odd about the fact that it was not to John Pierpont or even to Joseph Morgan, the Revolutionary soldier, that a statue was built, but to the farmer and sergeant of militia, Miles, in order to exhibit the "antiquity" of the Morgan line. Humble Miles was one of those ancestors who shine in the reflected glory of their descendants. If it were possible it was he who ought to have erected a statue to his descendant, Pip Morgan.

J. Pierpont Morgan was born April 17, 1837, in Hartford, two years before John D. Rockefeller. The day of his birth all of the banks in New York suspended specie payment. The next day those of Hartford followed suit. The future money king came into the world amid the din of crashing banks. He was baptized in the Congregationalist Church in Boston by John Pierpont and was called John Pierpont Morgan. No stranger monument could have been dedicated to the old battler of the Lord interested "in the great breathing mass of humanity."

It is difficult to depict Morgan's youth and young manhood to those who hold to the hero-villain theory of history. To millions he was and remains the image of the unfeeling despot. Because he was the central figure in so many episodes as the vicegerent of the Money Devil, it is not an easy matter for the black-white theorists of human nature to credit the softer elements of his nature. The political leader charged with stealing public funds, robbing ballot boxes, slugging rival candidates, and consorting with criminals is set down by those who do not know him personally as a sort of monster. But, on the other hand, those who know him and can testify that he is a devoted father, a loyal friend, and a generous neighbor find it equally difficult to believe that he is a grafter and gangster.

Those who believe the black patches in a man's character are prepared to call him black; while those who are familiar with the white patches only are unwilling to believe there are any black ones. Prove that the district leader gives coal to the poor and worships his little daughter and you acquit him of robbing the public till. If Morgan venerated his father, lavished loving attention upon the purchase of a little bonnet for his mother, wept at singing the songs she taught him, folded an old schoolmate like General Joe Wheeler to his bosom, lifting him from the floor in an exuberant hug—then there was no water in U. S. Steel and the crime against the New Haven road is a fiction. It is almost impossible to establish in the popular mind the perfectly simple truth that a man may rob a railroad or pad a security issue or crush a business rival without being a monster.

Morgan seems to have had a very engaging youth. He did not go to school until he was nine years old. He went, in order, to the Point School, the Episcopal Academy in Hartford, the Pavillion School in Cheshire—a boarding academy—and three years later to the Public High School in Hartford.

In 1851 his father moved the family to Boston, where he became a partner in J. M. Beebe, Morgan & Company. And Pierpont was entered in the English High School where, a biographer observes, there was not to be found a single name of Irish, Italian, German, or any other nationality save English (unless we except Delano). There was nothing to poison the mind of the pure-blooded young American.

Two years later came the offer to Junius Morgan to join George Peabody in London. He accepted. European funds were moving in abundance into investment in the growing young continent. Peabody, a young Baltimore grocery clerk, had gone to old England, risen to power as a London banker, accumulated a vast fortune, and was now ready to retire to devote himself to philanthropy. His fortune had been made chiefly from handling British capital seeking investment in America. He wanted a young partner and knew and admired Junius Morgan, who had been handling some of his business in Boston.

When the Morgan family took up its life and residence in England, Pierpont was sent first to a select school at Vevey on Lake Geneva, called the Institute Sillig, which was a favorite with American families abroad. There he remained two years, when he was sent to the University of Göttingen. He registered for the classes in mathematics and philosophy. And after two years he concluded that his education was finished and prepared to leave for a business career. This was in 1857.

In these school years we see a more or less reserved boy, deeply attached to his family, a most faithful correspondent, with a fine mind for mathematics, but little taste for the humanities, little interested in athletics, fond of dancing, parties, the companionship of young ladies, faithful to his religious duties, keeping his money accounts meticulously, looking forward impatiently to going into business and longingly toward marriage—and with an American girl only.

"In Göttingen," says Professor Harry Thurston Peck, "he won such distinction by his mathematical work as to receive the offer of a *professor's chair* in that historic institution." This has been repeated many times, along with Peck's additional observation that "he inclined to the scholar's life." Professor Ullrich, a first-rate mathematician who taught him at Göttingen, advised Morgan against going into business and encouraged him by saying that after another year he could assure him a post as an instructor and, who knows, someday when the good Professor Ullrich should grow old, he (Pierpont) might look forward to becoming a professor of mathematics. Which is quite a different story. But Morgan was never the scholar type. He had a natural aptitude for figures and did well without too much effort.

He must have been an unusually straightforward boy. A letter brought to light by his son-in-law, Mr. Herbert L. Satterlee, written when he was only thirteen years old, exhibits him approaching a common problem of the schoolboy with a frankness, forthrightness, and directness that command admiration. Smarting under a punishment by his teacher, Miss Stevens, he wrote her with a most engaging directness:

I should like to inquire of you the reasons why you as a teacher and, of course, over me, only a scholar, should treat me in such an inhuman manner as to send me out of the class for laughing a little too loud which, I can assure you I am perfectly unable to control and which no punishment will cure me of. You cannot deny that I have not tried to behave better in class lately. If I wanted I could sit still (without saying a word) in a corner and suppose all the class were to do it would not you think that all the class were very stupid indeed and you would have to do all the talking, the scholars saying nothing.

Whereupon he informed her that he proposed to do something about it—namely, go to another class if she didn't mend her ways.

When he left school he had a more or less fragmentary education, but he had been exposed to a number of cultural infections, had lived among cultured people for a number of years, could both speak and write French and German. He was indeed one of the few American industrial or money kings of his day who had enjoyed these advantages.

————————————— III —————————————

In the late summer or early fall of 1857 the young man from the English school in Boston, the French school at Vevey, and the German University of Göttingen stepped ashore at New York. A week later he sat down at his desk in the office of Duncan, Sherman & Company at 11 Pine Street, where the Bankers' Trust building now stands. They were merchant-bankers, had close relations with George Peabody & Company of London, through whose influence young Morgan got this place. It wasn't much of a place at that, since the salary was zero. But it was another school where he could learn the business of foreign exchange.

As he had come into the world amidst the clatter of crashing banks in 1837, so now he made his start in business amidst the excitement of the crisis of 1857. Commercial houses were going down, banks suspended specie payments, long lines formed at their tellers' windows, dark news came from London that Peabody & Company were in difficulties, rumors terrified the young man at 11 Pine Street about his father's failure. Peabody & Company were in trouble. The Bank of England had to come to their aid with three million dollars. Duncan, Sherman & Company were in trouble, and Junius Morgan in London had to extend a helping hand to them across the Atlantic.

New York was a very different city from that great metropolis over which this youth would one day cast so large a shadow. It was not precisely little old New York, for it had a population of about

700,000. But very little of that vast and complicated modern business machine with which Morgan played was yet formed. Business was concentrated down around Wall Street—stores, theaters, newspapers, as well as banks and brokerage offices. The number of corporations were few. Outside of the railroads, men in business owned their enterprises and put their own names over their shops and countinghouses. In the railroads there had been a bit of stockjobbing, but they were small affairs. The railroad giants had not yet begun to assemble their security machine. Even old Commodore Cornelius Vanderbilt was still in the shipping business.

There were millionaires—William B. Astor and Peter Lorillard, Cornelius Vanderbilt, Peter Cooper, Robert Goelet, Henry Brevoort, Peter Schermerhorn, August Belmont, and old Daniel Drew, not yet concerned with railroads but already battling Vanderbilt on the seas. The Stock Exchange was in the Wall Street district, but most of the trading was done on the street. On the corner of Broad and Wall was a broker named Frank Baker, now forgotten, of course. But the "Corner" where he once thrived is now an institutional spot in the world of capital. Young Morgan took a room some distance uptown in West Seventeenth Street.

This young Pierpont Morgan was the complete model of the ambitious young Christian gentleman eager to go forward in business. He cultivated a large acquaintance among the best families, made it a practice to spend Sunday evenings at the homes of these families, particularly where there were personable young ladies, sang hymns with them around the fireside, wrote faithfully to his family in London, attended scrupulously and with intelligence to his business, joined St. George's Church at Stuyvesant Square, joined lustily in the hymn singing on Sunday mornings, and, when he went into business for himself, took his own pew.

He was paid nothing at Duncan, Sherman & Company and his first money was made in a speculation in coffee during a trip for the firm to New Orleans. He was learning the ways of the man with money and he itched to go into business for himself. And this he did sometime in 1860 or 1861. It was not a difficult plunge.

After all, George Peabody & Company—his father's London firm —was a wealthy and powerful dealer in American paper of all sorts, and the opening as a dealer in exchange was ready to hand for him. He took a small office at 54 Exchange Place, which he shared with an Englishman named James Tinker. Later he had some sort of partnership arrangement with Tinker, who thus got the distinction of being J. Pierpont Morgan's first partner. It did not last long and Tinker seems to have vanished out of New York life and memory.

About the time he went into business for himself he also fell in love with a young woman named Amelia Sturgis. And this romantic episode forms one of the most appealing incidents in the life of this grim man. It revealed in him depths of tenderness which his later life in Wall Street concealed wholly from the public. She was perhaps the first or at least among the first young women he met when he arrived from Europe. His attachment to her deepened slowly but it was probably begun in those first meetings at Newport in the very first week he spent in America. In the spring and summer of 1861 he was completely immersed in the personal problem created by Mimi Sturgis' condition. She had contracted tuberculosis. She was wasting away rapidly. There was very little that could be done then against the ravages of this dread enemy. Before the summer was over he made up his mind to marry Mimi, to give up his business and devote himself completely to saving her life.

Her parents tried to induce him to give up his chivalrous project. But he was not to be turned aside. And so in early October, in the Sturgis home in East Fourteenth Street, with only the family present, young Morgan carried the frail Mimi downstairs in his arms, held her at his side while the marriage ceremony was performed, and then tenderly lifted her again in his strong arms and bore her to the waiting carriage and on to the pier. They went to London and then to Algiers with its warm sun and then, as she continued to fade, to Nice. There she died four months after the marriage. Two months later, in May, he brought her body home and laid it to rest at Fairfield. This tragedy crushed him, for a time seemed to have broken his spirit and watered down his ambition to utter frustration. But slowly he took up the broken threads, brought his old Cheshire school friend, Jim Goodwin, into partnership with him, and set off again upon his course.

It is not pleasant to turn from this generous side and this instance of self-abnegation to a somewhat darker side of Morgan's character—to the side that, unfortunately, left the deepest traces upon his country. For after all, Morgan's generous impulses wrought their benefits upon that small number of men and women who were in his circle and in his class. His vast adventures in finance touched our whole society. If we would know why the young man who could carry a dying bride in his arms to marriage and abandon his business at its very start to save her life could be the same young man who could be the center of the two episodes we are now about to describe, the answer must be that Morgan was an insular man. In spite of all his widely scattered friends and interests over the whole world, he was a man who, spiritually and socially, lived upon a little island. That island, and the people on it—his family, his friends, those who moved close to him, his class —lay within the circle of Mr. Morgan's sentimental perceptions. Those who lived on all the other islands—the "great breathing mass of humanity" so dear to old John Pierpont—lived in another world with which his sentimental and ethical relations were quite different.

———————————————— IV ————————————————

On April 12, 1861, General Beauregard fired on Sumter in Charleston Harbor and, so far as the Civil War and America were concerned, the fat was in the fire. Lincoln called for 75,000 volunteers and then in July for 200,000 more. The calls were answered fully by men everywhere. But young Mr. Morgan did not go. He did not go because of his poor health, writes his son-in-law. He was not the only young man in business who did not go. Young Mr. Rockefeller did not go either. And a host of gentlemen, who were to become famous wealth getters and patriots and flag wavers later, did not go. Why one man goes to war and another remains at home is a problem in spiritual values not easy to resolve. Some remain away because they hate war. Some hold back because they hate the cause of the particular war. That sometimes takes more courage than going. Some go because they are too weak to refuse to go. Some go to escape other frustrations. Some go driven on by a romantic sense of patriotic duty. Others go because they like war, like guns, like the glamor and urge of military adventure. Many go through a quiet, heroic sense of simple duty.

War is a dirty business, messy, costly, and there are plenty of plain people whose lives do not matter to do the fighting. Why should precious lives, so full of promise, like Mr. Rockefeller's or Mr. Morgan's be offered up? Why Mr. Morgan did not go to war a year or two later is another matter. But it ought not to be difficult to understand why he did not go when the war began. In those early months, he was concerned not with killing but with saving. His mind was consumed with the hope of marrying Mimi Sturgis and taking her to the healing sunshine of northern Africa to save her life. And from August to May of the next year he was away from America; and her growing troubles were lost in his own tragedy.

But why did he not go later? When the draft came, because of the desperate need of men, Morgan hired a substitute, as did Mr. Rockefeller. This substitute he always referred to as the "other Pierpont Morgan" and, according to his family, always took an interest in him afterward. For *the* Pierpont Morgan, while the "other" Pierpont Morgan was fighting, there was more important work to be done.

Briefly, here is the story. The war caught the Federal government sadly unprepared. It needed arms, ammunition, horses, vessels, uniforms, and particularly rifles. Great numbers had been moved South and when the war came were quickly seized by the Confederate authorities. In addition to the 75,000 volunteers called in May, militia units were forming and frantic appeals for guns poured into the capital. These scarcities opened the way for the business adventurers of all sorts to prey upon the government.

Some years before the war, the War Department bought a large number of rifles known as Hall's carbines. In 1857 the army inspecting officers condemned a large number of these carbines because they were of obsolete pattern, unserviceable, and had a defect that made loading them dangerous. In fact, there were cases of soldiers shooting their thumbs off in the act of loading. The carbines were ordered to be sold November 5, 1857, in an order issued by the chief of ordnance. Many were sold but about 5000 remained in the arsenal at Governor's Island, New York, and the Frankford arsenal at Philadelphia.

In May, 1861, Arthur M. Eastman of Manchester, New Hampshire, offered to buy the remaining 5000 Hall carbines from the chief of ordnance, fixing one price for the better ones and a lower price for the more defective. The chief of ordnance agreed to sell them all to Eastman for $3.50 each—"serviceable and unserviceable." He insisted also that Eastman must take them all at once and pay for them before delivery. Eastman was satisfied with the price, and in June the chief of ordnance wrote him that he had notified the arsenals at Governor's Island and Frankford to deliver them on payments in cash.

Eastman, who had hoped to take the carbines out in lots, now confronted with a mass delivery, had to find the money. He made an arrangement with one Simon Stevens. Stevens had a more or less unsavory record in dealings with the government. But Eastman agreed to sell the carbines to Stevens for $12.50 each. Actually Stevens agreed to advance the money to Eastman—$20,000—to get the carbines and to take as his profit all over $12.50 he could get for them. Then on August 1, Stevens wired General John C. Fremont, in command in the West, that "I have 5000 rifled cast-steel carbines, breach-loading, *new*, at $22; government standard 48. Can I hear from you?" Fremont wired to ship with all possible haste.

It is necessary to have a clear picture of this transaction. When the offer to buy the guns was made men were being hurried South to the capital against a threatened attack from Virginia. Frantic efforts were being made in St. Louis, Fremont's headquarters, for the defense of Missouri and a movement down the Mississippi. Then in July came the great disaster at Bull Run and the call for 200,000 men. In the midst of these events Eastman and Stevens proposed to buy from one department of the army the government's rejected guns for $3.50 and sell them to another department of the army for $22. The guns would be shipped directly from one government arsenal to another.

This was possible only because the general in the field commanding in St. Louis did not know and could not know that the guns belonged to another army department when he bought them. The Ordnance Department could not know a general in the field was buying, since Fremont had no right to buy. There was a law against it. His right would have to depend on the extraordinary assumption of power by a commander in the field faced with an emergency. The schemers planned on a prospective investment of $17,500, a sale for $110,000, a profit of $93,000 less shipping, packing, and other costs, a profit made by selling to a general in the field guns that already belonged to the government and that the government did not send to him because they had been condemned.

Young Morgan, just starting in business, became a part of this conspiracy. Neither Eastman nor Stevens had the money and Morgan, through Stevens, agreed to furnish it. The transaction was carried through in the following manner. There were 4996 Hall carbines actually involved. Morgan sent his check for $17,486 to the Ordnance Department in payment of the whole purchase. The guns turned out not to be rifled. This had to be done. They were packed and shipped in lots. When 2500 had been shipped, the government's check for $55,550 was sent to Morgan. Before the next 2500 were paid for the facts became known, the transaction was denounced in Congress, and payment was withheld pending an investigation. There was an investigation by a Congressional committee which denounced the transaction in the strongest terms. Morgan then made a claim for the balance due—$58,000; the government appointed a commission composed of J. Holt and Robert Dale Owen (son of the famous Robert Owen), and this commission confirmed the Congressional charges, but decided that, since the government had kept the carbines, the sellers should be paid at a fair valuation which it held to be $12.50. It awarded the claimants an additional $11,000. Stevens filed a claim for the whole amount of $58,000 with the Court of Claims, which held that the government had made a contract, was bound by it, and awarded the whole sum.

Roughly, the operation worked out thus. The whole sum received for the carbines was $109,912. Of this Eastman was to get $62,462 at $12.50 per carbine. Less the $17,486 paid for the carbines this would give him a profit of $44,976. And this would leave $47,450 as Stevens' share to be split with Morgan. How it was split is not known. Morgan, of course, would get the money he advanced out of Eastman's share. I say these are rough figures, because there were certain charges for packing, rifling, and so on that reduced these profits.

The story was brought to light, so far as I can judge, by Gustavus Meyer, in 1910, in his widely read and quoted three-volume *History of Great American Fortunes*. It was repeated by many other writers. But J. P. Morgan never, during his life, made any reply or comment on it. Recently an attempt has been made by Mr. Herbert L. Satterlee to exculpate his deceased client and kinsman in a full-length biography. He makes the point that Morgan acted merely as a banker, lending money on a business transaction—one of hundreds passing over his desk daily—that he did not know Eastman, probably never heard of him, that Eastman had concealed even from Stevens that the guns were being bought from the government and were in its possession; that Morgan got merely his principal plus actual outlays and interest as his share; that he never made any claim on the government for anything; that in the investigations by the Congressional committee he was not called as a witness and was not mentioned in the proceedings save as having furnished the money, and that after he had received payment of his ordinary loan after the first shipment he had no further connection with the proceedings and no part in the suit before the Court of Claims, which was prosecuted by an entirely different banking house—Ketchum Sons & Company. He then adds with that superior air that characterizes all Morgan utterances that the original critic—Gustavus Meyer—made these charges without consulting the records and that others repeated them without attempting to verify them after the fashion of the reckless journalistic historian. Meyer's famous history is referred to as "a book published in 1910," which is the standard Morgan way of disdaining to dignify an unfavorable chronicler.

Of course Gustavus Meyer supplied in his book the completest record of the sources whence his material was drawn. Mr. Lewis Corey, who repeated these charges, did the same thing. Mr. Carl Sandburg, in his painstaking life of Lincoln, *The War Years,* also refers to it at length. I have read all the source material completely and it is quite obvious that Mr. Meyer, Mr. Corey, and Mr. Sandburg have done so. The most charitable explanation of Mr. Satterlee's account is that he did not, but depended probably upon some hired assistant to bring him the facts, which were brought to him to his taste.

The assertion that Eastman did not tell Stevens and therefore Morgan that the guns were in possession of the government is a shocking dismissal of facts too obvious on the record to be misunderstood. And in the same class is the assertion that Morgan probably never heard of Eastman—having dealt only with Stevens.

First of all Morgan, who was advancing the money for the deal, insisted on a lien on the carbines. Is it conceivable that he did not know where the merchandise that was the basis of his lien was located? And as the guns upon which Morgan was advancing money were purchased from the army by Eastman and not Stevens he must have known of Eastman in the transaction. But as a matter of fact Morgan handled and paid for all the expenses of rifling and packing the carbines, and his check was made out to the government and delivered to the arsenals in New York and Philadelphia. The entry by the Ordnance Department on the transaction was "August 7, 1861—amount of draft on assistant treasurer, New York, from J. Pierpont Morgan, Esq., in payment of Hall's carbines, purchased by A. M. Eastman, $17,486." When the carbines were paid for the check came from the government for $55,550 made out to J. Pierpont Morgan. The whole money transaction was handled by him and he knew that he had paid the army for the carbines and had been paid for them by the government. He could not possibly fail to know that this was a sale to the government of its own carbines and he could not fail to know that they were bought for $3.50 and sold for $22.

That this hard-boiled and patriotic young man exhibited no curiosity about a transaction so strange on its face, upon which he was advancing so much money in his very first business year, is not to be credited even if the facts did not completely nullify so charitable an assumption. That it was just one of hundreds of transactions that went through his office is equally ingenuous. He was a young man who had just started in business, and his establishment consisted of a room at 54 Exchange Place which he shared with another man. This was not the busy J. P. Morgan of later years with hundreds of transactions flowing through the hands of clerks.

Mr. Satterlee makes the bald statement that when the first check of $55,550 was made to him he deducted his advance and certain other charges and then disappeared wholly out of the transaction and that he never made any claims for any further sums. This, of course, is palpably untrue. The claim for the remaining $58,000 before the Holt-Owen commission is officially reported as "Commission on Ordnance and Ordnance Stores: Purchase of Hall's Carbines, Washington, June 12, 1862. The Commission Have the Honor to report as follows: Case No. 97—J. Pierpont Morgan, New York, Claim for payment of Ordnance Stores, Balance claimed $58,165."

Odd indeed is the claim that when the Congressional committee was investigating the case it did not call Mr. Morgan as a witness. The committee was making these investigations in December, 1861. And at that time Mr. Morgan with his young bride was in Egypt. He left New York, October 7, and did not return until May of the following year.

As for the Holt-Owen commission, it had completed its investigation before Morgan returned. But there was no point in calling him. The commission was not concerned with the division of the profits between Stevens and Morgan, but with the claim itself. It held that Stevens had actually paid out $65,228.05 to Eastman for the guns (the price of the guns plus the cost of rifling plus the packing and other costs), that Stevens had collected $55,550 of this sum, and that therefore he was entitled to the difference plus $1,330.70 brokerage fee which Morgan's office added and still claimed.

After the decision of the Holt-Owen commission, Morgan's name does not appear in still further pressing for the $58,000. Another banking firm appears—Ketchum Sons & Company. This phase of the transaction remains unexplained. Morris Ketchum was an intimate friend of Morgan. He had been at one time connected with Junius Morgan. Moreover, he enjoyed certain relationships with General Fremont. During all this time Morgan spent a great deal of time at Ketchum's home. Even the first draft of $55,550 was cashed by him. That first draft was not enough to cover the sum that Stevens was to pay Eastman for the rifles. That, doubtless, is why Morgan, associated with Stevens, made his claim to the Holt-Owen commission, for they had yet to get their profit. Whatever Stevens, Morgan, and Ketchum were to get out of this operation had to come out of that second payment.

What were the relative participations of Stevens, Morgan, and Ketchum is not clear. It is possible that Morgan, preparing to marry and leave America, put his interest in the hands of his friend Ketchum (we will see Morgan associated with Ketchum again during the war in a gold speculation), but that must be surmise. In the end they got it all as a result of the Court of Claims decision. But what remains for history is that this young man who, for whatever reasons seemed good, did not go to war then or later, did not also hesitate to engage in a transaction in which profiteers were buying guns out of a government arsenal for $3.5o and selling them to the army in the field for $22.

------------------------------ v ------------------------------

When the war got under way, gold became an object of the first importance. The government needed gold. So much had to be bought abroad, and the United States had by secession lost its greatest export commodity—cotton. Immediately the speculators went to work in the gold market. Salmon P. Chase, Secretary of the Treasury, went to New York and told the bankers that gold was more needed than troops and begged them to aid the government. The price of gold went up and down with the tide of war. When the Union was winning, gold went down. A Confederate victory sent it up again. Finally the Stock Exchange ended gold speculation. The papers denounced the speculators. But they continued their activities in the Gold Room in Exchange Place.

Morgan and Edward Ketchum, son of Morris Ketchum, who was mixed up in the Hall carbine affair, went into a gold speculation. Union victories had sent the price down. In September, 1863, it ranged between 126 and 129. The Federal army was threatening Charleston. The fall of Charleston would be a severe blow to the Confederacy. Importers and other buyers of foreign exchange who owed bills in London delayed paying them. They gambled that with the fall of Charleston gold would go lower.

Morgan and Ketchum gambled that Charleston would not be captured. Meanwhile the demand for exchange on London was piling up, but held in abeyance. What if they could add still further to the scarcity of gold? When the crisis arrived and merchants rushed to buy gold, the price would go up. If they had the gold they could reap the profit. They could produce the scarcity and provide themselves with the gold simply by buying at once and shipping it out of the country. The two young speculators, backed by the elder Ketchum, bought two millions of gold and shipped it to Peabody & Company in London. Charleston held out. Suddenly importers tried to buy sterling exchange. The price rose. As fast as those having gold sold, Ketchum, not known to be in the pool, bought it. Soon Morgan and his partner had in their hands much of the current supply. The price went to 171 before Morgan unloaded his stocks. He and his partner made $160,000 on the operation.

The newspapers poured scorn upon the heads of the speculators. Later *The New York Times* castigated the "knot of unscrupulous gamblers who care nothing for the credit of the country" for whom Congress ought to "order the erection of scaffolds for hanging." It became so embarrassing to the government that Congress passed the Gold Act to stop it. Thus Mr. Morgan got his first taste of a thing he was to hate savagely in later life—government "interference." He got his name in the paper again as one of a group of bankers that denounced the act as "one more instance of the utter lawlessness of Congress."

Mr. Edward Ketchum, Morgan's partner in this pretty business, kept up his gold speculations until he was ruined by the victory of the Union. He then stole $2,800,000 from his father's firm and forged a million and a half in checks, was indicted, and sent to prison for four and a half years. The devout Christian would probably insist that the hand of divine justice intervened here, as Mr. Morgan was one of his victims to the tune of $85,000—just about his share of his gold winnings plus interest.

These two incidents—the carbines and the gold affair—throw a flood of light upon the acquisitive soul of Morgan, and indeed of his type. Young, reared in an atmosphere of culture, away from the sordid influences of moneyless men on the make, religious or at least pietistic, piping up on Sunday mornings and evenings his hymns of praise to the Almighty, fully able to understand the terrible issues that plunged his country at that time into one of the bloodiest wars in history, not willing to bear his part in the struggle, he could yet remain behind the lines as a partner in two ugly conspiracies—one to defraud the government in a sharper's sale of arms, the other in a cold-blooded speculation against its most sensitive financial interests.

Why do men go to war? Why do other men remain away from war? The answer can be made only by some power capable of soul-searching more thorough than is open to us. Why did John Pierpont Morgan—when he was twenty-four to twenty-eight years of age—stay home and grow rich? Why did John Pierpont, his grandfather, at seventy-six enlist as a chaplain with the Twenty-sixth Massachusetts Regiment and go with them to the front until, camped on the Potomac, he had to leave because of his infirmities?

—————————————— VI ——————————————

When the war was over Morgan was a rich young man. He reported a taxable income of $53,286 in 1864. He had married again—Miss Frances Tracy, daughter of Charles Tracy, wealthy lawyer, later partner of Boss Tom Platt and candidate for Mayor of New York against Van Wyck and Henry George. Also he had formed a new partnership. The firm was Dabney, Morgan & Company. He had worked under Charles W. Dabney, in Duncan, Sherman & Company. Old George Peabody, full of years and dollars, retired in London to use his millions in philanthropy and the firm in London became J. S. Morgan & Company.

The war over, money and energy began to flow into the railroads. Resourceful enterprisers and adventurers like Vanderbilt and Gould and Fisk and Roberts and Scott began to pick up all the little roads and make them into larger systems and inundate them with stocks and bonds. They fought among themselves. Millions of English capital poured into America through the house of Junius Morgan. The young Morgan in New York handled much of that business. Railroads were the coming thing—Pierpont Morgan could see that. He had an eye open to shoulder in on that front. His opportunity came in 1869 in a battle over a little road only 142 miles long. It was called the Albany & Susquehanna Railroad and ran from Albany to Binghamton. At Binghamton it connected with the Erie. And that was what started the fight.

Jay Gould and Jim Fisk had just beaten old Commodore Vanderbilt for control of the Erie. They were deep in those many glamorous larcenies that made Wall Street gasp. Gould wanted to get control of the Albany & Susquehanna for the Erie.

The road had been built largely with money subscribed by some twenty-two towns through which it passed. Its president was Joseph H. Ramsey. Ramsey was allied with the Delaware & Hudson Canal Company, which was interested in the Albany & Susquehanna because it connected with its valuable coal properties. Ramsey and the Delaware & Hudson were prepared to fight Gould. And thus the struggle became a war between the Erie Railroad and the rich and powerful coal company.

It began with Gould quietly buying up the shares of some of the towns that had subscribed to them and were probably glad to get rid of them. Ramsey retaliated by issuing 9500 new shares to offset the Gould acquisitions. The annual election was to be held September 7 at the company's office, 262 Broadway, Albany. And both sides were busy getting votes.

As the election approached, Ramsey, at the suggestion of the Delaware crowd, asked J. Pierpont Morgan to take command of their fight. Morgan was still young—only thirty-two—but he had acquired a considerable reputation. Despite the fact that he was called to face two of the most audacious and unprincipled adventurers in America—the serpent Gould and the ruffian Fisk—he entered the battle full of zest. With Charles Tracy as his lawyer he went to Albany. The war had become a battle of lawsuits, injunctions, and contempt orders. Fisk was named receiver of the road in one proceeding before Gould's personal kept judge, the infamous Barnard. Ramsey had another receiver named before another judge. Gould and Fisk got possession of the road at the Binghamton end. Ramsey's forces operated it at the Albany end.

It was not only a battle of legal process servers. It became a war of thugs and guns. Gould and Fisk led out their inevitable West Side gangsters and seized locomotives and depots, engaged in pitched battles with Ramsey's men. Armed men stood in battle array on both sides of the track. Thus, running the road became impossible, and Governor Hoffman intervened by sending state troops and putting the road under the temporary management of a general of militia.

Thus matters stood as the rival forces, armed with proxies, appeared in Albany for the election. Jim Fisk arrived with a carload of thugs to whom proxies were delivered before they went to the railroad offices. He got a contempt order from a judge for the arrest of Ramsey, the president of the road, and when the election started Ramsey was held by the sheriff. By this time there were twenty-two lawsuits tying up the road, its officers, and its enemies. The office where the election was held was crowded with stockholders, officials, and about fifty of Jim Fisk's roughs, who were, however, prevented from using violence through the vigilance of the police. In fact, the rival factions refused to recognize each other. They organized separately, despite the crush, named two sets of tellers, and from noon to one o'clock held two elections, naming two sets of directors. Morgan was elected director heading the Ramsey crowd.

A curious fable about this election, illustrating the great physical prowess of J. P. Morgan, has been told many times and is repeated in the Satterlee biography. It is an excellent example of that irresponsible form of journalistic history in which sources are ignored, upon which Mr. Satterlee looks with so much scorn, but here adopts so blithely. The story as told by son-in-law Satterlee runs as follows:

A few minutes before the hour of the meeting, Jim Fisk and a bunch of his followers came in the street entrance of the building and started up the stairs to the office of the company. Looking up they saw Ramsey and Pierpont at the head of the stairs. When they got to the top something happened very quickly. The portly Jim Fisk was knocked off his

feet and fell back on the men who were coming up behind him. Those
who were nearest to him were also thrown down the stairs. For a few
minutes it was a free for all fight. The attacking party was completely
taken by surprise and retired in disorder in the belief that there was a
strong force up in the dark hallway behind Pierpont and Mr. Ramsey.
Very punctually at the time for the meeting Pierpont and Mr. Ramsey
somewhat hot and dishevelled, went into the office, locked the door and
held the election.

It happens that the facts of this election were exhaustively examined by the Supreme Court in Albany and are on record in the
Supreme Court Reports (55 Barbour, page 344 *et seq.*). Ramsey,
one of the heroes of this mighty fracas, was under arrest and held
by the sheriff in an adjoining room when Fisk and his gang arrived. All of them—some fifty or more were counted by witnesses
—entered the offices unmolested. Fisk and his colleagues and his
mobsters held an election in the same room with Morgan. Both
elected boards and the whole proceeding was carried on quite
peaceably. The tale of Morgan and Ramsey hurling Fisk and fifty
gangsters down the stairs and putting them to flight is the kind of
story Pharaohs had inscribed on their tombs.

The rival boards of course fled to the courts. The Supreme
Court in Albany somehow managed to combine all of the multitudinous suits into one and decided that Morgan's board was the
legally elected one. Immediately upon the victory and on the day
of the election Morgan went to New York and executed a lease
of the Albany & Susquehanna to the Delaware & Hudson. He had
whipped Gould and Fisk, who had whipped everybody else including Vanderbilt.

His shadow lengthened in Wall Street. He moved his family to
a bigger house at 6 East Fortieth Street. He extended his energies
to very respectable civic affairs. He took an active interest in organizing the YMCA, the Metropolitan Museum of Art, acquired
a country estate at Cragston.

He had also outgrown his banking house. Anthony J. Drexel of
Philadelphia asked him to join the Drexels in a New York banking house. The firm of Drexel & Company of Philadelphia had

been founded by Francis M. Drexel, an immigrant portrait painter, the year Pierpont Morgan was born. Drexel had fought Jay Cooke's Northern Pacific adventure, calling it another South Sea Bubble, dominated the *Philadelphia Ledger*, contested in Philadelphia for banking leadership with Cooke. The sons, Francis, Anthony, and Joseph, had succeeded to the business and wanted to establish the firm in New York. Morgan dissolved the firm of Dabney, Morgan & Company, and Drexel, Morgan & Company was born. Morgan became a full partner in the Philadelphia house of Drexel & Company and held a dominating interest in the New York house of Drexel, Morgan & Company. It was this firm which, in 1895, became J. P. Morgan & Co.

Presently he crossed swords with Jay Cooke. The Federal government was planning a $300,000,000 conversion operation. Since the second year of the Civil War federal financing had been going to Jay Cooke who, in a sense, preceded Morgan as the first great modern American banking overlord. Cooke, as a pioneer booster, boomed real-estate lots at the age of sixteen in Sandusky, Ohio, served as railroad ticket agent in Philadelphia, clerk in a banking house and partner in Clark & Dodge at twenty-one. Very soon he set up for himself and, before he was forty, rose to national fame as the financier of the Civil War. He sold three billion dollars of government paper by extravagant ballyhoo, made millions out of his war services, and translated his new influence into valuable government franchises, took over the dying promotion of the Northern Pacific, developed the stock-watering and distribution technique to new heights, bought Congressmen, bribed a vice-president, wined reporters, purchased editors, gave church bells, supported impecunious ministers, combined the qualities of money getting, corruption, temperance, and piety in successful proportions, built a magnificent residence with fifty-two rooms and a theater, and was generally rated as the great master financier of America.

In 1873 Cooke sought the whole of a $300,000,000 government-bond refunding issue. Drexel, Morgan & Company headed a syndicate that demanded that the issue be split between it and Cooke. Morgan won out and collaborated with Cooke in managing the issue. But it was a complete failure. The bankers could not sell more than one sixth of the loan. Cooke intimated that his "distinguished associates" had hampered the operation. But it was a victory for Morgan, since the hold of Cooke on Federal finance was broken. But that hold was coming to an end soon anyhow. In the fall of that year the inevitable depression appeared. Cooke's fantastic Northern Pacific enterprise came its logical cropper. Cooke failed with it. His banking house closed and he disappeared as a factor in American finance. Cooke's exit left the financial stage without a leading character, a dominating and colorful figure. In time Morgan would assume that role.

In 1879 the door swung wide for his entrance on the stage as the great American banker. William H. Vanderbilt, son and heir of the old Commodore, famed for saying, "The public be damned," small-minded, arrogant, inept, timorous, owned eighty-seven per cent of the stock of the New York Central Railroad. That was too many eggs to have in one basket. The public thought so too, but for a different reason. They thought one man ought not to own so many eggs in so big a basket as this great railroad system. The New York legislature threatened the road as an attack on Vanderbilt. He decided to dispose of most of his holdings—rid the road of the curse of one-man control, rid himself of the dangers of loss. He selected J. Pierpont Morgan for the job. It had to be done secretly else the market price of the stock be ruined. A syndicate of Drexel, Morgan & Company, Morton, Bliss & Company, August Belmont, and Jay Gould bought 350,000 shares of Vanderbilt's stock at 120 and quietly eased it out, mostly into the hands of English investors, without causing a ripple in the market. As part of the bargain Morgan exacted from Vanderbilt the concession that he (Morgan) would sit on the board of directors of the Central. To sit on that board for Morgan was to dominate it. And with this operation he rose at once to a commanding position, as the banker for the richest man in America and as the fiscal agent of the New York Central and one of its directors. And with this his career in the reorganization of American railroads was launched.

——————————————————— VII ———————————————————

The modern arsenal of money-getting weapons now lay ready to hand for Morgan's use. For centuries men had been slowly fabricating the instruments for accumulating wealth. It was a far cry from the crude and barbarous simplicity of the ancient Egyptian system by which the Pharaoh, under the fiction of divine ownership of his subjects and of the land they walked on, could cut himself in for a share of the production of a whole nation. Slowly through the centuries one device after another was invented to enable the strong man to take for himself a fraction of the product of many men. Generally the strong men rendered some service in return for this levy—but also generally the toll taken was out of proportion to the service. But in time the weapons were multiplied and refined—money, merchandising, credit, banks, bills of exchange, checks, machines, corporations, classes of securities, speculative exchanges with their bag of tricks.

All of these were available to Morgan. Pioneers had preceded him for centuries, experimenting with them and perfecting the techniques. The corporation—the mightiest weapon of all—was just coming into its full flower. Corporation charters were granted by legislative act and were few in number. Generally, industrial corporations consisted of a few stockholders who were the active managers as well as owners of the business. But the railroads had many stockholders. The corporation manager dominated the property. But even here in many cases the manager was the owner, as in the case of William H. Vanderbilt and his eighty-seven per cent of the New York Central stock. But already the promoter had squeezed himself in between the owners (stockholders) and managers, as in the case of Gould and Fisk. And this promoter was coming more and more to be a banker. This is what happened when Morgan sold Vanderbilt's stock, leaving him a minority.

He made his entry to the board of directors part of the bargain. Before many years passed William H. Vanderbilt dropped dead. And Morgan became and remained the dictator of the Central. He would have done so even if Vanderbilt had lived.

Later the easy issuance of corporate charters by mere registry would be developed and along with that would come the holding company—the right of one corporation to hold shares in another. A West Virginia Secretary of State would go to New York with the state's seal and sell charters to anyone who wanted them on the easiest terms. New Jersey would adopt a corporation law legalizing holding companies, and one state after another would enter the competition for what was called "liberalized" corporation laws that would incorporate every exploitive and larcenous gadget that the rising tribe of corporation lawyers could invent. An Englishman named Ernest Terral Hooley in the early 'nineties would discover the precious device of preferred stock. He merged ten plants in England, worth $10,000,000; issued $10,000,000 in preferred and $10,000,000 in common against them. John W. Gates and Elbert Gary would hear about it and put the invention to work in America.

After that the primrose path of the promoter spread broad and unpoliced for the sharp-witted men. Morgan, of course, invented none of these things. But he conferred upon them one attribute they sadly needed. That was respectability. He possessed then and he acquired later upon a grander scale a thick encrustation of respectability. What Morgan did any adventurer in Wall Street could do without fear of branding as a rogue. He did what Gould did, though he resorted to none of those outright criminal stratagems that Gould used *in extremis*. But when he did them they lost the stigma of Gould.

Morgan, however, was something more than the financial adventurer that Gould was. He saw, as many did, that the railroads had for the most part fallen into the hands of adventurers. They were loaded with debts. Parallel lines had been built by men who were not so much interested in operating railroads as in building them. The construction company to build a road was a source of quick and fabulous profits. Hence roads were built without very much regard to their economic or commercial necessity. Sometimes they were built just for the builder's profit. Sometimes there was the extra expectation of blackmailing the road with which they competed.

To J. P. Morgan this was intolerable. Competition was a force he surveyed with a hatred deeper even than Rockefeller's. He was a lover of order—particularly of order administered by J. Pierpont Morgan. He liked peace, but a Roman peace—the Pax Morgana. He had another reason for condemning the existing railroad disorder. England continued to offer rich fishing grounds for Americans seeking investment money. Morgan's firm, through Junius Morgan in London, had placed millions of English money in America. His English clients were deeply disturbed by their losses. He was now interested in railroads as a director and fiscal agent. Such lines were threatened. And thus he was drawn more and more into efforts to reorganize certain roads and finally into a comprehensive policy for intersystem agreements under which gradually the smaller roads could be absorbed into the bigger ones and the bigger ones would operate within agreed territorial limits. Today we call this "consolidation."

His first important adjustment or rearrangement project was in connection with the New York Central and the Pennsylvania. He was fiscal agent for both. The two roads were at war about two small parasites that paralleled them.

The Western—a new road—paralleled and plagued the New York Central. The South Pennsylvania competed with and harassed the Pennsylvania. Each road accused the other of starting its special small enemy for blackmail purposes. Roberts of the Pennsylvania and William H. Vanderbilt of the Central were at sword's point over this. In the end the Western went into bankruptcy and Morgan stepped in with a plan. He reorganized the Western, and after immense difficulty induced Vanderbilt to buy it, while he persuaded Roberts to buy the South Pennsylvania. Thus he established peace between these two great systems.

Morgan now went from one reorganization to another—the Baltimore & Ohio in 1887, the Chesapeake & Ohio in 1888, the Northern Pacific in 1891, the Erie, the Reading, and various smaller roads. His method was always the same, where possible. He rearranged the capital structure, scaled down bonds, preserved control in the stockholders, went on the board or put an agent there, and centered control of the road in his hands through a five-year voting trust.

Most important of these Morgan adventures in railroad reorganization was the creation of the Southern system. In 1893 the Richmond & West Point Terminal Company was a more or less loosely integrated system which, due to mismanagement and looting, was in receivership. Morgan reorganized it, brought together forty corporations into a single well-knit system with 7,000 miles of road, called it the Southern Railway, and took the whole thing completely into his control through a voting trust. But he increased its capital fatally and for twenty years this system did not pay a dividend.

By 1900 he was the most powerful figure in the railway world. Four men dominated the greatest systems—Morgan, Harriman, Gould, and Hill. Morgan's power extended to the New York Central and Vanderbilt lines (19,500 miles), the Pennsylvania lines (18,220 miles), Hill's Great Northern and Northern Pacific (10,373 miles), and to the roads he dominated more directly (19,000 miles).

Through all these chapters, out of which he was making a million or two or three every time he doctored a road, to say nothing of the profits of his continuous fiscal relations with them, he was hammering at the principle that competition among the roads was disastrous, that they should be formed into large integrated systems, and that these systems should operate under agreements to control rates, new construction, costs. Ultimately many years later the government would come around to this view and seek, very weakly and futilely, to bring about consolidation in the public interest. Morgan worked for that end, but he wanted it under an oligarchy of railroad presidents dominated by a few bankers, himself the chiefest. The scandals, crimes, and discriminations against shippers had finally in 1886 brought about the passage of the Interstate Commerce Law, but the law was feebly enforced and flouted by the managers and bankers.

Therefore, in 1888, he brought the leading road chiefs together at his home, talked harshly to them about their sins, and after much wrangling formed the Interstate Commerce Railroad Association to make effective his "community of interest" theory, to end rate wars and set up an agency to arbitrate differences. He called it a gentleman's agreement. It was signed in January, 1889. But it achieved little. Then in 1890 he called the Western presidents and their bankers together. It was a more ambitious scheme to set up a self-governing agency over the Western roads. An advisory board was formed. Morgan thought it a great constructive step. "Think of it!" he exclaimed. "All competitive traffic between St. Louis and the Pacific in the hands of thirty men." Nothing could have seemed more perfect to him save to have it in the hands of fifteen men—or better still five—or best of all one man, and that one J. Pierpont Morgan.

To Morgan in his many battles and designs victory became a habit. But one man drove him to cover. That was Edward H. Harriman. Harriman, son of an impecunious Long Island minister, started life during the war as a quotation boy on the Stock Exchange, speculated, had enough to buy a seat on the Exchange when he was twenty-one, and staged raid after raid, acting alone, until he had his own small fortune. He married the daughter of William J. Averill, who owned a small upstate railroad, became interested in that, bought out all the other stockholders, got a taste of railway management, and sold it to the Pennsylvania at a big profit. Still adding to his fortune as a combination broker and floor trader on the Exchange, he forced his way into Stuyvesant Fish's Illinois Central directorate, then drove Fish out, hocked the credit of the Illinois Central to buy control of the Union Pacific when it collapsed in 1893, and when Collis P. Huntington died bought the Southern Pacific from his widow. He had ranged behind him the millions of the Standard Oil gang. He was small, frail, with a large head and secretive manner, a lone wolf in his operations, unhampered by Christian scruples though not lacking in Christian piety, was razor-sharp and lightning-swift in action, lacking in education but intellectually the superior of Morgan. This Harriman, with the Union Pacific, the Illinois Central, and the Southern Pacific and some small roads—a vast railroad empire of 26,000 miles—took J. Pierpont Morgan on the most disastrous battle of Morgan's life for possession of the Northern Pacific Railroad.

There were three great railroads in the Northwest—the Northern Pacific controlled by Morgan, the Great Northern of James J. Hill (allied with Morgan), and the Union Pacific of Harriman.

There was also the Burlington (Chicago, Burlington & Quincy). Hill and Morgan wanted it in order to give the Great Northern and Northern Pacific entry into Chicago. Harriman wanted it also, for several reasons. He went into the open market quietly to buy its stock. But he couldn't get enough. Hill at the same time was negotiating to get the Burlington and succeeded. The Northern Pacific and Great Northern bought it together, adding 8000 miles to their systems. Harriman asked Hill and Morgan to admit him and his Union Pacific to a third interest. He was refused. He notified Morgan and Hill in the grand manner of an offended sovereign that he considered this an unfriendly act. But, thought Morgan, what can he do about it? Morgan went to Europe well pleased. He disliked Harriman intensely.

But Harriman could do something. If he could not buy the Burlington, maybe he could buy Morgan's Northern Pacific which owned half of the Burlington. Secretly, cautiously, he began buying stock. Robert Bacon, Morgan's partner who was in charge of Morgan's interests, was apparently quite naïve and suspected nothing, even though Harriman's buying pushed the price of Burlington up. Another market operation on the floor, doubtless!

So completely did Harriman mask his movements that when the price of Northern Pacific went to 117, some Morgan allies unloaded to get the profit. One associate sold 30,000 shares. J. P. Morgan & Company sold 10,000. Northern Pacific directors sold a lot of the company's own stock. It was all dropping into the Harriman net. Canny old Jim Hill, off in the Northwest, alarmed, hurried to New York. He roused Bacon from his innocent negligence. He went to Kuhn, Loeb & Company, Harriman's bankers, and protested. Then he learned the truth. It was too late. Harriman had a majority of the common and preferred stock combined. Both classes of shares could vote.

A cable went to Morgan in Paris. He was in a towering rage. He stormed into the Paris office, lifting his voice and not in hymns. He wired to buy 150,000 shares. Morgan had one hope. Harriman had a majority of preferred and common combined, but not of common by itself. If Morgan could hold a majority of common, his board could call the preferred and thus kill Harriman's majority. The contest for the common raged in one of the greatest Wall Street battles—Morgan's immense resources against the bottomless moneybag of the Standard Oil gang behind Harriman.

The inevitable result was a corner—with Morgan and Harriman in possession of all available stock. The price of the stock went to 1000. The shorts were trapped. The rest of the market tumbled. U. S. Steel went from 46 to 24. Morgan formed a $20,-000,000 syndicate to support it. He and Kuhn, Loeb agreed to settle with the shorts for 150. Harriman wanted to fight on, maintaining that calling of the preferred would be illegal. But the Standard Oil gang wanted to settle.

Morgan returned to America. A treaty was arranged. Five vacancies were created on the Northern Pacific board. Harriman was named to one of them. Morgan held control, but Harriman was inside. That was full of danger. To make all secure against another Harriman attack, Morgan and Hill organized the Northern Securities Company. Its stock was all owned by Great Northern and Northern Pacific. Their controlling shares of the Burlington

stock were transferred to the Northern Securities Company—a
holding company. Hill was made president. Morgan had twelve of
the fifteen directors, Harriman three. The Union Pacific was still
left out, and Harriman was angry. Three years later Theodore
Roosevelt started his famous antitrust suit against the Northern
Securities Company and the Supreme Court held the company illegal. The market went into another panic.

Morgan had won, but he and Hill had had a narrow escape.
It was a severe blow to Morgan's prestige. It was a blow at his
pride. When the legal attack on Northern Securities was launched,
Morgan went to the White House. He said to the President: "If
we have done anything wrong send *your man* to *my man* and
they can fix things up." Roosevelt's man was the Attorney General. Morgan's man was his counsel. It would be as easy as that,
he thought. It was the peeved suggestion of an angry monarch
to a rival potentate. Morgan learned to his chagrin, disgust, and
humiliation that there was a power higher than his. The decision
was a difficult problem in unscrambling. Morgan said to his counsel: "You will have a pretty time of it unscrambling the eggs,
putting them back in the shells and returning them to the original
hens."

But the job was done. And when Harriman's Union Pacific got
back its shares, it ultimately sold them for a profit of $58,000,000.
Harriman was younger than Morgan. There was no other warrior worthy to do battle with him save Morgan and then only
because of his superior position. What Harriman might have
done later must remain an academic question. For the man was
already ill, wasting away in the fires of his own fierce energies.
Five years later he died, dominating directly or indirectly nearly
60,000 miles of track.

———————————————— VIII ————————————————

Up to 1895 Morgan's fame in the financial world was larger
than among the masses. In 1895 he attained that popular fame

that John D. Rockefeller already possessed—fame of the same dubious variety. He became the central figure in a historic episode of national finance which hoisted him at once in the Populist West to notoriety as America's Money Devil Number One.

All through 1894 and 1895 the country was in the grip of a baffling depression—unemployment, Coxey's Army on the march, labor uprisings, the great railroad strike and Debs' arrest, the farmers in despair, government revenue falling, the great gold-silver war brewing, the President and Congress at war.

The government had decided to redeem the greenbacks issued during the war. There were $350,000,000 of them outstanding. There was $150,000,000 of gold in the Treasury. A hundred million was deemed sufficient for redemption purposes.

But foreign exchange was running against us. Importers had to ship gold to Europe. They could take greenbacks to the Treasury and get gold. They did so in such volume that the Treasury's gold was almost depleted.

On January 7, 1894, there was only $68,000,000 of gold left in the Treasury. Secretary of the Treasury Carlisle sold $50,-000,000 of 5 per cent bonds at 117 through the New York bankers. That should have raised the gold reserve above a hundred million. It did—for a few weeks. But subscribers to the bond issue took greenbacks to the Treasury, redeemed them for gold, and gave that gold to the government in payment of the bonds. It produced but little new gold. Of all the gold paid in for the bonds, $24,000,000 came out of the Treasury.

Gold began flowing out of the Treasury again on note redemptions for shipment abroad. In November another loan of $50,000,000 was got through a banking syndicate and again half the gold to pay for the bonds was taken out of the Treasury.

In January, 1895, the Treasury's gold was disappearing so rapidly that a crisis was at hand. In February there was only $45,000,000 left and $2,000,000 a day was flowing out to redeem notes. In this extremity Secretary Carlisle went to August Belmont, Democratic banker, and J. Pierpont Morgan for help.

Morgan hastily organized a syndicate and proposed to furnish something over $65,000,000 in gold, taking U. S. bonds (4 per cent) at 104.4946 which meant 3.75 per cent interest. After much negotiation, during which Morgan and Belmont went to the White House for a long conference with Cleveland, the deal was closed. The government gave Morgan's syndicate $62,315,400 in 4 per cent bonds and got from it $65,116,244.62 of gold. Morgan agreed that none of the gold would be taken from the Treasury; that half of the bond issue would be sold abroad and that the syndicate would guarantee "as far as able to protect the Treasury from further drafts of gold during the performance of the contract." As a result of the bond issue the Treasury had $107,000,000 in gold by June.

This much debated transaction brought a scorching blast of abuse upon the heads of Morgan and the already much maligned Cleveland. The Western and Southern Senators said the President had sold out to the bankers. They charged that Morgan had squeezed the government. On the other side, there has been a lot of romantic nonsense about Morgan's rescue of the government's credit. "I had but one aim in the whole matter," he told a Senate committee, "to secure the gold that the government needed and to save the panic and widespread disaster that was to follow if the gold was not gotten."

Cleveland was denounced because this whole crisis was mixed up with the overshadowing money question. All United States bonds were payable in coin. This meant any coin—silver or gold. But Cleveland and the bankers wanted to change the law to make bonds payable in gold. Congress had resisted this. The silver groups declared it was an attempt to fasten the gold standard irrevocably on the government. Once the government elected to make its obligations payable in gold only, they felt the cause of bimetallism was lost. The episode assumed the character of a crucial test in the rising war between the silverites and the gold bugs and Cleveland and Morgan were looked upon as the arch devil bugs of gold. When the loan was made there was a stipulation for a lower rate of interest—3 per cent—if Congress would authorize gold bonds, and this infuriated the silver leaders, who of course ignored the proposal.

But Morgan was denounced also because of the hard bargain he had driven with the government—the high interest rate and the low price paid for the bonds. There is not the slightest doubt that he squeezed the inexperienced Cleveland, who was no financier, and the necessitous government he headed. He forced Cleveland to pay 4 per cent on $100 bonds to be sold for $104½ when outstanding 4 per cent U. S. bonds were selling on the market for 111. And these same bonds for which the Morgan syndicate paid 104½ it sold in the open market for from 112 to 124—a fact that enraged the critics. "The terms," says the conservative Alexander Dana Noyes [3] "were extremely harsh; they [the bankers] measured with little mercy the emergency of the Treasury."

Did Morgan save the credit of the United States? First of all, the credit of the United States was not near exhaustion. A government whose existing bonds are selling at a premium of 111 is not wanting in credit. And this new issue was oversubscribed six times in New York and ten times in London, men standing in line to get their shares at high prices. The fact that the bonds when issued went as high as 124 within two months of their release refutes the claim that the government's credit was in danger.

There was a quarrel between the President and Congress about the government's fiscal policy. The President wanted to make gold the basis of American bonds; bimetallists wanted to coin the seigniorage on silver. The government had silver for which it had paid $156,000,000. Congress wanted to coin that into $218,-000,000 silver dollars—a seigniorage profit of $62,000,000. Congress passed the law to do that and Cleveland vetoed it. There were grave defects in the greenback redemption law and in the silver purchase law. All these resulted in a drain on gold that had to be corrected.

[3] *Forty Years of American Finance* by Alexander Dana Noyes.

The bond issues hitherto issued did not correct this. And neither did Mr. Morgan's bond issue. As a matter of fact, that bond issue did not meet the government's problem any more than any of the preceding ones. Morgan's guarantee to protect the Treasury against withdrawals of gold was unsuccessful. He attempted to do this by controlling international exchange. He took all of the bankers and banks in New York into the syndicate, and as the New York banks were the medium through which foreign exchange was handled, he effected a monopoly of that and thus expected to control it. He used his credit and that of the syndicate to establish large credits in London and for a time he did prevent the flow of gold out of the Treasury. The syndicate pushed the price of sterling exchange up to $4.90, shaving a good profit on that. And the inevitable competition was drawn into the market. When that happened Morgan's control of foreign exchange was broken and gold began to move out of the Treasury.

Bond buyers and importers were again using greenbacks to redeem gold and send it abroad. By December the Treasury again had only $68,000,000 of gold. Cleveland had to resort to another bond issue and this time a bigger one than before—$100,000,000. But this time he did not make an exclusive contract with Morgan. He threw the issue open to the public. Over $580,000,000 was subscribed and the government got all the way from 110 to 120 for its bonds, instead of the 104½ paid by Morgan. The whole operation proved the groundlessness of Morgan's contention to Cleveland that a popular offering would be a failure. And it disproved equally the claim that Morgan had acted as a patriot and that he had saved the credit of the nation. He was a banker, with the usual glass eye, scooping out of the opportunity the last ounce of profit for himself. He was the same Morgan who had shipped gold to London in a speculative scheme when the Treasury said gold was more needed than troops and who had participated in the sale of Hall's carbines to the government. He was also the same Morgan who later told Owen Wister that a man always has two reasons for what he does: "the reason he gives and the real reason."

In the end the government was rescued by a series of events, crop failures in Europe and rich harvests at home, hence big grain exports and a reversal of the gold movement. Moreover, new methods of extracting gold from ore appeared and new gold mines were opened. Nature did the job, not Morgan.

----------------------- IX -----------------------

In the 'nineties the era of combination was in full swing. The antitrust law forbidding this sort of thing was passed in 1890. And this seemed to set into swift motion the very evil at which it was aimed. Cleveland and Harrison ignored the law. All sorts of little enterprises were uniting into larger ones. Many small plants were being brought together into local monopolies, regional monopolies. The age of steel had arrived, and steel plants of all sorts were growing larger. The industry was split up into provinces, each making certain standard shapes or products—iron, steel ingots, plates, tubes, rails, wire, and so on. In each of these lines there were numerous independent producers all engaged in vigorous, sometimes savage competition. They entered pools, cartels, trade agreements, in defiance of law, to curb competition, keep up prices, regulate production—the old struggle of enterprisers to govern the economic system in the interest of profits. Then they began to unite into larger units and then still larger ones until in the end the movement culminated in that colossal combination that is looked upon as J. Pierpont Morgan's chef-d'oeuvre.

Each of these steel provinces produced its special Napoleon. Thus the wire and nail industry had its John W. Gates. Gates was the product of an Illinois village, had little or no schooling, turned barbed-wire salesman at twenty-two and quickly set up his own outlaw mill in St. Louis, defying patent laws. He spread out into four other plants and then in 1892 formed an

amalgamation of these in the $4,000,000 Consolidated Steel &
Wire Company. Four years later he promoted the union of this
local amalgamation into a Western combination—the $24,000,000
American Steel & Wire Company of Illinois. Gates was a rotund,
burly, jovial adventurer, born gambler, who would bet a thousand on a race between raindrops flowing down a railroad win-
dowpane, sit in the Waldorf bar and play whist for ten dollars
a point or croquet with H. H. Rogers for a thousand dollars a
game, who combined organizing ability with his daring salesmanship and his gambling instincts. In these adventures in combination he was assisted by a collaborator of a very different
stripe, the pious, Sunday-school picnicker and hymn-singing
Elbert H. Gary, prosperous Chicago lawyer, who looked with
puritanical distaste upon some of the simpler forms of guile but
was the active and cunning and resourceful partner of Gates and
later Morgan in one of the greatest stock-watering jobs in financial history.

Gary formed the Federal Steel Company, which was the fruit
of a series of smaller combinations culminating in the company
of which Gary became president, abandoning his law practice.
And these Gary operations were done with the financial assistance of J. Pierpont Morgan.

By 1900 the steel industry had been pretty well trustified into
a group of similar combinations—Federal Steel, National Steel,
American Steel & Wire, American Steel Hoop, American Bridge,
National Tube, American Tin Plate. Overshadowing all of them,
of course, was Andrew Carnegie's great Carnegie Steel.

Carnegie built one of the greatest of American fortunes. Born
in Dunfermline, Scotland, coming to America at thirteen, bobbin
boy in a textile mill, and getting his start as assistant to Tom
Scott of the Pennsylvania Railroad, he bought a sixth interest
in a small iron-ore concern and built it, by dint of great organization ability, extraordinary gifts of leadership, and ruthless competitive practices, to the greatest steel enterprise in the world.
He differed from almost all of the industrial barons of his day. He

had a grain of religion—only a grain—but he was a nonconformist and had none of the sanctimonious habits of men like Rockefeller, Gary, Harriman, and Morgan. He had a strong streak of
social consciousness, was shocked when at thirty years of age
he found he had made $50,000 in a year, vowed never to make
more and forgot that vow bravely, tinkered with ideas about
education and peace, and, around 1900, was toying with the
notion of unloading his whole vast steel empire upon someone
else.

Carnegie might well be the subject of a whole chapter in this
book, were it not that his fortune, his methods, his place in the
development of industry and money-making were of the same
type as Rockefeller's and were overshadowed by his. With the
exception of Carnegie all of the men who dominated these various
steel combinations were promoters—Gates, Gary, the Moore
brothers, Daniel G. Reid, Converse. It was the age of the promoter. Many combinations then were made not because combination was essential for the industry but because it was a device
by which promoters could make fabulous riches overnight.

The technique was simple. Brown and Smith own plants. They
represent investments of $10,000,000 each. The promoter induces
Brown and Smith to combine their plants. A new corporation is
formed with $40,000,000 of stock divided into preferred and
common. Brown and Smith each get $10,000,000 of preferred
and $10,000,000 of common. The stock is listed on the Stock
Exchange; by careful manipulation the price is forced up and
unloaded on the public. Brown and Smith each have their
$10,000,000 investment in cash and yet still hold a preferred
claim for the same amount against the industry, in which, perhaps, they retain enough common to dominate the directors. The
promoter who manages this gets a huge slice of the loot. And, in
very large combinations where numerous plants were merged, the
promoter sometimes turned up with the lion's share and perhaps
at the head of the corporation as in the case of the cunning Gary.
In all of these combinations a huge volume of this watered stock

had been created and distributed among the promoters. The promoters received millions in stock for which nothing was paid. In fact, when all of these combinations were completed and before the U. S. Steel Corporation was formed, the promoters had got $63,306,811 in fees and preferred stock. And all this water was in the constituent companies before Morgan combined them.

Morgan did this final job in 1901. He did not vision it himself. He had to be sold on the idea. There has been no lack of highly fictionized accounts of the parturition process that preceded the determination of the great man to bring about the merger. The impeccable, endlessly patient and subservient Gary did the chores, Morgan supplying the final "yes" or "no" and the moral grandeur and power to force the constituent promoters into line. The complete product—the United States Steel Corporation— still survives as a perfect example of the most modern method of growing rich, the method that was to be the most widely used from that day to this and from which countless millionaire fortunes were born.

Morgan organized a new corporation—United States Steel. This great holding company then purchased the stocks of Carnegie Steel, Federal Steel, National Steel, American Steel & Wire, American Tin Plate, American Sheet Steel, American Steel Hoop, National Tube, American Bridge, Lake Superior Consolidated Mines, and some smaller companies. The latter company was owned by John D. Rockefeller and had and has one of the richest iron-ore deposits in the world.

The United States Steel Corporation issued $1,402,846,423 in capital securities divided as follows:

5% bonds	$303,450,000
Underlying bonds (assumed)	80,963,680
Preferred stock	510,205,743
Common stock	508,227,000

The United States Commissioner of Corporations who investigated the combination reported that the value of the plants acquired was $682,000,000. This estimate had the tacit confirmation of Judge Gary. The average market value of the stocks of the companies combined was $700,000,000. Morgan supplied $25,000,000 cash for working capital. So the combined companies had an asset value, including Morgan's cash, of not over $750,000,000. The total amount of the bonds and preferred stock issued for this was $813,655,743, or more than $50,000,000 more than their actual value. Thus, much of the preferred and all of the common—another half a billion—was pure water.

Thus, Morgan, the great constructive stabilizer and conservator, had evoked the greatest reservoir of watered stock in history. The man who posed as the archfoe of Gould and Fisk had now outdone them.

What did the Morgan firm get out of this? It acted as the manager of the banking syndicate that underwrote the whole operation. As manager it sold the 1,300,000 shares that the syndicate obtained. It received for these $90,500,000, according to the Commissioner of Corporations. After deducting the $25,000,-000 cash paid the Steel Corporation, the $3,000,000 expenses of organization and of running the syndicate, there was left a clear profit of $62,500,000. This tremendous sum is what the bankers got for their work. Of this sum Morgan's firm got $12,500,000 as syndicate managers before any part of the profit was distributed. It also shared in the division of the remaining $50,000,-000 according to its share in the syndicate, which we may be sure was very large.

The stock of the U. S. Steel Corporation, as soon as issued, was listed on the New York Stock Exchange. And Morgan, as syndicate manager, proceeded to sell it. It belonged to the various organizers, as you will recall, so that whatever they sold it for went not to the corporation or into the steel industry but into the pockets of the promoters. Having listed it Morgan employed James R. Keene, greatest of market manipulators, to "make a market" for the stock by manipulation—buying and selling through various dummies and staging fake activity so that the price would be forced up and the shares could be unloaded on the public. During the first year the preferred sold from 69 to 101.3 and the common from 24 to 55. The promoters unloaded most of these shares on the public and translated their stock profits into cash. What they finally got for it all, of course, must be left to surmise. But it was one of the biggest hauls in Wall Street.

The entire issue of 5 per cent bonds ($303,450,000) was given to Andrew Carnegie along with $188,566,160 of the preferred stock as the price of Carnegie Steel. The balance of the preferred and common was distributed among the owners of the other constituent companies and the bankers.

Gould or Harriman or Vanderbilt or any of the great freebooters never did anything rawer than this. But this was not done by Gould or Fisk or Harriman, but by the eminently respectable, the almost painfully respectable and aristocratic J. Pierpont Morgan, and there flowed over its surface the gilt from the name of this great pious magnifico who presided over the hospitality of Syndicate House. In the coming years Morgan would repeat this dose many times. But much worse, thousands of great and little *chevaliers d'industrie* would repeat it, in their village industries, in their local state industries, and in all the great national utility and industrial and mercantile enterprises of the country until, in time, American industry would become engulfed in the inundation of corporate water mixed with red ink.

——————————— x ———————————

This period was one of extraordinary development because of the wave of revolutionary inventions that had created great new industries—the telephone, the telegraph, electricity in all its forms, power, light, transportation; the age of steel with its revolutionary consequences to construction; the age of amazing technological expansion and perfection—with its monster child, mass production—and of course along with these the swift expansion and perfection of the instruments of credit and control.

As quickly as one group of men either invented or developed a prosperous or promising enterprise around any new device, the banker-promoters pounced upon it with their bag of tricks for turning the ownership into liquid form—all if not most of it liquid water—and pouring this water out upon the nation's investors in return for good hard cash. And foremost in these escapades was the great Morgan.

He began penetrating the telephone industry in 1902, and by 1906 he had the American Telephone & Telegraph Company under his thumb. Theodore Vail, for all his massive and leonine magnificence, was a compliant tool of the Morgans—so pliant indeed that during the war he illegally loaned $20,000,000 of the A. T. & T. funds to Great Britain, Morgan's ally, and had to borrow the funds to do it. The A. T. & T., since Morgan took it in tow, has borrowed a billion dollars through the Morgan bank, and the Morgan firm has collected $40,000,000 in commissions from it.

In 1902 Morgan amalgamated five agricultural machinery corporations, including the big McCormick Harvester Company, into the International Harvester Company at an immediate profit to the firm of nearly $3,000,000. The company, of course, fell under the Morgan yoke through a voting-trust arrangement in which Morgan's partners, Henry P. Davison and George W. Perkins, held control.

He reorganized and got control of the General Electric Company and superintended the spread of the General Electric—manufacturing company—into the field of power producer, acquiring power plants all over the country and building up one of the great power octopuses of the country, from which the plants were ultimately freed by the government.

There is no point in enumerating all of the departments of our economic life into which this powerful man thrust his arm because he had access to the money and had built up slowly a control over banks and insurance companies and industrial corporations and sources of raw materials and the men who operated all these things.

Many men, of course, made millions out of his plans, but it is difficult to say what happened to the countless investors on whom the promoters unloaded their stock. The buyers of United States Steel shares saw them go down to eight dollars a share three years after the organization. One of his creations was the International Mercantile Marine. He merged the Atlantic Transport, the American, Leyland, White Star, Dominion, and Red Star lines—American and British. The Cunard Line went in at first but pulled out. The Hamburg-American Line refused to have anything to do with it. The International was shockingly overcapitalized. Morgan put $50,000,000 into it, taking all the bonds, which he sold. He got besides $27,500,000 of stock. And he got complete control. He set out to market the issue but ran into trouble. Foreign countries countered with subsidies, while the American government failed to yield to the well-oiled conspiracy for American subsidies. The earnings of the lines were higher before the combination. The International Mercantile Marine suspended interest payments in 1914, just after Morgan's death, and went into receivership. It did not pay dividends for twenty years.

Most disastrous to investors of all his adventures was in his own native New England, where, seemingly, he set out to exhibit his might. He took a perfectly sound railroad, the New York, New Haven & Hartford, organized it into an elaborate system of railroads, steamships, and trolley lines. He unloaded upon it a group of streetcar lines and smaller roads, many of which he had got possession of. He increased the mileage from 500 to over 2000 miles. He increased the capital from $93,000,000 to $417,-000,000. Over $200,000,000 of this increased stock and bonds was used to buy up other properties, many of his own. He paid the most fantastic prices for what he bought. He gave $36,000,000 for the New York, Westchester & Boston which his man, Mellen, New Haven president, said was not worth ten cents a pound.

Morgan dominated the whole crazy patchwork with an iron hand. His arrogance was growing. His intolerance of discussion had become absolute. With a fist on the table he shut off debate. The road's president, Mellen, said: "I have been called the office boy. I was proud of his confidence. I regard the statement that I was his man as a compliment." The stocks and bonds of the New Haven were eased into the hands of over 25,000 stockholders, mostly in New England, and over 10,000 of them held no more than ten shares each. These securities were passed off upon New England investors by the persistent and corrupt debauchery of the New England press. Mellen testified the road paid out to a thousand little dailies and weeklies $400,000 a year. It held $400,000 of the bonds of the *Boston Herald*.

When this road failed, as was inevitable, it reduced to poverty thousands of aged people who had put their all into its securities upon their faith in the magician. No adventure of the reckless men who disgraced the financial world of the nineteen twenties— the Insulls, the Mitchells, the Wiggins—was worse than Morgan's New Haven operation. The New York *World*, at the time, declared that the New Haven investors were "swindled, ruined and robbed by cold, calculating villainy." All the cold, shameful facts about the New Haven infamy did not become known until after Morgan's death. Then his son contended that Mellen had withheld from Morgan his illegal acts. Of course that defense will not stand for a moment. Doubtless there were many minor rascalities of Mellen that Morgan did not know of. But he was the architect and builder and ruthless dictator of the whole criminal structure.

XI

In 1907 Morgan was seventy. He was now the magnifico. He had grown to look like an awesome moving-picture extra portraying Ghengis Khan or Tamerlane or some Mongol conqueror or Teutonic tribal chieftain. In October, 1907, he was in Richmond at Rutherford House surrounded by his favorite bishops—the Morgan "college of cardinals." Theodore Roosevelt was hunting bear in the cane country of Louisiana. And in New York deep and terrifying tremors were heard under that boiling volcano, Wall Street.

Many farseeing men had warned the frenzied dollar hunters that they were riding for trouble. But always they knew better. The abuse of banking through the rise of the trust companies saw New York trust banks with only a dollar and a half in cash for every hundred dollars in deposits. "The stupid fetish of cash reserves," laughed the ever-sapient superior persons along Broad Street. Fears of depression? "Old fogys!" said the sophisticates, "who do not realize that there will never be such things as 1873 and 1893 again." The banker-promoters hurled into the market billions in securities. The beast was stuffed. It was getting ready for the regurgitation. By September plenty of this sophisticated confidence was gone. Then came the Heinze and Morse failures. Morse, ship and ice magnate, had got the National Bank of North America and his friend, F. Augustus Heinze, copper baron and gambler, had got the Mercantile National Bank. They used them in their personal speculations. Copper crashed. The market went to pieces. The Morse bank and the Heinze bank were facing bankruptcy. The vestrymen bankers lifted their pious eyebrows in horror at the unregenerate Morse and Heinze.

Essentially they were no worse than the other desperadoes—merely a little less refined and without the odor of sanctity, and that is all. Heinze had United Copper, which was underselling the Rockefeller Amalgamated, and the Standard Oil gang was out to get him. It took advantage of the market weakness to raid his United Copper stocks, send the price down, ruin him and his bank that he had misused as they had theirs. The Clearing House forced Heinze and Morse to withdraw. The Clearing House was dominated by Morgan. The speculators blamed Theodore Roosevelt, off in the Louisiana canebrakes.

The frightened bankers called for Morgan to return. He was in the Episcopal convention where the good dominies were jittery as the vote was being counted on some world-shattering amendment to the *Book of Common Prayer*. To calm the angry Christians Morgan rose alone and began singing: *Oh Zion Haste! Thy Mission High Fulfilling!* The convention took up the canticle and the angry theological emotions were dissolved in song. Then came to him a call from his partners, Perkins and Steel: "Oh Morgan Haste! Thy Mission High Fulfilling!" He left at once, got to New York Sunday just before the Clearing House demanded Heinze's and Morse's exit from New York banking as the price of rescuing the two banks.

Morgan went to his marble library, where he found many of the leading money kings of New York. Next day crowds lined up before the Knickerbocker Trust Company of James Tracy Barney. Barney was leagued with Morse and Heinze. Barney begged for aid. J. Pierpont Morgan refused it. The National Bank of Commerce, a Morgan-controlled bank, announced that it would not clear checks for the Knickerbocker Trust any more. The Knickerbocker closed its doors, and Barney committed suicide. With this most of the banks in New York City felt the strain of fleeing deposits. George Cortelyou, Roosevelt's Secretary of the Treasury, went to New York. On October 25, to save the banks, at Morgan's urgence, he deposited $25,000,000 of government money in them. A few moments later J. P. Morgan authorized Ransom H. Thomas, president of the New York Stock Exchange, to go over to the Exchange floor and announce that the banks would lend $25,000,000 of call money to the brokers. It was eight years later, at the Pujo Committee hearings, before it was learned that the government's money had been used not to strengthen the banks but to relieve the call-money situation on the Stock Exchange and save the price of stocks—many of them worthless.

But this did not end the storm. Morgan sat in the west room of his library, playing solitaire, while partners and bankers sat in the east room, bringing proposals of rescue to him at intervals, like so many secretaries, and getting his imperial "yes" or "no." His librarian asked him why he didn't go into the other room and tell them what to do. He told her he didn't know what to do, but that sooner or later they would hit on something. They did—Clearing House certificates instead of money. Morgan approved that and presently the convulsion came to an end.

But not before he had made good his statement that "I won't take on all this unless I get what I want."

Moore & Schley was supposedly one of the solidest brokerage houses in the Street. The firm held an immense amount of Tennessee Coal & Iron stock as collateral for loans. The stock had sunk in value, and Moore & Schley were faced with suspension. Colonel Oliver H. Payne, Standard Oil millionaire, a friend, loaned them large sums to tide them over and he was threatened with loss if Moore & Schley were not saved. Payne went to Morgan and suggested that United States Steel should buy Tennessee Coal & Iron. This would save Moore & Schley and Payne.

Gary wanted this company but was prevented by fear of anti-trust laws from swallowing it. Gary and H. C. Frick went to Washington that night, called on Roosevelt before breakfast and told him the Steel Corporation was urged to take over the Tennessee Coal & Iron Company because an important house held great gobs of its stock and would crash if not thus saved. The name of the house was not disclosed, and Roosevelt supposed it was a trust company. He promised them immunity from prosecution, and before ten that morning Gary telephoned Morgan that the way was clear to grab the Tennessee Coal & Iron Company. It was not until the Stanley Commission investigation that it was learned that the whole operation was staged on one side to save, not a trust company, but a stockbroker, and on the other to enable the Steel Corporation to gobble up another competitor.

Before the transaction was completed it required an exertion
of Morgan's power. Stories of the weakness of the Trust Company of America made their way into the press. A run began on
that bank. Oakleigh Thorne, its president, went to Morgan's
library for help. He got the help. But he had to agree to give up
a huge block of stock of Tennessee Coal & Iron he held as
security for a loan made to Payne and others and accept U. S.
Steel stock instead. He owned 12,500 shares of unpledged stock
himself and these too he had to give up to the Steel Corporation.
The Steel Corporation, through Morgan, rounded up about
$32,000,000 of these shares from banks and brokerage houses.

---------------------------- XII ----------------------------

What was the secret of all this power? What was it that made
it possible for Morgan to compel bankers to disgorge shares they
wished to hold; to issue orders to corporation executives, to
bang his fist on the table and order a vote of directors? The
explanation is simple. The investment banker sells stocks and
bonds. His clients are corporations. He sells them to those who
have money. The nation's money is lodged in its banks, insurance
companies, trust companies, corporation treasuries. Morgan's
technique, therefore, was to get control of or to dominate directly
or indirectly the corporations that issued securities; also to rule
the money companies—banks, trust companies, and insurance companies—which had the money to buy or to lend.

For this reason, therefore, little by little he penetrated one
railroad and industrial corporation after another by getting directorships for himself and his partners and his numerous satraps,
by getting absolute control in many cases by means of voting
trusts. Also slowly he made his way into the domination of many
banks, trust companies, and insurance companies by the same
means. The story of this spider's web of interlocking interests
and directorates has been told many times and has hardly been
exaggerated. When the elder J. P. Morgan was alive the Pujo

Committee of the House found that Morgan and his partners
and the directors of his controlled trust companies and the First
National and National City banks together, both Morgan financial provinces then, held:

118 directorships in 34 banks and trust companies with resources of
$2,679,000,000.

30 directorships in 10 insurance companies having total assets of
$2,293,000,000.

105 directorships in 32 transportation systems with a total capital of
$11,784,000,000.

63 directorships in 24 producing and trading companies with total
capitalization of $3,339,000,000.

25 directorships in 12 public utility corporations with capital of
$2,150,000,000.

341 directorships in 112 corporations with aggregate resources or
capitalization of $22,245,000,000.

These are the figures of Justice Brandeis and they are, as he
observes, an understatement of the empire that Morgan built
before he died.

It was this access to other people's money that made his
power possible. This is why it was possible for Mr. Morgan to
say to a seeker after capital, with the air of one who owned it
all, that he would let him have millions. They were his to command. And they were his to command for two reasons that have
not been sufficiently stressed. Mr. Morgan was a man of immense
personal power, but all his commanding psychic fluids, his blazing eyes and ruthless manner would not have served him but
for two other weapons. One of them, of course, was the fact that
he was in command on both sides of most situations; he was
running the negotiations on both sides of the counter. He was,
as banker, representing himself; as director, or voting trustee,
representing the corporations from which he got his security
issues, and as director, representing the bank or trust company
or insurance company that supplied the money. Had some clerk
in the purchasing department of a railroad been caught in such
a transaction he would have been cashiered and prosecuted.

Apparently the simple and direct injunction of Jehovah who said, "Thou Shalt Not Steal," and of Christ who said, "No man can serve two masters," did not apply to this pious superman. He would give praise to the Lord in the twenty-five hymns he knew by heart but he would make his own rules of behavior.

The other weapon was even more reprehensible and has been less understood. It is the preferred list. The House of Morgan when putting out an issue of stocks could allot a few hundred or a few thousand shares to exalted persons who were useful to them. Then, when the shares were listed and manipulated into good prices for distribution on the Exchange, these preferred persons would reap swift, handy, and rich profits, usually without putting up a cent. The men who enjoyed these favors were the presidents of the corporations who had securities to issue and the banks, trust companies, and insurance companies who had direct control of funds. Subservience to the House of Morgan meant continuous access to these pretty profits; disobedience meant being cut off from them. It was, then, nothing less than commercial bribery. The Steel Corporation was a Morgan client. The officers of that corporation were its employees. When they accepted money favors from Mr. Morgan they were not better than any small-bore clerk who takes money from the man who deals with his employer and who can be prosecuted for commercial bribery.

Mr. Justice Brandeis, in his famous little volume, *Other People's Money*, has made the best description of how this worked:

J. P. Morgan (or a partner), a director of the New York, New Haven & Hartford Railroad, causes that company to sell to J. P. Morgan & Co. an issue of bonds. J. P. Morgan & Co. borrow the money with which to pay for the bonds from the Guaranty Trust Company, of which Mr. Morgan (or a partner) is a director. J. P. Morgan & Co. sell the bonds to the Penn Mutual Life Insurance, of which Mr. Morgan (or a partner) is a director. The New Haven spends the proceeds of the bonds in purchasing steel rails from the United States Steel Corporation, of which Mr. Morgan (or a partner) is a director. The United

States Steel Corporation spends the proceeds of the rails in purchasing electrical supplies from the General Electric Company, of which Mr. Morgan (or a partner) is a director. The General Electric sells supplies to the Western Union Telegraph Company, a subsidiary of the American Telephone and Telegraph Company; and in both Mr. Morgan (or a partner) is a director. The Telegraph Company has an exclusive wire contract with the Reading, of which Mr. Morgan (or a partner) is a director. The Reading buys its passenger cars from the Pullman Company, of which Mr. Morgan (or a partner) is a director. The Pullman Company buys (for local use) locomotives from the Baldwin Locomotive Company, of which Mr. Morgan (or a partner) is a director. The Reading, the General Electric, the Steel Corporation and the New Haven, like the Pullman, buy locomotives from the Baldwin Company. The Steel Corporation, the Telephone Company, the New Haven, the Reading, the Pullman and the Baldwin companies, like the Western Union, buy electrical supplies from the General Electric. The Baldwin, the Pullman, the Reading, the Telephone, the Telegraph and the General Electric companies, like the New Haven, buy steel products from the Steel Corporation. Each and every one of the companies last named markets its securities through J. P. Morgan & Co.; each deposits its funds with J. P. Morgan & Co.; and with these funds of each, the firm enters upon further operations.

There was nothing new about all this. On a smaller scale it had been used by Gould and Fisk and others on the railroads. But it was reprobated and frequently called by its right name. Morgan, however, developed it, spread it to every conceivable area of business, sanctified it as he strode through the world with clergymen and bishops and men of power and position bowing and scraping before him. After his advent it became the pattern of American money getting. It came to its full flower in the 'twenties, when in all the little and big Wall Streets, in all the villages and cities of the land, little Morgans and bigger ones learned how to use this fatal and immoral device.

But while Morgan rose to power and approval among the large business interests, there was a rising tide of distrust, criticism deepening into anger. Roosevelt had denounced the "malefactors of great wealth," looking toward Morgan, at a Gridiron dinner. Men like Bryan and La Follette had kept up an

incessant barrage against all that he stood for. The muckrakers
were in full career. The economic system began to tremble during Taft's administration. There was no "glamour boy" in the
White House now to save, while he castigated, them. And early
in 1912, as the parties made ready for the campaign that would
make Woodrow Wilson President, the House of Representatives,
on the motion of Congressman Pujo of Louisiana, ordered an
investigation of the "money trust."

The late Samuel Untermeyer, distinguished New York lawyer
and the most devastating of investigators, was named counsel
of the committee. And then, for the first time, the methods, the
back-stage scene-shifting, thunder-making, storm-making devices
were brought to light, the schemes, conspiracies, leagues, secret
agreements by which the vast power of the bankers was attained
were made plain. That investigation is the most important document in the history of the times. Of course it did not prove that
there was a money trust in the sense that one man controlled
all the money power in America. But it did prove that a few
powerful men, by various devious, corrupt devices, had attained
a power over vast areas of the money world that was fatally
antisocial.

The high point in the investigation was the appearance of
Morgan on the witness stand in December, 1912. He was seventy-
six years old. He answered the questions asked with apparent
freedom. All that is remembered of it now is the statement quoted
as if it were a text of Scripture, that a man's credit is not based
primarily on money or property but upon character. No one
recalls how Untermeyer completely blasted that answer by showing how Morgan, like all other lenders of call money, loaned it
out on the Stock Exchange to brokers who could hand over the
securities and that the firm cared nothing about the persons who
got the loans. His testimony, on the whole, was unimportant.
Many if not most of his answers were preposterous. He not only
denied that there was a money trust, but he denied that he exercised any power whatever—not the slightest—in any department

of industry. He did not, so he insisted, control his own firm. He never acted for both sides in a transaction, even when he was banker for one side and director for another; a voting trust did not put any power to control in the hands of the trustees; those who could dictate the election of directors could exercise no control over the directors. It was all quite foolish were it not for the majestic figure of the witness.

But the investigation itself did prove much and out of it came that series of reforms inaugurated in the first term of Woodrow Wilson. But so far as changing the course of our development is concerned, turning aside the tide of combination, monopoly, bigness, it was all a waste of time. Much might have been done. But the war ruined it all. With the coming of the Great War, all of the "malefactors of great wealth" flocked to the capital to become patriots. Many of the corporations that were floundering in difficulties in the approaching depression were saved. The war deepened and intensified the whole drift toward combination and, along with the new technological developments that were just then taking on commercial value, laid the groundwork for the mad era that followed.

On January 4, following the inquisition by Untermeyer, Morgan sat in his library on Thirty-eighth Street, going through his papers and putting great numbers of them into the fire. He had been ill. He probably knew his summons might come at any moment. He was burning the evidence. On January 7, he sailed for a vacation in Egypt. He was taken ill in Egypt and hurried to Rome. There he died on March 31, 1913.

Index

515

ABOUT THE AUTHOR

JOHN T. FLYNN *has written extensively on economics in newspapers, books, and magazines. His* Country Squire in the White House *was an outstanding best seller in 1940.* God's Gold, *his life of Rockefeller, was widely read several years ago. He writes regularly on finance for the Scripps-Howard newspapers and he is a staff contributor to* Collier's. Men of Wealth *is the result of more than five years' work.*

CPSIA information can be obtained
at www.ICGtesting.com
Printed in the USA
BVHW082251240121
598585BV00002B/35